Intelligence Analysis Fundamentals

In an era defined by strategic surprise, pervasive disinformation, and the accelerating fusion of artificial intelligence with traditional tradecraft, the demands on intelligence analysts have never been greater—or more complex. This fully revised and expanded second edition of *Intelligence Analysis Fundamentals* equips both aspiring and veteran analysts with the enduring principles and cutting-edge practices required to transform fragmented data into actionable foresight.

Since the first edition appeared, the global threat landscape has been reshaped by Russia's full-scale invasion of Ukraine, the protracted Gaza war and its ripple effects across the Middle East, Houthi disruptions of Red Sea shipping lanes, and the transformative role of commercial space systems—most notably SpaceX's Starlink constellation and the emerging Starshield intelligence architecture. Simultaneously, generative AI, large language models, and autonomous sensing platforms have begun to reshape collection, processing, and analytic judgment itself. These developments are not theoretical; they are already altering how intelligence is gathered, analyzed, and disseminated in real time. Written by a practitioner–scholar with decades of operational experience across military, law enforcement, and corporate intelligence environments, this edition integrates declassified and open-source case studies—from the predictive failures preceding October 7, 2023, to the rapid exploitation of commercial satellite imagery in Ukraine—that illuminate both best practices and the recurring pitfalls that lead to intelligence failure. Sixteen comprehensively updated chapters follow the complete intelligence cycle, enriched with new sections on OSINT in contested environments, AI-assisted analysis and its cognitive risks, counter-deception in the information age, and structured analytic techniques proven to mitigate bias. Designed as the definitive textbook for undergraduate and graduate intelligence studies programs—and as an essential desk reference for working professionals—this second edition combines conceptual clarity with practical immediacy. End-of-chapter exercises and red team simulations enable students to apply rigorous tradecraft to contemporary problems, while seasoned analysts will find fresh frameworks for navigating today's hybrid and hyperconnected threat environment. *Ancillaries including an Instructor's Manual with Test Bank and chapter PowerPoint slides for classroom presentation are also available for this book and can be provided for qualified course instructors.*

Intelligence Analysis Fundamentals, Second Edition is more than an update; it is a field-tested guide to mastering the craft of intelligence in an age of permanent disruption. Whether you are preparing for a career in the intelligence community, teaching the next generation of analysts, or seeking to sharpen your professional edge, this book delivers the foundational knowledge and practical wisdom required to anticipate, understand, and outthink tomorrow's adversaries.

Intelligence Analysis Fundamentals

Second Edition

Patrick McGlynn

CRC Press
Taylor & Francis Group
Boca Raton London New York

CRC Press is an imprint of the
Taylor & Francis Group, an **informa** business

Designed cover image: Getty Images (metanorworks)

Second edition published 2027
by CRC Press
2385 NW Executive Center Drive, Suite 320, Boca Raton FL 33431

and by CRC Press
4 Park Square, Milton Park, Abingdon, Oxon, OX14 4RN

CRC Press is an imprint of Taylor & Francis Group, LLC

First edition published by CRC Press 2019

ISBN: 9781032911748 (hbk)
ISBN: 9781032911724 (pbk)
ISBN: 9781003561712 (ebk)

DOI: 10.4234/ 9781003561712

Typeset in Sabon
by Deanta Global Publishing Services, Chennai, India

Access the Instructor and Student Resources:
https://www.routledge.com/9781032911748

Contents

About the Author

Patrick McGlynn is a retired U.S. Army Intelligence Major with over three decades of operational and analytical experience in military, interagency, and joint environments. A veteran of multiple combat tours in Iraq, Afghanistan, and the broader Middle East, he served in senior theater-level intelligence positions and contributed directly to strategic assessments at the Defense Intelligence Agency (DIA). His classified portfolio includes lead authorship of high-impact strategic reports on terrorism, irregular warfare, weapons of mass destruction proliferation, and information operations.

A recognized authority in analytic tradecraft, Major McGlynn designed and delivered flagship training programs for the U.S. Military and allied partners in Counter-IED analysis, Counterinsurgency (COIN), Collection Management, Network Targeting, Terrorism Analysis, and Information Operations. He is a graduate of the U.S. Army Command and General Staff College and holds an M.Ed. in Adult Education and Industrial Technology from Georgia Southern University.

Since retiring from active duty in 2007, he has remained a leading voice in the discipline, publishing extensively in professional journals and law enforcement reviews. His widely adopted advanced textbook, *Taking Intelligence Analysis to the Next Level* (CRC Press, 2022), is considered a standard reference for structured analytic techniques and critical thinking in the intelligence profession.

In this second edition of *Intelligence Analysis Fundamentals*, Major McGlynn distills lessons from the front lines of both classified operations and today's open-source revolution to prepare the next generation of analysts for the challenges of great-power competition, hybrid warfare, and the AI-augmented intelligence landscape.

CHAPTER 1

Defining Intelligence Analysis

INTRODUCTION TO INTELLIGENCE ANALYSIS

Introducing the world of Intelligence Analysis is akin to unlocking a treasure trove of insights and revelations (see Figure 1.1). In the exhilarating journey that begins here, we embark on a quest to unravel the enigmatic nature of intelligence. No longer confined by singular definitions, we navigate through myriad perspectives, each offering a glimpse into the intricate tapestry of intelligence analysis.

FIGURE 1.1 Unveiling the treasure trove of intelligence analysis (www.shutterstock.com).

DOI: 10.4324/9781003561712-1

This chapter serves as our compass, guiding us through the labyrinth of divergent viewpoints and illuminating the common threads that bind them. As we delve deeper, a comprehensive definition of Intelligence Analysis emerges, serving as our beacon amidst the vast sea of information.

LEARNING OBJECTIVES

1. **Differentiate** between "intelligence" and "intelligence analysis."
2. **Describe** the most basic similarities between law enforcement and military intelligence analysis.
3. **Analyze** the origins of intelligence analysis and understand the most prevalent similarities between the original concepts and modern-day processes of intelligence analysis.
4. **Comprehend** the function of intelligence analysis within the scope of the Homeland Security problem set.
5. **Compare** the analysis phase with the synthesis phase of intelligence.
6. **Explain** the reason a standard definition of intelligence analysis remains so elusive today.
7. **Understand** how the factual and the relational descriptive requirements of intelligence complement each other.

But our exploration does not end there. We unveil the cornerstone of our journey: The Framework for Analytic Cognition (FAC). Originating from the essence of analytical thought, the FAC stands as a testament to the artistry of intelligence analysis. While other processes may lurk in the shadows, the FAC takes center stage, casting its brilliance across the pages of our course (see Figure 1.2).

In the chapters to come, we will unravel the FAC's intricacies, explore its advantages, dissect its structure, and uncover its myriad applications. But first, we must understand the genesis of analysis: the requirements. Like seeds planted in fertile soil, these requirements sprout into the bedrock of our analytical journey, each category and subtype a testament to its real-world relevance.

Yet, our odyssey is not confined to theoretical realms alone. We bridge the gap between academia and reality as we delve into Crime Analysis and Military Intelligence. With each case study, we confront the challenges of Homeland Security Intelligence Analysis, standing vigilant

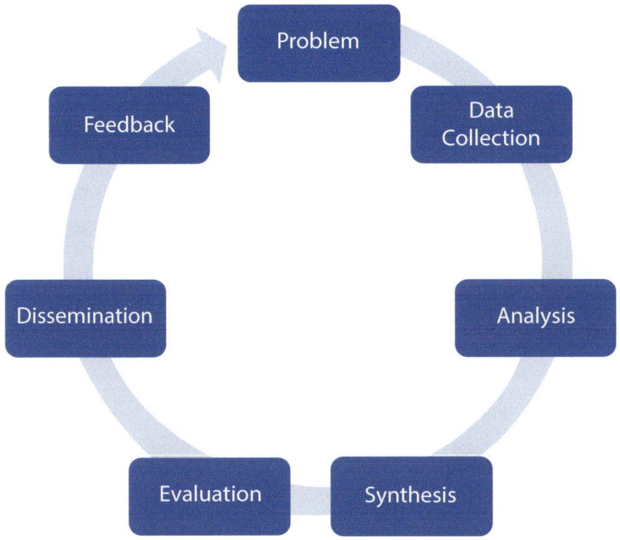

FIGURE 1.2 Flowchart: Framework for Analytic Cognition (FAC) process.

against the specter of the hybrid threat while providing real-world examples from history and modern times. See the following example.

> ***Example:***
>
> *In late 2023, intelligence agencies detected CyberAv3ngers attempting to exploit a known vulnerability in Israeli-made Unitronics PLCs (Programmable Logic Controllers) widely used in U.S. and Israeli water treatment plants, potentially allowing them to manipulate water levels and distribution; based on this intel, authorities proactively alerted affected facilities, enabling them to patch the vulnerability and implement enhanced security measures, effectively thwarting a large-scale cyberattack on critical water infrastructure across multiple countries by CyberAv3ngers (see Figure 1.3).*

So, join us as we embark on this exhilarating expedition into the heart of Intelligence Analysis. Let us unravel the mysteries, decode the enigmas, and forge a path toward clarity and understanding in a complex world.

WHAT IS INTELLIGENCE ANALYSIS?

Intelligence analysis, a cornerstone of modern security and decision-making, encompasses a multifaceted process to distill information into

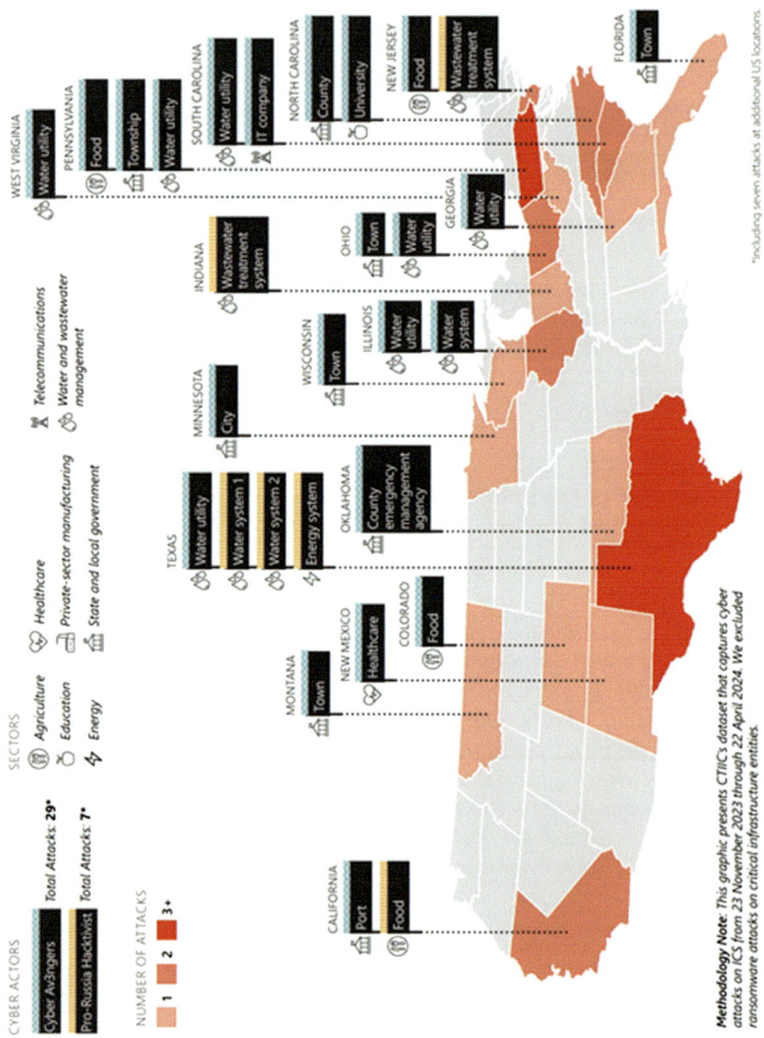

FIGURE 1.3 Reported cyberattacks on U.S. ICS, 23 November 2023 through 22 April 2024.

actionable insights. However, defining this pivotal concept remains elusive, reflecting the diverse perspectives within the Intelligence Community. For instance, the Federal Bureau of Investigation (FBI) emphasizes alignment with policymakers' needs, while the military focuses on serving commanders' interests.

According to the RAND Corporation, renowned for its research in this field, intelligence analysis involves leveraging collected data to address immediate operational queries or anticipate future adversary action.

> *Intelligence analysis is the process by which the information collected about an enemy is used to answer tactical questions about current operations or to predict future behavior.*[1]
>
> **RAND Corporation**

Differences

The complexity of intelligence analysis is further underscored by its myriad classifications, including:

- Varied data sources (e.g., Human Intelligence, Imagery Intelligence, Signals Intelligence, Open-Source Intelligence)
- Diverse end-user domains (e.g., Business Intelligence, Military Intelligence, Political Intelligence)
- Utilization of single or multiple sources (e.g., single-source vs. all-source analysis)
- Distinct types (e.g., strategic, tactical, scientific/technical)
- Consideration of product usability (e.g., actionable vs. non-actionable intelligence)

Commonalities

Despite this diversity, the core mental processes underpinning intelligence production remain consistent. Across the Intelligence Community (IC), analysis processes typically involve two essential phases: analysis, where information is dissected into its constituent parts, and synthesis, where these parts are integrated to form a coherent whole.

While variations exist in terminology and emphasis, the fundamental elements of analysis and synthesis endure across IC organizations.

For simplicity, this textbook adopts a holistic view of intelligence analysis, encompassing all activities from problem exploration to the delivery of final intelligence products, be they assessments, imagery, signals reporting, or other formats.

FRAMEWORK FOR ANALYTIC COGNITION

This textbook employs a cutting-edge framework called the Framework for Analytic Cognition (FAC), designed to streamline and enhance the intelligence analysis process. The FAC offers a comprehensive and adaptable structure, informed by scientific research, to empower intelligence analysts in their tasks. A study conducted by the Air Force Research Laboratory (AFRL) on intelligence analysis processes and extensive literature research identified the FAC as a recommended framework.[2]

Central to the FAC is its focus on equipping analysts to tackle intelligence questions and challenges within their areas of expertise, whether initiated internally or posed by external sources.

ANALYSIS REQUIREMENTS

At the heart of intelligence analysis lies the imperative to produce descriptive and explanatory outcomes, offering insights into current circumstances and, ideally, forecasts of future events.

Irrespective of the specific domain of intelligence analysis, the process invariably begins with one or more unanswered questions or unresolved problems. These questions, also called "requirements," serve as the genesis of the analytical journey. Intelligence analysis requirements typically fall into three primary categories: descriptive, explanatory, and anticipatory, as illustrated in Figure 1.4.

By recognizing and addressing these foundational requirements, analysts embark on a structured, informed approach to uncovering insights and generating actionable intelligence.

Whether they stem from internal inquiries or external demands, these analysis requirements provide the essential starting point for the analytical process. They guide analysts in determining the scope, objectives, and methodologies needed to address the intelligence challenges at hand.

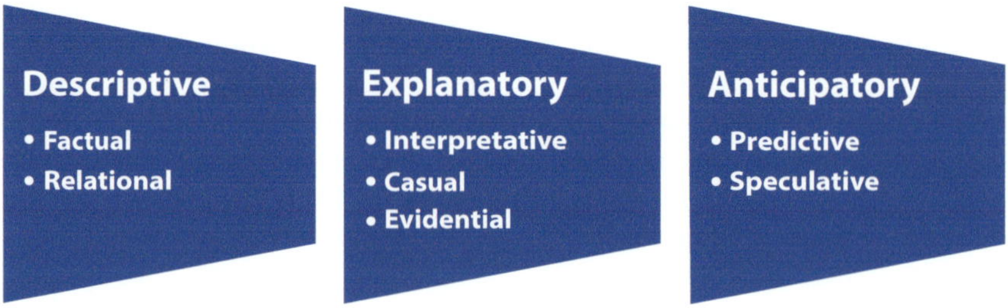

FIGURE 1.4 Analysis requirement categories.

Descriptive Requirements

Descriptive requirements entail providing a detailed depiction of existing conditions, events, or phenomena. Explanatory requirements seek to delve deeper, uncovering the underlying reasons or causes behind observed phenomena. Anticipatory requirements push the boundaries further, aiming to forecast future events or developments based on current trends and patterns.

Figure 1.4, Analysis requirement categories, serves as a visual aid to illustrate the multifaceted nature of intelligence analysis requirements, highlighting the diverse range of inquiries that analysts must address.

By understanding and categorizing these requirements, analysts can tailor their approaches and methodologies to effectively meet the information needs of stakeholders and decision-makers across various sectors, including military, law enforcement, and homeland security.

Through a systematic and rigorous analytical process anchored in identifying and analyzing requirements, intelligence analysts play a pivotal role in enhancing situational awareness, informing strategic decision-making, and safeguarding national security interests.

This comprehensive approach, underpinned by the FAC and structured analytical techniques, equips analysts with the tools and methodologies necessary to navigate the complexities of the contemporary intelligence landscape.

Focus of Descriptive Requirements

Descriptive intelligence requirements focus on providing factual or relational information. Factual requirements are concrete and unambiguous, akin to the essential elements often referred to as the "five Ws" in journalism: **W**ho, **W**hat, **W**here, **W**hen, and **W**hy (though the "Why" is frequently more explanatory). For instance:

1. Who? (e.g., green force, red force, friendly, enemy)
2. What? (e.g., five soldiers, two tanks, three submarines)
3. Where? (e.g., crossing the border, leaving port)
4. When? (e.g., 06:30, Tuesday, 15 July)
5. Why? (This aspect delves more into the reasons behind events, bordering on explanatory rather than purely factual)

Relational requirements describe connections, associations, or comparisons between elements. For example, one might analyze the similarities between tanks used by different forces, as illustrated below:

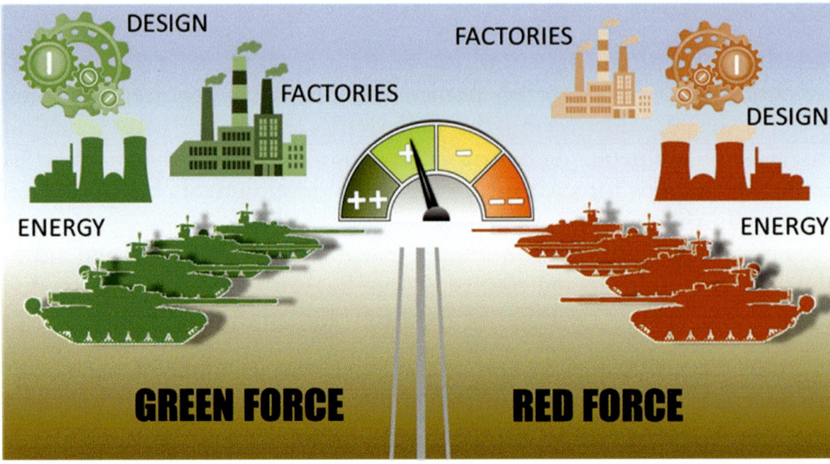

FIGURE 1.5 Analyzing shared origins: A comparative study of Green and Red Force tanks.

Example:

A comparison of Green and Red Force tanks reveals fundamental similarities, suggesting a shared supplier for heavy weapons (see Figure 1.5).

Explanatory Requirements

Explanatory requirements aim to interpret, understand causality, or gather evidence. Interpretive perspectives seek meaning in data, while causal viewpoints explore the reasons behind phenomena. Evidential-oriented requirements focus on acquiring data to support or refute hypotheses. Consider the following example.

Example:

Requirement Hypothesis Statement: *South American drug traffickers are utilizing a specific coastal property for ongoing drug processing destined for the United States.*

Intelligence Surveillance Reconnaissance (ISR) Collection Data:

- Commercial imagery collected over the past week shows no signs of activity, with a "For Rent" sign displayed prominently.
- Periodic imagery from the last month displays similar vacancy, with corroborating reports from real estate agents indicating no recent tenants.

- Human intelligence from local sources reinforces the absence of activity, with reports from neighbors confirming the property's lack of use.

Anticipatory Requirements

Anticipatory requirements focus on predicting future events or scenarios, encompassing predictive and speculative analyses. Predictive requirements seek to determine the likelihood of specific outcomes, while speculative requirements explore potential future scenarios based on varying assumptions.

Examples:

- **Example of a predictive analysis requirement:** What is the probability of the Jalisco New Generation Cartel (CJNG)[3] becoming the dominant drug cartel in Mexico within the next five years, with a likelihood more significant than 50%?

- **Example of a speculative analysis requirement:** How might the CJNG evolve over the next five years if host nations maintain current drug interdiction efforts? Provide insights into staffing, territorial control, smuggling operations, market share, and political influence.

These categories of requirements serve as essential guidelines for intelligence analysts, guiding their efforts in gathering and analyzing information to inform decision-making processes effectively.

CRIME ANALYSIS AND ITS APPLICATIONS

Crime analysis serves a vital function within law enforcement. It systematically examines crime patterns and trends to enhance operational effectiveness and support investigative efforts. By analyzing patterns, identifying suspects, and developing crime prevention strategies, law enforcement agencies can allocate resources more efficiently. While quantitative social science methods are commonly employed in crime analysis, qualitative approaches, such as analyzing police report narratives, also contribute.[4]

Definition of Crime Analysis

Crime analysis is a multifaceted law enforcement function systematically examining crime data and information to identify patterns, trends, and relationships. It encompasses collecting, collating, analyzing, and disseminating crime-related data to support law enforcement operations, investigative efforts, and crime prevention strategies. Crime analysts utilize various quantitative and qualitative methods to uncover insights into criminal activities, such as mapping techniques, statistical analysis, and examination of police reports and other sources of information. The ultimate goal of crime analysis is to provide actionable intelligence to law enforcement agencies, enabling them to allocate resources effectively, identify suspects, detect emerging crime trends, and develop targeted crime prevention initiatives.[5–7]

Advantages and Limitations of Crime Analysis

Crime analysis offers advantages and limitations when applied to homeland security threats. One advantage lies in criminal analysts' deep institutional and street-level knowledge, enabling them to identify and understand criminal enterprises effectively. Additionally, their familiarity with known criminal organizations allows them to leverage existing profiles to uncover unknown criminal networks.

However, crime analysis tends to be reactive, primarily responding to crimes after they occur rather than proactively seeking vulnerabilities or disrupting criminal activities. Analysts must navigate the complexities of legal prosecution, ensuring that their analyses can withstand scrutiny in court. Moreover, the effectiveness of crime analysis may be hindered by territorial borders and limited access to data resources. See the following example scenario.

> ***Example Scenario:***
>
> *Consider a scenario where a local law enforcement organization near the U.S. southern border apprehends a drug smuggler who provides a comprehensive confession implicating accomplices and connections to global terrorist groups. However, local law enforcement lacks the analytical and jurisdictional authority to pursue the leads effectively. Their jurisdictional boundaries, compounded by limited collaboration with other law enforcement agencies, impede their ability to follow the trail beyond their immediate jurisdiction. Even with cooperation from county, state, and federal authorities, jurisdictional constraints often hinder efforts to pursue leads across international borders (see Figure 1.6).*
>
> *This scenario underscores the challenges law enforcement agencies face in addressing transnational crime and highlights the importance of collaboration and information sharing across jurisdictions to combat complex criminal networks effectively.*

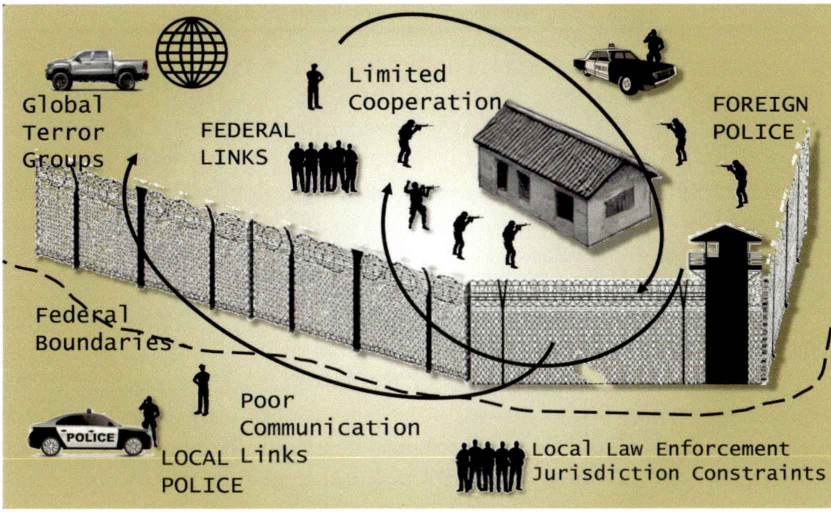

FIGURE 1.6 Barriers to effective border law enforcement.

MILITARY INTELLIGENCE: SCOPE AND CHALLENGES

Military intelligence analysis plays a pivotal role in ensuring the success of military operations and safeguarding national security. Unlike other forms of intelligence, such as crime analysis, military intelligence emphasizes forecasting and preparing for future challenges in complex and often volatile environments. It involves assessing adversaries' capabilities, identifying vulnerabilities, and anticipating their intentions to provide actionable insights for tactical, operational, and strategic decision-making. This process requires a proactive and aggressive approach, focusing on understanding the present and shaping the future battlefield through informed strategies and precision targeting. Military intelligence is a cornerstone of modern defense, offering critical insights that enable military forces to adapt to evolving threats and seize opportunities in dynamic operational landscapes.

Definition of Military Intelligence Analysis

Military intelligence analysis is a complex process that involves collecting, analyzing, and disseminating information about military threats, capabilities, intentions, and vulnerabilities. This process is essential to support military planning, operations, and decision-making at all levels, from tactical to strategic.

Characteristics of Military Intelligence Analysis

Military intelligence analysis is characterized by a proactive and aggressive approach focused on assessing adversaries' capabilities and vulnerabilities to identify potential threats and opportunities. Unlike crime analysis, which primarily examines past criminal activities, military analysis anticipates and prepares for future challenges in warfare and security. Military analysts prioritize identifying critical vulnerabilities in adversaries' resources necessary for significant military capabilities and proposing strategies for attack, degradation, or interdiction.

However, military intelligence analysis faces significant legal and jurisdictional constraints, particularly concerning information collection on U.S. persons. Department of Defense (DoD) Directive 5240.01 outlines strict limitations on military personnel's authority to collect intelligence on U.S. citizens, except under specific circumstances. This restriction poses challenges for military analysts, as it may impede their ability to investigate and analyze criminal or terrorist activities perpetrated by U.S. nationals, especially if detected outside the United States and its territories.[8]

Military intelligence agencies often collaborate with law enforcement and intelligence agencies to overcome these challenges, sharing information and coordinating efforts to address transnational threats effectively. This collaborative approach enables the pooling of resources and expertise, enhancing the overall effectiveness of intelligence analysis and counterterrorism efforts.

HOMELAND SECURITY AND THE HOMELAND SECURITY PROBLEM SET

Established in 2002 in response to the 9/11 attacks, the Department of Homeland Security (DHS) integrates 22 federal departments and agencies into a unified cabinet agency to secure the homeland (see Figure 1.7).

FIGURE 1.7 DHS seal.

DHS's core missions encompass preventing terrorism, enhancing security, managing borders, administering immigration laws, securing cyberspace, and ensuring disaster resilience. These missions are further categorized into six key areas:

1. Counterterrorism and Homeland Security Threats Securing and Managing Borders
2. Secure U.S. Borders and Approaches
3. Secure Cyberspace and Critical Infrastructure
4. Preserve and Uphold the Nation's Prosperity and Economic Security
5. Strengthen Preparedness and Resilience
6. Champion the DHS Workforce and Strengthen the Department[9]

The DHS threat problem set encompasses a range of challenges, including terrorism (both foreign and domestic), cyber threats (foreign and domestic), and border security issues such as smuggling and illegal immigration.

To address these challenges, DHS leverages various components, including law enforcement agencies such as Customs and Border Protection (CBP), Immigration and Customs Enforcement (ICE), and the United States Secret Service. Additionally, while possessing military capabilities, the U.S. Coast Guard operates under Title 14 USC 89, granting authority for law enforcement activities on U.S. waters and territories. The Office of Intelligence and Analysis (I&A) serves as DHS's intelligence arm, providing analytical support and intelligence products to inform decision-making and operational activities.[10]

While other organizations within DHS also contribute to addressing the problem set, the focus is primarily on these four key elements for instructional purposes.

Addressing the Hybrid Threat

When criminals, terrorists, and other malicious actors collaborate to leverage their personnel, resources, and efforts, the resulting threat to society becomes a "hybrid" menace, often more sophisticated and perilous than its components.

Given the hybrid nature and scope of the Homeland Security threat/problem set, characterized by elements of criminality, terrorism, and beyond, traditional military or law enforcement approaches alone are insufficient to address the multifaceted threat landscape effectively.

While there is no universally agreed-upon definition of "hybrid threats" across military, academic, or open-source sources, for instructional purposes, this text adopts the U.S. Army's definition: "the diverse and dynamic combination of regular forces, irregular forces, and/or criminal elements all unified to achieve mutually beneficial effects."

Aligning with the U.S. Army's definition of hybrid threats and comparing it with the Homeland Security Mission Statement underscores the necessity for DHS threat analysis groups to consider hybrid, criminal, and terrorism-based threats comprehensively. By integrating perspectives from both military intelligence and crime analysis, Homeland Security analysts can leverage the strengths of each while mitigating their limitations.

Homeland Security analysts benefit from extensive access to criminal records and databases of crime organizations, as well as multiple terrorist data resources. Through a combined approach that merges military intelligence and crime analysis methodologies, DHS intelligence analysts can prioritize identifying capabilities and vulnerabilities within threat organizations, enabling targeted actions to disrupt them at their weakest points, rather than solely focusing on areas where legal constraints may impact prosecution efforts.

GLOSSARY OF TERMS

Here is a glossary of key terms introduced and discussed in Chapter 1 to enhance your understanding of the material:

Actionable Intelligence: Information that can be immediately acted upon to make decisions or take operational steps, such as preventing an attack or addressing a security threat.

All-Source Analysis: The process of integrating intelligence from multiple sources (e.g., HUMINT, SIGINT, IMINT) to create a comprehensive view.

Analytic Bias: The tendency of an analyst to interpret information in a way that confirms their preexisting beliefs or expectations.

Analytic Tradecraft: The principles, practices, and techniques intelligence analysts use to ensure rigor, transparency, and credibility.

Anticipatory Intelligence: Intelligence designed to forecast future events, scenarios, or threats based on current trends.

Collection Discipline: A category of intelligence collection methods, such as:

- HUMINT (Human Intelligence)
- SIGINT (Signals Intelligence)
- OSINT (Open-Source Intelligence)
- IMINT (Imagery Intelligence)

Counterintelligence: Activities aimed at identifying and neutralizing threats posed by adversaries' intelligence services or activities.

Cyber Av3ngers: An Iranian IRGC-affiliated cyber persona (also known as CyberAveng3rs or Cyber Avengers) that has claimed responsibility for numerous attacks against critical infrastructure organizations, primarily in the water and energy sectors in the United States, Israel, and other countries.

Fusion Center: A collaborative effort between multiple agencies to analyze and share intelligence, often used in Homeland Security contexts.

Hybrid Threats: A combination of regular forces, irregular forces, and/or criminal elements unified to achieve strategic objectives.

Indicators and Warnings (I&W): Specific signals or events that suggest the likelihood of a particular outcome, such as an impending attack or policy change.

Industrial Control Systems (ICS): ICS is a category of Operational Technology (OT) that focuses on automating or remotely controlling physical processes. This contrasts with Information Technology (IT), which focuses on manipulating, recording, and conveying data.

Intelligence: Information that has been processed and analyzed to inform decision-making.

Intelligence Cycle: The process of planning, collecting, analyzing, and disseminating intelligence to support decision-making.

Intelligence Product: The output of the intelligence analysis process, which may take various forms (e.g., reports, briefings, visualizations).

Operational Intelligence: Intelligence focused on supporting immediate or short-term operational needs.

Programmable Logic Controllers (PLCs): A programmable logic controller (PLC) is a small industrial computer responsible for executing specific physical subprocesses, such as logic, timing, counting, communication, and data and file processing.

Red Teaming: A method of challenging assumptions, plans, or processes by adopting an adversary's perspective to identify vulnerabilities.

Strategic Intelligence: Long-term, big-picture analysis used to support policy and strategic decision-making.

Structured Analytical Techniques (SATs): Formalized methods designed to improve the rigor and objectivity of analysis, such as brainstorming, hypothesis testing, and scenario planning.

Tactical Intelligence: Intelligence used to inform decisions and actions at the tactical level, typically in real-time or near-term scenarios.

Threat Vector: An adversary's path or method to achieve their objectives, such as a cyberattack or physical incursion.

Verification Bias: The inclination to favor information that confirms existing hypotheses or beliefs.

This glossary serves as a quick reference for understanding key terms and concepts from the chapter. Feel free to revisit it as you progress through the material!

CHAPTER SUMMARY

This chapter introduced the foundational concepts and processes of intelligence analysis. Key takeaways include:

1. **Definition and Purpose:** Intelligence analysis distills collected information into actionable insights for decision-making, with variations in focus across military, law enforcement, and other domains.
2. **Framework for Analytic Cognition (FAC):** The FAC is an innovative approach to streamlining intelligence processes and supporting analysts through a structured and adaptable framework.
3. **Analysis Requirements:**
    - **Descriptive:** Focused on current conditions and events.
    - **Explanatory:** Explores causality and evidence-based insights.
    - **Anticipatory:** Predicts future scenarios or outcomes.
4. **Crime Analysis:** A systematic examination of crime patterns and trends to inform law enforcement strategies, leveraging quantitative and qualitative methods.
5. **Military Intelligence Analysis:** Proactively assesses adversaries' capabilities and vulnerabilities, supporting operational readiness and decision-making.
6. **Homeland Security Challenges:** DHS's mission addresses diverse threats, including terrorism, cyber risks, and border security. Hybrid threats amplify the need for integrated intelligence efforts.
7. **Hybrid Threats:** Unified actions of criminals, terrorists, and irregular forces necessitate collaborative approaches that combine military and crime analysis methodologies.

Key Concepts Covered

- **Intelligence Analysis Defined:** Intelligence analysis is the systematic process of evaluating information from multiple sources, integrating relevant data, and producing insights that support informed decision-making. The goal of intelligence analysis is to transform raw data into meaningful assessments that help decision-makers understand current situations and anticipate future developments.

- **Analysis and Synthesis:** At its core, intelligence analysis involves two complementary cognitive processes. **Analysis** breaks complex information into component parts, allowing relationships, patterns, and anomalies to be identified. **Synthesis** then integrates those components into a coherent interpretation or assessment that explains the significance of the information.
- **Framework for Analytic Cognition (FAC):** The **Framework for Analytic Cognition** (FAC) provides a structured approach to analytical thinking. It organizes how analysts frame problems, evaluate information, generate hypotheses, and develop conclusions. The FAC emphasizes disciplined reasoning, structured analytical methods, and the application of professional analytic tradecraft.
- **Intelligence Requirements:** All intelligence analysis begins with a question or problem known as an **intelligence requirement.** These requirements define the scope of the analysis, guide collection priorities, and determine the analytical methods used to produce intelligence.
- **Descriptive Requirements:** Descriptive requirements focus on understanding **what is happening now.** They typically involve factual information and relationships, answering questions such as who is involved, what occurred, where events took place, and when they happened.
- **Explanatory Requirements:** Explanatory requirements seek to determine **why events are occurring.** Analysts examine causes, motivations, relationships, and evidence to understand the underlying drivers and produce deeper insights into complex situations.
- **Anticipatory Requirements:** Anticipatory requirements focus on **future possibilities and probabilities.** Analysts attempt to forecast potential developments by examining current conditions, trends, indicators, and potential scenarios.
- **Crime Analysis:** Crime analysis is a law enforcement discipline that examines crime patterns, trends, and relationships to support investigations, allocate resources, and develop prevention strategies. Analysts use statistical analysis, geographic mapping, and investigative data to identify criminal networks and emerging threats.
- **Military Intelligence Analysis:** Military intelligence analysis focuses on evaluating adversary **capabilities, intentions, vulnerabilities, and courses of action.** It supports operational planning and decision-making by helping commanders anticipate threats and exploit adversary weaknesses.
- **Homeland Security Intelligence:** Homeland Security intelligence integrates elements of law enforcement, intelligence

community practices, and national security analysis to address threats such as terrorism, cyber-attacks, border security challenges, and transnational crime.
- **Hybrid Threats:** Hybrid threats arise when **criminal organizations, terrorist groups, irregular forces, or state actors collaborate** to pursue shared objectives. These threats combine tactics and capabilities from multiple domains, creating complex challenges that require coordinated intelligence efforts across agencies and disciplines.
- **Integrated Intelligence Approaches:** Modern intelligence problems often require combining insights from multiple analytical domains—such as military intelligence, crime analysis, and homeland security intelligence. By integrating these perspectives, analysts can develop more comprehensive and accurate assessments of complex threats.

Learning Objectives Accomplished

By completing this chapter, you should now be able to:

1. **Differentiate** between "intelligence" and "intelligence analysis."
2. **Describe** the most basic similarities between law enforcement and military intelligence analysis.
3. **Analyze** the origins of intelligence analysis and understand the most prevalent similarities between the original concepts and modern-day processes of intelligence analysis.
4. **Comprehend** the function of intelligence analysis within the scope of the Homeland Security Problem Set.
5. **Compare** the analysis phase with the synthesis phase of intelligence.
6. **Explain** the reason a standard definition of intelligence analysis remains so elusive today.
7. **Understand** how the factional and the relational descriptive requirements of intelligence complement each other.

Practical Application

During this chapter, you explored several practical intelligence analysis concepts through real-world inspired examples, including:

- **Identifying Intelligence Requirements**: Determining whether a requirement is descriptive, explanatory, or anticipatory.
- **Analyzing Criminal Intelligence Scenarios**: Examining how crime analysts identify patterns, trends, and relationships in criminal activity.

- **Evaluating Military Intelligence Challenges:** Understanding how analysts assess adversary capabilities, vulnerabilities, and intentions.
- **Exploring Homeland Security Threats:** Recognizing how criminal organizations, terrorist groups, and irregular actors can combine to form hybrid threats.
- **Applying Analytical Thinking Frameworks:** Understanding how the Framework for Analytic Cognition (FAC) helps analysts structure their thinking when addressing intelligence problems.

Reflection Questions

1. Why is it difficult to create a single universal definition of intelligence analysis?
2. How do descriptive, explanatory, and anticipatory intelligence requirements differ, and why are all three important to analysts?
3. In what ways do crime analysis and military intelligence analysis differ in their objectives and methods?
4. Why do hybrid threats present unique challenges for Homeland Security analysts?
5. How can structured analytical frameworks, such as the **Framework for Analytic Cognition (FAC)**, improve the quality and reliability of intelligence analysis?

Excellent work completing this chapter. Continue developing your analytical mindset and tradecraft—each concept you master strengthens your ability to interpret complex information and transform it into meaningful intelligence.

PRACTICAL EXERCISE: THE HYBRID THREAT (STUDENT HANDOUT)

The instructor will provide a Practical Exercise Sheet dealing with a hybrid threat and facilitate the learning activity. Read the Hybrid Threat scenario and be prepared to participate in a facilitated discussion. While reading the scenario, look for answers to the following questions:

- Is the criminal activity described as multi-jurisdictional?
- Are there aspects of a terror threat associated with criminal activity?
- What are some of the crimes identified in the scenario?

- What is the host nation's law enforcement involvement in criminal activities? Are they interdicting the flow of drugs and arms?
- Do these criminal activities fall under DHS? If yes, why? If no, then who and why?

FICTIONAL (BUT REPRESENTATIVE) FEDERAL LAW ENFORCEMENT REPORT

Title: Clandestine Drug Tunnel, Discovered on the U.S. Southern Border

Details: A secret underground tunnel was shut down due to the U.S. Federal and San Diego PD raid. The tunnel, equipped with electricity, lighting, hydraulic doors, ventilation, and a rail system, was being used for smuggling drugs between a San Diego industrial park and Tijuana, Mexico, officials said on Thursday.

The tunnel zigzags nearly 600 meters, linking warehouses in Tijuana (*Vic Grid AB 123456*) and a San Diego industrial park (*Vic Grid AB 134478*).

Analyst Comment: A 600-meter-long tunnel requires hundreds of thousands of labor hours and millions of dollars to construct and maintain.

Border Control and Drug Enforcement Administration (DEA) agents seized more than 19,000 pounds of marijuana, 500 pounds of cocaine, two million dollars in cash, and five million counterfeit dollars from the tunnel, in addition to hundreds of small arms including assault rifles, hand grenades, tons of explosives, a rented warehouse where the passageway ended on the U.S. side, and arrested three men in a night raid on Wednesday.

Analyst Comment: The industrial area, populated with several non-descript warehouses, provides good concealment for trucks being loaded with drugs/weapons.

HUMINT Source (CI 2345187) provided intelligence that led up to the raid. The source went on to say that the Sinaloa drug cartel is believed to have built and operated the cross-border tunnel. Local host nation authorities are allegedly aware of the tunnel and associated criminal activity. The cartel allegedly collaborates with Hezbollah agents from Venezuela to move weapons across the border.

Source Information:

- Source is registered CI and is monetarily compensated for information
- Motivated by monetary compensation and hatred for drug cartels, which reportedly assassinated his brother (brother's death confirmed, responsible party—unknown)

Has reported on Sinaloa cartel reliably in the past:

- Reporting based upon secondhand conversations among known drug smugglers in the area, overheard at a local cafe.

Asset Controller: Reports no reason to consider source untrustworthy at this time.

Details of Items Impounded:

- **Drugs:** 19,125 lbs. of marijuana, 507 lbs. of cocaine (98% pure)
- **Weapons Confiscated:** 120 automatic 9mm Makarov PM pistols, 95 AKS-74U 7.62mm 55 RDG5 hand grenades, 2.5 tons of commercial explosives, 200 meters of det cord, assorted fuses and blasting caps
- **Cash:** $2,210,765.00, used non-sequential, multidenominational bills
- **Counterfeit Currency:** $5,000,000.00, sequential $20s and $50s
- **Personnel in Custody:** Three males; two without identification, one with a fraudulent driver's license, have not spoken since being placed in custody. Descriptions follow:
    - Approximately 30 years old; nationality unknown; overheard speaking Spanish; 5'-10", brown hair/brown eyes, 1" scar over right eye, MS-13-related gang tattoos on arms and neck; see Figure 1.8, in possession of California Driver's License for a Steve Rodgers of San Diego, DL processed through DMV and verified as fraudulent; fingerprints to follow
    - Approximately 25 years old; nationality unknown; has not spoken; 5'-11", brown hair/brown eyes, several 2" scars on left arm, MS-13 gang tattoos; photos, fingerprints to follow
    - Approximately 25 years old; nationality unknown; has not spoken; 6'-1", brown hair/brown eyes, no visible scars, several tattoos in Arabic on both arms; photos, fingerprints to follow

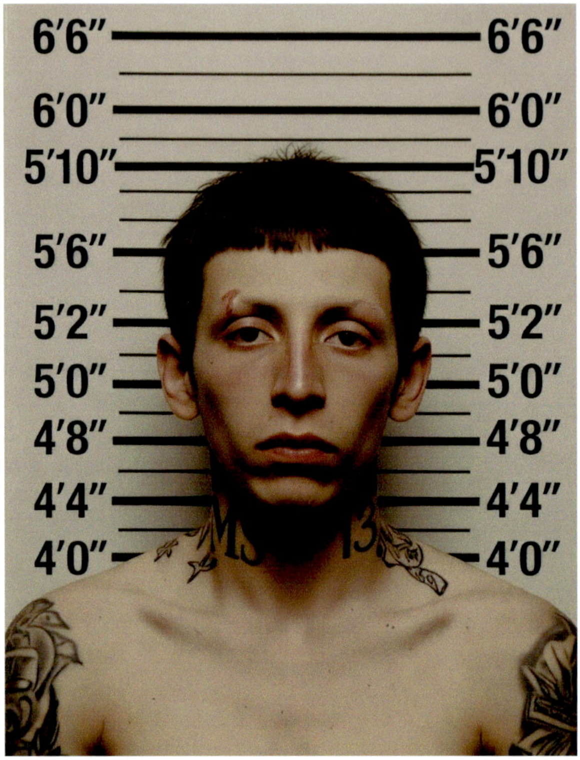

FIGURE 1.8 True name: Unknown, AKA Steve Rodgers.

NOTES

1. RAND Corporation, *Intelligence Analysis*, Retrieved 16 February 2024, http://www.rand.org/topics/intelligence-analysis.html.
2. Air Force Research Laboratory, *Framework for Analytic Cognition (FAC): A Guide for Doing All-Source Intelligence Analysis* (AFRL-RH-WP-TR-2012-0109), Melinda Marsh, 2012.
3. Vanda Felbab-Brown, *How Mexico's Cartel Jalisco Nueva Generación Rules*, Brookings, Retrieved 29 May 2022, https://www.brookings.edu/articles/how-mexicos-cartel-jalisco-nueva-generacion-rules.
4. International Association of Crime Analysts (IACA), *Definition of Crime Analysis*, Retrieved 16 February 2024, http://www.iaca.net.
5. Rachel Boba, *Crime Analysis with Crime Mapping*, Sage Publications, February 2022.
6. John Eck and Ronald Clarke, *Crime Analysis for Problem Solvers in 60 Small Steps*, U.S. Department of Justice, Office of Community Oriented Policing Services, 2017.

7. National Institute of Justice (NIJ), *Crime Analysis*, Retrieved 16 February 2024, https://nij.ojp.gov/topics/articles/crime-analysis.
8. U.S. Department of Defense (DoD) Directive 5240.1, *DoD Intelligence Activities*, 27 August 2014.
9. U.S. Department of Homeland Security, *Mission Statement and History*, Retrieved 16 February 2024, https://www.dhs.gov/mission.
10. U.S. Code, Law Enforcement, Title 14, Chapter 5, § 89.

CHAPTER 2

The Intelligence Cycle

INTRODUCTION TO THE INTELLIGENCE CYCLE

Welcome to Chapter 2 of *Intelligence Analysis Fundamentals*. This chapter will explore the Intelligence Cycle, a foundational framework for transforming raw data into actionable intelligence. Whether applied to national security, law enforcement, or corporate risk management, the Intelligence Cycle enables analysts to connect the dots, anticipate trends, and inform decision-making.

You will learn how the six phases—Requirements, Planning and Direction, Collection, Processing and Exploitation, Analysis and Production, and Dissemination—work together in dynamic environments. We will compare law enforcement and military approaches and examine real-world applications through detailed examples and exercises.

LEARNING OBJECTIVES

By the end of this lesson, students will be able to:

1. **Define** the Intelligence Cycle and explain its significance in the intelligence process.
2. **Identify** and describe the five key phases of the *Military Intelligence Cycle* (Planning and Direction, Collection, Processing, Analysis, and Dissemination).
3. **Apply** the principles of the Intelligence Cycle to hypothetical scenarios.
4. **Evaluate** the challenges and limitations associated with each phase of the cycle.
5. **Discuss** the ethical considerations in intelligence operations.

DOI: 10.4324/9781003561712-2

UNDERSTANDING THE PULSE OF INTELLIGENCE

The intricate world of intelligence analysis, where every detail holds some hidden significance, from the grand strategies of military campaigns to the clandestine maneuvers of criminal enterprises. We observe and decode various entities' subtle nuances and behavioral cues in this realm, shedding light on their intentions and future actions.

The journey begins with collecting raw information, akin to gathering puzzle pieces scattered across a vast landscape. Yet, in the meticulous analysis of these fragments, the true essence of intelligence emerges. Here, we transcend mere data, weaving together threads of insight to paint a comprehensive picture of the ever-evolving landscape of threats and opportunities.

At the heart of this endeavor lies the Intelligence Cycle, a meticulously crafted framework that guides the journey from information to actionable intelligence. From the initial gathering of raw data to the strategic dissemination of refined intelligence, each phase unfolds with precision, propelling us toward informed decision-making and proactive measures.

Embedded within this cycle are the foundational principles that resonate across diverse sectors, from law enforcement to the military and the business community. Despite nuanced variations, the core components remain steadfast, serving as the bedrock of intelligence training and operational methodologies worldwide.

Exploring the symbiotic relationship between intelligence agencies, we uncover the subtle distinctions between the U.S. Military's Intelligence Cycle and the FBI's framework (as shown in Figure 2.1) for crime analysis. While both share common objectives, subtle nuances

FIGURE 2.1 FBI Intelligence Cycle graphic (FBI).

such as the emphasis on mission requirements and the centrality of active collaboration underscore the tailored approach to each domain.

As one can see, the intelligence analysis operates in diverse contexts, from counterterrorism to corporate security. At its core, intelligence is a process of identifying patterns and answering critical questions to inform decision-making. This requires analysts to:

- **Recognize relevance:** Identify data that matters amid vast information streams.
- **Bridge gaps:** Develop insights where information is incomplete.
- **Anticipate the future:** Use predictive methods to foresee trends and actions.

According to Lowenthal, intelligence is both an art and a science, blending creative problem-solving with systematic methodologies. Successful intelligence analysis requires discipline, critical thinking, and collaboration across agencies and sectors.[1]

Unveiling the Intelligence Cycle

The Intelligence Cycle is a step-by-step process designed to produce actionable insights (see Figure 2.2). While variations exist across sectors, the core framework remains consistent.

Following is an overview of the six phases:

- **Requirements:** Define the intelligence questions that need answering.

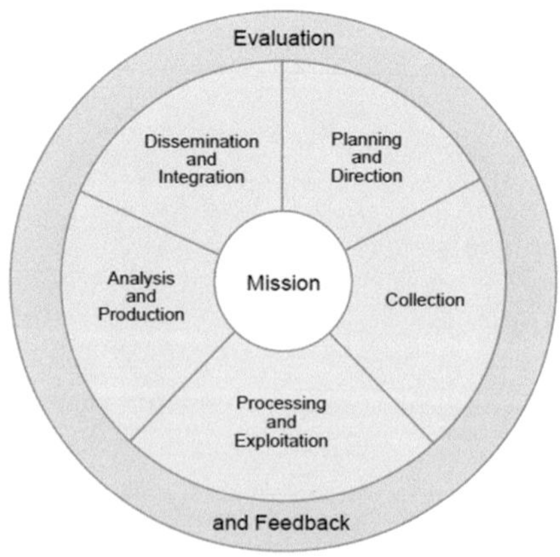

FIGURE 2.2 Military Intelligence Cycle (Department of Defense [DoD], Joint Publication 2.0, Joint Intelligence).

- **Planning and Direction:** Outline objectives, allocate resources, and prioritize tasks.
- **Collection:** Gather data from sources such as human intelligence (HUMINT), signals intelligence (SIGINT), and open-source intelligence (OSINT).
- **Processing and Exploitation:** Convert raw data into a usable format through techniques like decryption or translation.
- **Analysis and Production:** Synthesize processed information into actionable products.
- **Dissemination:** Share intelligence with stakeholders in a timely and secure manner.[2]

The Intelligence Cycle consists of six interrelated phases of intelligence operations typified by broad activities conducted by intelligence groups and organizations to provide clients, consumers, and decision-makers with relevant and timely intelligence. To limit confusion, the text mainly uses the Law Enforcement version of the Intelligence Cycle for explanation and discussion (see Figure 2.1).

The two graphics, Figure 2.1 and Figure 2.2, depict intelligence process cycles, in which the analysis process is only one phase of the overall process. The first graphic is from the Federal Bureau of Investigation (FBI), representing the Federal Law Enforcement version of the Intelligence Cycle. The second graphic depicts the military version, and its source is Joint Publication 2.0.[3] Notice that the "Analysis and Production" phase is in the exact location in both figures.

Illuminating Perspectives

The chapter describes and briefly explores the process of taking known information or data about situations and entities (military, criminal, or other threats) and characterizing the known and (with appropriate statements of probability or risk) predicted future trends and actions in those situations/entities.

There are negligible differences between the military and crime-oriented intelligence cycles. The only visible differences in the two graphics are (1) there is a separate "Requirements" phase in the FBI graphic ("Requirements" is synonymous with "Mission"), and (2) "Active Collaboration" is in the center of the FBI graphic ("Active Collaboration" and "Evaluation and Feedback" are synonymous processes).

AUTHOR'S NOTE: UNRAVELING THE NUANCES OF INTELLIGENCE METHODOLOGY

While seasoned professionals may view the disparities between the military and FBI intelligence cycles as inconsequential, a deeper examination by the Intelligence Community (IC) reveals intriguing insights into the evolution of intelligence practices. ***The overt emphasis on a Requirements phase within the FBI's framework, distinct from the military's approach,*** *sparks curiosity regarding the underlying philosophies shaping these methodologies.*

Newcomers to intelligence analysis may rightfully question the equivalence of "Requirements" to "Mission," signaling a fundamental exploration of terminology and its implications within the intelligence domain. Yet, beyond semantics lies the potential for paradigm shifts in intelligence conceptualization. ***Could the FBI's distinctive portrayal signify a progressive reinterpretation of intelligence processes, signaling a departure from traditional constructs?***

Despite rigorous inquiry, the quest for clarity often leads to convoluted discussions, underscoring the intricacies inherent in intelligence discourse. As we navigate through these complexities, it becomes evident that the differences between intelligence cycles serve as catalysts for introspection, prompting a reevaluation of established norms and fostering innovation within the field.
Therefore, since this is a fundamental text directed at the intelligence analysis novice, ***the text will treat the "Requirements phase to be synonymous with the Mission phase" rationale.***

SIX PHASES OF THE FBI'S INTELLIGENCE CYCLE

The FBI's Intelligence Cycle comprises six phases: beginning with Requirements, Planning and Direction, Collection, Processing and Exploitation, Analysis and Production, and ending with Dissemination. A continuous evaluation and feedback process is associated with each phase, known as "Active Collaboration" (see Figure 2.1).

Requirements

As discussed in Chapter 1, regardless of the intelligence analysis field, there is always at least one unanswered question or unsolved problem at the beginning of the process. The unanswered or unsolved problem is an intelligence (or analytical) requirement.

Identifying stakeholders' intelligence needs sets the stage for effective intelligence operations. This phase involves determining the information necessary to address specific challenges or support ongoing operations. However, user needs are often misunderstood, resulting in poorly defined requirements. It is essential that the intelligence consumer and the analyst thoroughly understand the requirements, and it is a shared understanding. Otherwise, intelligence resources and effort go to waste, and the analytical result will disappoint the intelligence end-user. The following is an example of a vague and poorly understood intelligence requirement.

> ***Example Scenario:***
>
> *A DHS intelligence consumer submits an intelligence requirement (IR): Provide intelligence on illegal border crossings of the Canadian border (see Figure 2.3, Analyzing intelligence requirements).*

FIGURE 2.3 Analyzing intelligence requirements.

Discussion: What is wrong with this request? The following bullets outline but a few of the vague and possibly misleading aspects of the requirement:

- *The complete Canadian Border? ... or just a portion? (Does the IR need greater specificity?)*
- *For what period? (the time period not stated)*
- *When is the information required? (Intelligence has an expiration date!)*
- *Illegal traffic across the border in which direction? (south, into the U.S. or perhaps north?), etc.*

Without further guidance, the analyst is expected to make assumptions to address these questions (contained in the bullet points), and these assumptions may be correct ... or perhaps not.

A More Refined IR: What is the volume and timing of illegal border crossings along a 10-mile stretch of the Canadian border near Blaine, WA, during the next 30 days? Focus on nighttime crossings involving organized criminal groups.

Intelligence Requirement (IR) Refinements

The analyst then performs some basic research on the intelligence problem. A period of requirements refinement should also take place to identify the "must-know" information. This "must-know" information is called the commander's critical information requirements (CCIR) in military circles.

CCIR is a comprehensive list of information requirements identified by the commander as critical in facilitating timely information management and the decision-making process affecting successful mission accomplishment. The CCIR should result from an exchange between the intelligence officer and the client. In the military's case, the client is the commander. Others will use finished intelligence products; they are the "consumers" or "end-users," but the "client" is the stakeholder in the requirements negotiation process, which has the last word. The following is an example of an unrefined intelligence requirement.

Another Example of an Information Requirement (IR):

Unrefined IR: *Will terrorists attack? If so, where, when, and how will the attack manifest itself?*

These CCIRs may be valid client concerns, but the requirements are multiple, broad, and so vague that they are virtually impossible to satisfy. In the previous Canadian border scenario, the analyst(s) is tasked to:

- *Reduce the number of requirements (preferably to one);*
- *Further develop the specifics (e.g., "where," a two-mile strip of the border; "terrorists," which terror group/cell; etc.); and*
- *Determine the client/commander's end purpose (or decision) that drives the intelligence need (knowing the end purpose is essential for molding collection planning).*

Example of an IR, 1st Refinement:

(Based upon client discussions and some level of research and intelligence collaboration effort (military term: wargaming).

Will the Islamic State of Iraq and the Levant (ISIL) attack the United States in the next two months?

(This first refinement has narrowed the threat scope and the time span, making the collection effort more practical but still very difficult.)

Understanding the Operational Environment

Knowing how the operational environment affects friendly and adversary operations also weighs into planning.

Example of an IR, 2nd Refinement:

Is ISIL more likely to attack the United States in the next two months using affiliates from outside U.S. borders or by using assets already in the U.S.?

(The second refinement is likely the result of a growing analytical draft hypothesis to determine the "most likely" threat course of action. Since it is impossible to look at "everyone, everywhere, all the time," the analyst(s) must develop a more workable hypothesis based on an appropriate threat model.)

Military Intelligence professionals refer to the process of creating a "workable hypothesis/threat modeling" as the "Intelligence Preparation of the Operational Environment" (*formerly Intelligence Preparation of the Battlefield/Battle Space*). Since DHS (friendly forces) are not alone, the threat (or enemy) also has "operational environment" constraints. Therefore, they must consider threat and friendly factors in the planning phase. Figure 2.4 depicts the effects of the "operational environment on the intelligence planning process.[4]

For example, a terror group may try to encourage sympathizers within the U.S. to attack. However, the terror group must weigh other factors. What controls do they have on who, what, where, or when their

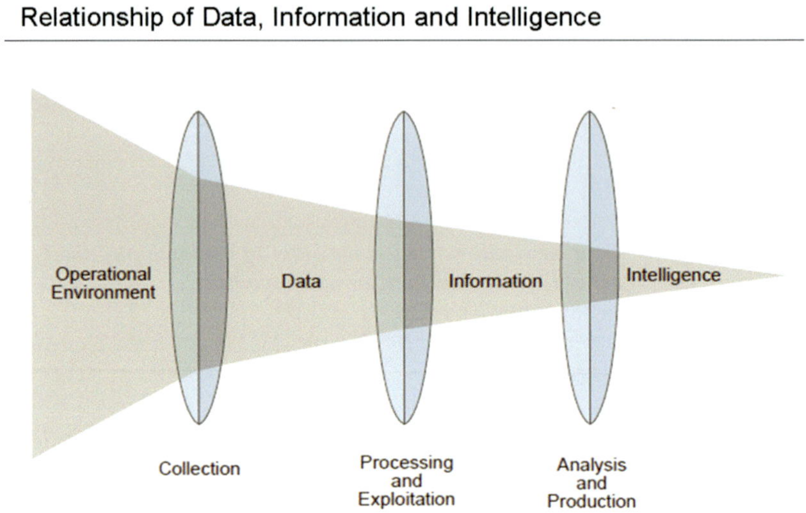

FIGURE 2.4 Relationship of the environment on the intelligence process.

sympathizers attack? Unless reasonable command and control (C2) ties exist between the sympathizer and the terror C2 element, target types and timing are complicated, and unless the sympathizer(s) have ample personal resources (weapons, explosives, transport, access, staffing, etc.), the logistics issues for the terror group become more complicated.

Understanding the operational environment reveals potential threat C2 vulnerabilities (weaknesses), providing intelligence collection opportunities. The analyst has now modified the hypotheses toward a "most likely" threat scenario where the terror group would use sympathizers, potentially already in the U.S., and plans and tasks collection requirements around this hypothesis (see the third refinement example).

Example 3rd Refinement:

Are ISIL C2 elements (see collection plan for specifics) using messenger services or commercial communications (directly) or the internet (indirectly) to contact potential sympathizers already in U.S. borders as part of an attack planning process, which may occur in the next two months?

(The third refinement is the result of a more mature hypothesis. It contains a finite defined target set to direct collection assets; the collection manager also understands that the collection plan will focus

on using signals intelligence [SIGINT] platforms [possibly HUMINT if feasible], and those SIGINT collection assets would need to signal/ message content.)

Checklist for Refining Intelligence Requirements

1. **Define Scope:** Specify the geographic area, time frame, and nature of the problem.
2. **Engage Stakeholders:** Collaborate to ensure alignment with decision-making needs.
3. **Prioritize Needs:** Focus on critical information that drives actionable outcomes.
4. **Anticipate Constraints:** Consider limitations in data, resources, and time.
5. **Clarify Outputs:** Determine intelligence final products' desired format and timing.

Planning and Direction

Strategic planning is crucial to guide intelligence activities. In this phase, objectives are outlined, resources are allocated, and priorities are set to ensure efficient intelligence operations.

The Planning and Direction phase will plan and generate, at a minimum, the initial tasking for all subsequent phases of the Intelligence Cycle. Analysis and production responsibilities assigned during the planning and direction phase establish the anticipated flow of information and the development of the appropriate intelligence dissemination architecture.

Analysts will make many assumptions throughout the intelligence process. One of those assumptions appears at the start of the "Planning and Direction" phase. Analysts must assume there exists a "clear and common" understanding of the requirements provided. If this is not the case, they should make every effort to rectify the situation. Failure to obtain a "clear and common" understanding of the requirements (between analyst and client) imperils further planning steps and all results from further analysis and collection efforts.

DHS all-source intelligence production is a collaborative/federated information-sharing process, often between many geographically dispersed and diverse organizations (Federal, State, and local Law Enforcement, and occasionally foreign governments). This approach involves dividing the analysis and production effort among intelligence facilities and law enforcement organizations (often worldwide) to meet DHS intelligence needs.

Collection

The collection phase focuses on gathering relevant data and information from various sources. Whether through human intelligence (HUMINT), signals intelligence (SIGINT), or other means, this phase acquires raw materials for analysis.

The "Collection" phase involves planning for and tasking "collection assets" (e.g., aerial surveillance, wiretaps, etc.). Analysts must understand "what is being asked" and "why the information is needed" to generate collection requests properly. The "what" and "why" help to define the collection plan better. Collection asset requests are generated by a "collection manager" and then routed to higher levels for approval and scheduling.

(Note: Planning for "what" information needs collection is identified in the previous Planning and Direction phase.)

The collection plan specifies the types of information and data required. It does not specify the collection platform. The collection plan should also state when the information is needed (e.g., the "not later than" or NTL date is JUN 4). Without the NTL date, the required information may be collected, but it may also arrive when it is no longer of value. The length of the collection period and frequency must also be determined based on the "why aspect" of the requirement (see the following example).

Example Scenario:

Determining illegal crossing activity along a specified two mile portion of the U.S. southern border is the subject of the collection effort. The information will drive border patrol staffing, scheduling, and interdiction efforts. The developed collection plan outlines a continuous 24-hour video collection effort for one month, starting one week from today's date. A quick terrain study shows that only foot traffic is possible along that particular stretch of the border. Therefore, the collection manager adds remote ground vibration sensors to the video surveillance package (see Table 2.1).

Processing and Exploitation

In this phase, raw data undergoes processing to convert it into usable intelligence. Information is organized, categorized, and analyzed to extract valuable insight.

TABLE 2.1 Comparing Intelligence Disciplines

Discipline	*Source*	*Strengths*
HUMINT	*Human sources (agents, informants)*	*Access to intentions and plans*
SIGINT	*Electronic communications*	*High-volume data, global coverage*
OSINT	*Publicly available information*	*Broad accessibility*
IMINT	*Aerial and satellite imagery*	*Geospatial accuracy*
MASINT	*Scientific and technical sensors*	*Unique forensic insights*

Source: Office of the Director of National Intelligence (ODNI), What is Intelligence? https://www.dni.gov/index.php/what-we-do/what-is-intelligence, Retrieved 28 February 2026.

The processing and exploitation phase converts raw collected data into usable forms more readily understood by clients, decision-makers, intelligence analysts, and other intelligence consumers. Processing and exploitation are becoming increasingly automated today, especially in IMINT, SIGINT, and MASINT. However, much processing is still manual. The processing and exploitation phase also combines and collates the data to fill the information gaps.

Not all raw data forms are understandable to the consumer. Even most imagery forms must first be processed and interpreted. Something as basic as an aerial photograph may require mensuration (measuring geometric magnitudes, lengths, areas, and volumes) to determine the proper scale/size of depicted objects for identification and targeting.

Similarly, not all data confirms or denies the hypothesis. Some data is erroneous or misleading; therefore, multiple collections help to provide a more thorough understanding and complete picture. HUMINT collections generally require credibility and reliability evaluations.

Other processing and exploitation may be required, such as signals decryption, documents or recorded voice translations, explosive forensics, or technical exploitation of a piece of equipment (e.g., a laptop computer).[5] Even translating an unencrypted document into English for further exploitation and analysis is an involved process (see Figure 2.5).

Highlighting Challenges

- **Data Overload:** With increasing sensor technology, analysts face overwhelming volumes of raw data. Tools like artificial

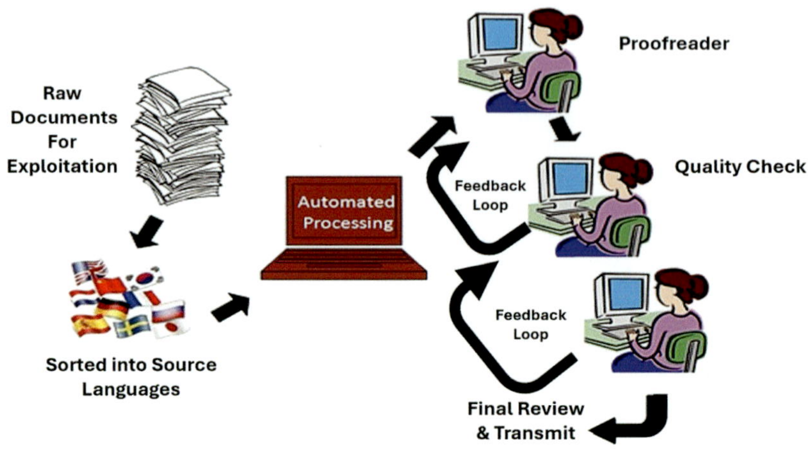

FIGURE 2.5 Simplified diagram of unencrypted document exploitation.

intelligence (AI) and machine learning (ML) are essential for triage and prioritization.

- **Biases and Errors:** Automated systems may amplify biases in the source data. Analysts must cross-check results with human validation.[6]

Analysis and Production

The analysis and production phases are at the heart of the cycle. Intelligence analysts dissect processed information, uncover patterns, and generate actionable intelligence products for decision-makers.

Collection capabilities assigned or attached to the DHS and other government/law enforcement-related groups gather information and raw data for analysis. The analysis and production phase creates the final intelligence products using the refined, compiled, and processed information and data from subordinate units and external organizations. All available processed information is integrated, evaluated, analyzed, and interpreted to create products that satisfy the information/intelligence requirements (IRs). Intelligence products can take many presentation forms. They may be oral presentations, hard-copy publications, or electronic media. All-source intelligence products are the result of multidiscipline fusion efforts.

A recent beneficial refinement to IC all-source intelligence processing is the requirement to comply with *Intelligence Community Directive 203*, Analytic Standards.[7] Before the creation of ODNI analytic standards, all-source processing, analysis, content, and quality control of intelligence products could vary from one member of the IC to the next.

This section only introduces the Analysis and Production phase as part of the Intelligence Cycle. Later chapters discuss and explain the Analysis Phase, including multiple and varied analysis methods and their utilization.

Dissemination

The final phase involves disseminating intelligence products to relevant stakeholders. Effective communication ensures decision-makers receive timely and accurate intelligence to inform their actions.

The purpose of the dissemination and integration phase is to appropriately distribute and deliver finished intelligence to the intelligence consumer or end-user to complete their organizational missions. Various mechanisms facilitate dissemination. Product classification, availability of viable distribution pathways, and the end-user's needs determine the mechanisms for delivery of finished intelligence products. If the dissemination route is appropriately accredited and certified, delivery can utilize computer networks, couriers, registered mail, and other delivery systems.

The multiplicity of dissemination paths underpins the need for interoperability between communications and computer systems among the IC and law enforcement.

Best Practices for Dissemination

1. **Tailor Content:** Adapt reports to the audience's expertise and needs.
2. **Use Secure Channels:** Ensure dissemination methods align with security protocols.
3. **Follow-up:** Confirm that recipients understand and can act on the intelligence provided.[8]

Active Collaboration: A Continuous Feedback Loop

Active collaboration and feedback are integrated into each phase of the Intelligence Cycle. This continuous evaluation ensures alignment with evolving requirements and priorities, fostering effective intelligence operations (see Figure 2.6).

PRACTICAL EXERCISE

The learning activity helps develop your skills to refine information/intelligence requirements. Your supervisor gives you an assignment: there is a fictitious Alaskan ECO-Terror group threatening to attack U.S. business interests. You have been given a "Draft" IR that is poorly

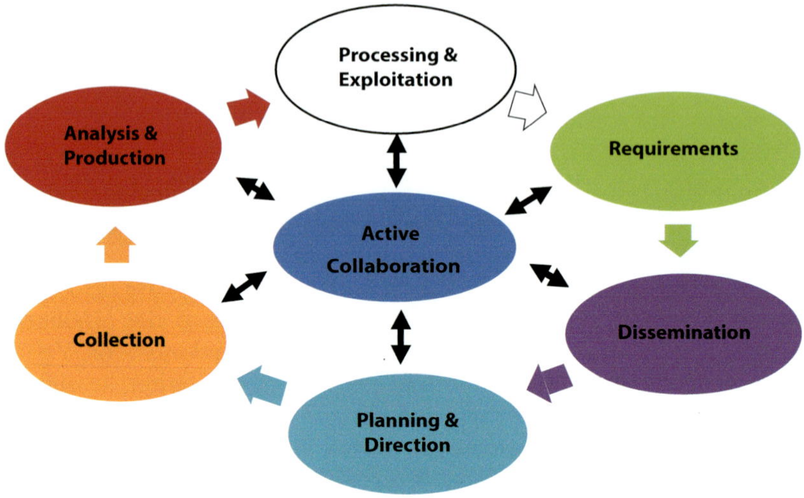

FIGURE 2.6 Analytical collaboration feedback loop diagram.

defined. Refine the IR as a more meaningful and observable requirement as a facilitated group exercise.

> ***Example Scenario:***
>
> *Your DHS supervisor has emailed you an information/intelligence requirement (IR) or has provided you with one directly. The IR reads as follows (see Figure 2.7):*
>
> *Your supervisor wants you to comment/collaborate on the IR and assist him in the refinement process.*

Exercise Instructions

The instructor will facilitate the group discussion. Using the IR and associated scenarios provided, refine the requirement into a meaningful and observable requirement.

Practical Exercise: (Student Handout)

Additional Guidance

- Reduce the number of requirements (preferably to one).
- Further develop the specifics.
- Determine the client/commander's end purpose (or decision).

CLASSIFICATION: "SECRET/NOFORN – Training Purposes Only"

To: "Your name"

From: Your supervisor

Date: "Today"

Subject: Homegrown terror group

We have received reliable reporting that indicates a radical Native Alaskan ECO-Terror group known as the Aleutian Green Warriors (AGW) has recently formed and may attack U.S. Business interests.

IR: Where, where, and in what strength will AGW attack? Identify what weapons they will use.

CLASSIFICATION: "SECRET/NOFORN – Training Purposes Only"

FIGURE 2.7 Example information/intelligence email.

- How does the operational environment affect friendly and adversary operations?
- *What is the "most likely" threat course of action? ... most deadly?*

CHAPTER SUMMARY

Congratulations on completing Chapter 2, *The Intelligence Cycle*. This lesson introduced you to the foundational framework that underpins intelligence analysis across various domains, from national security to corporate risk management.

This chapter briefly described and explored the process of taking known information or data about situations and entities (military, criminal, or other threats), characterizing the known (and the information gaps), and (with appropriate statements of probability or risk) predicting future trends and actions in those situations/entities. U.S. Military and Federal law enforcement versions of the Intelligence Cycle are essentially the same. Here is a recap of the key takeaways.

Key Concepts Reviewed

1. **The Intelligence Cycle Framework**
   - Six interconnected phases, *Requirements, Planning and Direction, Collection, Processing and Exploitation, Analysis and Production, and Dissemination*, work together to transform raw data into actionable intelligence.
   - Active collaboration and feedback enhance the cycle, ensuring adaptability and precision.

2. **Requirements**
    - Defining clear and specific intelligence questions is critical to success.
    - Poorly defined requirements can lead to wasted resources and irrelevant analysis.
3. **Planning and Direction**
    - Strategic planning aligns resources, priorities, and objectives, laying the groundwork for subsequent phases.
    - Clear communication between stakeholders and analysts is essential to avoid misinterpretations.
4. **Collection**
    - Data is gathered using various methods, such as HUMINT, SIGINT, OSINT, and IMINT.
    - A well-crafted collection plan ensures the relevance and timeliness of collected information.
5. **Processing and Exploitation**
    - Raw data is converted into usable formats through tools, technologies, and expertise.
    - Automation and human validation work together to mitigate data overload and errors.
6. **Analysis and Production**
    - Analysts synthesize processed data to produce intelligence products.
    - Methods like link analysis and scenario analysis help uncover patterns and predict future actions.
7. **Dissemination**
    - Intelligence is delivered to stakeholders securely and tailored to their needs.
    - Effective dissemination ensures decision-makers receive actionable insights on time.
8. **Active Collaboration**
    - Continuous feedback loops across all phases refine processes and align them with dynamic requirements.

Learning Objectives Accomplished

- **Understand** the purpose and phases of the Intelligence Cycle.
- **Recognize** the importance of well-defined requirements and iterative feedback.
- **Identify** the distinct roles of collection, analysis, and dissemination in intelligence operations.
- **Apply** best practices for refining vague or broad intelligence requirements.

Practical Application

You were introduced to real-world scenarios, such as:

- Refining intelligence requirements (e.g., Canadian border scenario, AGW threat).
- Developing a collection plan based on operational needs and constraints.
- Visualizing the flow of the Intelligence Cycle through feedback-driven collaboration.

Reflection Questions

1. Which phase of the Intelligence Cycle do you think is the most challenging? Why?
2. How can active collaboration improve the refinement of intelligence requirements?
3. How does understanding the operational environment affect the planning and collection phases?

Thank you for your engagement and effort in this chapter. Keep building your analytical skills to become a master of the intelligence craft!

GLOSSARY OF TERMS

Here is a glossary of key terms introduced and discussed in Chapter 2 to enhance your understanding of the material:

Active Collaboration: A continuous feedback process that ensures alignment with evolving requirements and priorities at every phase of the Intelligence Cycle.

Analysis and Production: The phase of the Intelligence Cycle where processed data is evaluated, integrated, and synthesized into actionable intelligence products.

Collection: The process of gathering raw information and data from various sources, such as human intelligence (HUMINT), signals intelligence (SIGINT), and open-source intelligence (OSINT).

Commander's Critical Information Requirements (CCIR): A list of critical information needed by a commander to facilitate timely decisions and mission success.

Dissemination: The final phase of the Intelligence Cycle, involving the secure delivery of finished intelligence to stakeholders in a usable format.

HUMINT (Human Intelligence): Intelligence gathered through interpersonal contact, such as agents, informants, or interviews.

Intelligence Cycle: A structured process consisting of six phases—Requirements, Planning and Direction, Collection, Processing and Exploitation, Analysis and Production, and Dissemination—designed to produce actionable intelligence.

Intelligence Preparation of the Operational Environment (IPOE): A systematic methodology for analyzing the operational environment to predict adversary actions and develop actionable insights.

MASINT (Measurement and Signature Intelligence): Technical intelligence derived from the analysis of physical properties, such as radar signals, chemical composition, or acoustic data.

Operational Environment: The conditions, circumstances, and influences that affect the planning and execution of operations, including both friendly and adversary factors.

OSINT (Open-Source Intelligence): Intelligence gathered from publicly available sources, such as newspapers, social media, and academic publications.

Planning and Direction: The phase of the Intelligence Cycle that involves defining objectives, allocating resources, and setting priorities to guide intelligence activities.

Processing and Exploitation: The conversion of raw data into usable forms through techniques like translation, decryption, or interpretation.

Requirements: The initial phase of the Intelligence Cycle where specific intelligence needs or questions are identified to drive the analysis process.

SIGINT (Signals Intelligence): Intelligence derived from intercepted electronic signals, such as communications or radar transmissions.

Threat Modeling: The process of developing hypotheses to predict an adversary's most likely and most dangerous courses of action.

This glossary serves as a quick reference for understanding key terms and concepts from the chapter. Feel free to revisit it as you progress through the material!

NOTES

1. Mark M. Lowenthal, *Intelligence: From Secrets to Policy* (8th ed.). CQ Press, 2020.
2. U.S. Department of Justice, *FBI Intelligence Cycle Overview*, Retrieved 2023, https://www.fbi.gov/how-we-investigate/intelligence/intelligence.
3. Department of Defense (DoD), *Joint Publication 2.0, Joint Intelligence*, Retrieved 2024, http://www.dtic.mil/doctrine/new_pubs/jp2_0.pdf.
4. Department of Defense (DoD), *Joint Publication 2.0, Joint Intelligence*, http://www.dtic.mil/doctrine/new_pubs/jp2_0.pdf.

5. Department of Defense (DoD), *Joint Publication 2.0, Joint Intelligence*, http://www.dtic.mil/doctrine/new_pubs/jp2_0.pdf.
6. M. Taylor and R. Lewis, 'AI in Intelligence Processing: Opportunities and Risks', *Journal of Intelligence Analysis*, 15(2), 45–59, 2022.
7. Office of the Director of National Intelligence (ODNI), Intelligence Community Directive 203, *Analytic Standards*, 2015, http://www.dni.gov/files/documents/ICD/ICD%20203%20Analytic%20Standards.pdf.
8. Office of the Director of National Intelligence (ODNI), *IC Directive 501: Dissemination of Intelligence*, 2021.

CHAPTER 3

Thinking about Thinking

INTRODUCTION

Imagine you are tasked with uncovering a complex puzzle hidden beneath layers of uncertainty and incomplete information. This is the daily reality of an intelligence analyst. In this chapter, we embark on an intriguing exploration of the mind's power, uncovering the intricate processes that underpin effective intelligence analysis. Rather than a dry academic exercise, this is a journey to enhance your cognitive toolkit, unlocking sharper insights and more reliable conclusions.

We delve into the fascinating realms of critical thinking, reflective thinking, and higher-order thinking, investigating how these skills transform raw data into actionable intelligence. From mitigating biases to embracing creativity, this chapter challenges you to reframe problems, question assumptions, and apply structured methodologies to complex scenarios. Together, we will navigate the human factors influencing thinking quality and uncover strategies to overcome them, ensuring your analytical skills evolve to meet any challenge (see Figure 3.1 and Table 3.1).

Understanding the neural underpinnings of cognitive functions is central for enhancing analytical proficiency. Figure 3.1 is a cross-sectional diagram of the human brain, illustrating key regions associated with critical thinking, reflective thinking, and higher-order thinking.

So, prepare to be inspired, question, and evolve as we dissect the intricacies of thinking about thinking to transform and potentially improve the way you think. Embrace the cognitive journey that lies ahead, for it promises to enrich your analytical capabilities and redefine your approach to intelligence analysis.

Welcome to Chapter 3, where mastering your mind begins as you embark on a journey through the mind of an intelligence analyst, where we explore the art and science of Thinking about Thinking. This chapter is not merely an academic discourse but a thrilling expedition into

DOI: 10.4324/9781003561712-3

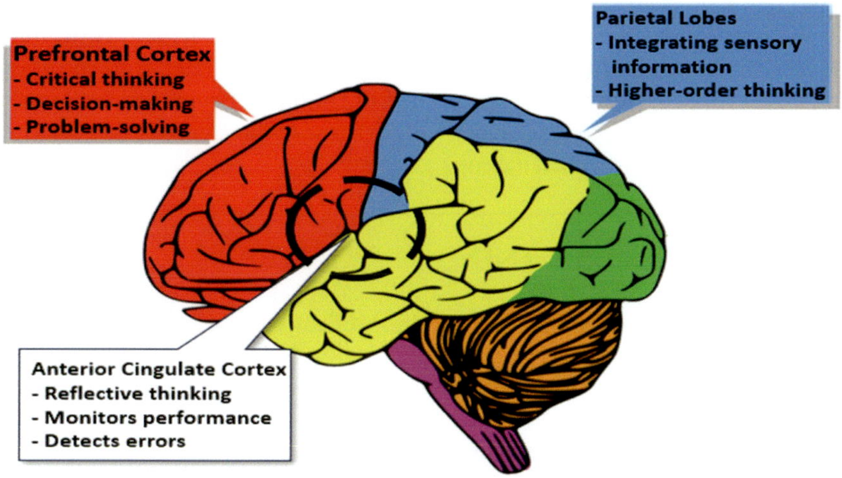

FIGURE 3.1 Where critical thinking, reflective thinking, and higher-order thinking happen.

TABLE 3.1 Cognitive Processes and Associated Brain Regions

Cognitive Process	*Brain Region(s)*	*Function*
Critical Thinking	*Prefrontal Cortex (PFC)*	*The PFC is responsible for higher-order cognitive functions such as decision-making, planning, problem-solving, and working memory.*[1]
Reflective Thinking	*Default Mode Network (DMN), including the Medial Prefrontal Cortex and Posterior Cingulate Cortex*	*The DMN is active during introspection and self-referential thinking, facilitating self-awareness and evaluation of past experiences.*[2]
Higher-Order Thinking	*Prefrontal Cortex, Parietal Lobes, Temporal Lobes*	*These regions collaborate to support complex cognitive tasks such as analysis, evaluation, and creation, integrating information across different domains.*[3]

the cognitive domain, where every analyst's primary tool, their mind, is sharpened and honed. We unravel the mysteries of critical thinking, reflective thinking, and higher-order thinking, diving deep into the cognitive factors that influence the quality of thought. Beyond mere definitions, we present a dynamic arena where these thought processes are the linchpins of successful intelligence analysis.

LEARNING OBJECTIVES

1. **Define** and differentiate critical, reflective, and higher-order thinking.
2. **Apply** the Dewey Sequence to structured problem-solving scenarios.
3. **Identify** and mitigate cognitive biases in analysis.
4. **Evaluate** the reliability of information using structured techniques.
5. **Analyze** how modern tools like AI assist in intelligence analysis.

PROBLEM-SOLVING

The art of problem-solving is a cornerstone of intelligence analysis, demanding a blend of creativity, critical thinking, and methodical strategy (see Figure 3.2). It transcends the mere identification of solutions, focusing instead on understanding the pathway to these solutions. This process is fundamental for replicating results and identifying any logical missteps.

At its inception, problem-solving involves categorizing problems as poorly defined or well-defined. A well-defined problem, such as receiving a bill, presents clear outcomes and straightforward remedies. Conversely, a poorly defined problem embodies complexity, requiring multiple steps and considering a number of variables, making the path to resolution less apparent.

Richards J. Heuer, Jr., an authority in analytical thought, emphasizes that the human mind's limited working memory often complicates intelligence analysis. To navigate this, he advocates for two pivotal techniques: decomposition and externalization. Decomposition involves breaking down a complex problem into manageable parts, facilitating clearer thought processes on each segment. Meanwhile, externalization involves transferring these problems onto a tangible medium, illustrating the interconnections between different components and variables. This

FIGURE 3.2 The art of problem-solving (www.shutterstock.com).

practice clarifies thought processes and aids in organizing and analyzing information.[4]

These strategies, decomposition and externalization, are not just techniques but essential tools in the analyst's arsenal. They enable them to dissect and understand each challenge's intricacies. Chapter 7 will delve deeper into these concepts, providing a framework for defining problems and crafting effective solutions.

CRITICAL THINKING

Critical thinking in intelligence analysis transcends traditional boundaries, offering a lens through which analysts can refine their thought processes to achieve unparalleled clarity and efficiency (see Figure 3.3). Defined as the disciplined practice of engaging with one's thoughts to organize, clarify, enhance efficiency, and identify biases, critical thinking is essential not for direct problem-solving but for improving the methodology of thought. This introspective journey is crucial for the intelligence analyst, whose primary objective is to distill unbiased, logical insights from a sea of information.

Key attributes of critical thinking include:

- The capacity to dissect raw data, critically assess evidence, and rigorously evaluate both arguments and the processes that led to them.

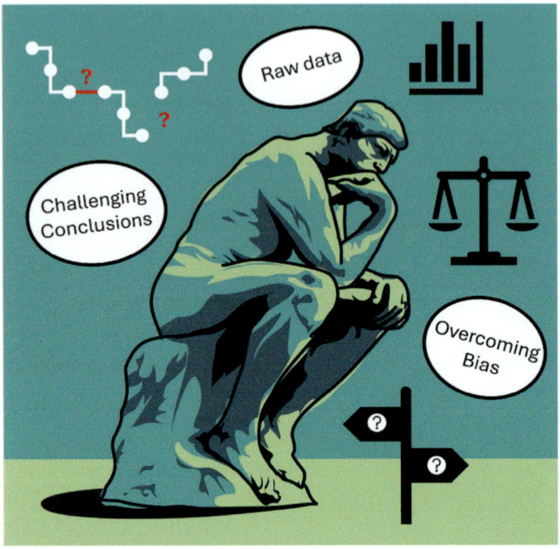

FIGURE 3.3 The concept of critical thinking (www.shutterstock.com).

- An acute awareness of logical connections and the discernment to identify when they are absent.
- A proactive stance toward challenging one's conclusions, driven by a quest for truth rather than the comfort of confirmation bias.
- The flexibility to reassess and realign one's belief systems when they obscure objectivity or logic.[5]

In intelligence analysis, where the stakes often involve national security, minimizing personal biases and recognizing logical fallacies is not just beneficial but imperative. Cultivating critical thinking skills ensures that analysts can navigate the complex web of information with a clear mind, ensuring that their conclusions are as accurate and unbiased as possible.

REFLECTIVE THINKING

Intelligence analysts should have a firm understanding of multiple problem-solving methods, which they can use as tools to break down, scrutinize, and continuously develop their analysis processes. Reflective thinking is a recognized and tested problem-solving procedure (see Figure 3.4).

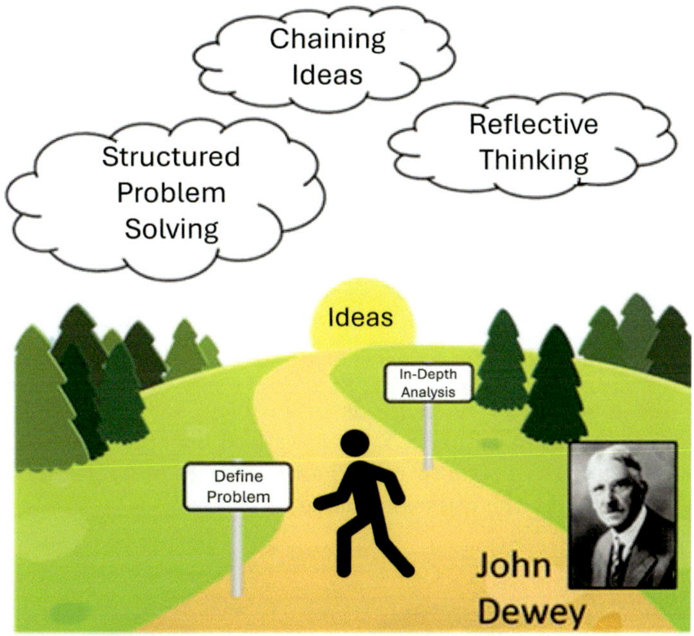

FIGURE 3.4 Dewey's concept of reflective thinking.

Reflective thinking is a basic thought model developed by John Dewey in the last century. It differs from random thought in its "chaining" feature, which entails a consecutive ordering of ideas so that each idea establishes its successor while referring to its forerunner. "Reflective thinking," as described by John Dewey, "is like retracing your steps on a hike to ensure you are on the right path. Each thought builds on the last, creating a coherent trail."[6]

As John Dewey delineated, reflective thinking is not merely a method but a transformative process that empowers intelligence analysts to critically evaluate and refine their problem-solving methodologies. This structured approach, distinct from spontaneous or random thought, involves a deliberate "chaining" of ideas, where each concept paves the way for the next, ensuring a cohesive and comprehensive analysis.

The Dewey Sequence, a cornerstone of reflective thinking, guides analysts through systematically exploring problems. This sequence begins with defining the problem, including clarifying ambiguous terms and concepts. It then progresses to an in-depth analysis of the problem's history, causes, symptoms, existing solutions, and their limitations, setting the stage for identifying criteria for viable solutions.

Proposing solutions involves brainstorming and other creative techniques, followed by a critical evaluation of these solutions against the established criteria. A solution is selected based on carefully balancing its advantages and potential drawbacks, considering immediate and long-term implications.

Finally, the implementation phase focuses on gaining support, outlining specific steps for execution, and establishing mechanisms for the solution's evaluation and validation. This rigorous process facilitates effective problem-solving and fosters a continuous learning and improvement culture among analysts.

Dewey Sequence Problem-Solving

One of the most effective methods of problem-solving is the Dewey Sequence, as shown in Figure 3.5. This method uses the reflective thinking process, which is a structured, organized series of questions. See the process described by the questions listed to follow.

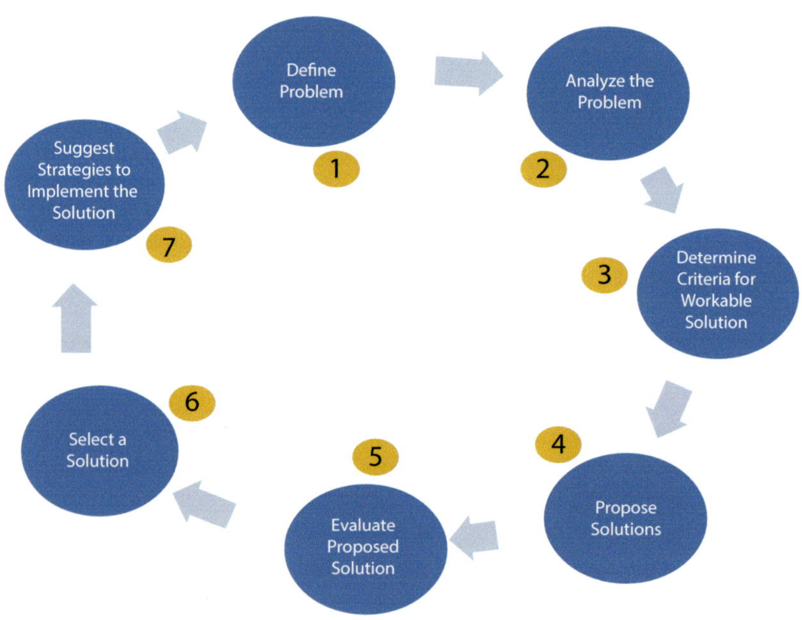

FIGURE 3.5 Dewey's sequence problem-solving process.

Step 1: Define the Problem

a. What is the specific problem?
b. Identify what terms, concepts, or ideas need defining or further explanation.

Step 2: Analyze the Problem

a. What is the history of the problem?
b. What are the causes of the problem?
c. What are the symptoms of the problem?
d. What methods currently exist to deal with the problem?
e. What are the limitations of these methods?

Step 3: Determine Criteria for a Workable Solution

What are the guidelines for a workable solution?

Step 4: Propose Solutions

After the analyst(s) has (have) analyzed the problem, suggest criteria for a solution (e.g., brainstorming).

Step 5: Evaluate Proposed Solutions

After compiling a list of possible solutions, evaluate the solutions using the following questions:

a. Are there any disadvantages to the solutions? Do the disadvantages outweigh the advantages?
b. Do the solutions conform to the formulated criteria (see Step 3)?

Step 6: Select a Solution

a. Weigh merits and deficiencies.
b. If adopted, would this solution have long-term and short-term adverse effects?

Step 7: Suggest Strategies to Implement the Solution

a. How can the analyst(s) gain support and approval for the proposed solution? What is the internal/external review process?
b. What specific steps are necessary to implement the solution?
c. How can the solution be evaluated/validated?[7]

Practical Exercise: (Student Handout)

This learning activity uses the Dewey Sequence Problem-Solving Process to develop and evaluate a solution to the problem.

Break into groups of more than two but less than five. The instructor will facilitate the exercise. Use the Dewey Sequence Problem-Solving Process to develop and evaluate a solution to the problem provided.

Problem Scenario

You are member of a fictitious intelligence analysis cell working for the DHS. Your job is to identify, quantify, and structurally analyze terror threats to the homeland to determine the level of threat and possible organizational weaknesses and vulnerabilities.

Your supervisor walks in the door and tosses a newspaper in front of your group. The headline reads: ***Islamic State (ISIS, ISIL) in the United States, All 50 States!***

"We have investigations of people in various stages of radicalizing in all 50 states," said the FBI Director, adding: "This is not a New York phenomenon or a Washington phenomenon. This is all 50 states and in ways that are very hard to see."

The FBI Director goes on to say: "Those people exist in every state. I have homegrown, violent extremist investigations in every single state. Until a few weeks ago there were groups in 49 states; Alaska had none, which I couldn't quite figure out. But Alaska has now joined the group so we have investigations of people in various stages of radicalizing in all 50 states; ISIL in particular is putting out a siren song with their slick propaganda through social media."

Your supervisor wants you to read the paper, analyze the problem, and provide some possible solutions.

Exercise Instructions

Based upon the scenario provided, use the Dewey Sequence Problem-Solving Process to identify solutions and select one to solve the problem. You have 45 minutes to discuss, develop, and document your solutions. Be sure you answer all questions to the best of your ability. Feel free to collaborate with other groups and/or use the internet to assist your process. Be prepared to share your results with the whole class.

Practical Exercise: (Student Handout)

Step 1: Define the Problem

- What is the specific problem?
- Identify what terms, concepts, or ideas need defining or further explanation.

Step 2: Analyze the Problem

- What is the history of the problem?
- What are the causes of the problem?

- What are the symptoms of the problem?
- What methods currently exist for dealing with the problem?
- What are the limitations of these methods?

Step 3: Determine Criteria for a Workable Solution

What are the guidelines for a workable solution?

Step 4: Propose Solutions

After the analyst(s) has (have) analyzed the problem and suggested criteria for a solution (e.g., brainstorming) .

Step 5: Evaluate Proposed Solution

After compiling a list of possible solutions, evaluate the solutions using the following questions:

- Are there any disadvantages to the solutions? Do the disadvantages outweigh the advantages?
- Do the solutions conform to the formulated criteria (see Step 3)?

Step 6: Select a Solution

- Weigh merits and deficiencies.
- If adopted, would this solution have long-term and short-term effects?

Step 7: Suggest Strategies to Implement the Solution

How can the analyst(s) gain support and approval for the proposed solution? What is the internal/external review process?

- What specific steps are necessary to implement the solution?
- How can the solution be evaluated/validated?

HIGHER-ORDER THINKING

The concept of higher-order thinking skills (HOTS), introduced by Dr. Benjamin Bloom in 1956, is a cornerstone of cognitive development that encompasses the processes of "Analyzing," "Evaluating," and "Creating," as shown in Figure 3.6. These skills are pivotal in nurturing an analytical mindset, especially for intelligence analysts who are tasked with dissecting complex information to forge new insights and strategic solutions.[8]

Analysis

It would seem intuitive that intelligence analysts would need to be analytical. However, the intelligence analyst takes analysis to a new level of complexity. They not only need to be able to analyze bits of data, imagery, and other information provided to solve problems or satisfy an IR, but they must be critical of the information sources, their potential personal cultural biases, and at the same time, be able to identify and

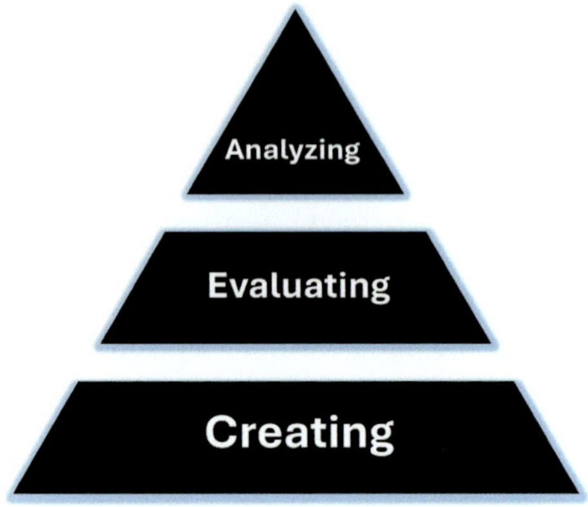

FIGURE 3.6 The elements of higher-order thinking.

analyze the process they used for the original analysis. Simply put, they analyze the source information, themselves, and the analytical process.

As defined by Robert Marzano, analysis consists of matching, classifying, error analysis, generalizing, and specifying. By engaging in these processes, intelligence analysts can use what they are learning about a threat or problem to create new insights and invent ways of using information in new situations. When analysts use analysis skills to determine the validity and worth of a particular piece of information, they are engaging in critical thought.[9]

Evaluation

The evaluation phase requires analysts to critically assess the information's reliability and relevance. This involves comparing new intelligence with existing data, examining source credibility, and evaluating the information's coherence and consistency. This meticulous approach ensures that conclusions drawn are not only based on solid evidence but also devoid of personal or systemic biases.

To evaluate information, analysts need to be able to distinguish essential data from information that is simply interesting. They must be able to identify core themes, form and support opinions, and identify inconsistencies, bias, or lack of coherence or accuracy in a text. They must also be able to use background information, prior knowledge, and other textual sources to assess the validity of the text. For example, when reading a raw HUMINT intelligence report from a new source, analysts with strong evaluation skills might compare the reports of two other vetted sources. Questions analysts use to evaluate the original source and reporting might include:

- Where reporting topics overlap, do they agree with new source reporting? Are there inconsistencies? *(Comparing/Contrasting/Critiquing)*
- What are the "bona fides" of the new source? What are the source's motivations for providing the information? *(Assessing/Appraising)*
- Do they have reasonable placement and access to the information they provide? If yes, how did they obtain placement and access? If not, how did they obtain the information? *(Defending/Justifying/Supporting)*

Creating

It may not be immediately apparent to the non-professional as to why "creativity" is critical to analytic processes. However, creativity is often what distinguishes the good analyst from the extraordinary. Creativity allows the analyst to diverge from the mainstream group-thought perspective. They are the ones who "think outside the box."

Creativity in intelligence analysis transcends conventional thinking patterns. It involves envisioning scenarios, hypothesizing adversary strategies, and developing countermeasures. The DHS's Analytic Red Cell Program exemplifies how creative thinking is applied in real-world contexts to anticipate and mitigate potential threats through unconventional analysis. In Red Cell analysis, the analyst attempts to imagine themselves in the minds of adversaries and contemplate their next move.

The DHS established the Analytic Red Cell Program in 2004. The Red Cell compares results with terrorism analysis from Homeland Security's intelligence professionals, who examine real-life threat information. Written reports on Red Cell's sessions are then forwarded to terrorism analysts inside the department, local and state police, and security experts in private industry. Most Red Cell reports note they are "alternative assessments intended to provoke thought and stimulate discussion."[10]

Incorporating HOTS in intelligence analysis fosters a dynamic and flexible thinking process that is crucial for navigating the complexities of modern security challenges. By applying these skills, analysts can enhance their ability to interpret, evaluate, and innovate, thus contributing to more effective and strategic decision-making.

COGNITIVE FACTORS THAT AFFECT THINKING QUALITY

The exploration of cognitive factors impacting the quality of critical thought reveals inherent human limitations that significantly influence the effectiveness of intelligence analysis. These limitations encompass difficulties in managing complexity, navigating uncertainty, personal biases, and sometimes a shortfall in subject matter expertise.

According to Richards J. Heuer and other supporting research, the principal challenges of critical thought are often human limitations. Humans are limited in their ability to address complex issues and situations by their inability to handle uncertainty, by personal biases, and, often, by the lack of subject matter expertise.[11]

Complexity

The intricate nature of information and data within the analytical process often surpasses human cognitive capacities. While computer algorithms have somewhat mitigated this challenge by handling extensive computations, they fail to model complex datasets with nuanced interrelations and variabilities. Analysts frequently resort to oversimplification to make sense of this complexity, which might introduce bias and diminish the value of nuanced, statistically significant data over more immediate, albeit less relevant, information.

The complexity of information/data in the analysis stream can often be very complex, far beyond the human mind's ability to comprehend, creating a significant analytical challenge. Today, computer algorithms and data processing reduce some of that complexity. Automated processing is an excellent mechanism for handling thousands of simple and repetitive calculations. However, relationships and variability are more difficult to conceptualize into models or algorithms.

Analysts often try to simplify the problem to better deal with the more complex information sets. Simplifying strategies may lead to biased results, such as using analogous examples or valuing vivid, immediate cases rather than more abstract, bland statistical data that are often of much greater value.[12]

Uncertainty

In stark contrast to the more definitive outcomes possible in criminal investigations, intelligence analysis operates within a realm of inherent uncertainty. The predictive nature of intelligence work, compounded by fluctuating variables, resists easy quantification, making it challenging to assign precise confidence levels or risk assessments to analytical conclusions.

Unlike criminal investigations, where once evidence is compiled and meets a judicial level of satisfaction that leads to an arrest, suspect interrogation, and possibly confession, intelligence analysis rarely achieves similar levels of certainty. Intelligence analysis normally operates under varying degrees of uncertainty. Most real-world analytical problem sets, due to the associated variables, cannot easily fit into statistical equations, and therefore, it becomes difficult for the intelligence analyst to provide hard mathematical percentages defining the confidence level of the analysis or level of risk involved.

The following examples better describe this conundrum.

Examples:

Imagine you are trying to predict the likelihood of men walking on the moon in 1900. Where do you begin? (At this time, airplanes did not yet exist, and the concept of space flight resides within the pages of H.G. Wells's science fiction novels.)

It is the same problem, but the year is 1950. Can you see the difficulty? (Now airplanes are commonplace; even jets and ballistic missiles exist. However, Sputnik will not launch for another seven years.)

Note: Intelligence analysts often get similar information requests (e.g., How can we stop the flow of illegal drugs into the U.S.? What will be the next great technological advance of our adversaries? etc.)

Since it is often impossible to remove uncertainty in analysis, the analyst will describe or qualify the level of uncertainty in the final analytical product so that the intelligence consumer can better assess the value and/or usefulness of the information provided when integrated into the decision-making process.

The Office of the Director of National Intelligence (ODNI) provides a standard to help normalize the assessment of analytical uncertainty (see Table 3.2).

TABLE 3.2 ODNI Directive 203: Analytic Standard, Likelihood, or Probability Terminology[13]

Almost No Chance	*Very Unlikely*	*Unlikely*	*Roughly Even Chance*	*Likely*	*Very Likely*	*Almost Certain*
Remote	*Highly Probable*	*Improbable (Improbably)*	*Roughly Even Odds*	*Probable (Probably)*	*Highly Probable*	*Nearly Certain*
1–5%	*5–20%*	*20–45%*	*45–55%*	*55–80%*	*80–95%*	*95–99%*

Bias

Richards J. Heuer, in his seminal work *Psychology of Intelligence Analysis*, identifies several cognitive biases that can impede objective analysis. Understanding these biases, their causes, and implementing mitigation techniques are crucial steps toward enhancing analytical accuracy. Following is a visual diagram summarizing these elements.

Cognitive Biases in Intelligence Analysis

1. Confirmation Bias
   - **Description:** The tendency to search for, interpret, favor, and recall information that confirms one's preexisting beliefs or hypotheses.
   - **Cause:** Analysts may unconsciously prioritize evidence supporting their initial assumptions, overlooking contradictory data.
   - **Mitigation Techniques:**
     - Actively seek out information that challenges existing beliefs.
     - Employ structured analytic techniques like Analysis of Competing Hypotheses (ACH) to systematically evaluate alternative explanations.
     - Encourage peer reviews to provide diverse perspectives.

2. Anchoring Bias
   - **Description:** The tendency to rely too heavily on the first piece of information encountered (the "anchor") when making decisions.
   - **Cause:** Initial information unduly influences subsequent judgments, even if it is irrelevant or misleading.
   - **Mitigation Techniques:**
     - Delay forming conclusions until sufficient information is gathered.
     - Consider multiple perspectives and data points before making judgments.
     - Regularly reassess initial assumptions in light of new evidence.

3. Availability Bias
   - **Description:** Overestimating the importance of information that comes to mind quickly, often because it is recent or vivid.
   - **Cause:** Recent or memorable events disproportionately influence analysis, leading to skewed assessments.

- **Mitigation Techniques:**
  - Rely on comprehensive datasets rather than anecdotal evidence.
  - Use statistical analysis to evaluate the actual frequency or probability of events.
  - Maintain awareness of this bias to consciously counteract its effects.

4. Mirror-Imaging
   - **Description:** Assuming that others think and act the same way as oneself.
   - **Cause:** Projecting one's own cultural norms, values, and decision-making processes onto others, leading to misinterpretation of actions and intentions.
   - **Mitigation Techniques:**
     - Develop cultural empathy and understanding of the subject's background.
     - Study the historical and situational context of the individuals or groups being analyzed.
     - Consult experts familiar with the culture or mindset of the subject.

5. Groupthink
   - **Description:** The practice of thinking or making decisions as a group, often resulting in unchallenged, poor-quality decision-making.
   - **Cause:** Desire for harmony or conformity in a group leads to irrational or dysfunctional decision-making outcomes.
   - **Mitigation Techniques:**
     - Encourage open dialogue and dissenting opinions within the team.
     - Assign a "devil's advocate" to question assumptions and conclusions.
     - Break the group into independent teams to explore the same problem separately.

6. Overconfidence Bias
   - **Description:** The tendency to overestimate one's own abilities, knowledge, or the accuracy of one's predictions.
   - **Cause:** Analysts may place undue confidence in their judgments, leading to insufficient consideration of alternative scenarios.
   - **Mitigation Techniques:**
     - Regularly calibrate confidence levels with actual outcomes to assess accuracy.

- Encourage humility and acknowledgment of the limits of one's knowledge.
- Use probabilistic language to express uncertainty in assessments.

By recognizing these cognitive biases and implementing the corresponding mitigation techniques, analysts can enhance the objectivity and reliability of their intelligence assessments. Heuer's work underscores the importance of self-awareness and structured analytic methods in overcoming the inherent limitations of human cognition.

Selection Bias

In addition to Heuer's biases previously listed, there is another analytical bias referred to as selection bias. Selection bias is a significant hurdle in intelligence analysis and scientific research.[14] This form of bias involves the preferential selection (aka *biased sampling* or *cherry-picking*) of data that aligns with the analyst's preconceptions or client expectations while neglecting or undervaluing contradictory evidence.

Mitigating Selection Bias

Mitigating sampling bias requires a conscientious effort to adopt practices that promote objectivity and critical scrutiny. Effective strategies include engaging in rigorous peer review processes to challenge and refine analytical conclusions. Implementing robust quality assurance procedures ensures the integrity and reliability of the analysis. Utilizing diverse sources enhances the breadth and depth of the analytical perspective, helping to counteract the tunnel vision resulting from over-reliance on a narrow dataset.

Moreover, the explicit acknowledgment and integration of discordant findings within the final analysis enrich the nuance and credibility of the conclusions drawn. Soliciting the insights of an independent, external group to address the same analytical questions can provide a valuable external benchmark, offering alternative viewpoints and revealing potential oversights or biases inherent in the original analysis.

Adhering to these practices not only diminishes the impact of selection bias but also elevates the overall quality and trustworthiness of the analytical output.

Analytical Bias Summary

Eliminating analytical bias is challenging because it can occur unconsciously, but analysts (and researchers) can minimize it by conducting peer reviews, using quality assurance procedures, using multiple sources, including, and explaining contradicting results in the final product, and having an outside and independent group solve the same problem.

To enhance the objectivity and reliability of intelligence assessments, it is crucial to understand common cognitive biases and implement corresponding mitigation techniques. For your convenience, following is a matrix that identifies various cognitive biases germane to intelligence analysis and corresponding mitigation techniques (see Table 3.3).

TABLE 3.3 Cognitive Biases and Mitigation Techniques in Intelligence Analysis[15]

Cognitive Bias	*Description*	*Mitigation Technique*
Confirmation Bias	*Tendency to search for, interpret, and remember information that confirms one's preconceptions.*	*Use structured analytic techniques like Analysis of Competing Hypotheses (ACH) to consider alternative explanations.*
Anchoring Bias	*Relying too heavily on the first piece of information encountered (the "anchor") when making decisions.*	*Deliberately seek out and evaluate information from multiple sources to challenge initial assumptions.*
Availability Heuristic	*Overestimating the importance of information that comes to mind easily.*	*Cross-reference with empirical data and statistical analysis to ensure conclusions are based on comprehensive information.*
Overconfidence Bias	*Holding an unjustifiable faith in one's own knowledge and abilities.*	*Encourage peer reviews and critical feedback to provide checks and balances on individual assessments.*
Mirror-Imaging	*Assuming that others think and act the same way as oneself.*	*Develop cultural and contextual understanding of the subject to appreciate different perspectives.*
Recency Effect	*Giving undue weight to the most recently received information.*	*Maintain a comprehensive timeline of information to assess all data points objectively, regardless of their arrival time.*
Groupthink	*Prioritizing group consensus over critical evaluation of alternatives.*	*Promote a culture of dissent and assign a "devil's advocate" to challenge prevailing opinions.*

Subject Matter Expertise

Subject Matter Expertise (SME) is a critical asset in the realm of analysis. Yet, it is unrealistic to expect analysts to be experts across the vast spectrum of topics they encounter. Analysts employ structured analytical techniques and critical thinking to navigate this challenge, bridge knowledge gaps, and progressively enhance their understanding.

Utilizing methodologies such as regression analysis, Monte Carlo simulations, and cluster analysis enables analysts to dissect complex datasets systematically, even in areas where their expertise is initially limited. This analytical rigor, coupled with a commitment to continuous learning, facilitates the development of SMEs over time.

Another vital skill for managing information overload is strategic data segregation—discerning the relevant from the irrelevant. This selective focus ensures that analysts concentrate their efforts on data that significantly impacts their analysis.

In instances where complete data is not immediately available, educated assumptions can serve as temporary placeholders, allowing the analytical process to continue. These assumptions are later refined or replaced as more concrete data becomes available, ensuring that the analysis remains robust and adaptable.

The journey to becoming a subject matter expert is iterative, relying on a blend of analytical strategies, critical evaluation, and an ongoing commitment to learning and adaptation.

CHAPTER SUMMARY

In Chapter 3, our discussion explored several key aspects of intelligence analysis, critical thinking, analytical bias, and the development of subject matter expertise. This chapter equips you with essential cognitive tools to excel as an intelligence analyst. By mastering critical and reflective thinking, applying structured problem-solving methods, and understanding cognitive limitations, you can enhance your analytical rigor. Additionally, exploring higher-order thinking and modern tools prepares you to tackle the complexities of intelligence work with creativity and precision. The highlights of this chapter include:

- **Thinking about Thinking** emphasized the importance of various types of thinking processes like critical, reflective, and higher-order thinking in intelligence analysis. It underscored the need for analysts to be objective, methodical, and aware of cognitive biases.

- **Problem-Solving** discussed the significance of problem definition and categorization into well-defined and poorly-defined problems. It highlighted using critical thinking to improve one's thinking process rather than directly solving problems.
- **Critical Thinking** stressed intelligence analysts' need to interpret information, appraise evidence, and evaluate arguments thoughtfully. This section also underscored the importance of being aware of and adjusting for one's biases and cognitive limitations.
- **Reflective Thinking** outlined the Dewey Sequence as a method for reflective thinking, emphasizing the structured questioning process to guide analysis and decision-making.
- **Higher-Order Thinking Skills (HOTS)** reviewed Bloom's Taxonomy as a framework for encouraging complex thinking skills in analysis, including creating, analyzing, and evaluating.
- **Cognitive Factors Affecting Thinking Quality** addressed the challenges of complexity and uncertainty in intelligence analysis and strategies to mitigate these through structured analytical techniques and critical evaluation.
- **Analytic Bias and Subject Matter Expertise** covered methods to mitigate analytic bias, such as peer reviews and using multiple sources. It also discussed the value of subject matter expertise and strategies for its development over time.

Throughout the chapter, the emphasis was placed on the need for continuous learning, the application of structured analytical methods, and the critical evaluation of one's own thinking processes to enhance the quality and effectiveness of intelligence analysis.

Key Concepts Covered

1. **Metacognition (Thinking about Thinking):** Metacognition refers to the awareness and regulation of one's own thinking processes. In intelligence analysis, metacognition allows analysts to monitor their reasoning, question assumptions, and deliberately adjust their analytical approach when necessary.
2. **Cognitive Processes in Analysis:** Human cognition involves perception, memory, reasoning, and judgment. Analysts must understand how these processes influence the interpretation of information, the formation of hypotheses, and the development of conclusions.
3. **Mental Models:** Mental models are internal representations of how analysts believe the world works. While these models help analysts interpret complex information efficiently, they can also

lead to errors when outdated or incorrect assumptions guide analysis.

4. **Cognitive Bias:** Cognitive biases are systematic patterns of deviation from rational judgment that can influence analytical conclusions. Common biases affecting intelligence analysis include confirmation bias, anchoring bias, availability bias, mirror imaging, groupthink, and overconfidence bias.
5. **Perception and Interpretation:** Analysts interpret incoming information through the lens of prior experience, expectations, and cultural context. Recognizing the difference between observation and interpretation is essential for maintaining objectivity in analysis.
6. **Structured Analytical Techniques (SATs):** Structured analytical techniques are formal methods designed to improve analytical rigor and reduce the influence of bias. Techniques such as brainstorming, hypothesis testing, and alternative analysis help analysts challenge assumptions and consider multiple perspectives.
7. **Critical Thinking in Intelligence Analysis:** Critical thinking involves disciplined evaluation of information, careful reasoning, and the deliberate questioning of assumptions. Analysts apply critical thinking to distinguish reliable information from noise and to construct well-supported conclusions.
8. **Information Overload and Data Management:** Modern intelligence environments produce vast amounts of data. Analysts must apply filtering, prioritization, and structured reasoning to separate relevant information from irrelevant or misleading data.
9. **Self-Correction and Analytical Reflection:** Effective analysts regularly review their reasoning, reassess assumptions, and update conclusions when new information becomes available. This iterative process strengthens the reliability of intelligence assessments.

Learning Objectives Accomplished

By completing this chapter, you should now be able to:

1. **Define** and differentiate critical, reflective, and higher-order thinking.
2. **Apply** the Dewey Sequence to structured problem-solving scenarios.
3. **Identify** and mitigate cognitive biases in analysis.
4. **Evaluate** the reliability of information using structured techniques.
5. **Analyze** how modern tools like AI assist in intelligence analysis.

Practical Application

During this chapter, you explored several practical concepts related to how analysts think and evaluate information, including:

- **Recognizing Cognitive Bias:** Identifying how confirmation bias, anchoring bias, and availability bias can distort analytical conclusions.
- **Evaluating Mental Models:** Examining how prior knowledge and assumptions shape the way analysts interpret new information.
- **Applying Critical Thinking:** Practicing disciplined reasoning to distinguish between facts, assumptions, and interpretations.
- **Using Structured Analytical Techniques:** Understanding how formal analytical methods can help analysts challenge assumptions and consider alternative explanations.
- **Managing Information Overload:** Learning strategies for filtering, prioritizing, and organizing large volumes of information to support effective analysis.

Reflection Questions

1. Why is metacognition important for intelligence analysts working in complex and uncertain environments?
2. How can mental models both help and hinder the analytical process?
3. Which cognitive bias do you believe presents the greatest challenge to intelligence analysts? Why?
4. How can structured analytical techniques help analysts reduce the influence of bias in their work?
5. In what ways can analysts actively monitor and improve their own thinking during the analytical process?

Excellent progress. Developing awareness of how you think is one of the most powerful tools an intelligence analyst can possess. Continue strengthening your analytical discipline as you move forward—mastering the mind is the **first step toward mastering intelligence analysis.**

GLOSSARY OF TERMS

Here is a glossary of key terms introduced and discussed in Chapter 3 to enhance your understanding of the material:

Analytic Red Cell: A program simulating adversary perspectives to predict behaviors.[16]

Bias: A systematic deviation from objective judgment.[17]
Critical Thinking: Disciplined analysis to improve thought processes.[18]
Dewey Sequence: A structured problem-solving methodology.[19]
Higher-Order Thinking Skills (HOTS): Advanced cognitive skills such as analysis, evaluation, and creation.[20]
Reflective Thinking: Sequential reasoning to evaluate and refine ideas.[21]
Subject Matter Expertise (SME): An individual with deep knowledge in a specific area.

This glossary serves as a quick reference for understanding key terms and concepts from the chapter. Feel free to revisit it as you progress through the material!

NOTES

1. Saiful Islam, *What Part of the Brain Controls Critical Thinking? 5 Factors and* 7 Ways to Improve, Life Alofa, 27 March 2023, Retrieved January 2025, https://lifealofa.com/what-part-of-the-brain-controls-critical-thinking.
2. All Good Health, *The Neuroscience of Metacognition: Understanding the Brain's Role*, 4 August 2024, Retrieved January 2025, https://allgoodhealth.net/cognitive-goals/metacognition/the-neuroscience-of-metacognition-understanding-the-brains-role/.
3. Saiful Islam, *What Part of the Brain Controls Critical Thinking? 5 Factors and 7 Ways to Improve*, Life Alofa, 27 March 2023, Retrieved January 2025, https://lifealofa.com/what-part-of-the-brain-controls-critical-thinking.
4. Richards J. Heuer Jr., *Psychology of Intelligence Analysis*, Central Intelligence Agency, 2019.
5. R. Paul and L. Elder, *Critical Thinking: Tools for Taking Charge of Your Professional and Personal Life* (2nd ed.), The Foundation for Critical Thinking, 2020.
6. J. Dewey, *How We Think: A Restatement of the Relation of Reflective Thinking to the Educative Process*, Boston, MA: Heath & Co Publishers, 1933.
7. J. Dewey, *How We Think: A Restatement of the Relation of Reflective Thinking to the Educative Process*, Boston, MA: Heath & Co Publishers, 1933.
8. B. S. Bloom, *Taxonomy of Educational Objectives: The Classification of Educational Goals*, Addison-Wesley Longman Ltd, 1956.
9. R. J. Marzano, *Designing a New Taxonomy of Educational Objectives*, Corwin Press, 2000.
10. John Mintz, 'Homeland Security Employs Imagination Outsiders Help Devise Possible Terrorism Plot', *Washington Post*, 18 June 2004, Page A27.
11. Richards J. Heuer, Jr., *Psychology of Intelligence Analysis* (2nd ed.), Pherson Associates LLC, 2007.
12. Douglas H. Harris and V. Alan Spiker, *Ergonomics – A Systems Approach, Critical Thinking Skills for Intelligence Analysis*, Chapter 10, Anacapa Sciences, Inc., 2012, Retrieved April 2025, www.intechopen.com.

13. Office of the Director of National Intelligence (ODNI), *Intelligence Community Directive #203, Analytic Standards*, 2015, http://www.dni.gov/files/documents/ICD/ICD%20203%20Analytic%20Standards.pdf.
14. Richards J. Heuer, Jr., *Psychology of Intelligence Analysis* (2nd ed.), Pherson Associates LLC, 2007.
15. Richards J. Heuer Jr., *Psychology of Intelligence Analysis*, Martino Fine Books, 2019.
16. John Mintz, 'Homeland Security Employs Imagination Outsiders Help Devise Possible Terrorism Plot', *Washington Post*, 18 June 2004, Page A27.
17. Richards J. Heuer, Jr., *Psychology of Intelligence Analysis* (2nd ed.), Pherson Associates LLC, 2007.
18. R. Paul and L. Elder, *Critical Thinking: Tools for Taking Charge of Your Professional and Personal Life* (2nd ed.), The Foundation for Critical Thinking, 2020.
19. J. Dewey, *How We Think: A Restatement of the Relation of Reflective Thinking to the Educative Process*, Boston, MA: Heath & Co Publishers, 1933.
20. B. S. Bloom, *Taxonomy of Educational Objectives: The Classification of Educational Goals*, Addison-Wesley Longman Ltd, 1956.
21. J. Dewey, *How We Think: A Restatement of the Relation of Reflective Thinking to the Educative Process*, Boston, MA: Heath & Co Publishers, 1933.

CHAPTER 4

Perception and Deception

INTRODUCTION

For the uninitiated, the intelligence analyst's duties only encompass collecting information on an adversary, analyzing the data, and creating and distributing the report. However, this limited view of the analyst's responsibilities is sorely lacking.

As illustrated in Figure 4.1, in Chapter 4, we navigate the shadowy realms where adversaries excel in concealment, challenging analysts to pierce through the veil of misinformation and subterfuge. This chapter unravels the complex interplay between an analyst's psyche and the deceptive stratagems employed by opponents, revealing how one's mental biases can unwittingly become the enemy's ally.

"Perception and Deception" delves deep into the psyche's intricate dance with reality, illuminating how our senses and cognitive processes shape, and sometimes warp, our understanding of the world around us. Through a blend of theory and real-world examples, we examine the sophisticated deception tactics wielded by military factions and criminal elements designed to mislead even the most astute observers. This chapter uncovers the mechanisms of self-deception, where our minds betray us, and arms analysts with a repertoire of analytical tools and methods to counter these illusions.

This chapter elevates the reader's comprehension of the analytical process by dissecting the multifaceted nature of intelligence work. It highlights the necessity for a disciplined and critical approach to data interpretation. Prepare to embark on an intellectually stimulating expedition into the heart of intelligence analysis, where every piece of information holds the potential for both revelation and misdirection.

DOI: 10.4324/9781003561712-4

FIGURE 4.1 What is real and what is a lie?

LEARNING OBJECTIVES

1. **Define** key terms related to perception, deception, and misperception.
2. **Explain** how biases and sensory inputs affect analytical judgment.
3. **Identify** and analyze historical examples of deception.
4. **Apply** the Congruity/Incongruity Rule in practical scenarios.
5. **Develop** strategies to detect and counter deception in intelligence contexts.

PERCEPTION

What is human perception? The *Oxford Advanced Learner's Dictionary* defines "perception" as "the ability to see, hear, or become aware of something through the senses" or "the awareness of something through the senses."[1]

However, analytical perception skills need to transcend the basic functionality of the five senses, embodying a sophisticated synergy between the reception of sensory stimuli and the cognitive operations that interpret these signals. This dynamic process facilitates the brain's capacity to derive a unified, meaningful comprehension of the myriad complexities within our environment. More than a mere sensory conduit, perception is a critical bridge linking the tangible external reality with our subjective internal interpretations. This connection is foundational for our ability to effectively navigate through diverse settings, engage in meaningful interactions, and adapt to the challenges presented by our surroundings. The brain's role in this process is intricate and pivotal, employing complex mechanisms to filter, enhance, and synthesize sensory data. This enables identifying and recognizing specific patterns, familiar visages, cherished melodies, and evocative scents, all of which hold profound personal relevance. Through this elaborate interplay of sensory input and cognitive processing, perception shapes our understanding of the world, coloring our experiences and influencing our interactions.

In lay terms, psychologists view perception as the human sensory experience of their environment. It involves the recognition of sensory stimuli and actions in response to them. Human beings gain information about their environment through perceptual stimuli to survive; for example, the stove is hot.

Perception includes the five senses: touch, sight, taste, smell, and taste. It also consists of the cognitive processes required to process sensory information, such as recognizing a favorite song, a friend's face, or the smell of grandma's cookies.

PRACTICAL EXERCISE #1: PERCEPTION SCENARIO

Objective

This exercise is designed to encourage participants to utilize their perception skills effectively. Participants will learn to interpret sensory inputs innovatively by engaging in a hands-on scenario.

Scenario

Imagine yourself in a corridor flanked by three unlit switches. Down this corridor lies a room, out of sight, housing three incandescent bulbs, each corresponding to one of the switches. Your challenge is to deduce which switch controls which bulb with a single visit to the bulb room, as illustrated in Figure 4.2.

> ***Hint:*** *Besides those who have already seen the exercise, the most successful participants depend on multiple sensory stimuli to perceive their environment.*
>
> *Note: The Instructor's Guide contains the solution.*

Misperception

Misperception intricately affects human survival, swaying it toward either advantage or peril. The intricacies of perception hinge on three pivotal elements: the observer's viewpoint, the nature of the object in question, and its environmental context. These elements collectively orchestrate the depth and accuracy of our perceptual experiences, guiding our interaction with the world around us.

Observer

Each observer wields a unique lens, shaped by personal experiences and perspectives, to decode their surroundings. This individual variance is evident in scenarios involving multiple eyewitnesses, such as a crime scene, where divergent accounts often emerge. These discrepancies can be attributed to differences in physical vantage points, which alter the scene's visual presentation and to each observer's unique mental and sensory capacities. Factors like age, attentiveness, and preexisting biases further color their interpretations, highlighting the subjective nature of human perception.

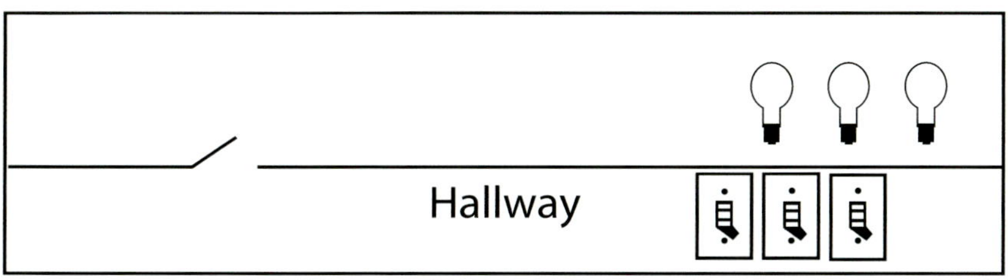

FIGURE 4.2 Sensory perception exercise.

Object Being Perceived

The focal object is critical in drawing or diverting an observer's attention. Elements that typically capture our focus include urgent signals like the flashing lights of a police vehicle or the sound of sirens. In contrast, distractors could range from undesirable sights, such as public disputes, to the discomforting wails of a child in distress.

Background and Surroundings

The backdrop against which an object is set can significantly influence perception. For instance, camouflage and ambient noises might obscure detection, while stark contrasts or distinctive scents can enhance observability. These environmental factors, in concert with the observer's predispositions and the inherent attributes of the object, determine the precision of cognitive perception or the occurrence of misperception.

This nuanced understanding underscores the complexity of human perception, revealing it as a dynamic interplay between the observer, the observed, and the setting. Recognizing these facets allows us to better comprehend the roots of perceptual diversity and the potential for misinterpretation in our daily encounters.

DECEPTION

Deception, distinct from misperception, involves a calculated attempt to manipulate the observer's understanding of reality. This manipulation is not always about fabricating falsehoods but often involves skewing perception through partial truths or strategic omissions. Deception operates through various mechanisms, including propaganda, distraction, misdirection, camouflage, and concealment, each designed to craft and propagate beliefs that serve the deceiver's purpose.

Unlike misperception, where the observer inadvertently misperceives the object due to experience or circumstance, deception is a deliberate effort to alter the observer's perception.

Example:

Focus on the figure at right. As your eyes observe from left to right, are the figures of the three men gradually getting larger, or smaller, or remaining the same size (see Figure 4.3).

You, the observer, perhaps already suspect trickery and falsely assume your initial assessment that "the figures were getting larger" is erroneous. Therefore, the optical pattern of converging lines and personal bias

FIGURE 4.3 Optical illusion (www.shutterstock.com).

(your assumption of the figure was purposely misleading) combine to fool your mind into believing the figures are approximately the same size. However, they are getting larger (from left to right).

To detect deception, a skill vital to the gatherer of intelligence, one must first understand what deception is and how it works. A broad definition of deception embodies terms such as deceit, bluff, disorientation trick, and other acts to create and spread untrue beliefs. Additionally, not all deceptions are complete lies. The most effective deceptions use some truth or leave out critical facts (half-truths or significant omissions). Deception comes through propaganda, distraction, misdirection, camouflage, and concealment.

Deceptions can be elaborate or quite simple and obvious. Therefore, one might think they should be relatively easy to detect.[2] In practice, this may not be the case.

Adversarial deception can easily mislead intelligence analysts, primarily because, unless prompted otherwise, they do not look for it and, therefore, assume it is not present. According to Richards J. Heuer, analysts often reject the possibility of deception because they see no evidence of trickery. Heuer persuasively argues that if an adversary plans and executes the deception properly, the analyst should not expect to see evidence of the deceit.[3]

TABLE 4.1 Terror/Criminal Deceptive Practices

Terror Group	*Criminal Organization*
Hezbollah sent operatives to South America to learn Spanish and blend with the local population.	*Use of semi-submersibles to move drugs from South/Central America north for distribution and sale.*
Use of border tunnels (Gaza/Israeli Border) for smuggling and other illicit activities.	*Use of border tunnels (U.S. southern border) for smuggling, drug running, and other illicit activities.*
ISIS/ISIL laundering millions of oil dollars from illicit Syrian oil trading.	*Cartels laundering millions of drug dollars from the illicit drug trade.*
Terrorists, posing as a TV news team, assassinate Ahmad Shah Massoud, leader of the Afghan Northern Alliance, on 9 Sep 2001.	*Human trafficking under the guise of Eastern European "mail-order brides."*
Terrorist organizations use websites and social media to recruit new followers or elicit donations.	*Human traffickers luring children into sex slavery.*

Most analysts can more easily understand deception by a nation-state, such as China, Russia, or Iran, exercising elaborate deception schemes. However, visualizing criminal or terrorist organizations using deception is often more complex. Many illicit, deceptive practices fall under various government classifications or are, by nature, "law enforcement sensitive;" therefore, they cannot be discussed here. However, the following table contains a sampling of the more notable real-world examples describing criminal organizations and terror groups using deception against the U.S. and other nations.

To cultivate an acute awareness of deception, one must grasp its essence and the subtleties of its execution. Deception is not solely about disseminating outright lies but also about the artful distortion of the truth. Effective deceptions often weave in elements of truth or strategically omit key information to mislead the target. Such tactics are not limited to grand schemes by nation-states but are also employed by criminal and terrorist organizations to achieve their objectives (see Table 4.1).

Each of the deceptive practices listed in the table is an attempt by an adversary to conceal or deceive to avoid discovery or true intent—all instances are typical examples of classic deception.

PRACTICAL EXERCISE #2: DECEPTIVE ADVERTISING

This exercise aims to sharpen the analytical skills necessary to discern the nuanced layers of deception in various contexts. By engaging with real-world examples and hypothetical scenarios, analysts can develop a more refined approach to identifying and countering deceptive tactics.

Background

The capacity to detect and understand deception is crucial for intelligence analysts, who must constantly question the veracity of the information they encounter. As Richards J. Heuer argues, recognizing the absence of evidence as a potential sign of well-executed deception is key to maintaining a critical stance toward seemingly straightforward data. Understanding deception in its many forms, from the elaborate ruses of nation-states to the more subtle manipulations of smaller entities, is essential for effective intelligence gathering and analysis (see Figure 4.4).

Instructions

1. **Introduction (5 minutes):** The facilitator will briefly discuss the significance of detecting deception in intelligence analysis and explain how advertisements can serve as practical examples of deceptive practices.
2. **Presentation of the Advertisement (5 minutes):** Students open their texts to the "SlimShaper Gummies" advertisement and read and analyze the content individually. See the SlimShaper advertisement in Figure 4.4:

Get Fit Fast with SlimShaper Gummies! Our revolutionary gummies are scientifically proven to help you shed up to 20 pounds in just two weeks—no exercise required! SlimShaper Gummies are your ultimate

FIGURE 4.4 Misleading advertisement (www.shutterstock.com).

solution for effortless weight loss, packed with all-natural ingredients like Superberry extracts and fat-burning enzymes. Limited stock available—order now and transform your body today!

3. **Group Analysis (15 minutes):** You will divide students into small groups to analyze and identify deceptive elements, truths or half-truths, and the intended psychological effects on consumers by brainstorming for potential consequences of the deception.
4. **Research Component (15 minutes):** Research online claims made in the advertisement, such as the efficacy of Superberry extracts for weight loss. Record findings and highlight discrepancies between claims and evidence.
5. **Discussion and Debrief (15 minutes):** When the class reconvenes, your group presents its findings and suggests strategies to counteract the deception (e.g., verifying claims, recognizing urgent language as a red flag). Then, discuss how these analytical techniques apply in broader intelligence contexts.

Scenario

Following is a scenario involving a deceptive practice known as a misleading advertisement. Analyze the ad by identifying the deceptive elements, the truth or half-truth used, and the intended effect on the observer's/potential customer's perception. Discuss the possible outcomes of the deception and strategies for uncovering the truth.

The following Author's Note box highlights a dozen phrases that are used, in one form or another, in consumer scams.[4]

AUTHOR'S NOTE

*According to a state consumer protection office, nearly every new scam is just a variation on one or more of these tried-and-true classics. If you come across any of these typical pitch lines, be careful—**there is likely to be some element of a scam involved!***

- *It is your lucky day! You won the foreign lottery!*
- *Burn fat while you sleep!!!*
- *Free cash grants! Never repay!*
- *This free seminar can change your life!*
- *Make BIG money working from home!*
- *THIS JUST IN: Fake news site delivers the latest scam!*

- *Enhance your love life! More energy! Greater stamina!*
- *Free golf clubs for 90 days!*
- *Big senior discounts on prescription drugs!*
- *A free vacation getaway for you!*
- *You have won $X million in the Australian (or some other place's) Sweepstakes!*
- *Bad credit or no credit? Not a problem!*

Personal (or Self-)Deception

Self-deception is a complex psychological phenomenon involving individuals convincing themselves of a "truth" that contradicts logical and accurate evidence. Sackeim and Gur further explore this concept, defining self-deception through specific criteria: the simultaneous holding of two contradictory beliefs, which are inaccessible to the individual's awareness due to a motivated act. This process distinguishes self-deception from mere misunderstanding or ignorance, as it involves an active effort to ignore or rationalize conflicting evidence or logic.

Sackeim and Gur define and empirically demonstrate "self-deception," which incorporates many essential elements postulated by other psychologists and philosophers, such as Plato, Freud, Fingarette, and Sartre.[5,6,7] Sackeim and Gur argued that specific criteria were necessary and sufficient to attribute self-deception to any event. One must:

1. Simultaneously,
2. Hold two contradictory beliefs,
3. One of which the individual is not aware of,
4. Because of a motivated act.

Using these criteria, self-deception contrasts with other types of deception and is thought to occur when individuals confront aspects of themselves that they find difficult to accept.

Self-deception is a situation where an individual denies or rationalizes away the significance, factual basis, or substance of conflicting evidence or logical argument. Self-deception involves convincing oneself to believe something as "factual" so that one does not realize they are discounting logical and trustworthy arguments and deceiving oneself. To emphasize the point, refer to an infamous and classic example of self-deception, Custer's Last Stand (see Figure 4.5).

FIGURE 4.5 General Armstrong Custer (www.shutterstock.com).

The phenomenon is not merely academic but has practical implications, as seen in historical events like Custer's Last Stand. Despite multiple reports indicating a prodigiously large enemy force, General Custer's overconfidence in his and his troopers' abilities led him to ignore these warnings, resulting in a tragic defeat. This instance exemplifies how self-deception can lead to disastrous outcomes when individuals allow personal biases and desires to cloud their judgment and decision-making processes.

Custer was not the brilliant tactician history books might imply. However, he was decisive and unafraid to take risks. Custer strongly exhibits these character traits when he disregards multiple reports of a massive enemy force awaiting his troops in the Little Bighorn River Valley.[8] Custer was said to have been grossly overconfident of the 7th Cavalry's ability to handle the hostiles. Self-assurance developed from years of actual Civil War combat, but by comparison, few and brief battlefield engagements fighting the Sioux Nation. In Custer's limited experience of fighting the Plains Indians, the common thread seems to be that when his troops attacked the Sioux war parties, the Sioux generally did not stand and fight. Therefore, the General erroneously assumed, at Little Bighorn, that the Sioux warriors would retreat in the face of the 7th Cavalry's determined assault.

In addition to ignoring hostile strength reports, estimates of 1,500 to 2,500 warriors from his Crow scouts, and the sound advice of his subordinate, Major Reno, and his superior, General Terry, Custer made the tactical decision to attack an overwhelmingly large force.[9] Adding insult to injury, Custer made several other severe tactical mistakes, namely spurning the offer of reinforcements (he only had 210 soldiers with him at his last stand), leaving two Gatling guns in the rear, dividing his forces into smaller and physically separate elements (Reno had roughly 350 troops in another location); therefore Reno was not capable of providing any timely support.[10]

Custer's actions at the Little Bighorn fit perfectly with the concept of self-deception. He convinced himself to believe something as "factual" (he and the 7th Calvary alone could defeat a significantly larger force) to the extent that he did not realize he was discounting logical and factual arguments.

Self-deception is a significant concern for analysts. To avoid self-deception, analysts must use multiple procedures to mitigate its adverse and possibly catastrophic effects. Such methods include peer reviews, structured analytical techniques (SATs), parallel collaboration, alternative analysis, and others, which will be discussed later in the text.

Analysts, particularly in intelligence and strategic fields, must be vigilant against self-deception to ensure accurate assessments and decisions. Techniques such as peer reviews, structured analytical techniques, parallel collaborations, and alternative analyses are essential tools to counteract the potential adverse effects of self-deception by fostering a culture of critical thinking and open-mindedness toward conflicting information.

PRACTICAL EXERCISE #3: SELF-DECEPTION QUIZ

This learning activity, developed by psychologists, aids individuals in assessing the presence of personal, or "self," deception in their character profile.[11]

Quiz Instructions

Take the following quiz, circling the appropriate number to the right. Do not feel embarrassed; no one will see your answers but you. Try to answer honestly and not overanalyze the question. Once complete, add up the numbers and wait for further guidance (see Table 4.2).

TABLE 4.2 Questions: (not *at all) 1 2 3 4 5 6 7 (very much so)*

1.	Have you ever felt hatred toward either of your parents?	1 2 3 4 5 6 7
2.	Do you ever feel guilty?	1 2 3 4 5 6 7
3.	Does every attractive person of the opposite sex turn you on?	1 2 3 4 5 6 7
4.	Have you ever felt like you wanted to kill somebody?	1 2 3 4 5 6 7
5.	Do you ever get angry?	1 2 3 4 5 6 7
6.	Do you ever have thoughts you do not want other people to know that you have?	1 2 3 4 5 6 7
7.	Do you ever feel attracted to people of the same sex?	1 2 3 4 5 6 7
8.	Have you ever made a fool of yourself?	1 2 3 4 5 6 7
9.	Are there things in your life that make you feel unhappy?	1 2 3 4 5 6 7
10.	Is it important to you that other people think highly of you?	1 2 3 4 5 6 7
11.	Would you like to know what other people think of you?	1 2 3 4 5 6 7
12.	Were your parents ever mean to you?	1 2 3 4 5 6 7
13.	Do you have any bad memories?	1 2 3 4 5 6 7
14.	Have you ever thought that your parents hated you?	1 2 3 4 5 6 7
15.	Do you have sexual fantasies?	1 2 3 4 5 6 7
16.	Have you ever been uncertain as to whether or not you are homosexual?	1 2 3 4 5 6 7
17.	Have you ever doubted your sexual adequacy?	1 2 3 4 5 6 7
18.	Have you ever enjoyed your bowel movements?	1 2 3 4 5 6 7
19.	Have you ever wanted to rape or be raped by someone?	1 2 3 4 5 6 7
20.	Have you ever thought of committing suicide to get back at someone?	1 2 3 4 5 6 7

HOW TO DECEIVE

Deception, as articulated by Barton Whaley in his seminal work *Textbook of Political-Military Counter Deception*, is an intricate dance of misdirection and illusion that serves both offensive and defensive strategic purposes. Whaley's exploration of the art of deception is unparalleled. He draws from various disciplines, including magic, politics, propaganda, and military strategy, to comprehensively understand the subject.

Barton Whaley's 10-Step Deception Process

Dr. Barton Whaley, a scholar in the science of deception, received his doctorate in Strategic Deception Analysis at MIT in 1969. He was a military intelligence officer, historian, and amateur student of magic. During the Korean War, he served in the U.S. Army Psychological Warfare Intelligence unit headquartered in Tokyo. In later years, he served as a research professor at the U.S. Naval Postgraduate School.

Barton Whaley's 10-Step Deception Process is a systematic approach developed through Whaley's extensive research and practical experience. This process serves as a blueprint for designing and executing deception operations effectively:

1. *Define the Mission Goals*: Understand the specific objectives of the deception operation. Whether it's to entertain, distract the enemy, or cover an operation, defining the goal is the first critical step.
2. *Desired Reaction*: Determine precisely how you want the target to respond. This step goes beyond mere distraction, aiming to provoke a specific action or decision that benefits the deceiver.
3. *Target's Perception*: Decide what you want the target to believe. This involves crafting the narrative or illusion the target will perceive as reality.
4. *Concealment and Revelation*: Strategically choose which facts or events to hide and which to reveal. This manipulation of information is crucial to steering the target's perception.
5. *Analyze and Adapt*: Study the actual situation to identify key characteristics to alter or emphasize in the deception plan.
6. *Design the Deception*: Develop a plausible alternative scenario or object that serves the operation's goals, ensuring it aligns closely enough with reality to be believable.
7. *Select the Means of Presentation*: Consider the available resources and constraints to determine how best to present the deception to the target.
8. *Operational Phase*: Transition from planning to action, where the designed deception is implemented.
9. *Open Channels*: Ensure the deceptive messages reach the target through accessible and monitored channels.
10. *Target's Acceptance*: For success, the target must perceive the deception as intended without recognizing the manipulation.

For an illusion to be successful, the target must accept, or "buy," the effect. This means the target perceives the illusion as genuine and regards it as fact. The illusion's effectiveness depends entirely on the target's willingness or ability to accept what is presented as reality. The deception will fail at this point only if the target takes no notice of the presented effect, notices but judges it as irrelevant, misconstrues its intended meaning, or detects its method. Conversely, the target will:

1. Take notice if the effect is designed to attract his attention;
2. Find it relevant if the effect can hold his interest;
3. Form the intended hypothesis about its meaning if the projected pattern of characteristics is congruent with patterns already part of his experience and memory; and
4. Fail to detect the deception if none of the ever-present, incongruent characteristics are accessible to his sensors.

Effective deception planning must anticipate all four contingencies, seek feedback, and monitor the target's responses to ensure they are being met.[12]

Whaley emphasizes the necessity of anticipation and adaptation throughout the deception process. The deceiver must constantly evaluate the target's reactions and adjust the strategy to maintain the illusion. This dynamic interplay requires a deep understanding of the target's perceptions, biases, and possible reactions.

Effective deception is not just about misleading the enemy; it's about controlling the narrative to achieve strategic objectives. Whaley's 10-step process provides a structured approach to crafting and executing deception operations, highlighting the importance of creativity, adaptability, and a thorough understanding of the target.

Whaley's work remains a cornerstone in the study of deception, offering valuable insights for military strategists, intelligence analysts, and anyone interested in the complexities of human cognition and behavior in the context of conflict and competition.

HOW TO DETECT DECEPTION

There are dozens of specific theories, principles, and methods for detecting deception. However, all have been adopted in one or more other disciplines, particularly by consistently successful analysts who deal regularly with deception. Of these many theories, principles, and methods, only three are covered here and are particularly appropriate for use by intelligence analysts.

Dr. Whaley surveyed 143 fields and disciplines to identify the key to detecting deception. The key presented itself as "congruity/incongruity analysis," or, for short, incongruity analysis.[13]

The process of detecting deception, as meticulously analyzed by Dr. Whaley and other experts, revolves around identifying congruities and contradictions within a given context. This approach is grounded in the scientific method, emphasizing observation, hypothesis formulation, prediction, and experimentation to validate or refute hypotheses. A key element of this method is methodological skepticism, a critical mindset crucial in scientific inquiry and equally vital in deception detection. It encourages us to question, challenge, and test our assumptions, leading to a deeper understanding of the truth.

Finding Patterns of Congruity and Incongruity (Scientific Method)

We start with the process many learned in grade school, the Scientific Method. The Scientific Method comprises several interlocking methods, a set of principles and procedures that scientists must follow when doing research.

Having defined the set of facts appropriate to their specialty, the scientist then observes them, a crucial step in the scientific method. This observation leads to the formulation of a guess (develop a "hypothesis") about their nature or relationship, then predicts that, if this guess were accurate, we should expect to see the predictable outcome, and ends with an experiment to test that prediction (and its underlying) hypothesis. If the theory is not disproven, scientists tentatively accept it, subject to repeated test experiments ("replication"). It is a method that places great value on skepticism. This skepticism extends to all steps in scientific investigation, observation and data collection accuracy, hypothesis formation, experimental design, analytical methods, and conclusions.

All discoveries or detections in science and technology are made by perceiving either a new congruity or an unexpected incongruity. These fresh perceptions can arise during an experiment using some systematic ("scientific") method or from chance observation of a natural event.[14]

Congruity

Congruity refers to the harmony or compatibility between elements, where everything fits together seamlessly. In normal science, congruity represents the expected routine, where established theories and knowledge are applied to solve problems. Anomalies or unexpected results are initially attributed to errors in procedure or equipment, assuming that proper adherence to scientific methodology will eventually yield the anticipated outcomes. However, on rare occasions, persistent anomalies signal a revolutionary discovery, indicating that the underlying hypothesis or theory might be flawed.

If two things fit together perfectly, they are congruous. If they do not fit, they are incongruous. Every coincidence is a perceived congruity. Normal science is the master of congruity. It busies itself by applying currently fashionable theories and received knowledge to immediate problems. Such plodding and systematic experimental procedure gives us precise tables of measurements and data that fill the handbooks of medicine, chemistry, engineering, physics, astronomy, and other sciences. Without it, there would be no scientists, only mechanics and philosophers.

Normal science is intolerant of surprises. Suppose a test or experiment gives an unexpected result. In that case, the scientist will dismiss it as either "experimenter error" (failure to follow the procedures called for) or "instrument error" (defective or maladjusted apparatus). The scientist then reviews the methods used, checks the apparatus, adjusts the measuring instruments, and proceeds to repeat the experiment. Usually, this will give the expected test result and eliminate the anomaly. If, in those rare and significant cases where the anomaly persists, the scientist will tend to question their competence, and, in most cases, this will be the complete and correct explanation. There is, however, an infrequent occasion when the unexpected observation is not a phantom conjured up by either bungled technique or faulty equipment.[15] Good scientists now realize they have been working from a flawed hypothesis or theory. This realization is the moment of truth, the tipping point where the scientist is on the brink of a revolutionary discovery, a moment filled with excitement and anticipation.

Incongruity

Any unexpected observation in science is said to be an anomaly. Incongruity is simply the most common term most physical scientists use for peculiarity. It is what some military deception planners, magicians, and computer scientists call a discrepancy, what some forensic scientists mean when they declare findings inconsistent, what some social psychologists call dissonance, etc. These anomalies, or incongruities, are not just deviations from the norm but crucial elements in scientific discovery, enlightening and informing scientists across disciplines.

Incongruities arise in science in only two circumstances: during mental play or by accident. The first and the most usual occurs whenever a scientist toys in their mind with possible connections between two phenomena and comes up with an unlikely pair that seems to fit together.

As Dr. James D. Watson's highly personal account, *The Double Helix* (1968), recalls, this frequently happened during his three-year, winding intellectual journey toward the revolutionary co-discovery (with Bernard Crick) in 1953 of the double-helix structure of the DNA molecule.[16]

The other, less usual, source of an unpredictable event is an accident. However, an accident of an exceptional kind, namely one that is first noticed, then perceived to have relevance to science, then stated as a formal hypothesis that can be "verified" (tested), and finally proved by what is called a "crucial experiment," as shown in Figure 4.6.

FIGURE 4.6 A crucial experiment.

The scientist's opposite path to creativity is by recognizing an incongruity, in other words, a puzzling chance occurrence. One example must suffice: Italian physicist Dr. Enrico Fermi was a year into researching the newly discovered neutron at the University of Rome in October 1934 when he and his team observed a puzzling anomaly in the silver samples they were irradiating with neutrons. They detected that the silver became much more radioactive when the experiments were done on a wooden table instead of a marble bench. A few days later, Fermi tried an experiment by placing a radiation filter between the neutron stream and the target metal. He had decided on lead as the filter. However, at the last moment, he noticed a handy slab of paraffin and, on a whim, used it instead. To everyone's surprise, the rates of nuclear activity increased by a hundredfold. Baffled by what all these unexpected events could mean, he went home for lunch and a nap. He was alone. At three that afternoon, he returned to his lab with the answer. The paraffin molecules had slowed the bombarding neutrons to the point where these slow neutrons could produce more effective collisions with the target than typical fast neutrons. Fermi had instantly invented a new branch of experimental physics (neutron-induced radioactivity). Four years later, it won him a Nobel Prize.[17]

This precious ability to perceive an "incongruity" (or puzzling observation) and devise a new theory that will make it "congruous" (or understandable) is what creates all "revolutions" in science.[18]

Balancing Congruities and Incongruities

Whenever a scientist or mathematician expresses a conclusion in an equation, it proves he has perceived and proved a congruity (identity or analogy) between the terms on both sides of the equation. These equalities range from the simple $2 + 2 = 4$, through the complex approximation $\pi = 3.1416$, to the Nobel Prize-winning $E = mc^2$.

However, to perceive and prove an incongruity, one must assess the authenticity of the observed. To do this, one must ask the following three basic questions:

- What is there that should not be there?
- What is missing? (i.e., What is not there that should be?)
- What is there, if anything, that should not be?[19]

Incongruity Analysis

Because nature never deceives, there can be no incongruities in nature. Consequently, whenever we find an incongruity (discrepancy, anomaly), we are entitled to draw three inferences:

Incongruity Analysis assumes that our instruments or sensors give false readings and need adjusting. Then, if the incongruity persists, we must infer that:

1. We have misread our instruments or sensors and need to double-check. *Then, if the incongruity persists, we are on the verge of an exciting discovery, namely that:*
2. Our relevant hypothesis is incorrect. In this case, there are two possible causes: *either there is some fundamental characteristic in nature that requires us to adjust our hypothesis to incorporate this newly perceived characteristic. Or …*
3. A Human deceiver has introduced some false characteristics. In that case, Incongruity Analysis will, in theory, reveal one or both of the two incongruities created by every deception, namely the real thing the deceiver is trying to hide (dissimulate) and the false thing being shown (simulated) in its place.

Because the process of detecting deception is fundamentally simple in both theory and practice, a sure sign of an ineffective deception analyst is one who subscribes to and applies complex theories, at least at the beginning. Conversely, an effective deception analyst is one who systematically applies Incongruity Analysis.

The Plus or Minus Rule

Each real thing has a large but finite number of identifiable characteristics. In other words, every real object must have its own set of defining characteristics, not one more or one less. All imitations will share at least one, and often many, of these characteristics. However, every imitation must lack at least one characteristic that marks the real thing, and it will usually have additional ones that are not in the original. Even identical twins have different histories starting in the womb.

Then, if either a plus (added) or a minus (missing) characteristic is detected, the imitation stands revealed. Note that a significant outcome of this Plus or Minus Rule is that the analyst does not need to discover all or even many discrepancies or contradictions. A single false characteristic, whether plus (added) or minus (missing), is sufficient to prove fakery. This is why complicated deceptions tend to be weak. For example, the corpse of *The Man Who Never Was* (Operation Mincemeat was a successful British disinformation plan during the Second World War) had died from the wrong cause (poison-induced pneumonia rather than drowning); his body was far too decomposed for the pretended time since death, and the personal effects bore not his but another man's fingerprints.[20] At least three absolutely or presumptively incongruous characteristics existed, any one of which, if detected by the enemy, would have completely blown the deception or at least raised grave suspicions about that major British military operation.

Military examples of the Plus or Minus Rule are common. They are most common in ambush situations where the only life-saving warning is a vague awareness of something wrong, a sense that something should not be (a seemingly abandoned knapsack perhaps), or something is missing (an empty village square during rush hour).

The Plus or Minus Rule helps the analyst identify the critical pieces of evidence to focus on. Therefore, we may conclude that the greater the number of uniquely distinguishing characteristics we know about something, the greater our chances of recognizing it as counterfeit if either (1) any incongruous characteristic is present, or (2) any congruous characteristic is missing.

The Congruity/Incongruity Rule and the Analyst's Advantage

Every real thing is always wholly congruent with all its distinguishing characteristics. Conversely, every false thing will display at least two incongruities. Because every deception involves simultaneously showing at least one false thing and hiding a corresponding real thing, the Congruity/Incongruity Rule tells us that the detective has two independent chances to detect any deception. Thus, deception will be confirmed if we detect the simulated or dissimulated half. Moreover, even this half-disclosure focuses the detective's guesses about the remaining part, thereby greatly simplifying the effort to detect it. This one simple fact gives the detective a crucial advantage against every deceiver.

American art expert and museum curator Thomas Pearsall Field Hoving applied his version of the Congruity/Incongruity Rule to his particular specialty:

> *Embedded in every art forgery, no matter how ambitious or paltry, is a stupid mistake left by the faker, a physical property that did not exist in ancient times, a kind of aging that cannot be natural, or an amusing error in style a blunder that anybody with concentration and common sense might be able to spot.*[21]
>
> **Thomas Pearsall Field Hoving, Former Curator**
> **Metropolitan Museum of Art**

Two other recent examples where the direct detection approach failed, yet the indirect one succeeded, were the mole-hunting cases of Aldrich Ames (in the CIA)[22] and Robert Hanssen (in the FBI).[23] Ames's extravagant lifestyle was significantly incongruent with his $60,000 a year salary, and a confidential informant purchased Hanssen's identity from a mole in the Soviet government.

PRACTICAL EXERCISE #4: DETECTING DECEPTION THROUGH CONGRUITY AND INCONGRUITY (FTD/ CLASSMATES.COM—PARTICIPANT GUIDE)

Background: This practical exercise reinforces theoretical concepts and provides students with hands-on experience in applying these principles in real-world-like scenarios, thus enhancing their analytical skills and critical thinking abilities.

Objective: To engage students in applying congruity and incongruity analysis for deception detection, fostering critical thinking, observational skills, and an understanding of methodological skepticism.

Case Summary: FTD, Classmates.Com pay $11 million for misleading advertising.[24]

Settlement Overview

- In a lawsuit brought by 22 states, FTD and Classmates.com faced allegations of misleading advertising and billing practices. These practices included:
  - **Negative Option Marketing:** Consumers were unknowingly enrolled in subscription services that automatically renewed.
- *A lawsuit by 22 states charged that the companies, affiliates until 2013, used "negative option marketing" to lure consumers into deals they did not know they were signing up for, including self-renewing subscriptions to Classmates.*
  - **Data Pass:** The companies shared consumers' personal and financial information with third-party marketing partners, leading to unauthorized charges.
  - **Lack of Transparency:** The terms of these transactions were not clearly disclosed to consumers, resulting in financial losses and frustration.
- The settlement required the companies to pay $11 million (Classmates.com and floral delivery company, FTD) to resolve allegations of misleading advertising and billing practices. This included reimbursements for affected consumers and investigatory costs for the states involved. While no wrongdoing was admitted, the companies eliminated the disputed programs.

Step-by-Step Instructions

Step 1: Introduction (5 minutes)

- Brief overview of the case summary.
- Note key deceptive practices:
  - Misleading subscription renewals.
  - Unauthorized sharing of credit card information.
- Discuss the importance of identifying patterns of deception in real-world scenarios.

Step 2: Analyze the Case (15 minutes)

- Group tasks:
  - Identify congruities (what makes sense and aligns with standard practices).
  - Highlight incongruities (elements that raise red flags or seem contradictory).
  - Apply the Plus or Minus Rule to detect missing or added characteristics indicative of deception.

Step 3: Group Discussion (15 minutes)

- Within their groups, participants:
  - Discuss their findings and propose hypotheses about the deceptive elements.
  - Debate potential motivations behind the deceptive practices.
  - Suggest strategies the companies could have used to improve transparency and compliance.

Step 4: Class Presentations (10 minutes)

- Each group presents:
  - The deceptive elements they identified.
  - Their reasoning using the Congruity/Incongruity and Plus or Minus Rules.
  - Potential consumer outcomes (e.g., financial loss, mistrust) and mitigation strategies.

Step 5: Facilitator-Led Debrief (10 minutes)

PARTICIPANT OBSERVATION SHEETS: (FTD/ CLASSMATES.COM—PARTICIPANT GUIDE)

Instructions: Use these points to record your observations during the exercise.

1. **Congruities**
   - What aspects of the company's practices aligned with industry norms or credible behavior?
   - Examples: Use of legitimate subscription services and established vendor relationships.
2. **Incongruities**
   - Identify elements that raise red flags or seem inconsistent with standard practices.
   - Examples: Automatic renewal without consent, lack of clear disclosures about data sharing.
3. **Plus or Minus Rule**
   - **Plus:** Note characteristics that should not be present (e.g., unauthorized sharing of credit card details).
   - **Minus:** Identify characteristics that are missing but should be present (e.g., explicit consumer consent).
4. **Patterns**
   - Are there recurring tactics or behaviors that suggest a deliberate attempt to deceive? For example, repeated failure to notify consumers of billing practices and reliance on hidden terms and conditions.

PRACTICAL EXERCISE #5: DETECTING DECEPTION THROUGH CONGRUITY AND INCONGRUITY CYBERSECURITY CASE STUDY—TREASURY DEPARTMENT HACK (2024)

Background

In December 2024, the U.S. Department of the Treasury experienced a significant cybersecurity breach attributed to Chinese state-sponsored actors. The attackers exploited vulnerabilities in a third-party software provider, BeyondTrust, to gain unauthorized access to unclassified documents and workstations within the Treasury Department. This case illustrates the dangers of supply chain attacks and the importance of robust cybersecurity measures.

Objective

To analyze a real-world cybersecurity incident, identify deceptive practices used by attackers, and apply analytical frameworks to detect and mitigate such threats in the future.

Scenario Key Details

1. **Unauthorized Access:** Attackers obtained an API key for Beyond Trust's cloud-based service, granting them remote access to Treasury Department workstations.
2. **Exploitation of Trusted Relationships:** By compromising a trusted third-party vendor, the attackers leveraged established trust to infiltrate the Treasury's network.
3. **Legitimate Software Use:** Attackers used legitimate tools and credentials, making their activities blend with normal network traffic.
4. **Evasion through Normalcy:** The attackers operated within the bounds of expected system activity, using valid credentials and tools. This created a deceptive appearance of routine behavior, reducing the likelihood of raising immediate red flags.
5. **Absence of Alarming Indicators:** The attackers ensured their activities did not produce easily detectable anomalies, such as large, sudden data transfers. Instead, they used gradual infiltration to maintain their covert presence.

Analysis Framework

1. **Congruities**
   - The attackers used legitimate tools and trusted third-party software, which appeared routine and credible.
   - Trusted vendor relationships made initial access seem legitimate.
2. **Incongruities**
   - Anomalous behavior patterns in network activity.
   - Unexpected use of API keys in regions or times not typical for the Treasury Department.
3. **Plus or Minus Rule**
   - **Plus:** Unauthorized access through valid credentials.
   - **Minus:** Lack of additional verification or anomaly detection for third-party vendors.
4. **Strategies to Mitigate Threats**
   - Enhance monitoring for unusual patterns in network traffic.
   - Conduct regular security audits of third-party vendors.
   - Implement zero-trust architecture to verify access requests continuously.

Task Instructions

1. **Review the Case Key Details:** Carefully read the background and key details of the Treasury Department breach.
2. **Analyze the Case:**
   - Identify congruities and incongruities using the observation sheet provided.
   - Apply the Plus or Minus Rule to detect deceptive elements.
3. **Group Discussion:**
   - Collaborate with your group to propose strategies for improving vendor security and preventing similar breaches.
4. **Presentation:**
   - Present your group's findings to the class, focusing on actionable recommendations.

Reflection Questions

1. What patterns did you observe that indicated potential deception?
2. How can zero-trust architecture help mitigate supply chain attacks?
3. What lessons from this case can be applied to other cybersecurity scenarios?

CHAPTER SUMMARY

Throughout Chapter 4, we have explored the nuanced realms of intelligence analysis, deception detection, and the methodology of Barton Whaley in understanding and implementing strategies for creating and countering deception. Significant points include:

Intelligence Analysis and Deception: The chapter begins by distinguishing between misperception and deception, emphasizing that while misperception is unintentional, deception is a deliberate act to mislead. It underscores the importance of understanding one's own biases and the need for rigorous analytical techniques to mitigate self-deception.

Barton Whaley's Deception Framework: We delved into Barton Whaley's comprehensive approach to deception, mainly focusing on his 10-Step Deception Process. This process outlines a systematic approach for planners to create effective deceptions, from defining mission goals to ensuring the target's acceptance of the deceptive narrative.

Detecting Deception: The chapter also covers strategies for detecting deception based on Whaley's extensive research across various disciplines. The key to detection, "congruity/incongruity analysis," is discussed in detail, highlighting how discrepancies between expected and observed outcomes can reveal deceptive practices.

Application in Real-World Scenarios: Historical events such as Custer's Last Stand, Operation Market Garden, Classmates.co m, and 2024 Treasury Hack illustrate how self-deception and failure to recognize incongruities can lead to disastrous outcomes. These examples serve as cautionary tales for analysts and strategists.

Methodological Approaches: The scientific method's role in identifying patterns of congruity and incongruity is emphasized, along with the Plus or Minus Rule, which assists in identifying discrepancies that could indicate deception.

The Analyst's Advantage: Finally, the chapter discusses how the congruity/incongruity rule gives analysts a crucial edge in detecting deception, offering a dual pathway to uncovering deceit by identifying what is hidden and falsely presented.

In summary, this chapter provides a deep dive into the complexities of deception and its detection. It offers valuable insights and methodologies for intelligence analysts and strategists to navigate the deceptive landscapes they may encounter.

Key Concepts Covered

1. **Perception in Intelligence Analysis:** Perception refers to how individuals interpret sensory information and observations to form an understanding of events or situations. In intelligence analysis, perception shapes how analysts interpret incoming data, identify patterns, and construct meaning from incomplete information.
2. **The Role of Expectations:** Expectations strongly influence perception. Analysts tend to interpret new information in ways that align with their existing beliefs or mental models. While expectations can speed analysis, they may also lead to misinterpretation or overlooked anomalies.
3. **Perceptual Distortions:** Perceptual distortions occur when analysts interpret information incorrectly due to preconceived beliefs, incomplete data, or misleading signals. These distortions can lead to incorrect conclusions if analysts fail to critically examine their assumptions.
4. **Deception in Intelligence Operations:** Deception involves deliberately manipulating information to mislead an observer into drawing incorrect conclusions. Adversaries use deception to conceal capabilities, intentions, or vulnerabilities while presenting false indicators designed to influence analytical judgments.
5. **Types of Deception:** Deception typically occurs through two primary methods:
   - **Simulation** – Showing something that is false.
   - **Dissimulation** – Concealing or hiding something that is real.

Both forms of deception aim to manipulate an analyst's perception of reality.

6. **The Congruity/Incongruity Rule:** A key principle of deception detection states that real phenomena tend to be internally consistent, while deceptive actions often produce inconsistencies. Identifying anomalies, contradictions, or irregularities can provide important clues that deception may be occurring.
7. **The Plus or Minus Rule:** Authentic objects or situations possess a complete and consistent set of characteristics. Imitations or deceptive constructs often contain either missing characteristics

(minus) or additional features that do not belong (plus). Detecting these discrepancies can reveal deception.

8. **Indicators and Anomalies:** Analysts detect potential deception by identifying indicators, discrepancies, or patterns that do not align with expected behavior. Careful observation and comparison with known baselines help analysts identify unusual or suspicious activity.
9. **Countering Deception:** Effective analysts guard against deception by questioning assumptions, comparing multiple sources, and using structured analytical techniques to test alternative explanations.

Learning Objectives Accomplished

By completing this chapter, you should now be able to:

1. **Define** key terms related to perception, deception, and misperception.
2. **Explain** how biases and sensory inputs affect analytical judgment.
3. **Identify** and analyze historical examples of deception.
4. **Apply** the Congruity/Incongruity Rule in practical scenarios.
5. **Develop** strategies to detect and counter deception in intelligence contexts.

Practical Application

During this chapter, you explored several practical concepts related to perception and deception in intelligence analysis, including:

- **Recognizing Perceptual Bias:** Examining how expectations and assumptions can influence the interpretation of intelligence information.
- **Detecting Deception Indicators:** Identifying inconsistencies, anomalies, and discrepancies that may signal deceptive activity.
- **Applying Analytical Rules for Deception Detection:** Using principles such as the Congruity/Incongruity Rule and the Plus or Minus Rule to evaluate suspicious information.
- **Evaluating Competing Explanations:** Considering multiple possible interpretations of ambiguous or conflicting intelligence data.
- **Analyzing Deception Scenarios:** Reviewing examples where adversaries attempted to manipulate intelligence collection or analytical conclusions.

Reflection Questions

1. How does human perception influence the way analysts interpret intelligence information?
2. Why are expectations both helpful and potentially dangerous in the analytical process?
3. What are the key differences between **simulation** and **dissimulation** in deception operations?
4. How can identifying incongruities or anomalies help analysts detect deception?
5. What analytical methods can help intelligence professionals guard against deception attempts?

Outstanding work completing this chapter. Understanding perception and deception sharpens your analytical awareness and strengthens your ability to detect hidden threats. Continue refining your analytical skills as you move forward in mastering the craft of intelligence analysis.

GLOSSARY OF TERMS

Here is a glossary of key terms introduced and discussed in Chapter 4 to enhance your understanding of the material.

Application Programming Interface (API): An API key is a unique string of characters used to authenticate and identify an application or user when making requests to an Application Programming Interface (API), essentially acting as a password that allows access to specific application features.

Congruity/Incongruity Rule: A method to identify deception by analyzing consistencies and discrepancies in information.

Deception: Deliberate actions to mislead or manipulate others.

Misperception: Incorrect interpretation of sensory or contextual information.

Perception: The process by which individuals interpret sensory information.

Self-Deception: Convincing oneself of a false belief to ignore conflicting evidence.

Supply Chain Attack: A "supply chain attack" is a cyberattack where a malicious actor compromises a third-party vendor or supplier within an organization's supply chain to gain unauthorized access to the organization's systems or data, essentially using the trusted relationship with the vendor to infiltrate the target organization.

Zero Trust: A cybersecurity framework that operates on the principle of "never trust, always verify." Instead of assuming everything behind the corporate firewall is safe, Zero Trust assumes that the system will be breached and designs security accordingly.

This glossary serves as a quick reference for understanding key terms and concepts from the chapter. Feel free to revisit it as you progress through the lesson material!

NOTES

1. Oxford University Press, *Oxford Advanced Learners Dictionary*, 2015.
2. Barton Whaley, *Textbook of Political-Military Counterdeception*, National Defense College, 2007.
3. Richards J. Heuer, Jr., *Psychology of Intelligence Analysis* (2nd ed.), Pherson Associates LLC, 2007.
4. State of Connecticut, Dept. of Consumer Protection, Retrieved January 2025, https://portal.ct.gov/dcp/common-elements/common-elements/the-dirty-dozen-classic-scams-and-pitches?language=en_US.
5. R. C. Gur and H. A. Sackeim, 'Self-deception, Self-confrontation, and Consciousness', in G. Schwartz and D. Shapiro (eds.), *Consciousness and Self-regulation: Advances in Research and Theory* (Vol. 2, pp. 139–197), New York: Plenum Press, 1978.
6. H. A. Sackeim, Self-deception: A Synthesis', in J. S. Lockard and D. L. Paulhus (eds.), *Self-Deception: An Adaptive Mechanism?* (pp. 146–165), Englewood Cliffs, NJ: Prentice Hall, 1988.
7. Ruben C. Gur and Harold A. Sackeim, 'Self-deception: A Concept in Search of a Phenomenon', *Journal of Personality and Social Psychology*, 37(2), 147–169, 1979.
8. Charles Windolph, Frazier Hunt, Robert Hunt and Neil Mangum, *I Fought with Custer: The Story of Sergeant Windolph, Last Survivor of the Battle of the Little Bighorn*, University of Nebraska Press, 1987.
9. Donovan, James, *A Terrible Glory: Custer and the Little Bighorn*, Little, Brown, and Co., 2008.
10. James Donovan, *A Terrible Glory: Custer and the Little Bighorn – The Last Great Battle of the American West*, Back Bay Books, 2009.
11. Ruben C. Gur and Harold A. Sackeim, 'Self-deception: A Concept in Search of a Phenomenon', *Journal of Personality and Social Psychology*, 37(2), 147–169, 1979.
12. Barton Whaley, *Textbook of Political-Military Counterdeception*, National Defense College, 2007.
13. Barton Whaley, *Textbook of Political-Military Counterdeception*, National Defense College, 2007.
14. Barton Whaley, *Textbook of Political-Military Counterdeception*, National Defense College, 2007.
15. Barton Whaley, *Textbook of Political-Military Counterdeception*, National Defense College, 2007.
16. James D. Watson, *The Double Helix: A Personal Account of the Discovery of the Structure of DNA*, New York: Atheneum, 1968.
17. Dan Cooper, *Enrico Fermi: And the Revolutions in Modern Physics*, New York: Oxford University Press, 1999.

18. Barton Whaley, *Textbook of Political-Military Counterdeception*, National Defense College, 2007.
19. Barton Whaley, *Textbook of Political-Military Counterdeception*, National Defense College, 2007.
20. Denis Smyth, *Deathly Deception: The Real Story of Operation Mincemeat*, New York: Oxford Press, 2010.
21. Thomas Hoving, *False Impressions: The Hunt for Big-Time Art Fakes*, New York: Simon and Schuster, 1997.
22. Tim Weiner, David Johnston and Neil A. Lewis, *Betrayal: The Story of Aldrich Ames, an American Spy*, Random House, 1995.
23. David Wise, *Spy: The Inside Story of How the FBI's Robert Hanssen Betrayed America*, Random House Publishers, 2003.
24. Truman Lewis, 'FTD, Classmates.Com to Pay $11 Million for Misleading Advertising', *Consumer Affairs*, 26 May 2015, Retrieved January 2025, https://www.consumeraffairs.com/news/ftd-classmatescom-to-pay-11-million-for-misleading-advertising-052615.html.

CHAPTER 5

Knowing Your Audience

INTRODUCTION

The metaphor "don't kill the messenger" originates from ancient Greek literature. Plutarch, a Greek historian and biographer, in a quotation from *Plutarch's Lives* (The Parallel Lives), writes:

> *The first messenger that gave notice of Lucullus' coming was so far from pleasing Tigranes that he had his head cut off for his pains, and no man dared to bring further information. Without any intelligence at all, Tigranes sat while war was already blazing around him, giving ear only to those who flattered him.*
>
> **Plutarch**

Plutarch's tale of Tigranes's fatal mistake vividly illustrates the peril of killing the messenger, which originates in ancient wisdom. This chapter, "Knowing Your Audience," dives into the essence of intelligence analysis, drawing on the profound lessons of history to guide modern-day analysts.

Imagine the scene: Lucullus is advancing, yet Tigranes remains blissfully unaware, preferring the comfort of flattery over the harsh truths of impending war. This vivid parable prompts us to recognize a truth, no matter how unpleasant, is vital for survival and reminds us that our mission as analysts extends beyond the mere delivery of intelligence. We are the architects of understanding, crafting messages that inform and are eagerly received by our audience.

Information is abundant and fleeting in the fast-paced and interconnected world of modern intelligence analysis. To navigate this landscape effectively, analysts must master the art of understanding and engaging their audience. Imagine being an intelligence analyst tasked with delivering critical information to prevent a national crisis. Your words are not just data; they are the bridge between knowledge and action, the key to

DOI: 10.4324/9781003561712-5

influencing decisions that can change the course of events. This chapter, "Knowing Your Audience," transforms historical lessons and cutting-edge techniques into actionable strategies for today's analysts. By diving into the nuances of audience engagement, you will learn how to craft intelligence that informs and inspires action. Whether deciphering raw data, framing your findings, or anticipating questions before they are asked, this chapter equips you with tools to ensure your intelligence resonates with its intended audience, ensuring your message is heard and acted upon.

This chapter is more than a guide; it is a journey into the art of persuasion and presentation. You will learn to anticipate your audience's needs and expectations and engage them in a way that makes your intelligence indispensable. By embracing the strategies outlined here, you will ensure your analysis has an impact and is acted upon, transforming information into insight and insight into action.

LEARNING OBJECTIVES

1. **Define** the role of audience analysis in crafting intelligence products.
2. **Identify** methods for selecting and presenting evidence to different audiences.
3. **Apply** principles of logical reasoning and justification in intelligence reporting.
4. **Recognize and address** cognitive biases in both analysts and consumers.
5. **Utilize** modern technologies and feedback tools to enhance intelligence delivery.

IDENTIFY AND WRITE FOR YOUR AUDIENCE

Intelligence analysis is not just about gathering data; it is about transforming that data into actionable intelligence that captivates and motivates the audience. Analysts must become adept storytellers, weaving facts into narratives that resonate with their consumers' needs and

AUTHOR'S NOTE: TIPS ON "HOOKING YOUR AUDIENCE"

- *Remember, your first chance to get your reader's attention may be your last.*
- *Know what interests your audience.*
- *Give them what they want early.*
- *Do not make them look for it.*
- *Use simple and direct language.*
- *Pair the "hook" text with a visual (e.g., a graphic), if appropriate.*

interests. This is crucial, whether the subject is as immediate as the winning lottery numbers or as captivating as Hollywood's latest gossip.

Understanding your audience goes beyond knowing their interests; it involves intimate familiarity with their informational needs and decision-making processes. This principle is embedded in Chapter 2, specifically the Planning and Direction phase, where the foundation for audience-centric analysis is laid. The goal is to ensure that key insights are not buried but prominently featured, allowing the audience to grasp and act upon them quickly.

Therefore, since you have already identified "What" information the end-user needs or wants, do not make them search for it because it is buried three pages deep into the report.

Analysts, like novelists, must capture the intelligence consumer's attention early to get their message across, whether it is the "winning lottery number" or the latest Hollywood rumors about their favorite soap opera star. Generally, humans only want information they can "use" or that "interest them," but preferably "both."

Identifying your audience will do more than ensure you write clearly by including the most wanted information; it will also aid the analyst in focusing on the audience's "needs." See the following example scenario.

Example Scenario:

Consider the situation where the U.S. Drug Enforcement Agency (DEA) assigns a Department of Homeland Security (DHS) analyst with the task of identifying major drug smuggling routes across the Texas border into the U.S. This intelligence product's primary audience includes the DEA and the Customs and Border Protection (CBP) agents actively operating on the ground. A solid understanding of the audience's operational environment, constraints, and capabilities enables the analyst to create a useful and actionable intelligence requirement (IR) (see Figure 5.1).

Objective: Identify the major drug smuggling routes crossing the Texas border into the U.S. As a DHS analyst, you are responsible for rephrasing this information requirement (IR) and sending it to other units for collection.

Who is your audience? Is it the DEA? ... DHS? ... CBP Management? ... CBP Patrol Agents? ... Drug Smugglers?

Background: The collection requirement should logically be directed to the CBP agents stationed at the Texas border. Unless DHS has reliable, confidential informants (CIs) embedded within one or more of the drug smuggling cartels, the DEA (the IR originator), DHS (which is responsible for rewriting and forwarding the IR), and CBP Management (which lacks access or resources to obtain the information) would not serve as logical collection assets for this IR.

FIGURE 5.1 Revising the IR to meet the audience's needs.

Most Probable Workflow of the IR:

1. Task Origination (DEA): The DEA assigns a task to DHS to refine and forward the information requirement (IR). The DEA's request stems from its strategic goal of disrupting drug smuggling operations.

2. Intelligence Analyst Role (DHS):

   - *The analyst refines the IR to make it specific, actionable, and relevant to field operatives.*
   - *Refined IR: Identify primary smuggling routes used by drug cartels to transport cocaine through specific Texas border sectors, focusing on known chokepoints and patterns in cartel activity.*

3. Forwarding to Collection Entities (CBP Management):

   - *CBP Management is informed of the task, ensuring resources are appropriately allocated.*
   - *Example: Allocate surveillance assets and coordinate with CBP Patrol Agents.*

4. Field Collection (CBP Patrol Agents and other law enforcement officers, LEOs): On-the-ground CBP agents (and other LEOs) gather intelligence through:

   - *Monitoring and reporting suspicious activities in border areas.*

- *Reviewing patterns of seizures and interceptions.*
- *Coordinating with partner agencies for additional intelligence.*

5. Feedback Loop: Collected intelligence is returned to DHS analysts for synthesis and analysis. Refined insights are then communicated to CBP and DEA for operational action and strategic decision-making.

Audience Considerations:

- ***CBP Patrol Agents:*** *The primary audience for the IR, as they are best positioned to observe and collect the required intelligence.*
- ***DEA:*** *The originator of the IR needs the synthesized results to inform broader counter-narcotics operations.*
- ***CBP Management:*** *Is a secondary audience for oversight and resource allocation.*
- ***DHS:*** *Responsible for analysis, refinement, and coordination of the IR.*
- ***Other Law Enforcement Entities:*** *They may also be privy to historical drug seizure data.*

AUTHOR'S NOTE: FIRST ASK YOURSELF: WHAT DOES THE AUDIENCE ALREADY KNOW ABOUT THE SUBJECT?

How does one locate a "major drug smuggling route?"—are they labeled "major drug smuggling routes?"—not very likely. Although CBP agents would plausibly know what large drug shipments look like. For example, a couple of grams of cocaine found in the backpack of a non-U.S. national found outside El Paso, in this case, probably does not fit the IR criteria. However, the analyst will eventually start to see patterns form ***by plotting the large drug seizures identified in recent years on a map.*** *With enough data, those patterns will begin to show trafficking routes and potentially indicate amounts of throughput. CBP and other law enforcement organizations could provide the needed historical drug seizure data.*

In the example just outlined, CBP agents may not know of every potential smuggling route but can recognize patterns in reported drug seizures. The DHS analyst can tailor the request for information accordingly. By specifying the need for details on drug seizures greater than one kilogram within proximity to the Texas–Mexico land border, the analyst directly addresses the "what," "why," and "how" of the audience's informational needs.

IMPORTANCE OF INTEGRATING MODERN TECHNOLOGIES

The integration of modern technologies such as artificial intelligence (AI), machine learning (ML), and data visualization platforms has significantly enhanced intelligence analysis by improving accuracy, efficiency, and accessibility. AI and ML tools can process vast amounts of data at unprecedented speeds, identifying patterns and correlations that may be overlooked by human analysts. These technologies help predict audience needs, tailor intelligence products, and mitigate biases by offering data-driven insights. Additionally, data visualization platforms transform complex datasets into accessible and engaging formats, improving communication and comprehension among intelligence consumers. However, challenges remain, including the risk of algorithmic biases, ethical concerns surrounding AI decision-making, and the need for human oversight to interpret results effectively. Addressing these challenges requires ongoing refinement of these tools and the incorporation of ethical frameworks to ensure responsible and accurate intelligence analysis. Examples of these tools include Palantir or IBM Watson in analyzing data and predicting audience needs (e.g., AI-assisted sentiment analysis for tailored briefings).[1]

How Digital Tools and Social Media Analytics Are Transforming Intelligence Reporting

Digital tools and social media analytics have revolutionized intelligence reporting by enabling real-time data collection, enhanced situational awareness, and increased accessibility to open-source intelligence. Social media platforms generate vast amounts of data daily, providing intelligence analysts with valuable insights into public sentiment, emerging threats, and geopolitical developments. Tools such as sentiment analysis, geolocation tracking, and network mapping allow analysts to detect patterns, predict trends, and verify information more effectively. However, these advancements also present challenges, including misinformation, data overload, and the ethical implications of surveillance. By leveraging these tools responsibly and integrating them with traditional intelligence methods, analysts can improve the accuracy and timeliness of their assessments, ensuring decision-makers receive relevant and actionable intelligence.

Additionally, engagement with the audience does not end with the report's delivery. Feedback mechanisms, such as direct communication with CBP agents and others, ensure the intelligence provided is relevant, understandable, and, most importantly, actionable. This iterative process enhances the intelligence's quality and builds rapport with the audience, establishing the analyst as a trusted and valued source of information.

Example Scenario (continued): Other items that might be included in the IR ...

What does the audience (the CBP agents) need to know? The analyst must translate clear criteria to the CBP agents, which satisfies the "intent" of the DEA IR.

Answer: *Request information on all drug seizures greater than one kilogram reported in the vicinity (50 miles) of the Texas–Mexico land border. Specifics include weight, date, and time of seizure; names of the perpetrator(s) involved; gang/cartel/organizational affiliation; direction traveling when captured; reported origin, destination, and route information, if available.*

What other questions might the intelligence audience have?

Answer: *To save possible reiterations of drafting, revising, and resending the IR, the analyst might call or email a CBP office near the Texas border and bounce the IR off of a CBP agent. If it does not make sense to the agent, the analyst should listen to their audience's concerns and make adjustments before forwarding the IR for release. Knowing that their input to the IR is valued, the CBP agents will be more encouraged to execute the task.*

By adopting a more audience-centric approach, analysts can ensure their intelligence informs and inspires action, increasing its value and impact.

CHOOSING YOUR SUPPORTING EVIDENCE

To prevent misunderstanding, the text does not endorse the "selection of supporting evidence" for presentation based on "what agrees" or "does not agree with one's hypothesis." However, if, for instance, your audience generally does not accept (or prefer) certain types or forms of evidence (such as statistics or expert opinions), it will not matter how much statistical data or expert opinion-related evidence you possess; the consumer may ignore it or disregard it based on the "packaging" rather than the "content." If intelligence products are ignored or overlooked, in either case, you have failed. In intelligence analysis, one does not always get to choose the types of supporting information or available data. However, if different forms are available to support the analysis, the analyst should try to choose those forms that the consumer will most likely read.

Generally, an intelligence argument can be supported using three different methods. An analyst can use these methods separately or in combination, depending on its purpose and audience. The methods are

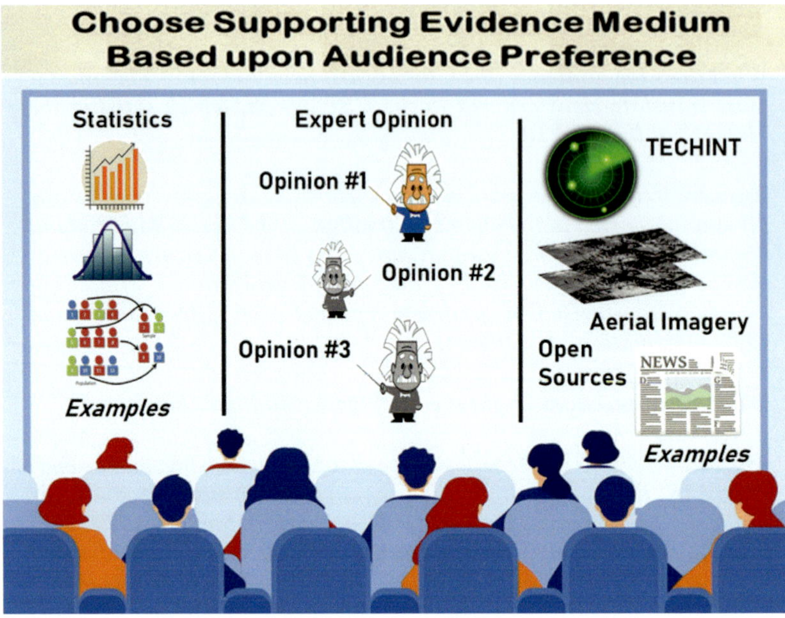

FIGURE 5.2 Choosing supporting evidence.

statistics, *examples*, and *expert opinion* (see Figure 5.2). From the perspective of an intelligence consumer, each form has its advantages and drawbacks. Strategically selecting evidence based on the audience's preferences and cognitive biases ensures the information resonates and influences decisions.

AUTHOR'S NOTE: TIPS ON CHOOSING SUPPORTING EVIDENCE

- *Evidence should be strategic and tailored to the audience's preferences, biases, and understanding level.*
- *Include recent developments in data visualization and interactive evidence presentation.*
- *Use narrative techniques to make examples more relatable and memorable.*
- *Present contradictory data along with an explanation so the user understands why the information is deemed invalid.*

Statistics

It is essential to contextualize statistics to demonstrate how different interpretations can lead to varied conclusions. Transparency in methodology and recognition of the limitations of using statistical data are crucial to prevent misinterpretation. While statistics provide seemingly unbiased evidence, their strength lies in the analyst's ability to narrate the story behind the numbers, making complex data understandable and relevant to the audience's concerns.

Some intelligence consumers want statistical evidence in their reports. Statistics can present information in a seemingly unbiased numerical format. According to Webster, "statistics" is a branch of mathematics dealing with the collection, analysis, interpretation, and presentation of masses of numerical data.[2] Therefore, one must understand statistical information can be presented in various factual ways and yet suggest dramatically different conclusions. The following example shows how factual statistics can be used to mislead.

Example Scenario:

Some may be familiar with the well-known statistic that 52% of car accidents occur within five miles of home, and 69% of all auto accidents happen within 10 miles. This fact may lead some to worry that, for some unknown reason, driving in the vicinity of their home is more dangerous than driving outside a 10-mile radius of it (see Figure 5.3). However, a casual skeptic may realize that no matter the destination or direction chosen (e.g., the store, work, golf course, etc.), one leaves home as the point of origin and returns almost 100% of the time. This means that, statistically, you will be within 10 miles of your home much more often and are more likely to have an accident within that 10-mile radius than anywhere beyond it.

FIGURE 5.3 Statistics example.

Utilizing statistics to support your analysis is most suitable if your audience is comfortable with statistical information and understands its limitations. However, not all datasets or numerical samples, especially small or skewed ones, readily accommodate statistical analysis. Because of these limitations in statistical calculations, the analytical results may be significantly flawed. As a result, statistical evidence is not always appropriate, even when consumers desire its inclusion in the overall analysis product.

AUTHOR'S NOTE: USE CAUTION WHEN USING STATISTICS FOR SMALL DATASETS

Using statistical analysis on small datasets can lead to erroneous conclusions due to several key issues:

1. ***Increased Variability (High Sampling Error):*** *Small samples exhibit more significant variability, meaning any observed patterns or trends may arise from chance rather than a true underlying relationship. A single outlier can disproportionately affect the results.*
2. ***Lack of Representativeness:*** *A small sample may not accurately reflect the larger population. If the sample is not sufficiently diverse, the results may be biased and not generalizable.*
3. ***Violation of Statistical Assumptions:*** *Many statistical tests presume a normal distribution of data, which is more challenging to achieve with small samples. Without a large enough dataset, the assumptions of normality, independence, and equal variance may be violated, leading to misleading outcomes.*
4. ***Increased Risk of Type I and Type II Errors:***
   - *Type I Error (False Positive): Detecting an effect when none exists is more likely in small samples, as randomness can create patterns that appear significant.*
   - *Type II Error (False Negative): The power of a statistical test diminishes with small samples, making it harder to identify a real effect when it is present.*
5. ***Overfitting and Lack of Generalization:*** *Small sample sizes can result in overfitting, where a model performs well on limited data but falters when applied to a broader dataset.*
6. ***Misleading Effect Sizes:*** *In small samples, effect sizes can become exaggerated because a few extreme values can*

heavily sway the mean or standard deviation, leading to misleading interpretations.

7. ***Confidence Intervals Are Wider:*** *The smaller the sample, the wider the confidence intervals, meaning that any estimate drawn from the data is less precise.*

Good and Bad Examples of Supporting Evidence

Analogies that compare two things (e.g., "a military force's position is like the Alamo or Thermopylae") often create vivid imagery for the reader; however, they may not always be factual. Factual examples (not analogies) that support or contradict the analyst's claims should be included. These examples should provide specifics and supporting details, often giving the analysis a visual description that captures and retains the intelligence consumer's attention. Types of evidence include HUMINT reporting, photographic evidence, video or audio recordings, and raw scientific or forensic data. Each example dataset requires additional contextual information (e.g., the date and time of the data, names of individuals in the photos and videos, voice recordings). Although some interpretation is required, it is generally minimal.

Analysts should organize examples logically or sequentially, whichever is easiest for the reader to comprehend and best supports the analysis. Contradictory data should also be included, accompanied by some explanation or rationale, so the user understands why the information is deemed invalid or irrelevant.

Some intelligence consumers resemble the characters from the old TV show *Dragnet*, which aired in the 1950s and later in the 1970s. The most famous line from the series came from Detective Joe Friday (played by Jack Webb), who would say, "All we want are the facts, ma'am." Like Detective Friday, intelligence end-users are not interested in opinions or intricate mathematical algorithms (regardless of their accuracy). They only want "the facts" (see Figure 5.4).

Expert Opinions

Factual evidence is the basis for expert opinions; however, expert opinions differ from facts because they are interpretations of facts.

For example, a physicist may consider mountains of data when determining whether a foreign chemical processing facility produces weapons-grade Uranium (U235) or peanut butter. The same dataset reviewed by multiple expert observers or subject matter experts (SMEs) may yield differing interpretations of the same information. Often, political

FIGURE 5.4 Joe Friday's famous line from *Dragnet* (www.shutterstock.com).

decisions on whether to do nothing, exercise sanctions, or bomb the facility are balanced based on which argument is most convincing (see Figure 5.5).

Intelligence analysts often must use SMEs to interpret data because they do not have the background information to weigh the facts presented properly. However, some consumers are not interested in highly

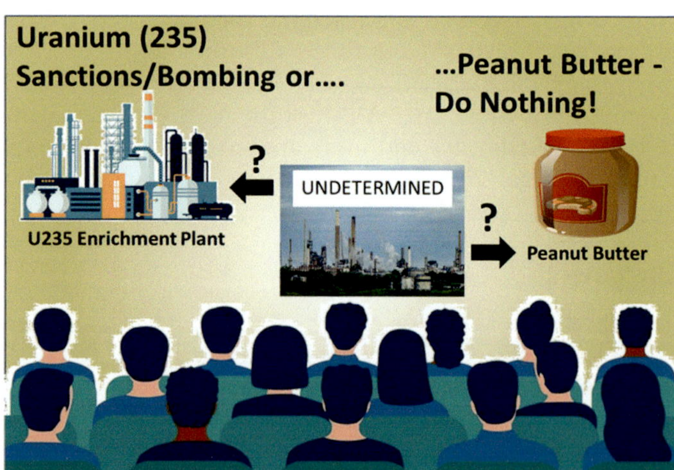

FIGURE 5.5 Decisions made from expert opinions.

technical and lengthy scientific reports. They want a clean, quick assessment. Nevertheless, by providing that "clean quick assessment" to the consumer, the analyst is not relieved of the burden of due diligence and performing thorough and complete analysis. Even if the analyst does not provide the raw scientific data as part of the deliverable, they should have it available and reference it in the final report.

ORGANIZING INFORMATION FOR THE USER

One should recognize that most intelligence consumers are like you and do not want to waste their time reading many pages of marginally related information to eventually find what they were looking for many pages into the document or, even worse, not at all.

To ensure the intelligence consumer can quickly locate desired reporting content, it is crucial for an analyst to have a well-structured and logical plan for presenting findings. This approach, whether based on a template or your own design, should instill confidence in your work. Whichever way you choose to present your findings, it should be consistent, verifiable, straightforward, and logically supportable.

Finding(s) (Intelligence Assessments)

Analytical findings (also known as your assessments) are based upon the evidence or information (e.g., facts, opinions, and statistics) collected and your analysis of that information. One must show the linkage between your findings and the supporting evidence. To demonstrate this linkage, an analyst typically states their claim/finding as the topic sentence of the paragraph, followed by the supporting evidence or information from which the claim or finding derives its support, as well as the justification or logical reasoning linking the evidence to their finding.

Example of Findings (Focused on the Audience)

Fictitious Analytical Scenario:

Imagine you are a DHS analyst and have been informed that notice of an alien invasion of Texas is being broadcast across the news channels. Your role is crucial as you must prepare a quick assessment for Federal, state, and local law enforcement as well as the National Guard units in affected areas to assist them in containing the situation.

- The IR reads: Determine size, strength, route(s), speed of movement, and intentions/destination(s) of space invasion force. Following are the first field reports and your first finding.

FIGURE 5.6 Sci-fi movie poster typical of the 1950s.

- Media and internet reports pour in:
  - A local TV news station announces "Invaders from Space" (see Figure 5.6), citing NASA public advisory announcements and video reports (using cell phone video sources and station video clips). This sensational reporting causes public concern and widespread unease.
  - Video clips show footage of spacecraft landing at five separate locations in Texas.
  - Local police reports corroborate the five landing sites. TV reports have yet to locate a landing site that the police have not already reported.

Analyst Comment: News agencies likely found landing sites based on police scanner reports and locals posting cell phone photos and video clips on social media and other internet platforms.

- Hundreds of cell phone video clips flood the internet.

Analyst Comment: Presently, only 25 video clips match up to military, air traffic, or police reports with any level of confidence.

- Seven other sightings are still under investigation.
- Multiple conspiracy theories circulating on social networks citing China, Russia, the CIA, angels, and creatures from outer space are attacking.

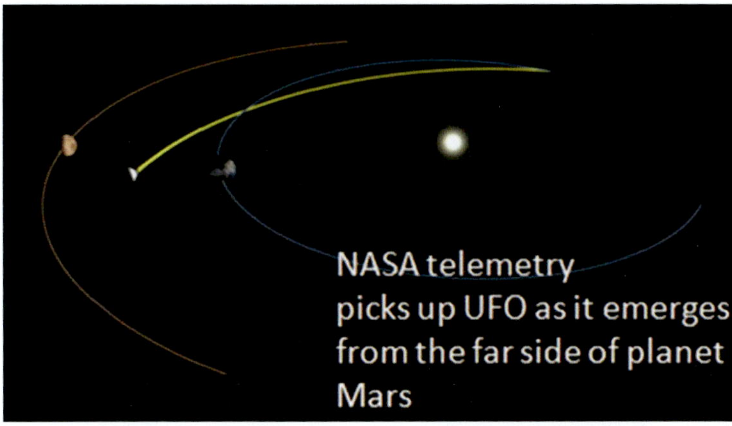

FIGURE 5.7 NASA's estimated trajectory of the invasion force.

- NASA reporting verifies alien craft trajectories originated from or near Mars. The craft was first suspected to be a series of asteroids that had a near miss on Mars. Later, after a series of course and speed changes, it was confirmed to be under intelligent control. Radio contact was attempted with no response. The ultimate origin cannot be confirmed at this time (see Figure 5.7).
- U.S. Military reconnaissance imagery depicts multiple large (300 yds long × 50 yds wide) spacecraft at multiple landing sites across Texas (>25 known sites, multiple more suspected). Cloud cover and commercial and private aircraft in the vicinity confuse observations (see Figure 5.8).

FIGURE 5.8 Drone photo of spacecraft.

FIGURE 5.9 Hovering ground vehicle image from highway traffic camera.

- Military and Federal Air Traffic Controllers also track on radar and attempt radio contact without response.
- Highway traffic cameras along Interstates 10 and 20 show more than 100 unidentified vehicles (approximately 30 feet long) moving east at approximately 50 mph. The forward limit of progress is roughly along the Texas–Louisiana border (see Figure 5.9).
- Local LEO reports:
  - Visible rays causing law enforcement officers (LEOs) at roadblocks to become physically nauseated and temporarily incapacitated; no further information (NFI).
  - Landing craft (visually reported to be over 200 yards long) are deploying multiple (>100 total) smaller craft/vehicles (each approximately 30 feet long), which hover above the ground (10 to 20 feet).
  - Multiple deployed craft/vehicles approach roadblocks; officers give verbal orders to stop in English and Spanish, as

well as hand signals and warning shots. Aliens responded with an incapacitating ray, unidentified backwash from hovering craft, brushing patrol cars and personnel aside as they bypass roadblocks and move eastward toward the interstate. Multiple reports were submitted with similar results. No known deaths have been reported at this time.

- Unidentified aquatic/amphibious craft being transported by other self-propelled vehicles.

Now, as analysts, we divide the information into the following categories: Supporting Evidence, Inferences, Assumptions, and Gaps

- Supporting Evidence (What do we know?)
  - *Military satellite imagery depicting large (300 yds long x 50 yds wide) spacecraft at multiple landing sites (>25 known sites, multiple suspected) across Texas.*
  - *NASA telemetry shows the point of origin to be the planet Mars, potentially.*
  - *Local LEOs' eyewitness reports:*
    - *Unable to contain in landing zones*
    - *Invaders using an unidentified incapacitating ray against any potential resistance*
    - *Large numbers (>100) of unidentified air and land craft levitating and moving east at 50 mph along Interstates 10 and 20*
    - *Other unidentified hovering craft in columns*
    - *Other hovering vehicles are transporting unidentified (possibly aquatic/amphibious) craft (see Figure 5.10)*

FIGURE 5.10 Police artist's drawing of the possibly aquatic craft being transported by hovering vehicles.

- Inferences (What do we suspect?)
  - *Possibly hostile; use of incapacitating ray to remove resistance, no reported attempts to communicate or respond to human attempts*
  - *Over 100 LEO reports of large numbers (>100) of unidentified air and land craft (if manned, one per craft, the number would be >100)*
  - *Movement based upon eyewitness reports: moving east at 50 mph along Interstates 10 and 20 (possibly I-30)*
  - *The intermediate destination is likely the Mississippi River:*
    - *The observation is based on unidentified craft carried by the hovering vehicles in columns that appear to be aquatic or amphibious.*
    - *Only a large body of water on the path for hundreds of miles on the path of travel is the Mississippi River (see Figure 5.11).*
      - *If they were heading to the Atlantic, they would have more likely landed closer to the coast.*
      - *They landed near I-10 and I-20, so they used the roads to travel east.*

- Assumptions (What must we assume?):
  - *Invaders are extraterrestrial, possibly from Mars, but could have originally come from another planet in the Solar*

FIGURE 5.11 Situation map, provided by Southwest Texas Fusion Center.

System or outside the Solar System and used the backside of Mars as a staging area.
  - *Perhaps looking for freshwater, otherwise they would have landed near one of the oceans.*
  - *The hovering vehicles' levitation mechanism may not work above bodies of water; otherwise, they would not need to carry aquatic (floatable) craft.*

- Gaps (What do we need to know?)
  - *Intentions and ultimate destination are unknown:*
    - *Hostile, conceivably. The purpose may be an occupation or possibly a raid. If a raid, what is the purpose? Perhaps supplies, ... freshwater? This may be the reason for going for a swim in the Mississippi ... Presently, the invader's intentions are not determinable.*
    - *The invaders are not indiscriminately killing or destroying property, but they are also not communicating.*
    - *Obviously, they are highly advanced technologically, but why are they not communicating?*
  - *Point of origin is unknown: NASA telemetry can only observe the side of Mars facing Earth.*
  - *The final destination(s) is (are) also unknown?*
  - *What are the propulsion systems of all craft unknown?*
  - *Are they living creatures? What is their physiology? There were no actual "being" sightings, only spacecraft and ground-effect vehicles. Therefore, all or some vehicles could be unmanned (robotic) spacecraft/vehicles.*

Enhancing Foundational Evidence

Foundational or supporting evidence is the information the analysts use to base their findings. Notice, under *Example Finding #1* (shown later) what sources (see *Source Footnotes* that follow *Findings*) are used to support the finding are specified, e.g., military satellite imagery, NASA telemetry, and local Law Enforcement Organization (LEO) Reports. Factual evidence generally speaks for itself. However, inferences need some level of explanation; assumptions should be recognized as "assumptions," and intelligence gaps need to be identified as collection requirements and explained in the final reporting.

Enhancing the supporting evidence underpinning the intelligence analysis ensures a nuanced understanding of the evidence's role in shaping assessment conclusions and recommended actions.

Facts

A fact is a piece of information considered to be "true." In the analytical field, that is generally a piece of information having multiple independent and known reliable sources. For example, a criminal report identifying a suspect by name is generally supported by solid evidence such as video, fingerprint, or DNA evidence. However, there may still be a chance that the video footage is misleading or the other biometric evidence is compromised, planted or somehow manipulated. However, the chances of this being the case are extremely small but they are not zero.

Foundational evidence forms the bedrock of intelligence analysis, serving as the basis for all findings. This evidence, ranging from military satellite imagery to NASA telemetry and reports from local LEOs, must be meticulously cited, allowing the reader to trace the origins of each claim. This not only bolsters the credibility of the analysis but also promotes transparency.

Inferences

Inferences, by their nature, are not facts. However, inferences should be supported by facts and described in the findings using presumptive or suggestive terminology, e.g., likely, highly likely, unlikely, etc. The destination of "the Mississippi River" is cited as a "likely" destination. The rationale for the probable destination is based upon the route of movement (east) and the unidentified, possibly aquatic, or amphibious craft being moved by hovering vehicles. The analyst's rationale for making the inference is usually included in the findings/final assessment to assist the intelligence consumer in understanding the analyst's perspective.

Assumptions

It may be reasonable to consider the possibility that the invaders are "extraterrestrial," given their apparent origins beyond Earth. Although there are numerous indicators, the lack of incontrovertible proof complicates this assumption. You have many indicators, but no incontrovertible proof. Other, albeit less likely, scenarios also exist, such as their origin from a parallel dimension or another time.

The pressing question then becomes how to secure undeniable evidence. No substantial proof may be at hand, leaving analysts in a bind unless they can capture and analyze a spacecraft or observe an alien encounter firsthand. Instead of expending valuable resources to chase after elusive or debatable data, the analyst must make logical assumptions and proceed accordingly.

Rather than wasting precious collection assets to obtain difficult or impossible-to-find data for the experts to argue over, the analyst makes a few logical assumptions and moves on.

While it could all be an elaborate hoax, such a ruse would require falsifying sensor data and video footage from multiple independent, and notably credible, sources. Limiting assumptions and clearly designating them as such within the analysis document is crucial. Additionally, conducting a risk analysis is essential to evaluate the consequences of potentially flawed assumptions. For instance, if a homicide detective prematurely concludes that a suspect is female, they may inadvertently overlook a significant portion of potential suspects.

Gaps

Would it be reasonable to assume that the invaders came from Mars? They may have appeared to have come from there on their way to Earth. *Take note*: They may have just been passing by the planet Mars when NASA picked them up on their sensors. NASA's telemetry supports the Mars-to-Earth portion of the travel route, but that is all that can be surmised from the available sensor data. Currently, the point of origin is beyond the reasonable scope of the evidence available and, therefore, is considered an intelligence "gap."

Intelligence "gaps" are unknowns. They may be questions left unanswered from the original IR or new questions generated during the analysis process. Analysts should submit collection requirements to address any intelligence gaps in either case.

Justification (Logical Reasoning)

It is not enough to present an assessment to the intelligence end-user. Explaining the thought processes used to arrive at the stated findings is necessary. Otherwise, the final intelligence assessment may be filled with useless information and conclusions that do not address the intelligence customer's requirements. One first categorizes the gathered information to aid in this explanation while focusing on the intelligence end-user's needs.

Understanding and Categorizing Information

Once information is collected, it must be meticulously sorted and categorized. This initial organization of collected datasets the stage for more effective analysis by clarifying which pieces of data are most relevant to address the specific questions or challenges faced by the audience. The analyst must keep the audience in mind throughout the process.

Audience Analysis

The intelligence's audience, lightly armed state National Guardsmen and law enforcement professionals, have specific operational capacities and responsibilities. Understanding these roles is crucial in making the intelligence actionable and relevant.

Example of the Justification Process:

Once collected, information is sorted into the appropriate categories, and after weighing all available data, one must make logical and justified assessments (findings) based on the sorted and analyzed information.

So, who is the audience?... **Answer:** *A combination of lightly armed state National Guardsmen and law enforcement professionals.*

What is our audience's most likely mission? ... Is it "defeat the invaders?" ... If this is the case, do they have the capacity? ... Does a state of "war" exist? ... Are the invaders attacking anyone? ... Note: There are no reported casualties (save the purported temporarily incapacitated police). ... or perhaps your audience's mission is to "Protect the public."

First, one must recall "exactly what the IR specified."

IR: Determine the size, strength, route(s), and speed of movement and intentions/destination(s) of the space invasion force.

Did the IR specify something like "Identify possible physical weaknesses for tactical exploitation?"

Answer: *No, the IR had no language requesting this information.*

AUTHOR'S NOTE

If necessary, the U.S. Military (and, in this case, NATO Forces) would be far better suited to attack the invaders.

Would it not be more advantageous for everyone if the police and National Guard were to focus their resources on evacuating civilian populations to prevent potential collateral casualties?

Should government leaders ultimately determine the situation to be a hostile invasion and the military order the military to engage, armed forces will need clear fields of fire.

There are many other questions one can try to answer, such as:

- *What if the invaders are not hostile?*
- *What if the extraterrestrials did not even know our planet was inhabited?*
- *What if we attacked and started a war that could have been avoided?*

The bullet points noted here may all be valid questions for some other intelligence customers, but they are not part of the IR received, and analysts should not waste precious time and resources looking for unrequested information.

Findings

- ***Finding #1:*** *Over 100 extraterrestrial spacecraft approximately 300 yds long × 50 yds wide (origins unknown) have landed in Texas at 25-plus confirmed locations.*[1] *Multiple* *smaller (approximately 30 feet long) ground-effect vehicles have emerged (specific numbers unknown, estimated to <5 per spacecraft based upon assessed mothership volume) from parent craft and are moving east along Interstates 10, 20, and possibly I-30 at approximately 50 mph.*[2]

- ***Finding #2:*** *Likely headed toward the Mississippi River (could cross Mississippi) at two, probably three, locations (I-10/I-20/I-30? bridges); intentions, friendly or hostile, unknown (no fatalities yet reported) and ultimate destination(s) presently unknown.*[3]
- ***Finding #3:*** *Unidentified ground effect craft are extremely mobile. However, vehicular movement patterns indicate a preference or may require a relatively flat surface to obtain/maintain the present speed (approximately 50 mph), resulting in preferential movement along interstates.*[4] *NFI.*
  - ***Assumption 1: Invaders are extraterrestrial in origin.***
  - ***Assumption 2: Invaders possess advanced technology, superior weapons, and propulsion capabilities.***

Source Footnotes:

1. *NASA ground station radar and satellite telemetry tracks, National OPIR imagery collection.*
2. *Southwest Texas Fusion Center collected and collated multiple state and local police reports and pertinent interstate traffic camera footage.*
3. *Analyst's assessment is based upon available field reports and pattern/movement analysis.*
4. *Analyst assessment based upon multiple eyewitness police reports, video, and traffic camera footage.*

Looking at each bulleted item above, ask yourself if the IR was answered yes, no, or partially. Regardless of the answer, was there adequate support for the presented finding? Remember, the IR response is more helpful when it focuses on the needs of the intelligence consumer (i.e., the audience).

CHAPTER SUMMARY

As the Introduction mentions, this chapter does not address "why" people associate bad news with the bearer. However, it does give the intelligence analyst tools and information on how to prepare intelligence products that users are more likely to read and appreciate. By fully understanding one's audience (the intelligence consumer) and their mission, the analyst tailors information requirements (IRs) to more accurately collect information and more precisely address the information needs of their customers, making the intelligence end-user feel better that their information request was understood and adequately supported.

Identify and Write for Your Audience

Identifying your audience will do more than ensure you write clearly by including the most wanted information. It also aids the analyst to focus on the audience's "needs."

Choosing Your Supporting Evidence

Generally, one can support an intelligence argument using three different methods. An analyst can use them separately or in combination, according to their purpose and audience. The types are statistics, examples, and expert opinion. From an intelligence consumer's perspective, each form has advantages and detractors. Knowing what type(s) the intelligence consumer is more receptive to increases the likelihood that an intelligence product will be appropriately received and the information contained will be understood and accepted.

Statistics

Using statistics to support your analysis may be most appropriate if your audience is comfortable with statistical information sets and understands their pitfalls. However, not all datasets or numerical samples (small or skewed datasets in particular) readily support statistical analysis. Because of this shortfall in statistical calculation, the statistical analytical results may be seriously flawed. Therefore, using statistical evidence is not always appropriate, even when the consumer desires that it be included in the overall analysis.

Examples

Examples play a crucial role in providing a visual description that can engage and hold the intelligence consumer's attention. Whether it's HUMINT reporting, photographic evidence, video or audio recordings, or raw scientific or forensic data, each example dataset brings the analysis to life.

Expert Opinion

Expert opinions are crucial as they provide interpretations of facts. Intelligence analysts often must use subject matter experts (SMEs) to interpret data because they do not have the background knowledge to weigh the facts presented properly. However, some consumers are not interested in highly technical and lengthy scientific reports. They want a clean, quick assessment. Nevertheless, by providing that "clean quick assessment" to the consumer, the analyst is not relieved of the burden of due diligence and performing thorough and complete analysis. Even if the analyst does not provide the raw scientific data as part of the deliverable, they should have it available and reference it in the final report.

Organizing Information for the User

To ensure the intelligence consumer can quickly locate desired reporting content, an analyst should have a logical plan to present your findings and support your case in a brief and logical fashion. The format can be based on a template (if driven by organization requirements) or of your own design. Whichever way you choose to present your findings, it should be consistent, verifiable, straightforward, and logically supportable.

Foundational Evidence

Foundational or supporting evidence is the information the analysts use to base their claim/finding. Factual evidence generally speaks for itself. However, inferences need some level of explanation, assumptions should be recognized as assumptions, and intelligence gaps need to be identified as collection requirements.

Finding(s) (Intelligence Assessments)

Analytical finding(s) (also known as "assessments") is (are) based upon the evidence or information (e.g., facts, opinions, and statistics) collected and your analysis of that information. One must show the linkage between your findings and the supporting evidence.

Facts

A fact is a piece of information considered to be "true." In the analytical field, that is generally a piece of information with multiple independent and known reliable sources. There is still a chance that the evidence is fake or somehow manipulated. However, the chances of this being the case are extremely low but not zero.

Inferences

Inferences should be supported by facts and described in the findings using presumptive or suggestive terminology, e.g., likely, highly likely, unlikely, etc. ... The analyst's rationale for making the inference is usually included in the finding/assessment to assist the intelligence consumer in understanding the analyst's perspective.

Assumptions

Analysts may use assumptions when there are many indicators but no incontrovertible proof. For example, suppose something is "self-evident" or conversely "extremely difficult to determine." Rather than wasting precious collection assets to obtain obvious information or impossible-to-find data, the analyst makes a few logical assumptions and moves on.

Assumptions should be few in number and clearly identified as assumptions in the analysis document.

Gaps

Intelligence "gaps" are unknowns. They may be questions left unanswered from the original IR or new questions generated during the analysis process. Analysts should submit collection requirements to address any intelligence gaps in either case.

Justification (Logical Reasoning)

Keeping the audience in mind, the analyst weighs all available data and makes reasonable and justified assessments (findings) based on that information. Once analysts have drafted their findings, they review them to ensure they are logical and defensible.

Key Concepts Covered

1. **Importance of Audience Awareness:** Effective intelligence analysis is not complete until it is communicated clearly to the intended decision-maker. Understanding the audience ensures that intelligence products are relevant, understandable, and actionable.
2. **Decision-Maker Needs:** Different consumers of intelligence—such as policymakers, military commanders, law enforcement officials, or corporate executives—have unique informational needs, priorities, and time constraints. Analysts must tailor their products to support those specific decision requirements.
3. **Levels of Decision-Making:** Intelligence supports decision-making at multiple levels:
    - **Strategic Level** – Long-term policy and national security planning.
    - **Operational Level** – Planning and coordination of campaigns or major initiatives.

- **Tactical Level** – Immediate actions and real-time operational decisions.

Understanding the level of decision-making helps analysts determine the scope, depth, and format of intelligence products.

4. **Communication Style and Clarity:** Clear, concise communication is essential in intelligence reporting. Analysts must avoid unnecessary jargon, explain technical terms when needed, and present conclusions in a manner that allows decision-makers to quickly understand the significance of the information.
5. **Bottom Line Up-Front (BLUF):** Many intelligence organizations use the **BLUF** format, which presents the key judgment or conclusion at the beginning of the report. This approach allows busy decision-makers to quickly grasp the most important insight before reviewing supporting details.
6. **Analytical Confidence and Uncertainty:** Intelligence assessments often involve uncertainty. Analysts must clearly communicate their level of confidence in judgments and explain the evidence, assumptions, and limitations associated with their conclusions.
7. **Visualization and Presentation Tools:** Charts, graphs, maps, and other visual tools can help decision-makers quickly understand complex information. Visualizations enhance comprehension and allow analysts to communicate patterns, relationships, and trends more effectively.
8. **Avoiding Information Overload:** Providing excessive detail can obscure the most important message. Effective analysts prioritize key findings and present information in a structured format that supports rapid decision-making.
9. **Maintaining Objectivity:** While analysts must understand their audience, they must also remain objective and avoid shaping intelligence conclusions to match what they believe the audience wants to hear.

Learning Objectives Accomplished

By completing this chapter, you should now be able to:

1. **Define** the role of audience analysis in crafting intelligence products.
2. **Identify** methods for selecting and presenting evidence to different audiences.
3. **Apply** principles of logical reasoning and justification in intelligence reporting.

4. **Recognize and address** cognitive biases in both analysts and consumers.
5. **Utilize** modern technologies and feedback tools to enhance intelligence delivery.

Practical Application

During this chapter, you explored practical methods for tailoring intelligence products to decision-makers, including:

- **Identifying Audience Needs:** Determining what information decision-makers require in order to support their responsibilities.
- **Adapting Intelligence Products to Different Levels:** Understanding how strategic leaders, operational planners, and tactical operators require different levels of detail and analytical focus.
- **Applying the BLUF Format:** Structuring intelligence products so that key judgments are presented clearly at the beginning of reports or briefings.
- **Communicating Analytical Confidence:** Explaining the level of certainty associated with intelligence judgments and identifying key assumptions or intelligence gaps.
- **Using Visual Communication Tools:** Employing charts, graphs, maps, and other visual aids to present complex information effectively.

Reflection Questions

1. Why is it important for intelligence analysts to understand the needs and priorities of their audience?
2. How might intelligence products differ when supporting strategic leaders versus tactical operators?
3. What advantages does the BLUF format provide to decision-makers?
4. How can analysts effectively communicate uncertainty without undermining the usefulness of their intelligence assessments?
5. In what situations might visual tools be more effective than written descriptions when presenting intelligence information?

Excellent progress. Mastering the ability to understand and communicate with your audience is a critical skill for intelligence professionals. Continue developing your analytical and communication abilities as you move forward in your study of intelligence analysis.

GLOSSARY OF TERMS

Here is a glossary of key terms introduced and discussed in Chapter 5 to enhance your understanding of the material.

Cognitive Bias: A systematic error in thinking affecting decisions and judgments.

Foundational Evidence (or Supporting Evidence): Core data and facts forming the basis of analysis.

Inference: A conclusion drawn from evidence and reasoning.

Intelligence Requirement (IR): A specific question or task requiring information collection and analysis.

NFI (No Further Information): An analytical abbreviation indicating that no other data is currently available. Used to indicate to the intelligence consumer further information on the subject is currently unavailable, thus saving the consumer from spending time looking for non-existent information possibly located elsewhere in the report.

Subject Matter Expert (SME): An individual with specialized knowledge in a particular field.

This glossary serves as a quick reference for understanding key terms and concepts from the chapter. Feel free to revisit it as you progress through the lesson material!

NOTES

1. J. J. Wirtz and M. E. Clarke, *Intelligence Analysis and Decision Making: Tools for the Digital Age*, 2021.
2. Merriam-Webster, *Dictionary*, Retrieved 24 March 2024, https://www.merriam-webster.com/dictionary/statistics.

CHAPTER 6

Analytical Communication

INTRODUCTION

Effective analytical communication in today's intelligence landscape goes beyond merely conveying information; it focuses on delivering precise, impactful, and actionable insights. Intelligence analysts must master the art of clear and structured communication to help decision-makers quickly grasp critical findings and respond confidently. Whether presenting to policymakers, military leaders, or corporate executives, analysts must hone their writing and briefing skills to produce concise and compelling products.

Imagine being tasked with delivering a high-stakes intelligence report to national security officials. The clarity of your message could mean the difference between timely action and missed opportunities. This chapter will equip you with the necessary techniques to sharpen your analytical communication skills, enhance collaboration with peers and external experts, and produce intelligence products that adhere to the highest professional standards.

Professional intelligence organizations, both governmental and commercial, rely on established writing standards and style guides to maintain consistency and professionalism in their communications. These guides cover everything from grammar and punctuation to formatting and stylistic conventions, ensuring that every document adheres to high-quality standards. This chapter underscores the importance of these standards and provides a roadmap for developing and using them effectively in your work.

By mastering the principles outlined in this chapter, you will enhance your ability to produce clear, persuasive, and professional intelligence products and significantly increase the impact of your work. Whether you are a seasoned analyst or new to the field, the insights and techniques presented here will elevate your communication skills and ensure that your analytical work has the maximum impact.

DOI: 10.4324/9781003561712-6

This chapter covers the following key areas:

> ***AUTHOR'S NOTE***
>
> *Be aware that by itself, this chapter cannot hope to develop good writing skills. At best, it may enhance or refine existing skills into a style that adds clarity, succinctness, and precision to your intelligence products.*

- **Formulating an Analytical Product Pitch:** Techniques for creating compelling and persuasive pitches that highlight the value and relevance of your analysis.
- **Peer-to-Peer Collaboration:** Strategies for effective communication and collaboration among analysts to enhance the quality and coherence of intelligence products.
- **Outreach to Experts:** Best practices for engaging with external experts to enrich your analysis and validate findings.
- **Formatting the Final Product:** Guidelines for presenting your analysis in a clear, professional, and accessible format.
- **Writing for Release:** Guidance on preparing intelligence products for dissemination, ensuring they meet the necessary standards and guidelines.
- **Checklists and Tools:** Practical checklists and tools to support you in producing high-quality, standardized intelligence communications.

LEARNING OBJECTIVES

By the end of this chapter, students will be able to:

1. **Define** analytical communication and explain its importance in intelligence analysis.
2. **Apply** the BLUF format to intelligence products.
3. **Utilize** digital tools to enhance analytical writing and visualization.
4. **Identify** and mitigate cognitive biases in intelligence reporting.
5. **Develop** clear and persuasive data-driven narratives.

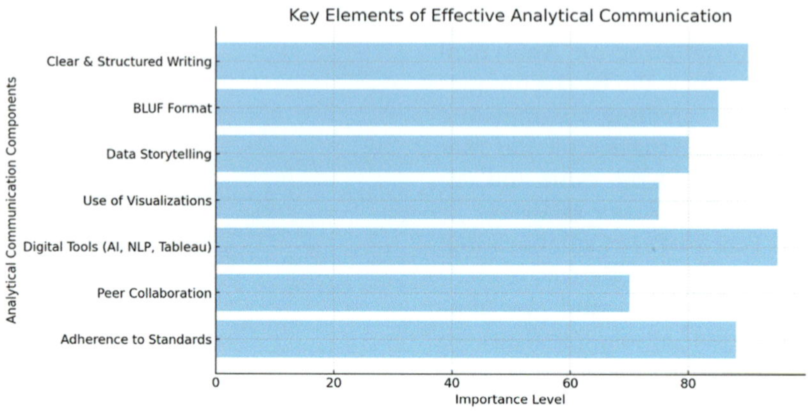

FIGURE 6.1 Key elements of effective analytical communication.

KEY ELEMENTS OF ANALYTICAL COMMUNICATION

Additionally, the chapter will cover the key elements of analytical communication (see Figure 6.1).[1–6] The following visual representation of the key elements of effective analytical communication illustrates their importance in intelligence reporting.

These key elements of effective analytical communication align with professional intelligence writing standards. Notice "Digital Tools" stands out as the most important.

DIGITAL TOOLS

So, why are digital tools the most important element in analytical communication? In modern intelligence analysis, digital tools hold the highest importance because they enhance accuracy, efficiency, and clarity, enabling analysts to deliver high-impact intelligence products with speed and precision. Following are five reasons why digital tools (AI, NLP, Tableau, and other analytics software) are the most critical component in effective analytical communication:

1. **Accelerate Data Processing and Analysis**
    - AI and NLP tools (e.g., OpenAI's GPT, IBM Watson, Palantir) automate the summarization of vast intelligence datasets.
    - Reduces manual workload and allows analysts to focus on interpretation rather than data extraction.

- *Example*: NLP can scan thousands of intelligence reports and extract key insights in seconds.

2. **Enhance Intelligence Writing and Clarity**
   - AI-powered grammar and style checkers (e.g., Grammarly, DeepL Write) ensure precision, consistency, and clarity in intelligence reporting.
   - Helps maintain adherence to professional standards (ICD 203, ODNI Analytic Standards).
     - *Example*: AI can recommend rewording complex intelligence statements for better readability.

3. **Data Visualization for Better Storytelling**
   - Tools like Tableau, Power BI, and ArcGIS allow analysts to transform raw data into interactive and actionable dashboards.
   - Visuals improve comprehension and ensure decision-makers can grasp insights quickly.
     - *Example*: Instead of reading a 10-page report on cyber threats, a policymaker can review an interactive heat map of the most targeted sectors.

4. **Improves Collaboration and Intelligence Sharing**
   - Secure platforms like Microsoft Teams, Trello, and Analyst's Notebook facilitate real-time intelligence collaboration.
   - Intelligence agencies can now share findings instantly across global teams in a classified environment.
     - *Example*: AI-assisted threat assessment models allow multiple analysts to work on the same intelligence case simultaneously.

5. **Reducing Bias and Increasing Objectivity**
   - AI-powered Structured Analytic Techniques (SATs) help mitigate human biases in intelligence analysis.
   - Digital Red Teaming tools simulate alternative viewpoints, preventing confirmation bias.
     - *Example*: AI cross-references intelligence sources to detect inconsistencies in reports.

Without digital tools, intelligence reporting would remain slow, error-prone, and difficult to interpret. By integrating AI-driven NLP, data visualization, and collaboration platforms, analysts can produce concise, data-driven, and bias-free intelligence products that improve decision-making at all levels. Thus, in today's fast-paced intelligence landscape, digital tools are not just useful; they are indispensable.

FORMULATING AN ANALYTICAL PRODUCT PITCH

In the realm of professional communication, analytical communication stands out for its necessity of precision and clarity. Given its critical nature, it requires meticulous preparation and a structured approach to ensure standardization and minimize the risk of miscommunication. Crafting an effective analytical product pitch is essential for conveying complex information in an understandable and impactful way.

Communication Preparation

Effective communication begins with thorough preparation. Regardless of the type of communication, be it a written report, a presentation, or a briefing, there are four fundamental steps to prepare effectively: analyzing the purpose, knowing your audience, determining the medium, and assembling the information.

Analyze the Purpose

Clearly define the goal of your communication. Are you aiming to direct, inform, influence, or motivate your audience? Understanding the purpose shapes the content and tone of your message.

Know Your Audience

The previous chapter covered this concept in detail. Before preparing your communication, consider who your primary and secondary receivers (audience) are, determine the medium(s) best suited to the task, and assemble the information to be used. Once the communication is drafted, utilize the proper review and coordination process to release the intelligence product for final decimation.

Primary Receiver

Identify the primary audience for your communication. Tailor your message to their level of understanding and their needs.

Secondary Receiver

Consider any indirect audience who might receive your message through the primary receiver. Ensure the content remains relevant and clear to them as well.

Determine the Medium

Choose the appropriate medium for your message, whether a formal intelligence product, a letter, or a memorandum. The medium should suit the message's purpose and the audience's preferences.

Assemble Supporting Information

Gather all necessary data, research reports, and background information. Ensure your analysis is well-supported with relevant and up-to-date information.

Coordinators/Facilitators

Recognize those involved in reviewing, processing, and disseminating your communication. Their role is critical in ensuring your message reaches the intended audience effectively.

Communication Execution

Once the preparation is complete, the execution of your message must be precise and impactful. Visualization and clarity are paramount to ensure your audience can easily understand and engage with your message.

Get to the Point Quickly

The "Bottom Line Up-Front" (or BLUF) format presents the initial main idea or conclusion. This approach ensures your audience immediately grasps the key message. Include all necessary context to support understanding.

Organize Logically

Arrange your thoughts and paragraphs in a logical sequence. Use clear transitions to guide your audience through your analysis, ensuring that they can follow your thought process effortlessly.

Ensure Clarity and Precision

Be succinct, by using clear, concise, and precise sentences. Avoid jargon and overly complex language that might obscure the message. Each sentence should contribute to the overall understanding of the analysis.

Succinctness

The essence of succinctness is the art of coming to conveying key points as efficiently as possible. To illustrate the point, two sentences with the same information are presented.

Succinctness Example:

Original Sentence:

- When it comes to analytical writing that is authoritative and professional in nature, there is a common misconception that analytical products must be written in a verbose manner in order to come across as an expert in the field.

Now look at the same sentence rewritten.
1st Rewrite:

- When it comes to authoritative and professional analytical writing, there is a common misconception that analytical products must be written verbosely to appear as experts in the field.

Now rewritten once more.
2nd Rewrite:

- A brief but accurate analysis product is superior to one that is wordy and imprecise.

What are the differences between the two sentences? See Table 6.1 for the answer.

Clarity

Analytical writing thrives on clarity. The report writer's rule: never use three words when one is sufficient is paramount to good analytical writing. The only exception to this rule is when reducing the word count confuses the message. Some guidelines to assist in clarifying intelligence products include:

- Avoid lengthy introductory clauses, e.g., the enemy guerilla forces, which had suffered seven major engagement losses this

TABLE 6.1 Revision Matrix for Succinctness Example

Original Sentence	*1st Rewrite*	*2nd Rewrite*
Passive	Less Passive	Active
39 words	28 words	15 words
Nonessential clause	No clause	No clause
Reading Level: 19.8 grade	Reading Level: 18.1 grade	Reading Level: 11.5 grade

year prior to yesterday's defeat, were beaten again today. (*Note*: The gist of the statement is the "enemy guerilla forces were defeated today," the rest of the clause adds wordiness without a great deal of information that the reader may already have.)

- Avoid nominalization, e.g., destabilize, not destabilization.
- Avoid "passive voice" and embrace "active voice." Using active voice is not always possible, but it should always be the goal.

> ***AUTHOR'S NOTE***
>
> *Notice that all sentences express essentially the same idea, but the rewritten sentences perform the task with fewer words, and they are easier to read.*
>
> *Analysts strive to keep intelligence products' reading levels at 12th grade or less. It is fair to assume that their audience (military, governmental, business, or law enforcement) will have a high school education or better.*

Precision

Precision in analytical writing is analogous to hitting the bull's eye in marksmanship. Analytical writers become more precise in their writing when they use more nouns and verbs and fewer adjectives and adverbs; more straightforward terms, such as "use," vice, "utilize," and avoid jargon.

Precision Examples:

Following are examples of increasing degrees of precision in noun and verb choice.

Examples of "Vague" to "Precise" Analytical Writing Style:

- *An Eastern European supplier provides armaments to terrorists.* (Vague)
- *Former Communist-bloc supplier provides arms to terrorists.* (Less vague)
- *Romanian arms dealer provides small arms to terrorists.* (Precise)
- *Romanian arms dealer sells Kalashnikov rifles to Taliban.* (More precise)
- *Nicolai Anatov*[7] *sells AK47s to Pakistani Taliban.* (Precise and actionable)

Observations: The examples progressively become more precise, using more specific nouns and verb usage. "An Eastern European supplier" becomes a proper name, and the action verb morphs from "provides" to the more accurate transaction "sells." The result is a sentence roughly the same length but less vague and providing more actionable information. By "actionable," we mean to use a proper name; analysts can now search databases, identify possible aliases, possibly make identifications, and further the intelligence collection process.

Summarize and Conclude

End with a summary of your communication's purpose and desired outcome. Reinforce the main points and leave your audience with a clear understanding of the following steps or the actions required, if any.

ENHANCING YOUR PITCH WITH ADDITIONAL STRATEGIES

To further enhance your analytical product pitch, consider the following strategies: storytelling, visualization tools, and end-user feedback. These strategies are based on research and best practices.

Narrative Techniques

Use storytelling elements to make your analysis more engaging. This can help illustrate complex points and make your message more memorable.[8] Storytelling techniques are essential in analytical communication because they enhance clarity, engagement, and retention of complex information. Intelligence analysis, by its nature, involves the synthesis of vast amounts of data into meaningful insights that influence decision-making. Storytelling provides a structured way to present this analysis, making it more accessible and compelling for diverse audiences.

1. **Enhancing Comprehension and Retention**
   People process and remember information better when it is framed as a narrative rather than a series of disconnected facts. A well-structured story has a beginning (context/background), middle (analysis), and end (conclusion), making it easier for decision-makers to absorb and recall critical intelligence insights.

2. **Creating a Persuasive and Impactful Message**
   Storytelling is inherently persuasive. Decision-makers often rely on intuition supported by evidence rather than pure data. Presenting analytical findings through a narrative structure allows analysts to highlight key issues, frame potential outcomes, and drive informed decision-making more effectively.

3. **Providing Context and Meaning**
Raw intelligence reports filled with statistics and facts can be overwhelming and difficult to interpret. A narrative approach allows analysts to contextualize data, explaining its significance and relevance to the audience's needs. This framing helps to bridge the gap between raw information and actionable intelligence.

4. **Engaging and Captivating the Audience**
Dry, technical reports often fail to hold the audience's attention, especially when decision-makers are pressed for time. Storytelling incorporates elements like real-world examples, hypothetical scenarios, or case studies that engage the reader and keep them interested in the analysis.

5. **Simplifying Complex Concepts**
Intelligence analysis frequently involves intricate relationships, probabilities, and abstract concepts. A well-crafted story can break down these complexities, using analogies or structured explanations that make the information more digestible.

6. **Facilitating Decision-Making under Uncertainty**
Decision-makers often operate under uncertainty, requiring intelligence products that highlight risks, opportunities, and possible courses of action. A narrative approach allows analysts to present information in a structured manner, guiding the audience toward a logical decision without overwhelming them with extraneous details.

7. **Humanizing Data-Driven Analysis**
Intelligence reports often deal with human behaviors, geopolitical tensions, or security threats. Storytelling allows analysts to incorporate a human perspective, making the analysis more relatable and impactful. This is especially valuable in intelligence briefings where emotional and psychological factors influence decision-making.

8. **Strengthening Collaboration and Communication**
Storytelling can be a valuable tool in peer-to-peer collaboration and when engaging with external experts. A clear narrative structure helps facilitate discussions, ensuring that all stakeholders have a shared understanding of the intelligence product.

By integrating storytelling techniques into analytical communication, intelligence professionals can enhance their ability to convey critical insights clearly, compelling, and actionable.

Visualization Tools

To complement your written analysis, incorporate visual aids such as charts, graphs, and infographics. Visuals can help convey data more effectively and highlight key insights.[9]

Analysts often ask if they should include visuals (e.g., graphics, photos, maps, etc.) in their intelligence products. The answer is "yes," provided the organization allows it. Everyone has heard the saying that a picture is worth a thousand words. However, there is more to it. Today, visual communication is omnipresent. Why? Visuals accomplish what text alone cannot. Visuals immediately affect us both cognitively and emotionally.

OTHER WRITING TIPS

- *Write with nouns and verbs. Though adjectives and adverbs are important, nouns and verbs are the key to concise, powerful writing.*
- *Avoid using power-draining qualifiers such as rather, very, little, or pretty.*
- *Use an active voice, which is usually stronger and more direct, as a rule.*
- *Use strong, active words by avoiding empty actors such as "it is," "there are," and all their variations because they interfere with clarity.*
- *Use clear verbs instead of hidden verbs, such as "implement, perform, and determine" vice "implementation," "performance," and "determination."*

- *Cognitively*: Graphics expedite and increase our level of communication. They increase comprehension, recollection, and retention. Visual clues help us decode text and attract attention to information or direct attention increasing the likelihood that the audience will remember.
- *Emotionally*: Pictures enhance or affect emotions and attitudes. Graphics engage our imagination and heighten our creative thinking by stimulating other areas of our brain (which in turn leads to a more profound and accurate understanding of the presented material).

FIGURE 6.2 Example of visualizing information for impact.

The computer/internet age has made its mark on the Intelligence Community. Not only are various graphics routinely included in IC web products, but also interactive media (e.g., maps, Google Earth, etc.) and hyperlinks to relate other information and reference sourcing are routinely imbedded into web-based intelligence products. "Pictures interact with text to produce levels of comprehension and memory that can exceed what is produced by text alone." Studies demonstrate that visuals imbedded in web-based intelligence products make the product more likely to be read and if read, more likely to have a greater impact. If you still doubt the impact of visuals in intelligence products, look at the picture and the text (see Figure 6.2), then ask yourself a question: Which has more impact, the text or the photo?

Feedback Loops

Establish a feedback loop with your audience to ensure your message is understood and gather input for improvement. This iterative process can enhance the clarity and impact of your communication.[10]

By integrating these strategies and adhering to a structured approach, you can ensure that your analytical product pitches are precise, professional, compelling, and influential.

In addition to the "Other Writing Tips" listed in the box, you are referred to the Office of the Director of National Intelligence (ODNI) Writing Guide, which is referenced in note 31 and provided in PDF form in the Instructor's Reference Materials available on the book's website associated with this text (www.routledge.com/9781032911748).

PEER-TO-PEER COLLABORATION

This section covers strategies for effective communication and collaboration among analysts to enhance the quality and coherence of intelligence products.

Effective communication and collaboration among analysts are vital for producing high-quality and coherent intelligence products. Peer-to-peer collaboration leverages the diverse expertise within a team, fostering a holistic approach to analysis and ensuring that multiple perspectives are considered. This section outlines strategies to enhance communication and collaboration among analysts, ultimately leading to superior intelligence outcomes.

Building a Collaborative Environment

1. **Foster a Culture of Openness**
   - **Encourage Open Dialogue:** Create an environment in which analysts feel comfortable sharing their ideas, questions, and concerns. Open dialogue promotes trust and transparency, both of which are essential for effective collaboration.[11]
   - **Active Listening:** Cultivate active listening skills within the team. This involves fully concentrating, understanding, responding to, and remembering what is said. It helps acknowledge and value each member's input, enriching the collaborative process.

2. **Promote Knowledge Sharing**
   - **Regular Briefings and Debriefings:** Implement regular briefings to share updates, insights, and findings. Debriefings after significant projects or tasks can provide valuable lessons learned and identify areas for improvement.[12]
   - **Centralized Knowledge Repositories:** Use centralized databases or knowledge management systems in which analysts can store and access reports, datasets, and relevant documents. This ensures that valuable information is readily available to all team members.

> ***AUTHOR'S NOTE***
>
> - *Communication can be oral or written. Of the many types of intelligence support activities, preparing and conducting intelligence briefings is one of the more common.*
> - *Because developing, preparing for, and conducting intelligence briefings is a critical but lengthy subject, the text has dedicated a full chapter to the subject.* *See Chapter 14, Intelligence Briefings, for more information.*

3. **Leverage Technology**
   - **Collaboration Tools:** Utilize digital collaboration tools such as *Slack*, *Microsoft Teams*, or *Trello*. These platforms facilitate

real-time communication, project management, and file sharing, making it easier for analysts to work together efficiently.[13]

- **Secure Communication Channels:** To protect sensitive information, ensure that all communication channels are secure. Use encrypted messaging and secure file transfer protocols to maintain data integrity and confidentiality.

Structured Collaboration Techniques

1. **Analytical Brainstorming Sessions**
   - **Diverse Participation:** Include analysts from different backgrounds and areas of expertise in brainstorming sessions. This diversity fosters creativity and leads to more comprehensive analysis.[14]
   - **Structured Formats:** Use structured brainstorming techniques, such as mind mapping or the Delphi method, to organize ideas and ensure that all voices are heard.

2. **Peer Review Processes**
   - **Regular Peer Reviews:** Establish a system for regular peer reviews of analytical products. This helps identify potential biases, errors, and areas for improvement, enhancing the overall quality of the output.[15]
   - **Constructive Feedback:** Train analysts to provide constructive feedback that is specific, actionable, and focused on the work rather than the individual. This encourages continuous improvement and professional growth.

3. **Cross-Functional Teams (Interdisciplinary Collaboration)**
   - **Form cross-functional teams with members from various departments or specialties:** This approach brings different perspectives and expertise, producing more robust and well-rounded intelligence products.[16]

Enhancing Collaborative Skills

1. **Training and Development**
   - **Communication Skills:** Offer training programs that enhance communication skills, including writing, presenting, and interpersonal communication. Effective communication is the backbone of successful collaboration.[17]
   - **Conflict Resolution:** Equip analysts with conflict resolution skills to handle disagreements constructively. This ensures that conflicts are managed to strengthen rather than hinder collaboration.[18]

2. **Team-Building Activities**
    - **Regular Team-Building Exercises:** Conduct regular team-building activities that promote trust, cooperation, and a sense of camaraderie among analysts. These activities can range from workshops and retreats to informal social gatherings.
    - **Mentorship Programs:** Implement mentorship programs where experienced analysts mentor newer team members. This facilitates knowledge transfer and helps build strong professional relationships within the team.[19]

By adopting these strategies, intelligence teams can significantly enhance their peer-to-peer collaboration, producing high-quality, coherent, and actionable intelligence products. Collaboration improves the analytical process and fosters a supportive and dynamic work environment where analysts can thrive.

ENGAGING WITH EXTERNAL EXPERTS

In the complex and ever-evolving field of intelligence analysis, engaging with external experts is a crucial strategy for enriching your analysis and ensuring its accuracy and relevance. External experts bring specialized knowledge, fresh perspectives, and valuable insights that can significantly enhance the depth and breadth of your intelligence products. This section explores the best practices for identifying, approaching, and collaborating with these experts. By leveraging their expertise effectively, analysts can validate their findings, uncover new dimensions of analysis, and produce more robust and credible intelligence outputs.

Identify Relevant Experts

Through diligent research and leveraging professional networking processes, relevant subject matter experts (SMEs) can be identified.

- **Research** – Conduct thorough research to identify experts with relevant expertise and experience in the area of interest.[20] Use academic journals, industry publications, professional networks, and online databases to find potential experts.[21]
- **Network** – Leverage professional networks and attend industry conferences, seminars, and workshops to establish connections with leading experts in your field.[22] Networking can provide direct access to thought leaders and innovators.[23]

Build Relationships

Once relevant SME(s) is/are identified and contacted, an analyst must next establish a level of trust. This is different and separate from the SME having the appropriate security clearance. The analyst must build up personal trust to ensure mutual understanding and professional cooperation. Additionally, there must also be regular and effective communication between experts and analysts.

- **Establish Trust** – Building a relationship based on trust and mutual respect is essential. Be transparent about your objectives and the scope of your analysis. Demonstrate your commitment to ethical standards and confidentiality.
- **Regular Communication** – Maintain regular communication with experts. This can involve periodic updates, consultations, and discussions. Consistent interaction helps in building a solid rapport and facilitates ongoing collaboration.[24]

Frame Your Inquiry Clearly

- **Specific Questions** – When contacting experts, specify what you seek. Clearly articulate your questions and the type of input you need. This clarity helps experts provide more targeted and relevant insights.
- **Contextual Information** – Provide sufficient background information to help experts understand the context of your inquiry. This includes the objectives of your analysis, the key issues at stake, and any preliminary findings you have.

Utilize Various Communication Channels

- **Direct Contact** – Whenever possible, initiate direct contact through emails, phone calls, or face-to-face meetings. Personalized communication can be more effective in building relationships and gaining trust.
- **Digital Platforms** – Utilize digital platforms such as webinars, video conferences, and collaborative online tools to facilitate expert interaction, especially when geographical barriers exist.[25]

Validate and Cross-Reference Findings

- **Multiple Sources** – Validate your findings by consulting multiple experts. Cross-referencing insights from different sources helps ensure the reliability and accuracy of the information.
- **Critical Evaluation** – Critically evaluate the input received from experts. Consider their perspectives, biases, and the context of

their expertise. Integrate their insights into your analysis while maintaining an objective and balanced view.[26]

Document and Acknowledge Contributions

- **Record Keeping** – Keep detailed records of your interactions with experts, including the information provided, the context of discussions, and any follow-up actions. This documentation is valuable for reference and transparency.
- **Acknowledgement** – In your final product, acknowledge the contributions of external experts. This gives credit where credit is due and strengthens your analysis's credibility.[27]

By following these best practices and additional strategies (see "Additional Strategies for Effective Expert Engagement" box), one can effectively engage with external experts to enrich the analysis, validate findings, and ultimately produce high-quality intelligence products that are credible and impactful.

FORMATTING THE FINAL PRODUCT

Presenting your analysis in a clear, professional, and accessible format ensures that your intelligence products effectively communicate their intended message. Proper formatting enhances readability, facilitates understanding, and lends credibility to the analysis. This section provides guidelines for formatting your final product, emphasizing the importance of consistency and clarity. Utilizing standardized product templates is a critical strategy in this process. Templates ensure document uniformity, streamline the writing process, and help maintain high-quality standards. By adhering to these guidelines and leveraging templates, analysts can produce polished and impactful intelligence products that meet the expectations of diverse audiences.[28,29]

Using Product Templates

Written products are far more common than oral products. Just as briefings have formatting guidance tools for performance, so do written intelligence products. An automated template is a type of formatting guidance tool that has become popular with the advent of electronic word processing.

So why use intelligence product templates? There are a multitude of reasons beyond uniformity or standardization. Not to discount uniformity and standardization, but meeting a minimum product standard and ensuring an analyst organizes information so that the intelligence consumer can quickly locate specific pieces of information are essential. Other reasons are efficiency, mitigating writer's block, facilitating the review routing process, etc.

Writer's block does not just affect novelists; analysts also suffer from it. Product template files provide analysts with a place to start. Not only do they give a starting point, but they can also promote team building. By looking at a blank template, the analyst sees a "to-do" list of the content they need to complete. The product template outlines and "cues" the analyst to what types of information they must collect, analyze, source, route for review, and deliver to the client or end-user. The template can also assist in the proper classification of the information contained.

AUTHOR'S NOTE: ADDITIONAL STRATEGIES FOR EFFECTIVE EXPERT ENGAGEMENT

- *Communication can be oral or written: Collaborative research projects engage in joint research projects with experts to deepen your understanding and foster long-term partnerships. Collaborative efforts can lead to more comprehensive and robust analyses.*
- *Expert panels and advisory boards: Establish expert panels or advisory boards to provide ongoing guidance and review of your analytical work.*
- *Training and workshops: Organize training sessions and workshops with experts to build internal capacity and enhance your team's analytical skills. These sessions can provide valuable insights and practical knowledge.*

Electronic product templates also allow for data access automation. Once the individual fields of a correctly linked and network-associated product or report template are in place, the information can become accessible and searchable by any linked database, allowing collaboration and data sharing that was unheard of just 20 years ago.

As mentioned previously, a properly executed product template file or series of product template files instills standardization and increases efficiency. Standards are created and enforced because the template file uses built-in product styles, identifies needed content and sourcing requirements, and more. Since these intelligence product attributes are preinstalled, they also create time savings and efficiency.

Using Digital Tools

As discussed at the beginning of the chapter, something new to analytical communications is Natural Language Processing (NLP) software, such as OpenAI's GPT models for drafting intelligence summaries and Tableau for visual analytics. GPT models assist in summarizing large volumes of intelligence reports by extracting key insights and structuring them in a clear and concise format, thereby reducing the time analysts spend drafting documents. Tableau enables analysts to create dynamic and interactive dashboards, helping them visualize complex data trends and relationships, which makes intelligence reports more accessible and actionable.

Sample Product Template

In the practical exercise, you will be provided an unclassified template similar to the ones used by the Department of Homeland Security (DHS) for Open-Source Information Reporting. It includes "boilerplate" material and explanatory information for required and recommended content. The document fields electronically link to databases to allow instant updates to searchable relational knowledge bases.

Government reports are replete with acronyms, and DHS is no exception. Following is a list of acronyms that appear in the Practical Exercise sample template and their meanings:

- CYB: Cyber
- DHS: Department of Homeland Security
- IA: Office of Intelligence and Analysis
- HSEC: Homeland Security
- OSCAR-MS: Open-Source Collection Acquisition Requirement Management System
- OSIR: Open-Source Information Report
- U: Unclassified

Note: Open-Source Collection Acquisition Requirement Management System (OSCAR-MS) is a web-based service sponsored by the Office of the Assistant Deputy Director of National Intelligence for Open Source (ADDNI/OS) to provide the National Open-Source Enterprise (NOSE) with an application for managing open-source collection requirements.[30]

PRACTICAL EXERCISE: USING A TEMPLATE

In this "analytical communications" practical exercise, you will take the information provided by your instructor and enter it into the OSIR template (provided by your instructor). After entering the information in the proper locations, save and print out the report and bring it back to class for review and comment.

Mastering the BLUF Format

This section attempts to answer two questions often voiced by new analysts in the IC: Why do intelligence analysts care about learning how to write in the BLUF format, and what makes it so great?

The BLUF format tailors products to meet the needs of intelligence consumers or end-users. These consumers may be high-ranking members of government or the military. Generally, they are busy men and women who rely on clear, concise, and accurate intelligence reporting to make daily decisions that affect U.S. national security and other critical issues. Arranging intelligence reporting in the BLUF format helps situate the required information more efficiently in a more understandable layout.

In the BLUF format, the first sentence of each paragraph summarizes the key information in the paragraph. The BLUF should address the essential information in a paragraph. If the paragraph contains information that does not fall under the BLUF, that information should be moved to a more appropriate paragraph, or the BLUF should be revised to include the additional information. The BLUF format organizes paragraph sentences by importance, allowing readers quickly grasp key points and can find information efficiently.

As stated previously in the "Communication Execution" section of this chapter, it is most effective to get the point immediately, which is why BLUF is the best way for intelligence analysts to communicate with their clients and consumers. Summarizing paragraphs in the first sentence allows decision-makers to skim intelligence products without sacrificing clarity. Other documents not in the BLUF format, such as academic white papers, texts, and research reports, may contain paragraphs with several vital ideas scattered throughout the document. Having the main idea and other more critical ideas scattered through the text may cause readers who skim these publications inadvertently to skip over key information. Most importantly, the BLUF format aids readers in locating information.

The BLUF formatted intelligence product typically contains the following sections:

- Executive Summary
- Introduction
- Analysis
- Background
- Conclusion

Title

The title is not a section; however it is essential because it "sells" the product.

The title, introduction, and executive summary will usually be the last parts of your product to be created because each summarizes the product's contents.

The title succinctly represents the product's contents, positioning the product and signaling the information it will provide. Creating an accurate Title is extremely important because it is often the first and only opportunity to catch the reader's attention.

> ***TIPS***
>
> - *The product title may be your hook for potential indirect intelligence consumers, so it must be accurate, concise, representative, and catch the reader's attention.*
> - *Do not use web-style "click bait" titles! Intelligence consumers are not pleased if they spend their valuable time searching for information associated with a sensational "click bait" title only to discover that they have been duped and their time has been wasted.*

Executive Summary and Introduction

A BLUF-formatted intelligence product usually starts with an "Executive Summary"-style section followed by an Introduction. The Introduction and Executive Summary (like the Title) are written last because each component must summarize everything in the product. The Executive Summary may be called "Executive Summary," "Key Findings, Key Judgments," etc. The name is not essential; what is important is that it is usually written last and summarizes the entire document. Therefore, once the product is written, the analyst only has to "cut and paste" the first sentence of each paragraph into the Executive Summary, and then review and revise for grammatical correctness. Sometimes, when an Executive Summary is used, the Introduction is omitted.

Generally, Executive Summaries can be provided as stand-alone documents of one to two pages that convey the analytical impact of the complete intelligence product (minus the details). An Introduction should briefly and generally sum up the main points of the paper, like a less-detailed Executive Summary.

Background

The Background section follows the Introduction and provides whatever background information the reader needs to understand the analysis contained. It is situated in the document to allow the following section to focus entirely on the analysis without being mired with unnecessary explanatory details and technical speak. The Background section allows the Analysis section to focus primarily on the analysis results rather than the research conducted to create it.

Analysis

The body of the BLUF-formatted intelligence product contains the analysis and sources used to create it and will generally be the longest part of the document. Call out sourcing in the document using footnotes or endnotes. Footnotes are preferred because they can provide "extra information" to aid the flow of paragraphs, provide needed definitions and background information, and reduce paragraph "clutter."

Document your analysis in a brief, accurate, and precise fashion. Writing clear and concise products forces analysts to carefully order their thoughts and think critically. Thus, avoiding accidental or intentional misrepresentation of the facts and improving the final analytical product.

There is no room for bias, opinion, or "gut feelings" in intelligence analysis. All analysis and subsequent inference or assessment must be supported and based on the facts. If included in the final product, any intelligence "gaps" identified during the process should be cited as "gaps." Likewise, any "assumptions" used in the analysis must be adequately identified so that the reader fully understands the basis of your analysis and appropriately weighs it into the decision process.

The title of the "Analysis" section is usually decided by organizational format or doctrine. Regardless of the organizational format, doctrine, or personal preference, the title should be appropriate to the contents (e.g., Body, Contents, Supporting Arguments, etc.).

Conclusion

The BLUF-formatted document ends with the "Conclusion" (also called the Summary or Outlook paragraph), which should efficiently summarize the document's content. As such, the conclusion should not introduce new material; it can expand upon previous material already addressed in the document's body.

Text Boxes

Text boxes are useful for helping to organize your product and provide additional information. Along with other visuals to improve the presentation of the product (or webpage), text boxes visually flow with the text to assist in readability.

Today, analysts commonly use text boxes in the body of intelligence products to draw attention to important concepts, findings, and assumptions, highlight anecdotal material, present alternative analysis, or dissent, administrative (or scope) notes, background information, or other appropriate uses. When using text boxes to highlight anecdotal material, the analyst is pointing out to the reader the subjective nature or unreliability of the information. Shaded or tented text boxes can highlight important information of particular significance, catch the reader's attention, and alert them that the material is necessary to understand one or more portions of the product.

Text box fonts, sizing, number of sentences, shading color, and titling are all functions of the style guidance and formatting of the parent organization/agency creating the product.

Some members of the IC use various color shades or tones to signify the purpose of the text box and will refer to the text box as a "tone box."

WRITING FOR RELEASE

This section provides guidance on preparing intelligence products for dissemination, ensuring they meet the necessary government, business, and law enforcement standards and guidelines.

Intelligence products have diminished value if we cannot share them with our friends, military allies, business associates, or legal and law enforcement organizations. Therefore, there are mechanisms available to facilitate that sharing process. Formally, releasing classified information is far different from covertly disclosing information to adversaries or the unauthorized leaking of classified documents to the press.

Often in the normal course of duties, intelligence analysts collect or create classified, sometimes highly classified, information, which may be of great value to our friends in law enforcement and allies in the joint effort to stem international crime and terrorism. Besides common causes, America shares intelligence with foreign partners for other reasons, such as quid pro quo, influence, or to encourage new partnerships. There are similar situations in business and law enforcement. Corporations would not want their competitors to have access to their high-value marketing analysis. Nor would law enforcement want criminals to have their sensitive crime analysis reporting.

Conversely, declassifying already overclassified information can be inefficient and needlessly time-consuming. Therefore, analysts are encouraged to "write for release." Writing for release means providing an intelligence product that meets a specific classification caveat threshold, which allows release to a specific partner.

For the U.S. government and military to succeed and avoid multiple declassification/reclassification iterations and reviews, the process usually starts with a product proposal meeting, which all intelligence stakeholders and reviewers attend. At this meeting, it will be determined if releasing the information to a given partner is even feasible. If so, the analyst creates a U.S. version and submits it through the release review chain and to the Foreign Disclosure Officer (FDO) if the product is to go outside U.S. custody. This is but a brief overview of the release process. Many other procedural requirements exist depending on the specifics of the information, the level of classification, and the specific organizational protocols of the origination intelligence organization.

Business organizations will have unique rules for keeping proprietary information and trade secrets safe.

Similarly, Law Enforcement Sensitive (LES) Information is non-classified information intended explicitly for official law enforcement use (generally unavailable to the public). It pertains to investigative data, reports, techniques, strategies, and other details that, while not explicitly classified, still bear significant relevance to the safety and security of the public or specific individuals. It is used predominantly by law enforcement agencies and other associated judicial establishments to maintain efficient and effective crime prevention, investigation, and prosecution measures.

PRACTICAL EXERCISE: STUDENT HANDOUT

In this "analytical communications" practical exercise, you will take the information provided by your instructor and enter it into the OSIR template.

Scenario

You are a DHS analyst tasked with writing an Open-Source Information Report (OSIR). The DHS Technical Intelligence (Tech-INT) group has already processed the URL and identified similar reporting (though for a different URL). Next is the (fictitious) "Local Police Report." Use the OSIR template provided by your instructor. After entering the information in the appropriate sections, save it, print out the report, and bring it back to class for review and comment.

LOCAL POLICE REPORT

Basic Facts:

Today's Date: 18 June 2016

1. On 12 June 2016, X (formerly Twitter) user @Irhabi.net (user name: CyberIrhabi) tweets a threat to a U.S. citizen (name: John Doe) and states that "He has nowhere to hide."

2. On 14 June 2016, X user @Irhabi.net (user name: CyberIrhabi) tweets a message to a U.S. citizen (name: John Doe) and directs him to go to website (www.ihabi.net/home) and click on his name (a hyperlink on the page) located on the webpage, under his photo. Mr. Doe did as asked and found all the information from his private Facebook page posted.
3. On 16 June 2016, X user @Irhabi.net (user name: CyberIrhabi) tweets a threat to a U.S. citizen (name: John Doe) and states that "He knows where John lives and works and who his family is."
4. On 16 June 2016, Mr. Doe contacted local law enforcement, who refers case to DHS for action.

Tech-INT Analyst Comment: For similar reporting, see OSIR DHS-OS-0123-16.

Tech-INT Analyst Comment: URL www.irhabi.net is a new address without any previous reporting and cannot be evaluated.

ANALYTICAL COMMUNICATIONS CHECKLISTS

Before making the first draft, the following checklist provides a "takeaway" for future use and as a tool to reinforce the analytical communications instruction covered in this chapter. Whether the analytical communication is written, verbal, or web-based, the checklist of typical self-test questions will aid the analyst in performing a quality control check.

1. First, did I outline all pertinent information, contacts, and organizations needed to collect the required information?
2. Did I use appropriate nouns and verbs and minimize the use of adjectives and adverbs?
   - Did I use solid and active words by avoiding empty actors such as "it is," "there are," and all their variations because they interfere with clarity?
   - Did I use precise verbs instead of hidden verbs, such as "implement," "perform," "determine," vice "implementation," "performance," and "determination?"
3. Did I avoid using power-draining qualifiers such as "rather," "very little," or "pretty?"
4. Did I use active voice, vice passive, whenever possible?
5. Am I writing as accurately and succinctly as possible?
   - Can I make my point with less text?
   - Is my language vague or precise?
   - Have my words conveyed my meaning?
   - Can someone be confused by what I said/wrote?

6. Did I use the bottom line up-front (BLUF) format?
7. Is each paragraph properly classified?
8. Did I focus on my audience, and is my content "written for release?"
9. If I had a template, did I follow it?
10. Does my text provide substantial factual information better presented in a graphic or visual form?
11. Do my text boxes effectively emphasize information that may otherwise be lost in the text?
12. Do I have so many text boxes that they detract from the text?
13. Do the fonts, sizing, number of sentences, shading color, and titling match style guidance and formatting?

CHAPTER SUMMARY

Effective analytical communication is fundamental to intelligence success. Analysts must master structured writing formats like BLUF, leverage digital tools for enhanced reporting, and employ data storytelling techniques to engage their audience. Additionally, mitigating cognitive biases ensures objectivity and accuracy in intelligence products. By integrating visual communication strategies and peer collaboration, intelligence professionals can create impactful and actionable intelligence reports. The content summary of each chapter section follows.

- **Formulating an Analytical Product Pitch:** Techniques for creating compelling and persuasive pitches that highlight the value and relevance of your analysis.
- **Peer-to-Peer Collaboration:** Strategies for effective communication and collaboration among analysts to enhance the quality and coherence of intelligence products.
- **Outreach to Experts:** Best practices for engaging with external experts to enrich your analysis and validate findings.
- **Formatting the Final Product:** Guidelines for presenting your analysis in a clear, professional, and accessible format.

Basic Workings of Analytical Communication

Professional communication generally requires thoughtful preparation, and "analytical communication" is no exception. Because of its critical nature, analytical communication requires a more rigorous and rigid structure to ensure product standardization and reduce the chances of misunderstanding and miscommunication.

Communication Preparation

One must take the time to carefully plan and prepare analytical communication to satisfy production requirements and avoid needless confusion. No matter what type of written communication instrument you are dealing with, according to the ODNI Writing Guide, there are four basic preparation steps: (1) Analyze the purpose, (2) Know your audience, (3) Determine the medium, and (4) Assemble the information.[31]

Communication Execution

After completing your preparation steps, visualize your message, making every effort to ensure it is clear and can be easily understood.

Product Writing Style

Adding clarity, succinctness, and precision enhances and refines your writing skills to produce a more professional style that is reflected in the quality of your intelligence products.

Briefings

Communications can be oral or written, of the many types of intelligence support activities, preparing and conducting intelligence briefings is one of the more common. See Chapter 14, "Intelligence Briefings," for details on developing, preparing for, and conducting intelligence briefings.

Digital Tools

New to analytical communications is Natural Language Processing (NLP) software, such as OpenAI's GPT models for drafting intelligence summaries and Tableau for visual analytics. GPT models assist in summarizing large volumes of intelligence reports by extracting key insights and structuring them in a clear and concise format, thereby reducing the time analysts spend drafting documents. Tableau enables analysts to create dynamic and interactive dashboards, helping them visualize complex data trends and relationships, which makes intelligence reports more accessible and actionable.

Using Product Templates

A type of formatting guidance tool, which has come into vogue with the advent of electronic word processing, is the automated template. Intelligence product templates provide efficiency, mitigate writer's block, facilitate review routing processes, etc. Electronic templates allow for data access automation.

Mastering the BLUF Format

The BLUF format tailors products to meet the needs of intelligence consumers or end-users; some may be high-ranking members of government or the military. Arranging intelligence reporting in the BLUF format helps more efficiently situate the information in a more understandable layout that is required.

In the BLUF format, the first sentence of each paragraph sums up all of the information in the paragraph. The BLUF should address all of the information in a paragraph. Following the BLUF format arranges the component sentences in the paragraph from most to least important and ensures readers immediately are aware of the intelligence product's most important points, allowing readers to locate information more easily.

As stated previously in the "Communication Execution" section in this chapter, it is most effective to get the point immediately, which is why BLUF is the best way for intelligence analysts to communicate with their clients and consumers. Summarizing paragraphs in the first sentence allows decision-makers the ability to skim intelligence products without sacrificing clarity.

The BLUF formatted intelligence product includes a product title and contains normally contains the following sections: Executive Summary, Introduction, Analysis, Background, and the Conclusion.

Writing for Release

America shares intelligence with foreign partners for other reasons, such as quid pro quo, influence, and to encourage new partnerships. Intelligence products have diminished value if we cannot share the information with our friends and allies. Therefore, there are mechanisms available to facilitate that sharing process. Formally, releasing classified information is far different from covertly disclosing information to adversaries or the unauthorized leaking of classified documents to the press.

Product Visuals

Product visuals that appear in intelligence products include visuals such as graphics, photos, maps, etc. Today, visual communication is omnipresent. Visuals accomplish what text alone cannot because visuals quickly affect us both cognitively and emotionally.

Text Boxes

Text boxes are useful for organizing your product and providing additional information. They effectively emphasize details that may otherwise be lost in the text. Today, analysts commonly use text boxes in intelligence products to highlight important concepts, findings, and assumptions, showcase anecdotal material, present alternative analyses or dissent, and include administrative (or scope) notes, background information, or other relevant content uses.

Analytical Communications Checklist

The provided checklist offers a takeaway for future reference and serves as a tool to reinforce the analytical communication instructions covered in this chapter. It includes a list of typical self-test questions to assist the analyst in conducting a written, verbal, or web-based quality control check of analytical communications.

Key Concepts Covered

1. **Analytical Communication:** The process of presenting intelligence findings in a clear, concise, and structured manner so that decision-makers can quickly understand the implications and take appropriate action.
2. **BLUF (Bottom Line Up-Front):** A writing structure that places the most important conclusion or assessment at the beginning of a report or paragraph, allowing busy decision-makers to quickly grasp the key point.
3. **Clarity, Precision, and Succinctness:** Effective intelligence writing emphasizes direct language, strong verbs, and precise terminology to eliminate ambiguity and improve comprehension.
4. **Digital Tools in Analytical Communication:** Technologies such as Natural Language Processing (NLP), artificial intelligence tools, and visualization platforms (e.g., Tableau or Power BI) can help analysts summarize large datasets and present insights more effectively.
5. **Data Visualization and Visual Communication:** Graphics, dashboards, maps, and charts can significantly improve comprehension by allowing decision-makers to quickly identify patterns, trends, and relationships.
6. **Cognitive Bias Awareness:** Analysts must remain vigilant against biases such as confirmation bias or mirror imaging that may distort analytical judgments.
7. **Peer Collaboration and Expert Engagement:** Collaboration with colleagues and external experts helps improve analytic rigor, validate assumptions, and strengthen the credibility of intelligence products.

Learning Objectives Accomplished

After completing this chapter, students should now be able to:

1. **Define** analytical communication **and explain** its importance in intelligence analysis.
2. **Apply** the BLUF format to intelligence products.
3. **Utilize** digital tools to enhance analytical writing and visualization.
4. **Identify and mitigate** cognitive biases in intelligence reporting.
5. **Develop** clear and persuasive data-driven narratives.

Practical Application

During this chapter, you explored practical methods that intelligence analysts use to communicate analysis clearly and effectively to decision-makers. These techniques are routinely applied in government intelligence agencies, law enforcement organizations, military units, and corporate intelligence environments. Key practical applications from this chapter include:

- **Structuring Intelligence Products Using BLUF:** Organizing intelligence reports so that the most important analytical judgment appears first, allowing busy decision-makers to immediately understand the key finding.
- **Writing with Clarity, Precision, and Succinctness:** Using strong nouns and verbs, minimizing unnecessary qualifiers, and avoiding overly complex language to ensure intelligence products are easy to understand.
- **Using Digital Analytical Tools:** Leveraging technologies such as Natural Language Processing (NLP), AI-assisted summarization tools, and visualization platforms to analyze large volumes of information and communicate insights efficiently.
- **Applying Visual Communication Techniques:** Using charts, maps, timelines, and dashboards to highlight patterns, relationships, and trends that might otherwise be difficult to identify in written text alone.
- **Collaborating with Peers and Subject Matter Experts:** Strengthening analytical rigor by incorporating peer review, interdisciplinary collaboration, and expert consultation when evaluating complex intelligence problems.
- **Identifying Assumptions and Intelligence Gaps:** Clearly explaining where evidence is limited, identifying assumptions used in

the analysis, and communicating the level of confidence associated with analytical judgments.
- **Using Structured Writing Standards:** Following established style guides and professional writing standards to ensure intelligence products maintain consistency, clarity, and credibility.

These practical communication skills are essential for intelligence analysts because the value of analysis depends not only on the quality of the research but also on how effectively the findings are communicated to those responsible for making decisions.

Reflection Questions

1. Why is it important for intelligence analysts to present conclusions clearly and quickly to decision-makers?
2. How can the BLUF format improve the effectiveness of intelligence communication?
3. In what ways can digital tools such as NLP or data-visualization software enhance analytical communication?
4. What are the risks of poor analytical communication, and how might they affect decision-making?
5. How can collaboration with peers or external experts strengthen the quality of an intelligence product?

Effective analytical communication is a skill that improves with practice. Continue refining your writing, questioning assumptions, and seeking feedback from peers and mentors. Mastering these skills will greatly enhance your ability to deliver intelligence that informs decisions and makes a meaningful impact.

GLOSSARY OF TERMS

Here is a glossary of key terms introduced and discussed in Chapter 6 to enhance your understanding of the material:

BLUF (Bottom Line Up-Front): A structured writing format that presents conclusions before details.
Cognitive Bias: Systematic errors in thinking that affect decision-making and analysis.
Data Visualization: The graphical representation of information and data.
Intelligence Product: A report, briefing, or analysis produced by intelligence professionals to support decision-making.

Metadata Analysis: The examination of data attributes to provide additional context or insights in intelligence reporting.
NLP (Natural Language Processing): AI-powered technology that helps analyze and generate human language.
Red Teaming: A structured analytic technique used to challenge assumptions and identify alternative scenarios.
Structured Analytic Techniques (SATs): Methods used to enhance intelligence analysis by reducing biases.
Structured Thinking: A logical and methodical approach to problem-solving and communication in intelligence writing.
Threat Analysis: The process of evaluating potential security risks and assessing their likelihood and impact.

This glossary serves as a quick reference for understanding key terms and concepts from the chapter. Feel free to revisit it as you progress through the material.

NOTES

1. Richards J. Heuer, Jr., *Psychology of Intelligence Analysis*, Central Intelligence Agency, Center for the Study of Intelligence, 1999.
2. Office of the Director of National Intelligence, *Intelligence Community Directive 203: Analytic Standards*, U.S. Office of the Director of National Intelligence, 2015.
3. Edward R. Tufte, *The Visual Display of Quantitative Information* (2nd ed.), Graphics Press, 2001.
4. Linchpin Analytics, *Best Practices in Intelligence Writing: The BLUF Approach*, 2022.
5. David McCandless, *Information Is Beautiful*, HarperCollins, 2009.
6. OpenAI Research Team, *Applications of Natural Language Processing in Intelligence Analysis*, 2023.
7. Note: Nicolai Anatov is a fictitious name. Any resemblance to real persons, living or dead, is purely coincidental.
8. Chip Heath and Dan Heath, *Made to Stick: Why Some Ideas Survive and Others Die*, Random House, 2007.
9. C. N. Knaflic, *Storytelling with Data: A Data Visualization Guide for Business Professionals*, Wiley, 2015.
10. D. A. Garvin and M. A. Roberto, *Change Through Persuasion*, Harvard Business Review, 2005.
11. A. C. Edmondson, *The Fearless Organization: Creating Psychological Safety in the Workplace for Learning, Innovation, and Growth*, Wiley, 2018.
12. A. Pentland, *The New Science of Building Great Teams*, Harvard Business Review, 2012.
13. R. Miller, *Mastering Collaboration: Make Working Together Less Painful and More Productive*, O'Reilly Media, 2019.
14. S. E. Page, *The Difference: How the Power of Diversity Creates Better Groups, Firms, Schools, and Societies*, Princeton University Press, 2007.

15. D. L. Sackett, S. E. Straus, W. S. Richardson, W. Rosenberg and R. B. Haynes, *Evidence-Based Medicine: How to Practice and Teach EBM*, Churchill Livingstone, 2000.
16. Paul S. Adler, Sung-Won Kwon and Charles Heckscher, 'Professional Work: The Emergence of Collaborative Community', *Organization Science,* 20(2), 359–376, 2009.
17. J. A. DeVito, *The Interpersonal Communication Book*, Pearson, 2019.
18. K. W. Thomas and R. H. Kilmann, *Conflict Mode Instrument*, CPP, Inc., 1974.
19. Tammy D. Allen, Lisa T. Eby, Mark L. Poteet, Elizabeth Lentz and Lillian Lima, 'Career Benefits Associated with Mentoring for Protégés: A Meta-Analysis', *Journal of Applied Psychology,* 89(1), 127–136, 2004.
20. N. Hara and R. Kling, 'Communities of Practice with and Without Information Technology', *The Information Society*, 18(5), 375–379, 2002.
21. J. S. Katz and B. R. Martin, 'What Is Research Collaboration?' *Research Policy,* 26(1), 1–18, 1997.
22. Mark S. Granovetter, 'The Strength of Weak Ties', *American Journal of Sociology,* 78(6), 1360–1380, 1973.
23. Rob Cross and Andrew Parker, *The Hidden Power of Social Networks: Understanding How Work Really Gets Done in Organizations,* Harvard Business Review Press, 2004.
24. Laura A. Lindenfeld, D. M. Hall, B. McGreavy, L. Silka and D. Hart, 'Creating a Place for Environmental Communication Research in Sustainability Science', *Environmental Communication*, 6(1), 23–43, 2012.
25. James Hemsley, Jordan Jacobson and Anastasia Gruzd, 'Social Media for Social Good or Evil: An Introduction', *Social Media + Society,* 6(1), 1–10, 2020.
26. A. Bryman, *Social Research Methods*, Oxford University Press, 2004.
27. J. W. Creswell and C. N. Poth, *Qualitative Inquiry and Research Design: Choosing Among Five Approaches*, Sage Publications, 2018.
28. W. Germano, *From Dissertation to Book,* University of Chicago Press, 2013.
29. S. J. Gerson and S. M. Gerson, *Technical Communication: Process and Product*, Pearson, 2016.
30. U.S. Army, *Army Doctrine and Training Publications – Intelligence* (ADRP 2-0), 31 August 2012.
31. Office of the Director of National Intelligence (ODNI), Writing Guide, 2011.

CHAPTER 7

Brainstorming Techniques Used to Define the Problem

INTRODUCTION

Intelligence analysis is only as good as the problem it seeks to solve. History has repeatedly shown that vague, misinterpreted, or poorly defined problems can lead to catastrophic failures in decision-making. Considering the intelligence failures leading up to the September 11 attacks, various agencies had fragments of critical information, but the inability to define the overarching threat resulted in missed opportunities to prevent the attack.

Today's intelligence analysis challenges include the fragmented nature of intelligence data, the urgency of decision-making, and the hidden threats that can lead to critical failures.

Defining the problem is foundational in determining an intelligence mission's success. Analysts are tasked with transforming ambiguous and sometimes conflicting consumer needs into clear, actionable intelligence requirements. This requires both critical thinking and structured brainstorming techniques.

This chapter will guide you through four essential brainstorming methods: dumping, testing, mapping, and role-playing, that help refine intelligence problems. Each technique serves a distinct function: generating ideas, critically evaluating solutions, visualizing complex relationships, or stepping into the adversary's mindset. By mastering these techniques, analysts can ensure they are addressing the right problem correctly, reducing uncertainty, and enhancing the quality of intelligence production.

Building on concepts introduced in Chapter 2, this chapter emphasizes the interpretive role of the analyst in transforming customer information "needs" into precise intelligence requirements that will steer the

DOI: 10.4324/9781003561712-7

production process. This transformation often begins with a straightforward dialogue between the intelligence producer and the consumer, evolving into a more nuanced analysis as the complexity of the intelligence problem unfolds. Whether faced with broad, open-ended questions or more tightly constrained scenarios, analysts must navigate the delicate balance of dialogue and analysis to define the problem accurately. This chapter will guide you through these challenges, providing insights and strategies to ensure that the problems you or your analytical team define are relevant and resolvable within the context of the intelligence mission.

LEARNING OBJECTIVES

By the end of this chapter, students should be able to:

1. **Explain the Importance of Problem Definition in Intelligence Analysis:**
    - Describe how clearly defining the problem influences intelligence accuracy and effectiveness.
    - Identify historical examples of intelligence failures due to poorly defined problems.
2. **Apply Brainstorming Techniques to Intelligence Problem-Solving:**
    - Differentiate between the four brainstorming techniques: dumping, testing, mapping, and role-playing.
    - Identify when each technique is most effective in intelligence analysis scenarios.
3. **Evaluate the Strengths and Limitations of Each Brainstorming Method:**
    - Analyze the advantages and drawbacks of each brainstorming technique in real-world intelligence contexts.
    - Assess how factors like time constraints, complexity, and available data impact the choice of technique.
4. **Demonstrate the Ability to Define and Refine Intelligence Problems:**
    - Transform broad or vague intelligence consumer requests into precise, actionable intelligence requirements.
    - Utilize problem taxonomy to classify intelligence challenges based on complexity and required analytical methods.
5. **Understand the Consequences of Poorly Defined Intelligence Problems:**
    - Explain how misallocating intelligence resources can lead to flawed decision-making.

- Describe methods analysts use to mitigate risks associated with ambiguous or misinterpreted intelligence needs.

6. **Use Visual and Interactive Tools to Enhance Problem-Solving:**
   - Construct concept maps to organize intelligence problems and identify key relationships.
   - Apply role-playing exercises to explore adversary perspectives and anticipate potential outcomes.
7. **Collaborate Effectively between Intelligence Producers and Consumers:**
   - Engage in iterative discussions to refine intelligence questions and ensure clarity.
   - Develop strategies to overcome communication gaps between analysts and decision-makers.
8. **Critically Assess Intelligence Hypotheses Using Testing Techniques:**
   - Break down intelligence problems into conceptual parts to validate assumptions.
   - Use systematic testing to identify and eliminate infeasible solutions while refining viable alternatives.
9. **Recognize and Avoid Cognitive Biases in Intelligence Analysis:**
   - Identify how biases like groupthink and confirmation bias can distort intelligence findings.
   - Apply structured brainstorming techniques to counteract cognitive biases and improve analytical accuracy.
10. **Participate in Practical Intelligence Analysis Exercises:**
    - Engage in small group brainstorming activities to define and refine intelligence problems.
    - Critically evaluate other groups' problem definitions using structured testing criteria.

THE CONSEQUENCES OF POOR PROBLEM DEFINITIONS

History is rife with examples of intelligence failures due to improperly defined problems. One of the most striking examples is the 2003 Iraq War, where intelligence agencies failed to correctly determine whether Iraq possessed weapons of mass destruction (WMDs). The problem was framed around confirming Iraq's WMD capabilities rather than objectively analyzing whether such weapons existed at all. This faulty problem definition led to intelligence biases, ultimately resulting in flawed policy decisions (see Figure 7.1).

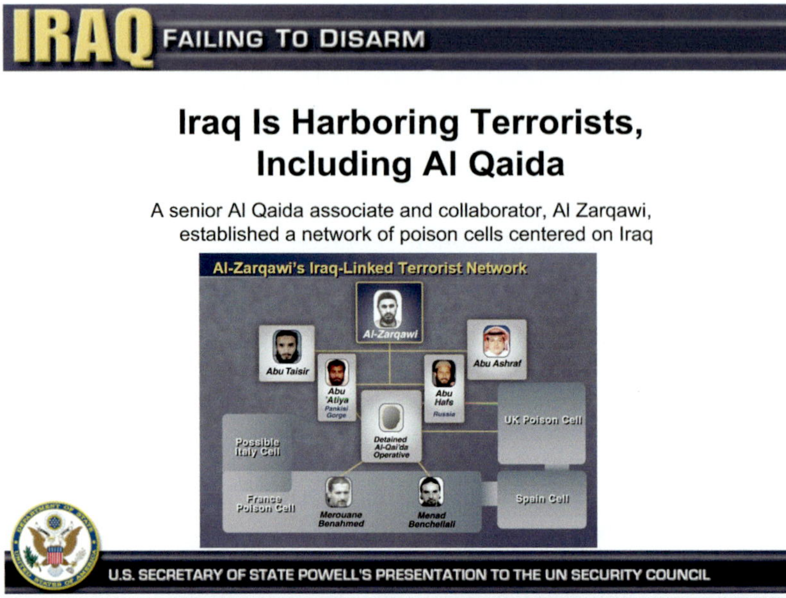

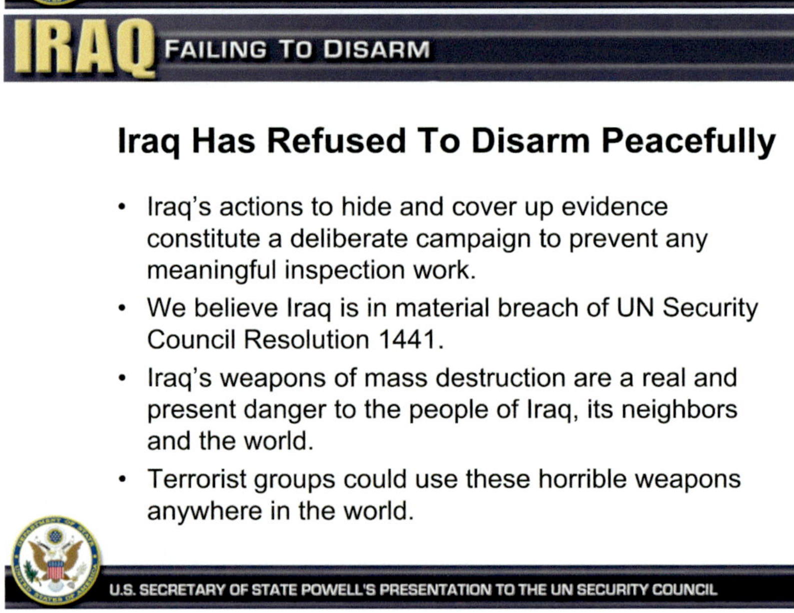

FIGURE 7.1 Unsuccessful problem definition (2003 Iraq War); two slides from General Colin Powell's speech and presentation to the United Nations.

FIGURE 7.2 Successful problem definition: WW2 Enigma code. (Left) Military model Enigma I circa 1930. (Wikipedia, Used per CC BY-SA 4.0, User: Alessandro Nassiri.) (Right) Enigma rotor assembly—three movable rotors are sandwiched between two fixed wheels: The entry wheel on the right and the reflector on the left.

By contrast, successful intelligence efforts, such as breaking the Enigma code in World War II, hinged on precisely defining the cryptographic challenge at hand. The British codebreakers at Bletchley Park refined their approach using systematic brainstorming techniques, allowing them to crack the German cipher and alter the course of the war (see Figure 7.2).

These cases underscore the necessity of defining the problem with precision. Without this clarity, intelligence resources may be wasted, and incorrect conclusions may have dire consequences.

NAVIGATING MULTIPLE CONTINGENCY SITUATIONS: EMBRACING COMPLEXITY

In the labyrinth of intelligence analysis, some problems have no clear boundaries and present many possible outcomes. Such situations, where potential scenarios are virtually limitless, demand a strategic approach. The analyst's first task is to pose or receive the right questions, driving the analysis forward. For example, the broad question of "When and where will the enemy attack?" encapsulates countless possibilities, each often with unique implications.

The lack of data can make anchoring the analysis challenging in these scenarios. Without concrete, measurable data (empirical or statistical), it becomes difficult to establish a solid foundation or reference point for analysis. Without reliable data, making accurate assessments, predictions, or conclusions is more challenging because there is nothing on which to anchor the analysis.

In other words, data serves as a crucial guide in analysis, and without it, the analysis can become speculative or less reliable. It is like trying to navigate without a map; you can still move forward, but your path is less specific and more prone to errors.

Therefore, the task often becomes one of elimination, narrowing down the field of possibilities to a more manageable scope. However, this isn't always feasible, and when it's not, the analyst must engage in a rigorous process of identifying, characterizing, and preparing for all potential outcomes.

This process is often akin to wargaming, where analysts brainstorm and role-play various scenarios, considering each from multiple perspectives, including the adversaries. By iterating this process, using different methods and participants, analysts can reduce variability and establish a measure of confidence in their conclusions. A well-defined problem emerges from this complex interplay of scenarios, allowing the intelligence team to move forward with clear, unambiguous, and actionable requirements.

BRAINSTORMING CONTINGENCIES: UNLOCKING CREATIVE POTENTIAL

Brainstorming is a powerful tool in the analyst's arsenal, designed to unearth every possible angle of a problem. It is a process that thrives on creativity, encouraging participants to let ideas flow freely without the constraints of immediate critique. This section explores how to harness brainstorming effectively as a group or individually.

The essence of brainstorming is to allow ideas to emerge organically, capturing them before any filtering or prioritization begins. The goal is to cover as many contingencies as possible, expanding the scope of possibilities that can later be refined. However, managing group dynamics is crucial to prevent dominant personalities from skewing the session's outcomes.

Four distinct brainstorming techniques: dumping, testing, mapping, and role-playing, offer different approaches to problem definition; each method has varied strengths and applications.

1. **Dumping:** This is the simplest method (see Figure 7.3), where analysts "brain dump" all their thoughts onto paper without inhibition. Speed and volume are essential to this method. Dumping quickly generates as many ideas as possible. Though

FIGURE 7.3 "Brain dumping" session.

the most valuable insights often emerge in the first few minutes, the full dumping session helps ensure nothing is overlooked. Organizing these ideas into a coherent list afterward helps the group review and refine the output.

2. **Testing:** Here, the focus shifts from creation to validation. Analysts take a concept and systematically dissect it, testing its components to see if they hold up under scrutiny. This method helps eliminate unfeasible ideas and surface viable alternatives that might have been missed in earlier brainstorming sessions.

3. **Mapping:** Visual thinkers will find mapping an invaluable tool. Analysts can visualize relationships, priorities, and connections among concepts by organizing ideas into a conceptual "map" on a board. This technique clarifies the structure of the problem, making it easier to identify critical focus areas.

4. **Role-Playing:** Putting oneself in the opponent's shoes can offer new perspectives essential for defining the problem. By understanding how the opponent thinks and acts, analysts can reveal potential scenarios that might be missed. This technique requires research and preparation but can yield insights crucial to understanding the problem from all angles.

Although there are several, we will introduce four analytical brainstorming techniques: dumping, testing, mapping, and role-playing. These four brainstorming methods can be combined or used individually.

Drawbacks of Brainstorming

The biggest drawback of brain dumping is its lack of structure. This lack of structure can lead to several specific challenges:

- **Disorganization:** Ideas generated through brain dumping are often scattered and unstructured, making it difficult to identify patterns, themes, or coherent strategies without extensive sorting and analysis.
- **Overwhelming Information:** The sheer volume of ideas produced can be overwhelming and counterproductive. Sorting through many potentially unrefined ideas to find valuable insights requires considerable time and effort.
- **Variability in Idea Quality:** Brain dumping encourages the expression of all thoughts, regardless of their viability or relevance. Variation in quality can result in a mix of high-quality and low-quality ideas, necessitating a rigorous filtering process to separate valuable insights from less useful ones.

These aspects of brain dumping can complicate the brainstorming process by requiring significant additional effort to organize and prioritize ideas effectively, potentially reducing the overall efficiency of the brainstorming session.

Situations Where Brain Dumping Is Best Used

- **Initial Exploration of a Problem:** Brain dumping is particularly effective at the beginning of the analytical process when the problem is not yet well-defined. It allows analysts to explore the problem space without the constraints of predefined structures, helping to uncover all possible angles.

WHY DUMPING WORKS BEST IN THESE SITUATIONS

Brain dumping is effective in these situations because it taps into the natural flow of ideas, allowing for a breadth of input that can be critical in the early stages of analysis. Not imposing immediate constraints fosters creativity and inclusivity, ensuring no potential solution or perspective is overlooked. Additionally, its speed and efficiency make it an ideal tool in fast-paced or high-pressure environments, where quick thinking and adaptability are essential.

- **When Facing Complex or Ambiguous Problems:** In situations where the problem is highly complex or ambiguous, brain dumping can help surface a wide range of ideas and perspectives, which are crucial for understanding the full scope of the issue.
- **Time-Constrained Analysis:** When rapid idea generation is needed, such as in crisis situations or when deadlines are tight, brain dumping allows analysts to quickly produce a comprehensive list of ideas or contingencies that can be further developed.
- **Overcoming Groupthink:** In scenarios where there is a risk of groupthink, brain dumping can help break the cycle by encouraging all participants to contribute independently before any ideas are critiqued. Blocking groupthink can lead to more diverse solutions and prevent consensus-driven bias.
- **Generating Hypotheses:** When analysts need to develop a wide range of hypotheses about a situation, brain dumping allows them to explore all possible explanations without prematurely dismissing any ideas, leading to a more thorough examination of the problem.

Strengths of "Testing" the Brainstorming Technique

- **Critical Analysis:** Testing allows for critically evaluating ideas by breaking them down into parts (see Figure 7.4). This analytical approach helps validate the feasibility and practicality of each idea, ensuring that only robust, well-thought-out concepts move forward in the process.
- **Idea Refinement:** Through the systematic critique and testing of ideas, this method helps refine and sharpen the concepts being considered. It encourages deeper thinking and can often significantly improve the original ideas.

FIGURE 7.4 Idea testing session.

- **Error Reduction:** By rigorously challenging assumptions and potential solutions, testing helps reduce the likelihood of errors or oversight in the later stages of a project. Error reduction is crucial for minimizing risk in critical or high-stakes environments.
- **Alternative Solutions Exploration:** Testing often leads to discovering alternative solutions or contingencies that may not have been initially considered. Testing provides a broader range of options for solving complex problems.
- **Consensus Building:** Testing ideas in a group setting can help build consensus among team members. As ideas are dissected and debated, a more precise understanding emerges, which can help align the team around the most viable solutions.

Situations Where Testing Is Most Effective

- **Complex Problem-Solving:** Testing is invaluable when faced with complex problems where the consequences of failure are significant. It ensures that every proposed solution is viable and all potential flaws are identified and addressed before implementation.
- **High-Risk Environments:** In scenarios where the stakes are high, such as in security, healthcare, or critical infrastructure projects, the rigorous examination of ideas through testing is crucial to avoid costly or dangerous mistakes.

WHY TESTING WORKS BEST IN THESE SITUATIONS

Testing works best in these situations because it emphasizes critical thinking, detailed analysis, and rigorous scrutiny of each idea. This approach is crucial when the cost of failure is high or the solution must be highly reliable. Testing helps avoid pitfalls that could arise from less scrutinized ideas by ensuring that each potential solution is thoroughly vetted. This method enhances the quality of the solutions developed and builds a strong foundation for effective decision-making and problem-solving in challenging environments.

- **Innovation Development:** Testing allows ideas to be challenged and refined for projects requiring innovative solutions. Testing is particularly important in technology or product development, where feasibility and functionality are critical.
- **Resource-Constrained Situations:** Ensuring that only the most viable ideas are pursued is essential when resources are limited. Testing helps prioritize efforts on solutions that are most likely to succeed, thus optimizing the use of available resources.

- **When Seeking to Improve or Optimize Existing Solutions:** Testing is ideal when the goal is to refine or improve existing solutions. It allows teams to dissect and analyze what works and what doesn't, leading to more effective enhancements.

The testing session takes an idea and breaks it down into multiple parts. Once there is agreement that all the conceptual parts are present and in order (if there is an order), the group describes how one would feasibly accomplish each portion of the selected idea. See the following example.

> ***Example:***
> *The multiple aspects of a terrorist smuggling a dirty bomb into the country and detonating it:*
>
> - *Target selection*
> - *Collecting the nuclear and explosive materials and other components*
> - *Moving the material and components into the country*
> - *Assembly, emplacement, and detonation*
> - *Escape*
>
> *An analytical team might assign each bulleted item to a different analyst or analytical group for a more detailed examination.*

Strengths of the "Mapping" Brainstorming Technique

- **Visual Clarity:** Mapping offers a visual representation of ideas and their relationships, which can clarify complex information and make abstract concepts more tangible (see Figure 7.5). Visual clarity helps participants see connections and patterns that might not be obvious in verbal or written formats.
- **Enhanced Engagement:** The visual and interactive nature of mapping can engage participants more deeply than some other methods. This engagement often leads to higher creativity and investment in the brainstorming process.
- **Facilitates Complex Problem-Solving:** By organizing ideas visually, mapping can simplify understanding complex problems. It allows participants to break down large issues into smaller, more manageable parts and see the relationships between different elements.
- **Encourages Holistic Thinking:** Mapping helps participants consider a wide range of factors and how they interact, promoting a more holistic approach to problem-solving. All-inclusive thinking is crucial when dealing with multifaceted issues where different elements influence one another.

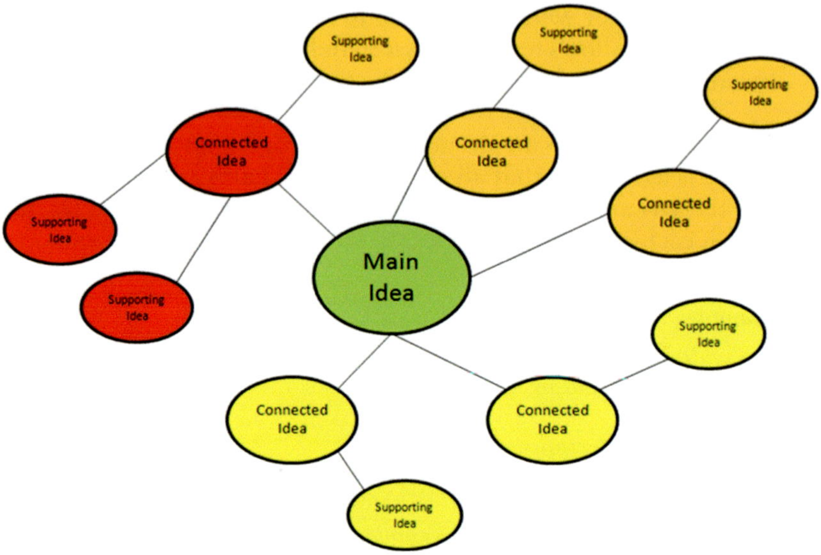

FIGURE 7.5 Mapping (brainstorming technique).

- **Dynamic and Flexible:** Mapping is a dynamic process that can easily be adjusted as new ideas emerge or relationships change. This flexibility makes it suitable for evolving discussions where ideas must be continuously integrated and re-evaluated.

Situations Where Mapping Is Most Effective

- **When Addressing Complex Systems or Processes:** Mapping is particularly effective when dealing with complex systems or processes that involve multiple interrelated elements. It helps visually organize these elements, making it easier to understand how changes to one part might affect the whole.

WHY MAPPING WORKS BEST IN THESE SITUATIONS

Mapping works best in these situations because it makes complex relationships understandable and manageable. The visual format helps participants grasp intricate systems and contributes to deeper analytical thinking by making abstract relationships concrete. Additionally, the collaborative nature of mapping can harness a group's collective insights, enhancing the depth and breadth of the brainstorming session. Mapping makes it particularly valuable in scenarios where understanding the interplay between different elements is crucial for developing effective solutions.

- **In Strategic Planning and Project Development:** Strategic planning often involves understanding how various aspects of a business or project interconnect. Mapping these interconnections can aid stakeholders in seeing the bigger picture and planning more effectively.
- **During Collaborative Sessions:** Mapping is ideal for sessions involving multiple stakeholders with different perspectives. It allows everyone to contribute their views and see how their contributions fit into the larger scheme.
- **For Enhancing Creativity in Teams:** When a team needs to explore new ideas or innovate, mapping can help stimulate creative thinking by visually exploring different possibilities and how they might be connected or expanded upon.
- **In Educational and Training Settings:** Mapping can be a powerful tool for learning and teaching, as it helps students and trainees visualize and remember complex information by relating concepts to one another in a structured format.

Situations Where Role-Playing Is Most Effective

Role-playing is a powerful technique in analysis, especially in intelligence and strategy fields, because it offers several distinct advantages that enhance the understanding of complex scenarios and the decision-making process (see Figure 7.6).

FIGURE 7.6 Role-playing tools.

- **Perspective-Taking:** Role-playing forces analysts to step into the shoes of others, be they competitors, adversaries, or other stakeholders. This shift in perspective can unveil insights about motivations, strategies, and potential moves that might not be apparent from an external viewpoint. Depending on the context, understanding the "why" behind actions can lead to more effective counter-strategies or more empathetic approaches.
- **Scenario Exploration:** By acting out different scenarios, participants can explore a range of outcomes and reactions in a controlled, risk-free environment. Scenario exploration helps

identify potential weaknesses, opportunities, and unforeseen consequences of decisions, allowing for better contingency planning.

- **Enhanced Creativity:** Role-playing encourages creative thinking by allowing participants to explore "what if" scenarios dynamically. Role-playing sessions can lead to innovative solutions and strategies that might not emerge through conventional brainstorming techniques.
- **Improved Communication and Teamwork:** Role-playing exercises can enhance communication and understanding among team members as they collaborate to navigate complex scenarios. Role-playing can improve team cohesion and alignment on objectives and strategies.
- **Stress Testing Plans and Policies:** Through role-playing, organizations can test how plans and policies work in practice before implementation. Role-playing can expose practical issues or flaws that might not be visible in theoretical analysis, allowing organizations to refine their approaches.
- **Training and Development:** Role-playing effectively helps participants develop essential skills such as negotiation, strategic thinking, and leadership. It provides a realistic setting to practice these skills, which can enhance an analyst's effectiveness in real-world situations.
- **Emotional and Behavioral Insight:** Role-playing can provide deep insights into emotional and behavioral responses that might occur in real situations that could be overlooked. Understanding these elements can be crucial when planning interventions or when trying to predict the actions of others.

WHY ROLE-PLAYING WORKS BEST IN THESE SITUATIONS

Role-playing works best in scenarios that require deep understanding, strategic foresight, and effective communication because it offers immersive, experiential learning and decision-making opportunities, such as crisis management, negotiation and diplomacy, military and business strategy, and competitive analysis.

Analysts and strategists can better understand their challenges and develop more robust, resilient responses and strategies by incorporating role-playing into their analytical processes.

PROBLEMS WITH INADEQUATE DEFINITION

Intelligence requirements do not always translate end-customer information needs into a workable intelligence collection plan. Even when the customer is confident that they know what the intelligence problem is and what the derivative information requirements should be, there is a need to vet the requirement(s) at a minimum. The vetting (or refinement) process described earlier in Chapter 2 is critical to ensuring the analysis process gets started correctly and limited collection assets are not wasted.

The level of unrestricted communication between the analytical group and the customer at this stage often determines the quality of the subsequent intelligence product produced and whether or not it meets customer needs. However, divergent perspectives between the intelligence customer and analytical group often complicate the negotiation process.

The analyst can use models to educate intelligence end-user customers and mold their expectations to aid negotiations. One of those models is a *Taxonomy of Problem Types.*

TAXONOMY OF PROBLEM TYPES

A taxonomy provides a structured way of classifying problem types, helping analysts and customers alike understand the nature of the intelligence challenge. The Taxonomy of Problem Types outlined in this section offers a model for defining intelligence scenarios, from the simplest to the most complex.

This framework helps identify the role of facts and judgments, the analytical tasks required, and the methods and instruments that might be used. By classifying the problem type, analysts can choose the most appropriate strategy for resolving it, whether through simple research, detailed analysis, or predictive modeling[1] (see Table 7.1).

The following examples show how an analyst might use the *Taxonomy of Problem Types* to understand some of the specifics and implications of various intelligence problems.

USING THE PROBLEM TAXONOMY TABLE

- *Does not provide answers*
- *Only aids the analyst in understanding the parameters associated with the problem*
- *Facilitates analytical planning*
- *Useful explanatory tool to educate customers and shape expectations and competitive analysis*

TABLE 7.1 Taxonomy of Intelligence Problem Types: A Framework for Clarity*

	Problem Types				
Characteristics	***Basic***	***Definable***	***Moderately Random***	***Severely Random***	***Undefined***
Role of problem type	(Easiest) Simple research	5 W's (Who, What, When, etc.)	Identify and rank outcomes	Identify and rank limitless outcomes	Predict future events/situations
Role of facts	Highest	High	Moderate	Low	Lowest
Role of judgments	Lowest	Low	Moderate	High	Highest
Analytical tasks	Find information	Collect sensor data, Find and/or develop calculation(s)	Generate all outcomes	Define all potential outcomes	Define future variables/factors
Analytical methods	Research sources	Match data to calculation(s)	Decision theory; utility analysis	Role-playing, brainstorming, wargaming, etc.	Analysis via predictive modeling/ scenarios
Analytical Instruments	Matching	Mathematical calculation(s)	Influence diagram, utility, probability	Subject evaluation of outcomes	Use of SMEs
Analytical outputs	Fact	Specific value, dataset, or number	Weighted alternatives or outcomes	Plausible outcomes	Elaboration of expected future(s)
Probability of error	Lowest**	Low**	Moderate**	High**	Highest**
Follow-up tasks	None	None	Periodically monitor for change	Continuously monitor	Exhaustive research

**Author comment:* The "Taxonomy of Intelligence Problem Types" depicted in Table 7.1 reflects minor edits and revisions from the original 1995 version.

**Dependent on data quality and reliability.

Example 1:

A "definable" intelligence problem – What will the weather conditions be for tomorrow's mission? (See Table 7.1, yellow highlighted information.)

Answer: Cloudy, 25% chance of rain, temperature 72°, winds out of the SW at four mph.

Example 2:

A "severely random" intelligence problem – Who will be the leading international terrorist ten years from today?

Answer: Most likely it will be someone alive today (and ten years from now), potentially an Islamic Extremist (but ten years from now, Islamic Extremism may not be a major international terror threat). Since terrorists rarely go from obscurity to international notoriety overnight, the "leading international terrorist" ten years from now is likely involved in radical/extremist or terror activities today (see Table 7.1, gray highlighted information).

Shared understanding between the analyst (intelligence producer) and intelligence customer (client and/or end-user) is essential. Ultimately, the analyst and the client must reconcile their differing viewpoints to agree on intelligence requirements and begin the collection process. Continuous free and open communication among the players fosters agreement on intelligence priorities and results in more usable and meaningful intelligence production. However, the communication process does not end with product delivery; customer feedback on production quality improves the definition of future intelligence problems and requirements.

PRACTICAL EXERCISE

The facilitator will provide a handout for this small group brainstorming exercise. You will be broken into groups of four to six and given a scenario. Using the scenario provided, take ten minutes to brainstorm the idea and conceptually map it out. Then, you will exchange your freshly mapped ideas with another group and conduct ten more brainstorming sessions to test the idea. After completing the second brainstorming session, be prepared to discuss your observations with the instructor.

CHAPTER SUMMARY: ENHANCING INTELLIGENCE ANALYSIS THROUGH BRAINSTORMING TECHNIQUES

Defining the problem is one of the most crucial aspects of intelligence analysis. Without a well-defined problem, intelligence efforts risk being misdirected, leading to faulty conclusions and ineffective decision-making. This chapter introduced four essential brainstorming techniques: dumping, testing, mapping, and role-playing, each serving a distinct function in the problem-definition process. Additionally, it explored the role of problem taxonomy in structuring intelligence challenges.

Customer "needs" often require interpretation or analysis by the intelligence service before becoming the intelligence requirements that drive the production process. This dialog between intelligence producer and customer begins with a simple set of questions and, if appropriate, progresses to a more sophisticated analysis of the intelligence problem. "Defining the problem" is the designation given to this exercise of combining dialogue and analysis to produce requirements.

The ability to refine intelligence requirements through structured brainstorming ensures that analysts work on relevant, resolvable problems, ultimately leading to actionable intelligence. Analysts must continuously assess whether they are asking the right questions, as the right question often determines the quality of the answers.

Brain Dumping

Brain dumping is characterized by its unstructured nature, allowing a free flow of ideas without immediate critique. It is especially useful in the initial stages of problem formulation, where capturing a broad range of ideas is more critical than their immediate relevance or feasibility. The main drawbacks include the potentially overwhelming volume of ideas and the lack of structure, making subsequent analysis challenging.

Testing

The testing technique critically analyzes ideas by breaking them down and evaluating their components. This method is invaluable when dealing with complex problems where the implications of errors are significant. Testing refines ideas and helps identify viable alternatives that were not initially considered. It is best used in environments where detailed scrutiny of concepts is necessary to ensure robustness and feasibility.

Mapping

Mapping excels in visual clarity and the organization of complex relationships. It is particularly effective in situations that require a clear understanding of how various elements interact within a system. By providing a visual representation of these interactions, mapping aids in strategic planning and complex problem-solving, making it an essential tool in collaborative and multistakeholder settings.

Role-Playing

Role-playing is a dynamic method that enhances understanding by allowing analysts to assume the perspectives of different stakeholders. This technique is particularly effective in scenarios such as crisis management, competitive analysis, and negotiation, where anticipating the actions and reactions of others is crucial. Role-playing facilitates a deep engagement with the material, promoting creative solutions and strategic foresight.

Each brainstorming technique discussed in this chapter offers unique advantages and is suited to specific analytical contexts within intelligence work. Understanding when and how to apply these techniques can significantly enhance the quality of analysis, leading to more informed decision-making and strategic planning. The choice of technique should align with the situation's specific requirements and the intelligence analysis's goals, ensuring that the process not only generates a wide range of ideas but also critically evaluates and refines these ideas into actionable intelligence insights.

Multiple Contingency Situations

When the problem has no boundaries and few defining characteristics, defining the problem can be difficult. The analyst begins the process by asking or being asked, the right questions.

When dealing with hypothetical situations, the most logical course of action would be to find a more manageable number by eliminating contingencies. However, that is not always achievable. Therefore, the analytical task now identifies, characterizes, and prepares for all potential outcomes. The analytical process is brainstorming (also called wargaming) various scenarios and role-playing the adversary's perspective.

Brainstorming Contingencies

Brainstorming is intended to encourage the analyst to use their creativity to help identify contingencies and define problems. Brainstorming is most effective as a group, but it works for individual analysts. Letting the mind run free without critiquing any ideas can provide new perspectives covering most, if not all, potential contingencies.

Although there are several, we introduced four analytical brainstorming techniques: dumping, testing, mapping, and role-playing. These four brainstorming methods can be combined or used individually.

Problems with Some Definitions

Intelligence requirements do not always translate end-customer information needs into a workable intelligence collection plan. Even when the customer is confident that they know what the intelligence problem is and what the derivative information requirements should be, there is a need to vet the requirement(s) at a minimum.

The level of unhindered communication between the analytical group and the customer at this stage often determines the quality of the subsequent intelligence product produced and whether or not it meets customer needs.

Taxonomy of Problem Types

To aid in the negotiations, the analyst can use models as tools to educate the customer and mold their expectations. Taxonomies provide a mechanism or model for classifying concepts, including the principles that underlie such classification. One such model for defining intelligence scenarios employs the Taxonomy of Problem Types.[2] The taxonomy illustrates the factors that intelligence customers and analysts may consider in expressing the nature of the intelligence problem and selecting a strategy for resolving it.

Key Concepts Covered

1. **Importance of Problem Definition:** Defining the problem is one of the most critical steps in intelligence analysis. Clearly identifying the intelligence problem ensures that analytical efforts, collection resources, and decision-making processes are focused on the right issues.
2. **Transforming Consumer Needs into Intelligence Requirements:** Intelligence consumers often express their needs in broad or ambiguous terms. Analysts must interpret these needs and refine them into precise intelligence questions and actionable requirements that guide analysis and collection.
3. **Consequences of Poor Problem Definition:** History demonstrates that poorly framed intelligence problems can lead to analytical bias, misallocation of resources, and flawed decisions. Clear problem definition helps prevent analytical errors and intelligence failures.

4. **Brainstorming as a Problem-Definition Tool:** Structured brainstorming techniques allow analysts to explore the full scope of an intelligence problem. These methods help generate ideas, identify assumptions, and uncover hidden aspects of complex analytical challenges.
5. **Four Brainstorming Techniques:** This chapter introduced four key brainstorming methods; dumping, testing, mapping, and role-playing. Each technique provides a unique approach to generating ideas, evaluating feasibility, visualizing relationships, and understanding adversary perspectives.
6. **Managing Multiple Contingency Situations:** Some intelligence problems have no clear boundaries and involve numerous potential outcomes. Analysts must identify, characterize, and evaluate multiple contingencies to reduce uncertainty and guide decision-making.
7. **Taxonomy of Problem Types:** The Taxonomy of Problem Types provides a framework for classifying intelligence challenges based on complexity. This model helps analysts determine the appropriate analytical methods, tools, and levels of judgment required.
8. **Collaboration between Intelligence Producers and Consumers:** Effective problem definition requires continuous communication between analysts and decision-makers. Collaboration ensures that intelligence requirements remain relevant, achievable, and aligned with operational needs.

Learning Objectives Accomplished

1. **Explain** the importance of problem definition in intelligence analysis.
2. **Apply** brainstorming techniques to intelligence problem-solving.
3. **Evaluate** the strengths and limitations of each brainstorming method.
4. **Demonstrate** the ability to define and refine intelligence problems.
5. **Understand** the consequences of poorly defined intelligence problems.
6. **Use** visual and interactive tools to enhance problem-solving.
7. **Collaborate Effectively** between intelligence producers and consumers.
8. **Critically Assess** intelligence hypotheses using testing techniques.
9. **Recognize and Avoid** cognitive biases in intelligence analysis.
10. **Participate** in practical intelligence analysis exercises.

Practical Application

During this chapter, you explored practical methods for defining and refining intelligence problems, including:

- **Applying Brainstorming Techniques:** Using dumping, testing, mapping, and role-playing to generate and evaluate possible solutions to complex intelligence problems.
- **Defining Intelligence Requirements:** Transforming vague consumer questions into clear and actionable intelligence tasks.
- **Conceptual Mapping of Intelligence Problems:** Visualizing relationships between actors, capabilities, vulnerabilities, and potential outcomes.
- **Testing Analytical Assumptions:** Breaking down ideas into their component parts to evaluate feasibility and identify weaknesses.
- **Exploring Multiple Contingencies:** Examining how different scenarios and adversary actions could influence intelligence outcomes.
- **Using Problem Taxonomy:** Classifying intelligence challenges according to complexity in order to select appropriate analytical methods.

Reflection Questions

1. Why is clearly defining the intelligence problem essential before beginning analysis?
2. How can brainstorming techniques help analysts uncover hidden assumptions or overlooked scenarios?
3. In what ways can collaboration between intelligence producers and consumers improve the definition of intelligence requirements?

Thank you for your dedication and engagement in this chapter. Continue developing your analytical discipline and curiosity—each well-defined problem brings you one step closer to mastering the craft of intelligence analysis.

GLOSSARY OF TERMS

Here is a glossary of key terms introduced and discussed in Chapter 7 to enhance your understanding of the material:

Brain Dumping: A brainstorming technique that involves rapidly listing all possible ideas without judgment.

Dirty Bomb: Also known as a radiological dispersal device (RDD), a dirty bomb is a type of explosive weapon that combines conventional explosives, like dynamite, with radioactive material. The primary goal of a dirty bomb is not to cause a massive explosion but to spread radioactive contamination over a wide area. This contamination can lead to radiation exposure, causing potential health risks and long-term environmental damage.

Groupthink: A psychological phenomenon where the desire for consensus overrides critical thinking.

Heuristic Analysis: A method of problem-solving based on experience and intuition rather than rigid rules.

Intelligence Requirements: Specific informational needs defined by intelligence consumers.

Mapping: A visual brainstorming technique that identifies relationships and structures within a problem.

Problem Taxonomy: A classification framework that helps analysts determine the nature of an intelligence problem.

Role-Playing: A method where analysts adopt different perspectives, such as that of an adversary, to anticipate potential outcomes.

Scenario Planning: A strategic technique used to anticipate multiple possible futures.

Testing: A critical evaluation process where ideas are dissected to determine feasibility.

Wargaming: A structured analytical approach where different potential actions and outcomes are simulated.

This glossary serves as a quick reference for understanding key terms and concepts from the chapter. Feel free to revisit it as you progress through the material!

NOTES

1. Morgan D. Jones, *The Thinker's Toolkit* (pp. 44–46), New York: Random House, 1995.
2. Morgan D. Jones, *The Thinker's Toolkit* (pp. 44–46), New York: Random House, 1995.

CHAPTER 8

Generate the Hypothesis

INTRODUCTION

The Power of Multiple Perspectives in Intelligence Analysis

Intelligence failures often stem not from a lack of information but from the inability to consider alternative explanations. One of the most infamous examples of this is the 2003 U.S. intelligence assessment regarding Iraq's weapons of mass destruction. Analysts were so convinced of Iraq's weapons program that they failed to generate and thoroughly assess alternative hypotheses. This case and many others illustrate a fundamental truth in intelligence work: *The most perilous assumption is that you already possess the correct answer.*

Hypothesis generation is the foundation of critical thinking in intelligence analysis (see Figure 8.1). A hypothesis is not merely a guess but a structured explanation that proposes an answer to a specific question based on available evidence. Analysts must resist the temptation to settle on the first plausible explanation. Instead, they must develop multiple hypotheses, exploring a range of possibilities before narrowing their focus.

This chapter introduces structured methods and strategies intelligence that professionals use to generate hypotheses effectively. From defining the core question to applying situational logic and theoretical models, you will learn to systematically approach intelligence problems with an open mind. Whether analyzing potential security threats, tracking illicit activities, or predicting geopolitical developments, mastering hypothesis generation will sharpen your ability to anticipate, assess, and act decisively.

DOI: 10.4324/9781003561712-8

FIGURE 8.1 Hypothesis generation.

LEARNING OBJECTIVES

By the end of this chapter, students will be able to:

1. **Define** and explain the concept of hypothesis generation in intelligence analysis.
2. **Apply** the six-step process for generating hypotheses to intelligence problems.
3. **Identify** cognitive biases that can affect hypothesis generation and apply strategies to mitigate them.
4. **Develop** and **evaluate** multiple hypotheses using structured analytical techniques.
5. **Demonstrate** the importance of generating alternative hypotheses through practical exercises and case studies.

THE HYPOTHESIS GENERATION PROCESS

> ***AUTHOR'S NOTE: TIPS FOR GENERATING HYPOTHESES***
>
> - *Involve additional analysts to gain diverse perspectives and generate more hypotheses.*
> - *Ensure that the hypothesis is measurable and testable.*
> - *Maintain an open mind.*

A hypothesis is an explanation that proposes an answer to a specific question based on a level of knowledge about a topic. This phase in the analysis process should identify all hypotheses worthy of detailed examination. Sometimes known as an "educated guess," a hypothesis rests upon some existing knowledge of a given subject. However, rather than a guess, we will propose an answer to a specific question based on a level of knowledge about a topic. It can be generated using the following six-step process (see Figure 8.2).

Note: An analyst does not have to use the specific method presented in the text. It belongs to the authors and evolved from the scientific method of hypothesis generation and many years of military and law enforcement experience.

1. Define the Core Question

Every hypothesis begins with a question—a clear, specific information requirement that the analyst seeks to answer. The question should be focused yet broad enough to allow for multiple hypotheses. For example, consider the problem of "finding cross-border tunnels" along the U.S.

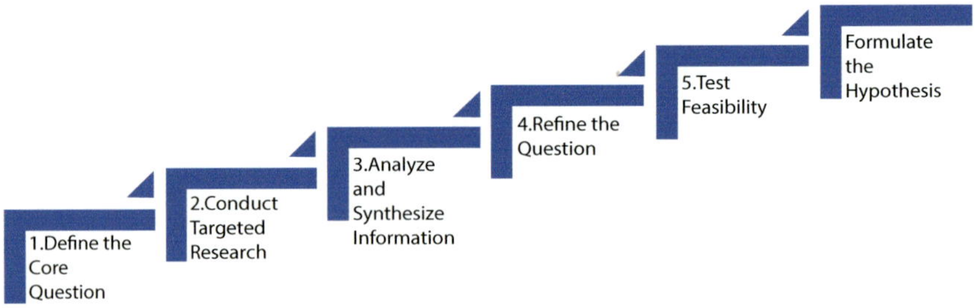

FIGURE 8.2 Six-step hypothesis generation process.

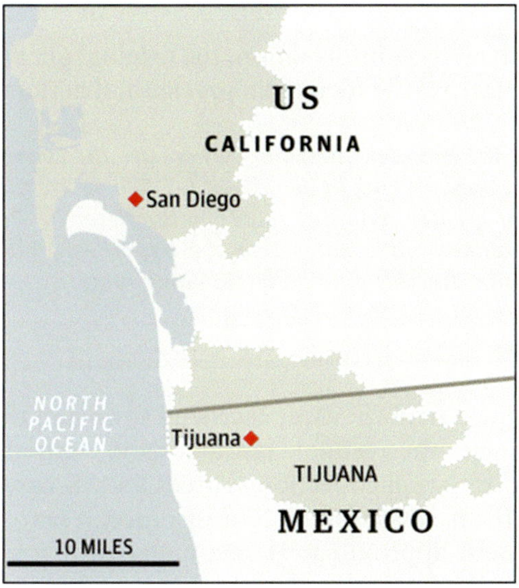

FIGURE 8.3 Map of California's border with Mexico.

southern border (Figure 8.3). This question sets the stage for hypothesis generation by identifying a critical intelligence need.

2. Conduct Targeted Research

The next step is to gather information about the topic. You may not need extensive research if you are already a subject matter expert, but staying updated on new developments and methodologies is important. This step involves a deep dive into relevant literature, reports, case studies, and expert opinions for those less familiar with the subject. The goal is to accumulate enough knowledge to form a well-grounded hypothesis.

3. Analyze and Synthesize Information

With research in hand, the analyst must now sift through the data to identify patterns, gaps, and insights that are relevant to the core question. This analysis may involve consulting with experts, reviewing case studies of past tunnel discoveries, or examining scientific methods used to locate underground structures. The aim is to transform raw information into actionable intelligence, laying the groundwork for hypothesis development.

4. Refine the Question

As you gather and analyze information, the original question may evolve. It is essential to narrow the focus to a precise and actionable question.

> *For example, the broader question "Where are the tunnels along the U.S. southern border?" might be refined to "Where are the illegal border tunnels of greater than one meter in diameter in the San Diego area?" This refinement ensures that the hypothesis will be specific enough to guide effective data collection and analysis.*

5. Test Feasibility

Before formulating a hypothesis, it is crucial to ensure that the question can be answered with the available resources and methods. This involves verifying that information collection sources (in this case, technical sensors will collect the necessary data). For instance, research indicates that operational tunnels, approximately one meter in diameter, in the San Diego area typically require electrical power, and power cables generate detectable electromagnetic fields (EMF). Knowing the relationship between situational activity and the collection platform (EMF sensor), the analyst can then confirm that EMF sensors are available and suitable for the task.

6. Formulate the Hypothesis

With a refined question and the assurance that it can be tested, the analyst is ready to articulate the hypothesis. This declarative statement posits a relationship between variables, an educated prediction based on the gathered knowledge.

> ***AUTHOR'S NOTE***
>
> - *Other scenarios, such as radar, tomography, Sonde (or beacon) locators, seismic measurements, electronic marker systems, and others, were available for detecting the tunnels. However, EMF detection was chosen because it is relatively straightforward and commonplace.*
> - *It is easier to construct the hypothesis by stating it as an "if ... then" statement.*

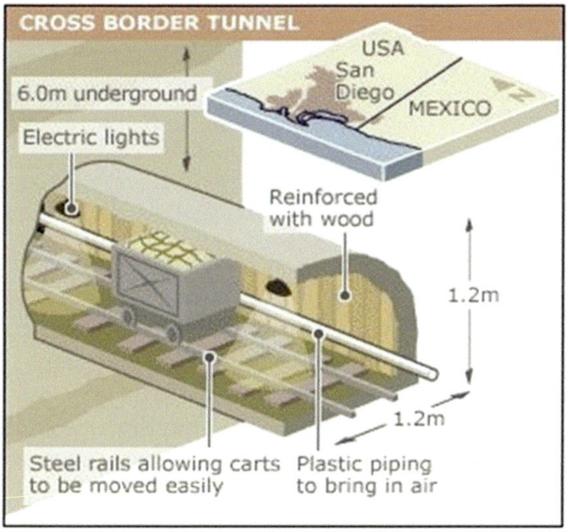

FIGURE 8.4 Diagram of a typical border tunnel.

> ***Example:***
>
> *If illegal border tunnels in the San Diego area (as illustrated in Figure 8.4) are operational and approximately one meter in diameter, they will produce a detectable EMF. This statement serves as a testable hypothesis that will guide subsequent data collection and analysis efforts.*

Strategies for Hypothesis Generation

Hypothesis generation is not a one-size-fits-all process. Analysts often employ three key strategies to develop and evaluate their hypotheses:

- **Situational Logic:** This strategy involves applying logical reasoning to a specific context or situation. By considering the unique circumstances of the problem, analysts can generate hypotheses tailored to the particularities of the case.
- **Application of Theory:** Drawing on established theories and models, analysts can generate hypotheses grounded in proven principles. This approach leverages the body of knowledge already existing in the field, applying it to new or evolving situations.
- **Comparison:** By comparing the current situation to similar cases or historical precedents, analysts can generate hypotheses informed by past experiences. This strategy helps identify patterns and outcomes that may apply to the present analysis.[1]

APPLICATION THEORY WEAKNESSES

- *It can blind analysts to the specifics of the current situation, which differentiates it from generalized theory.*
- *It is often psychologically challenging to overcome an interpretation based on theory, even in light of hard evidence to the contrary.*

Generating a robust, testable hypothesis is a cornerstone of effective intelligence analysis. Following this process, analysts can ensure that their hypotheses are well-founded, focused, and actionable. This chapter has provided a structured approach to hypothesis generation, equipping analysts with the tools to tackle complex intelligence challenges confidently and precisely. As you move forward, remember that the strength of your analysis hinges on the quality of your hypotheses. Get this step right, and the rest will follow.

HISTORICAL COMPARISON WEAKNESSES

- *Conveniently assumes that the current situation and a past situation are equivalent based on known similarities, which can cause incorrect conclusions.*
- *Vivid historical precedents often force themselves to the forefront of consideration.*

Situational Logic

Situational logic is one of the most powerful tools in the intelligence analyst's toolkit. It allows analysts to navigate complex, often ambiguous situations by grounding their hypotheses in the specifics of the case at hand. Unlike other approaches that rely heavily on theoretical frameworks or generalizations, situational logic focuses on the uniqueness of each situation, considering the particular details and circumstances that define it.

In the realm of intelligence analysis, every situation is distinct and shaped by a multitude of factors, including the actors involved, their motivations, the resources at their disposal, and the broader social and political context. Situational logic enables analysts to construct plausible scenarios by connecting these dots, helping to explain past events or anticipate future outcomes. This chapter explores how to effectively apply situational logic in generating hypotheses, offering insights into its strengths, limitations, and practical applications.

The Core of Situational Logic

Situational logic involves understanding a scenario as a unique instance rather than a mere example of a broader category. The analyst starts by immersing themselves in the specifics of the situation, examining the known facts, identifying the key players, and understanding the relationships between them. This process requires logical reasoning and a deep appreciation of context, as the situation's uniqueness often holds the key to unlocking its mysteries.

Situational logic is particularly effective in tracing cause-and-effect relationships, especially when dealing with means–end dynamics. By analyzing the goals of the actors involved and the means they have at their disposal, the analyst can construct a narrative explaining why certain actions were taken and the likely outcomes. This approach is not merely about linking events in a linear fashion; it is about building a coherent model that explains the interplay of various factors within the situation.

Constructing Scenarios with Situational Logic

The process of constructing scenarios using situational logic involves several key steps:

1. **Gathering and Analyzing Data:** The first step is to compile all relevant information about the situation. This includes intelligence reports, background information on the actors, historical data, and any other details that could influence the analysis. The analyst must then sift through this information, identifying patterns, inconsistencies, and gaps that need further exploration.
2. **Identifying Key Actors and Motivations:** Situational logic strongly emphasizes understanding the roles and motivations of the key players involved. The analyst must consider what the critical actors are doing and why they are doing it. This involves delving into their access to resources, goals, and the power dynamics at play in the situation. Understanding these elements helps form a more accurate picture of the situation.
3. **Building the Scenario:** With the data and understanding of the actors in hand, the analyst can begin constructing a scenario. This involves linking the identified elements into a plausible narrative that explains the situation. The scenario should account for the cause-and-effect relationships that have shaped the current situation and should be able to predict potential future developments.
4. **Testing the Hypothesis:** Once the scenario is constructed, the next step is formulating and testing a hypothesis. This involves

considering whether the scenario holds up under scrutiny and whether the hypothesized outcomes are consistent with the available evidence. If inconsistencies arise, the analyst may need to adjust the scenario to better fit the data.

Example of Situational Logic in Action:

Consider the following scenario, where situational logic is applied to generate a hypothesis:

Scenario: A series of intelligence reports indicate that John Doe (one of many possible leak suspects) joined an intelligence organization on April 1st of the previous year. By April 5th, Doe was granted access to classified materials. On April 10th, a security breach occurred, with classified files becoming public online. These files were part of the materials Doe had access to, though several thousand others also had access to them (see Figure 8.5).

FIGURE 8.5 Situational logic.

Additional Context:

- *The website that published the classified material is known for promoting anarchist ideologies.*
- *John Doe was involved with an anarchist group during his college years, though there has been no evidence of continued involvement since his college days. His initial reason for joining the group was social; he said he was dating someone involved with the group.*
- *John Doe has not yet undergone a counterintelligence (CI) or lifestyle polygraph.*

Formulating a Hypothesis Using Situational Logic:

Now, considering the noted scenario, the analyst develops an "if ... then" statement that can be used to validate or refute the available information. See the following draft hypothesis statement provided. If John Doe is the source of the leak, either knowingly or unknowingly, then he is likely to fail a polygraph or has somehow maintained ongoing direct or indirect contact with an anarchist group (as illustrated in Figure 8.5).

Testing the Hypothesis

To test this hypothesis, the analyst could recommend administering a CI/lifestyle polygraph to John Doe. If he fails the polygraph, covert surveillance could be conducted to determine whether he has ongoing contacts with anarchist groups or if there are other factors at play.

AUTHOR'S NOTE

- *The example hypothesis may not be correct, but the tests will quickly validate (or disprove) it.*
- *Also, notice that even if Doe fails the polygraph, further supporting (or possibly disproving) evidence is still pursued (e.g., covert surveillance).*
- *It is easier to construct the hypothesis by stating it as an "if ... then" statement.*
- *Never forget, even if Doe is proven to be a "leaker," it doesn't mean he wasn't part of a deception, or that he is alone!*

The previous example illustrates how situational logic enables the analyst to draw connections between seemingly disparate pieces of information, creating a narrative that can be tested and refined. The process involves logical reasoning and a nuanced understanding of human behavior and the social dynamics that influence it.

STRENGTHS AND LIMITATIONS OF SITUATIONAL LOGIC

Strengths

- **Broad Applicability:** Situational logic can be applied to a wide range of situations, making it a versatile tool for intelligence analysis.
- **Detail-Oriented:** It allows analysts to consider the unique details of a situation, which can be crucial in understanding complex scenarios.
- **Scenario Building:** Situational logic is particularly effective in constructing plausible scenarios to guide further analysis and decision-making.

Limitations

- **Complexity:** Situational logic can become complex, especially in situations with many variables or where information is incomplete or ambiguous.
- **Subjectivity:** The process relies heavily on the analyst's interpretation of the situation, which can introduce bias if not carefully managed.
- **Resource-Intensive:** Thoroughly applying situational logic may require significant time and resources, primarily when gathering and analyzing large volumes of detailed information.
- **Fails to Exploit Theoretical Knowledge:** Fails to exploit theoretical knowledge obtained from the study of similar cases.
- **May Miss or Misread Causal Effects:** Causal effects derived by situational logic may be symptoms of more fundamental events, which theory can explain.

Situational logic is an indispensable tool for intelligence analysts, offering a structured yet flexible approach to hypothesis generation. By focusing on the unique aspects of each situation, analysts can develop well-grounded hypotheses tailored to the specific circumstances they are investigating. While situational logic has limitations and challenges, its ability to provide deep insights into complex situations makes it an essential component of practical intelligence analysis. As you continue to hone your skills in this area, remember that the power of situational logic lies in its ability to transform raw data into a coherent and actionable narrative, one that can make the difference between success and failure in answering intelligence questions.

CHOOSING BETWEEN STRATEGIES

There is no "best" strategy. After generating as many relevant hypotheses as possible while making maximum use of all potentially relevant information and using all three strategies (as appropriate) at the early hypothesis generation phase, then methodically exclude the implausible and impossible until you have a workable handful of possible and probable hypotheses.

Table 8.1 compares and contrasts the applicability, advantages, and limitations of using situational logic, theory, and comparison as strategies for generating analytical hypotheses.

TABLE 8.1 Strategies for Hypothesis Generation: Summary

	Situational Logic	*Applying Theory*	*Historical Comparison*
Application	• Uses data sources that are available, but valid comparisons or theory applications are not suitable	• Uses multiple examples to generalize and fill gaps	• Uses an explicit conceptual model based on one or more similar situations from other times or places
Advantages	• Can be used for practically any situation • Able to integrate large amounts of data	• Enables an analyst to sort through a mass of less significant details	• Convenient shortcut, chosen when data is limited or theoretical cases are not available
Limitations	• Susceptible to personal bias • Fails to exploit theoretical knowledge obtained from the study of similar cases • Derived causal effects may be symptoms of more fundamental events	• It can blind analysts to the specifics of the current situation • Difficult for analysts to overcome an interpretation based on theory, even in light of contrary, hard evidence	• Assumes a current situation and a past situation are equivalent based on known similarities • Vivid historical precedents often dominate other available evidence

DEALING WITH MULTIPLE HYPOTHESES

In the complex field of intelligence analysis, dealing with multiple hypotheses is a crucial step that can significantly influence the accuracy and reliability of the final analysis. The hypothesis generation and evaluation processes involve identifying plausible explanations and systematically considering and testing a range of potential scenarios that fit the data. This approach helps to mitigate cognitive biases and ensures that the analysis remains objective, thorough, and resistant to premature conclusions.

Generating and Managing Multiple Hypotheses

Generating as many plausible hypotheses as possible ensures a comprehensive analysis. This process involves brainstorming and considering a wide array of scenarios, even those that might initially seem unlikely. The objective is to avoid early rejection of unproven hypotheses, as doing so may bias the analysis and close off potentially valid avenues of investigation. By reserving judgment and allowing a liberal definition of plausibility, analysts increase the likelihood of identifying all reasonable hypotheses.

No fixed number of hypotheses should be considered; the appropriate number depends on the complexity of the analytical problem and the analysis stage. In cases of high uncertainty or significant impact, more hypotheses should be considered to ensure that all possibilities are explored. However, managing too many hypotheses can become unmanageable. As a practical guideline, reducing the list to a manageable number, typically fewer than seven, by grouping similar hypotheses can make the analysis more efficient without sacrificing thoroughness.[2]

Strategies for Choosing among Competing Hypotheses

Selecting the most plausible hypothesis involves systematic evaluation rather than relying solely on intuition or first impressions. The scientific method emphasizes disproving rather than confirming hypotheses, a principle that should guide the analytical process. Screening out hypotheses that appear improbable is necessary, but care must be taken to distinguish between hypotheses that are merely unproven and those that have been disproven.

Eliminating Hypotheses

- *Is it really measurable or testable?*
- *Is it wrong/disproved?*
- *Collect evidence to prove/disprove.*
- *Use ACH to reduce biases.*
- *Preferentially try to disprove rather than prove.*

An unproven hypothesis lacks supporting evidence but is not incorrect. These hypotheses should remain in consideration until they can be conclusively disproven. For example, the hypothesis that an adversary is engaged in deception may seem unproven due to a lack of evidence. However, rejecting it outright without thorough investigation would be a mistake. In well-executed deception operations, evidence may be intentionally obscured, making it crucial to maintain a hypothesis until a systematic search for disconfirming evidence is completed.

Less Preferred Strategies for Hypothesis Selection

While systematic evaluation is ideal, intelligence analysts sometimes rely on less rigorous strategies when dealing with incomplete information and competing goals. These less preferred strategies, identified by Stanford University professor Alexander George, include:

- **Satisficing:** Selecting the first hypothesis that appears "good enough" rather than evaluating all alternatives to find the best one. This approach can lead to suboptimal conclusions if better hypotheses are overlooked.
- **Incrementalism:** Focusing on minor, incremental changes rather than considering the possibility of significant shifts in the situation. This can result in missing significant developments or changes in the environment.
- **Consensus:** Choosing the hypothesis that garners the most agreement or aligns with the preferences of decision-makers rather than the one most supported by evidence. This approach can be problematic when it leads to confirmation bias or groupthink.
- **Reasoning by Analogy:** Drawing parallels with previous situations to avoid past mistakes or replicate successes. While applicable in some cases, this strategy can lead to oversimplification and failure to recognize the unique aspects of the current situation.
- **Relying on Principles or Maxims:** Making decisions based on established rules or principles can be overly simplistic and fail to account for the situation's complexity.[3]

The Role of Intuitive Analysis

Intuitive analysis, which often involves focusing on confirming a single hypothesis, is a less reliable method that can lead to biased conclusions. This approach tends to give more weight to evidence supporting the favored hypothesis while discounting evidence contradicting it. While intuitive analysis can be quicker and less cognitively demanding, it is prone to errors and should be avoided in favor of more structured approaches.

> ***INTUITIVE ANALYSIS WEAKNESSES***
>
> - *Selective perception-only information that is relevant to the initial hypothesis is processed; if incorrect, information suggesting a different hypothesis is lost*
> - *Failure to generate appropriate hypotheses – Most people are unable to identify and choose from the full range of potential hypotheses*
> - *Failure to consider the diagnostic ability of evidence – Without a full range of alternative hypotheses, evidence applicable to current hypotheses, as well as others, may be used to mistakenly verify current hypotheses*

Though more cognitively demanding, simultaneously evaluating multiple hypotheses offers a more objective and reliable analysis. This approach is facilitated by methods such as the Analysis of Competing Hypotheses (ACH), developed by Richards Heuer during his time at the CIA. ACH provides a structured framework for systematically evaluating multiple hypotheses, drawing on principles from the scientific method, cognitive psychology, and decision analysis. By using ACH, analysts can reduce cognitive biases and improve the accuracy of their conclusions.[4]

Dealing with multiple hypotheses is a critical component of effective intelligence analysis. By generating a wide range of plausible hypotheses and systematically evaluating them, analysts can avoid premature conclusions and increase the likelihood of identifying the correct explanation. While intuitive and less rigorous methods may be tempting, especially under time constraints, using structured analytical techniques such as ACH is essential for maintaining objectivity and ensuring the reliability of the analysis.

Figure 8.6 illustrates a decision tree to help you visualize the process better. It allows analysts to choose between situational logic, theory, or historical comparison more easily.

CHAPTER SUMMARY

In the complex field of intelligence analysis, hypothesis generation is a critical process that shapes the direction and outcome of an investigation. This chapter provides a comprehensive guide to generating and

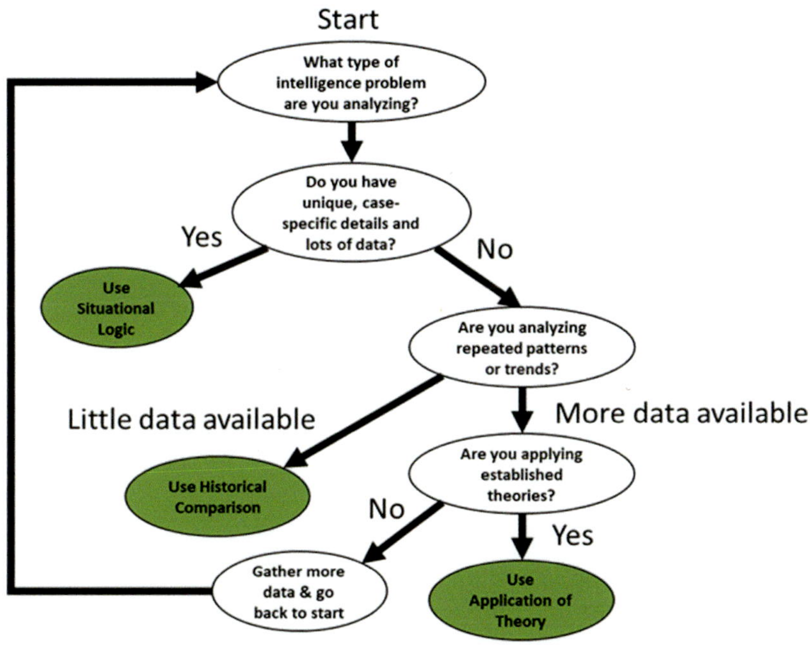

FIGURE 8.6 Decision tree: Choosing an analytical strategy.

evaluating multiple hypotheses, emphasizing the importance of considering a broad range of possibilities before arriving at a conclusion.

Introduction to Hypothesis Generation

The chapter begins by highlighting the significance of hypotheses in intelligence analysis. A hypothesis is a tentative explanation or prediction that guides the investigative process. Analysts must generate multiple plausible hypotheses rather than focusing on a single explanation to ensure a thorough and unbiased analysis.

The Hypothesis Generation Process

A structured six-step process is introduced for generating hypotheses:

1. **Define the Core Question:** Start with a specific, focused question that drives the need for analysis.
2. **Conduct Targeted Research:** Gather relevant information to build a strong foundation of knowledge.
3. **Analyze and Synthesize Information:** Identify patterns, gaps, and insights from the research.

4. **Refine the Question:** Narrow the focus to ensure the hypothesis is specific and actionable.
5. **Test Feasibility:** Ensure the hypothesis can be tested with available resources and methods.
6. **Formulate the Hypothesis:** Develop a testable statement that predicts a relationship between variables.

Three key strategies for generating hypotheses are explored:

1. **Situational Logic:** Focuses on the unique details of the situation to build a plausible narrative.
2. **Application of Theory:** Uses established theories to generate hypotheses based on proven principles.
3. **Comparison:** Compares the current situation with similar historical cases to identify patterns.

Situational Logic

The chapter delves into situational logic, emphasizing its effectiveness in dealing with complex and ambiguous situations. Analysts can construct scenarios that explain past events or predict future outcomes by understanding the specifics of a scenario, including the motivations of key actors and the cause-and-effect relationships at play.

Dealing with Multiple Hypotheses

Analysts are encouraged to generate as many plausible hypotheses as possible, avoiding premature rejection of unproven options. Managing multiple hypotheses involves reducing the list to a manageable number and systematically evaluating each one. The chapter discusses strategies for selecting the most plausible hypothesis, stressing the importance of disproving rather than confirming hypotheses.

Less Preferred Strategies and Intuitive Analysis

The chapter also reviews less preferred strategies for hypothesis selection, such as satisficing, incrementalism, consensus, reasoning by analogy, and relying on maxims. While these strategies may be used when information is incomplete, they can lead to suboptimal conclusions. Intuitive analysis often focuses on confirming a single hypothesis and is critiqued for its potential biases. The chapter advocates for a more structured approach, such as the Analysis of Competing Hypotheses (ACH), to ensure objective and reliable analysis.

In conclusion, the chapter reinforces the importance of generating and evaluating multiple hypotheses in intelligence analysis. By following a structured approach and avoiding reliance on less rigorous methods, analysts can improve their conclusions' accuracy and reliability, ultimately enhancing their work's effectiveness.

Key Concepts Covered

1. **Role of Hypothesis Generation in Intelligence Analysis:** Hypothesis generation is a critical step in the analytical process that helps analysts develop structured explanations for observed events or patterns. By proposing multiple possible explanations, analysts avoid premature conclusions and improve the reliability of their assessments.
2. **Definition of a Hypothesis:** A hypothesis is a structured, evidence-based explanation or prediction that proposes a relationship between variables. It is more than an educated guess; it is grounded in research, logical reasoning, and available intelligence reporting.
3. **Six-Step Hypothesis Generation Process:** Analysts can generate hypotheses using a systematic process:
   - Define the core question.
   - Conduct targeted research.
   - Analyze and synthesize information.
   - Refine the question.
   - Test feasibility.
   - Formulate the hypothesis as a testable statement.
4. **Situational Logic:** Situational logic examines the unique characteristics of a specific case. Analysts use known facts, motivations of actors, and contextual circumstances to construct plausible scenarios that explain current conditions or predict potential outcomes.
5. **Applying Theory:** Analytical theories provide generalizations derived from studying many examples. When certain conditions are present, theory suggests that particular outcomes may follow with some degree of probability, helping analysts interpret complex events.
6. **Historical Comparison:** Analysts may compare current situations with similar historical events to identify patterns or precedents. This approach can help fill intelligence gaps and suggest potential outcomes, though it must be applied carefully to avoid false equivalence.
7. **Managing Multiple Hypotheses:** Analysts should generate several plausible hypotheses and systematically evaluate them rather than focusing on a single explanation. Weak or impossible

hypotheses should be eliminated methodically until a manageable set of likely explanations remains.

8. **Avoiding Less Rigorous Analytical Approaches:** Analysts must guard against intuitive shortcuts such as satisficing, consensus bias, reasoning by analogy, or reliance on unsupported assumptions. Structured methods help ensure analytical rigor and reduce cognitive bias.

Learning Objectives Accomplished

1. **Define and Explain** the concept of hypothesis generation in intelligence analysis.
2. **Apply** the six-step process for generating hypotheses to intelligence problems.
3. **Identify** cognitive biases that can affect hypothesis generation and apply strategies to mitigate them.
4. **Develop and Evaluate** multiple hypotheses using structured analytical techniques.
5. **Demonstrate** the importance of generating alternative hypotheses through practical exercises and case studies.

Practical Application

During this chapter, you explored how analysts generate and refine hypotheses through practical examples and demonstrations, including:

- Developing a Hypothesis from an Intelligence Requirement: Using the cross-border tunnel detection scenario along the U.S. southern border to demonstrate how analysts move from a broad intelligence question to a refined, testable hypothesis.
- Applying the Six-Step Hypothesis Process: Defining a core question, conducting research, analyzing findings, refining the intelligence requirement, testing feasibility, and formulating a hypothesis.
- Using Multiple Hypothesis Generation Strategies: Applying situational logic, theoretical models, and historical comparisons to develop alternative explanations for observed events.
- Evaluating Competing Hypotheses: Identifying which explanations best account for known facts while eliminating those that are implausible, impossible, or unsupported by evidence.

Reflection Questions

1. Why is it important for intelligence analysts to generate multiple hypotheses rather than relying on a single explanation?

2. How can situational logic, theory, and historical comparison complement each other during hypothesis generation?
3. What risks arise when analysts rely on intuition or assumptions rather than structured analytical methods?

Thank you for your engagement and effort in this chapter. Continue practicing disciplined analytical thinking and structured hypothesis development—these skills will strengthen your ability to interpret complex intelligence problems and support sound decision-making.

GLOSSARY OF TERMS

Here is a glossary of key terms introduced and discussed in Chapter 8 to enhance your understanding of the material.

Analysis of Competing Hypotheses (ACH): A structured technique used to evaluate multiple hypotheses and minimize bias.
Anchor Bias: A cognitive bias where initial information disproportionately influences analysis.
Cognitive Bias: Systematic errors in thinking that affect decision-making and analysis.
Confirmation Bias: The tendency to search for, interpret, and remember information that confirms preexisting beliefs.
Historical Comparison: A strategy that uses past events with similarities to generate hypotheses about present situations.
Hypothesis: A proposed explanation for an observation or event, subject to testing and validation.
Red Teaming: A structured analytical technique where a group challenges assumptions and explores alternative hypotheses.
Situational Logic: An analytical method that constructs a hypothesis based on the specific context of an event rather than generalized models.
Sonde Locator *(or beacon locator)*: A device used in various industries, primarily utility locating, construction, and plumbing, to find and track the position of underground or hidden objects. It emits a signal that a locator above ground can detect.

This glossary serves as a quick reference for understanding key terms and concepts from the chapter. Feel free to revisit it as you progress through the lesson material!

NOTES

1. Don McDowell, *Strategic Intelligence: A Handbook for Practitioners, Managers, and Users*, Scarecrow Press, 2008.
2. Richards J. Heuer, Jr., *Psychology of Intelligence Analysis*, Central Intelligence Agency, Center for the Study of Intelligence, 1999.
3. Alexander L. George, *Presidential Decision-making in Foreign Policy: The Effective Use of Information and Advice*, Westview Press, 1980.
4. Randolph H. Pherson and Richards J. Heuer, Jr., *Structured Analytic Techniques for Intelligence Analysis* (2nd ed.), CQ Press, 2014.

CHAPTER 9

The Collection Process

INTRODUCTION TO THE COLLECTION PROCESS: THE LIFEBLOOD OF INTELLIGENCE ANALYSIS

In the vast and intricate intelligence world, the collection process is the foundation upon which all analysis is built. In this phase, raw data transforms into actionable intelligence, guiding decision-makers and shaping national security strategies. The success of any intelligence operation hinges on the sharpness of the analyst's mind and the richness, accuracy, and relevance of the information gathered. This step is far more than a mere formality; it is the heartbeat of the intelligence cycle.

Imagine being tasked with solving a complex puzzle, but many of the pieces are missing or hidden. This is the challenge faced by intelligence analysts every day. Often, the information they need may already be at their fingertips, buried in the vast archives of previously collected data, or ongoing collection efforts might actively seek it. However, when critical pieces are still missing, analysts must initiate new collection efforts or acknowledge these gaps in their final assessments. The quality of their conclusions is directly tied to the depth and breadth of the collection process, making it a pivotal element in the intelligence cycle.

Historically, intelligence collection has often relied on meticulous research and the ability to tap into available, usually public, information sources. For example, during the Cold War, Soviet intelligence agencies demonstrated the power of open-source intelligence, relying heavily on publicly accessible information to feed their vast intelligence apparatus, as shown in Figure 9.1. Remarkably, the FBI estimated that up to 90% of Soviet-collected intelligence came from open sources, an approach that continues to be relevant in today's intelligence practices.[1]

This chapter will delve into the collection process, focusing on how intelligence professionals identify and bridge information gaps and turn seemingly mundane data into valuable insights. By exploring open-source data, from public records to press reports, you will understand

DOI: 10.4324/9781003561712-9

FIGURE 9.1 Soviet collection during the Cold War.

the tools and techniques essential to the modern intelligence analyst's toolkit. Through realistic, unclassified examples and exercises, you will learn how to harness the power of open sources to fuel your analytical work, just as the Intelligence Community (IC) does in real-world operations.

As we embark on this exploration, remember that the collection process is more than just a step in the intelligence cycle. It is the lifeblood of effective analysis and the key to transforming information into actionable intelligence.

LEARNING OBJECTIVES

By the end of this chapter, students should be able to:

1. **Explain** the intelligence collection process and its role in transforming raw data into actionable intelligence.
2. **Understand** the critical role of the collection process in transforming raw data into actionable intelligence.
3. **Describe** the functions and importance of collection management within intelligence operations.
4. **Analyze** historical intelligence failures caused by inadequate collection processes.
5. **Differentiate** between various intelligence collection disciplines and their applications.
6. **Assess** the impact of emerging technologies on intelligence collection.

7. **Develop** effective collection plans by applying strategic concepts such as tipping and cueing, redundancy, mix, and integration.
8. **Identify** and evaluate various intelligence disciplines and sources, including their applications and limitations.
9. **Assess** common challenges and limitations in the collection process and propose mitigation strategies.
10. **Apply** open-source intelligence (OSINT) information to construct efficient collection plans.
11. **List** new technologies for enhancing intelligence gathering and analysis efficiency, speed, and accuracy.

CASE STUDY: INTELLIGENCE FAILURE DUE TO POOR COLLECTION

One of the most significant intelligence failures in recent history was the misjudgment of Iraq's Weapons of Mass Destruction (WMD) program in 2003. The U.S. Intelligence Community, relying on fragmented and unreliable sources, concluded that Iraq possessed active WMDs. However, post-invasion inspections revealed no such arsenal. The failure was largely attributed to poor intelligence collection—over-reliance on unverified HUMINT sources, lack of proper SIGINT validation, and insufficient cross-disciplinary verification. This case underscores the importance of accurate, multisource intelligence collection.

INTEGRATION OF NEW TECHNOLOGIES INTO INTELLIGENCE COLLECTION PROCESSES

Modern intelligence collection has evolved significantly due to the integration of artificial intelligence (AI), machine learning (ML), big data analytics, cyber intelligence (CYBINT), and quantum computing. These technologies enhance the efficiency, speed, and accuracy of intelligence gathering and analysis, allowing intelligence agencies to process massive amounts of information and extract meaningful insights more effectively. Following is a breakdown of how each technology contributes to intelligence collection.

- **Artificial intelligence (AI):** Used for predictive analysis and automating data sifting (see Figure 9.2).
- **Machine learning (ML):** Enhances pattern recognition in intercepted communications.

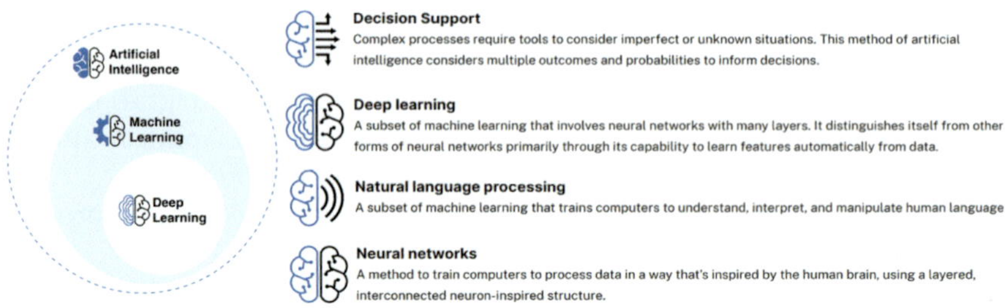

FIGURE 9.2 How artificial intelligence, machine learning, and deep learning fit together (NASA).

- **Big data analytics:** Processes massive datasets for real-time intelligence.
- **Cyber intelligence (CYBINT):** Extracts information from deep and dark web activities.
- **Quantum computing:** Expected to revolutionize cryptanalysis and decryption.

Artificial Intelligence (AI): Enhancing Predictive Analysis and Automating Data Processing

How AI is Integrated into Intelligence Collection:

- AI systems automate data processing by sifting through vast amounts of raw intelligence, prioritizing relevant data, and identifying key patterns.
- AI-driven predictive analytics helps intelligence agencies anticipate security threats before they materialize.
- AI can detect anomalies in communications and behavior, signaling potential terrorist activities or cyberattacks.

Example: AI in Counterterrorism

AI-powered intelligence platforms like IBM's Watson AI and Palantir Gotham analyze vast intelligence datasets to detect terrorist threats (see Figure 9.3).

After the 2015 Paris terror attacks, European intelligence agencies used AI-driven systems to analyze social media activities and intercepted communications, identifying potential threats in real time.[2,3]

Note: For information on Palantir Gotham, go to Palantir Gotham: https://www.youtube.com/watch?v=rxKghrZU5w8&t=256s.

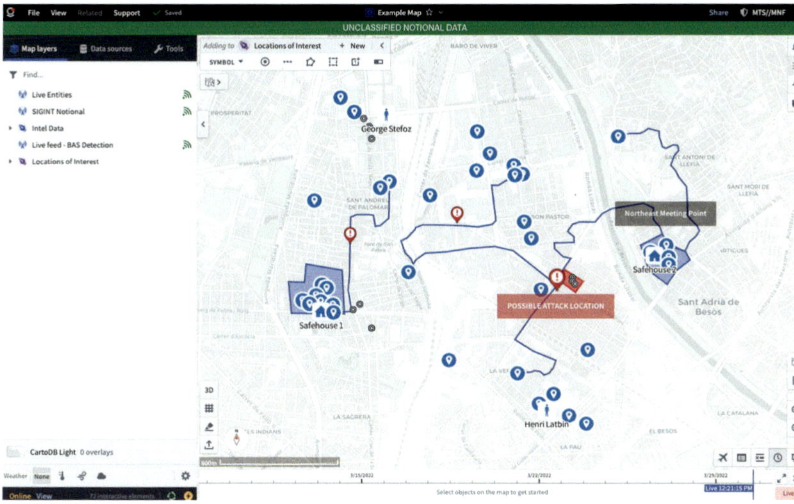

FIGURE 9.3 Screen capture of Palantir's Gotham™ AI application.

Machine Learning (ML): Enhancing Pattern Recognition in Intercepted Communications

How ML is Integrated into Intelligence Collection:

- ML algorithms analyze intercepted signals and messages for suspicious patterns.
- ML-powered natural language processing (NLP) systems translate and process foreign communications in real time.
- ML helps identify voice patterns in intercepted audio for speaker recognition in SIGINT operations.

Example: SIGINT and ML-Based Voice Recognition

The U.S. National Security Agency (NSA) uses ML-enhanced voice recognition software to analyze intercepted phone calls from suspected terrorist networks. By matching voiceprints to known individuals, ML systems can link conversations across different surveillance operations, aiding in tracking high-value targets.[4,5]

FIGURE 9.4 Conceptual image of big data analytics.

BIG DATA ANALYTICS: PROCESSING MASSIVE DATASETS FOR REAL-TIME INTELLIGENCE

How Big Data Analytics is Integrated into Intelligence Collection:

- Big data platforms process vast amounts of intelligence data from multiple sources, including IMINT (satellite images), SIGINT (electronic communications), and OSINT (public sources like social media).
- Enables real-time monitoring of global events by correlating social media posts, sensor feeds, and intercepted communications.
- Identifies hidden connections between individuals, groups, and activities.

Example: Big Data in Geospatial Intelligence (GEOINT)

The U.S. National Geospatial-Intelligence Agency (NGA) uses big data analytics to process satellite imagery, identifying real-time military buildups, infrastructure developments, and suspicious movements (see Figure 9.4). This capability was crucial in detecting Russia's military buildup on Ukraine's border before the 2022 invasion.[6,7]

Cyber Intelligence (CYBINT): Extracting Information from Deep and Dark Web Activities

How CYBINT is Integrated into Intelligence Collection:

- CYBINT tools scan the dark web for illicit activities, such as terrorist financing, arms trafficking, and cybercrime.
- Tracks cyber threats, state-sponsored hacking, and online radicalization.

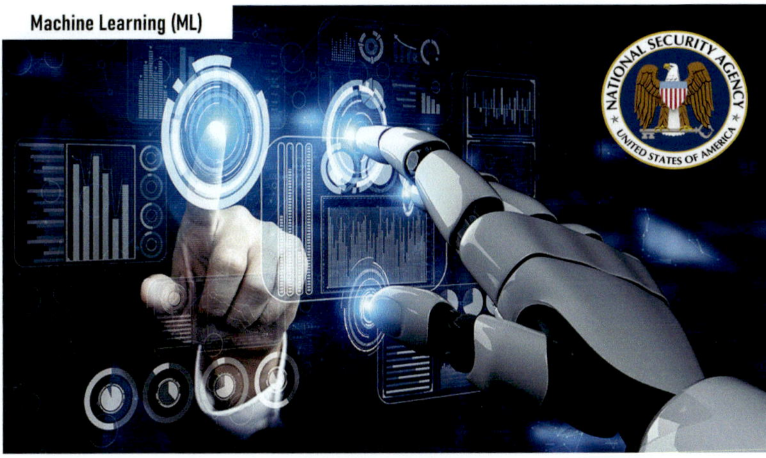

FIGURE 9.5 Conceptual image of CYBINT at GCHQ.

- Uses AI to map out cybercriminal networks by monitoring encrypted chatrooms and underground forums.

Example: Dark Web Monitoring for Counterterrorism

The UK's Government Communications Headquarters (GCHQ) developed Cyber Threat Intelligence (CTI) systems that scan encrypted dark web forums for ISIS recruitment activities (see Figure 9.5). In 2018, British intelligence disrupted an online ISIS propaganda network on Telegram, preventing the dissemination of recruitment materials.[8,9]

Quantum Computing: The Future of Cryptanalysis and Intelligence Decryption

How Quantum Computing will transform Intelligence Collection:

- Quantum computing is expected to break current encryption standards, revolutionizing SIGINT operations.
- Quantum systems can process intelligence at exponentially higher speeds, reducing decryption time from years to hours.
- Used in advanced cryptography and secure communications.

Example: Quantum Computing and NSA's Codebreaking

The NSA and China's National Cybersecurity Center are engaged in a technological race to develop quantum computers that break modern encryption algorithms (see Figure 9.6). If successful, these systems could decrypt intercepted state secrets, financial transactions, and diplomatic communications in real time.[10,11]

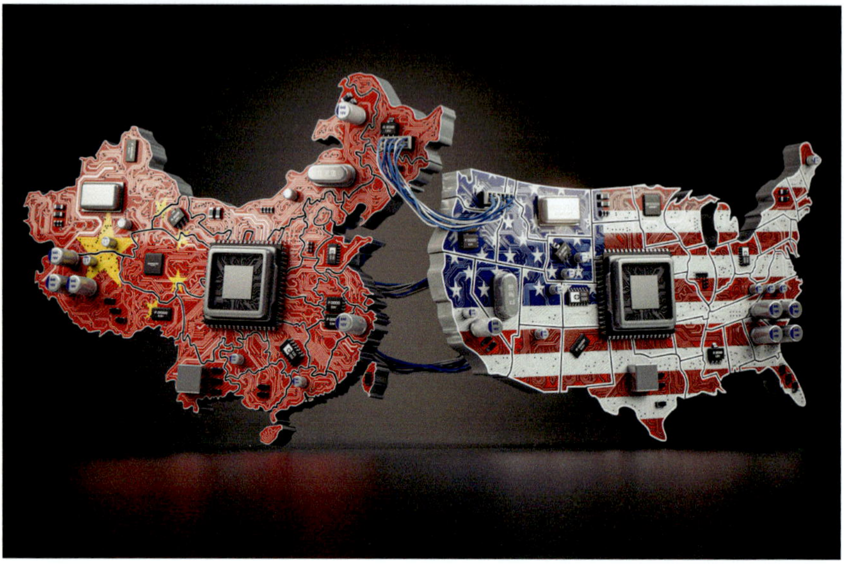

FIGURE 9.6 Conceptual image of the NSA and China's ongoing cyber conflict (www.shutterstock.com).

AUTHOR'S NOTE

China has several cyber units, including PLA Units 61398 and 61486 and the CAC.

- ***PLA Unit 61398*** *– Also known as (aka) APT1, a People's Liberation Army (PLA) unit accused of cyberattacks on U.S. companies. A Mandiant 2013 report, a U.S. cybersecurity firm, detailed evidence linking the unit to cyber espionage.*
- ***PLA Unit 61486*** *– Aka APT2, a bureau within the PLA's operation arm. The unit has been linked to cyberattacks on American, European, and Japanese aerospace and satellite industries.*
- ***Cyberspace Administration of China (CAC)*** *– The country's internet regulator/censor. In 2018, the CAC became the executive arm of the Central Cyberspace Affairs Commission. China's cyber operations are thought to combine espionage and entrepreneurship. For example, the Nortel/Huawei case involved espionage that caused the collapse of the Canadian telecommunications company.*

The Future of Intelligence Collection

Integrating AI, ML, big data analytics, CYBINT, and quantum computing into intelligence collection has significantly enhanced speed, efficiency, and accuracy. Intelligence agencies around the globe are utilizing these technologies to anticipate threats, monitor adversaries, and derive meaningful insights from vast amounts of data. However, as these technologies advance, new ethical and security challenges must be confronted to ensure that intelligence collection remains both effective and legally sound.

COLLECTION MANAGEMENT: THE NERVE CENTER OF INTELLIGENCE OPERATIONS

Collection management is the nerve center of intelligence operations, responsible for strategically coordinating data acquisition from a vast array of sources. In today's dynamic intelligence environment, collection management is more than just organizing and validating information; it is about ensuring that the correct data is gathered, verified, and delivered with precision and speed to those who need it most.

In a U.S. government or military intelligence organization, the collection management team is the gatekeeper of incoming data. While they perform basic validations, such as checking metadata, date, time, location, and more, they do not analyze the information's significance. Instead, they ensure the data is accurate and ready for the analysts who interpret it.

The process begins with the analyst reviewing the intelligence requirement (IR) to determine if an answer has already been generated. The analyst must confirm this answer's accuracy and currency, if necessary. Once validated, this intelligence is swiftly distributed to the end-user, ensuring timely decision-making. However, if the data is outdated or incomplete, the analyst embarks on further research, tapping into existing intelligence and readily available data sources to meet the IR.

The collection management process is illustrated in the U.S. Army's Collection Management Cycle, shown in Figure 9.7. This cycle underscores the importance of continuous monitoring and adaptation, as collection managers must constantly align intelligence requirements with available assets, ensuring that every piece of gathered data is a step closer to actionable intelligence.[12]

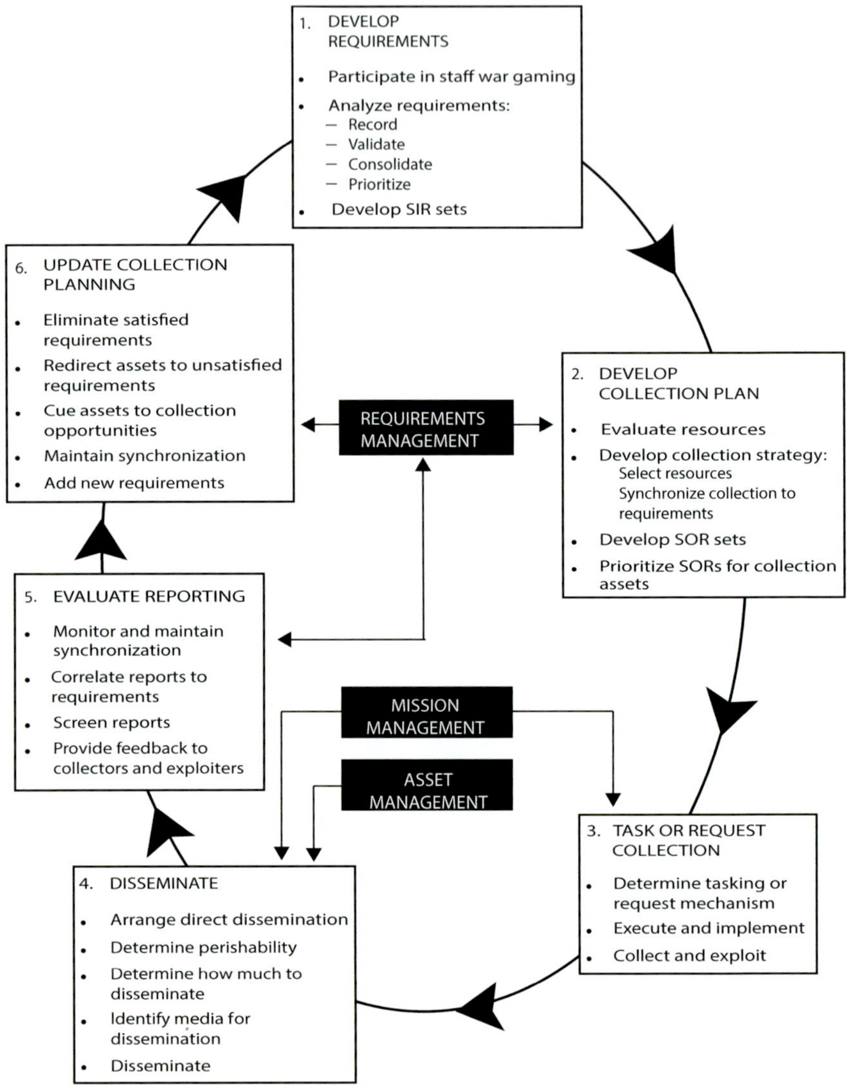

FIGURE 9.7 U.S. Army's Collection Management Cycle (U.S. Department of Defense).

Traditional Methods: From Shoeboxes to Digital Archives

In the early days of intelligence analysis, the process was often labor-intensive and rooted in physical data collection. Analysts would rely on their own carefully curated files, usually called an "analyst's shoebox." These shoeboxes contained everything from map references and 3 × 5 notecards to photographs and other tangible pieces of information. Each shoebox was a personal archive, built over time, filled with whatever data the analyst had previously gathered on a particular topic.

This method, while effective for its time, had obvious limitations. The reliance on physical documents made data retrieval slow and cumbersome. However, the underlying principle of applied research, systematically searching for, organizing, and analyzing information, remains unchanged. The transition from physical shoeboxes to digital archives has streamlined the process. However, the core methodology still relies on the analyst's ability to find relevant information, piece it together, and derive meaningful insights.

Modern Methods: Harnessing the Power of Advanced Technology

The landscape of intelligence analysis has undergone a dramatic transformation with the advent of modern technology. Today, the U.S. Intelligence Community (IC) has access to powerful algorithm-driven search engines and sophisticated software platforms that have revolutionized the research process. Tools such as Palantir™ Gotham (Figure 9.8), used by agencies like the Department of Homeland Security (DHS),

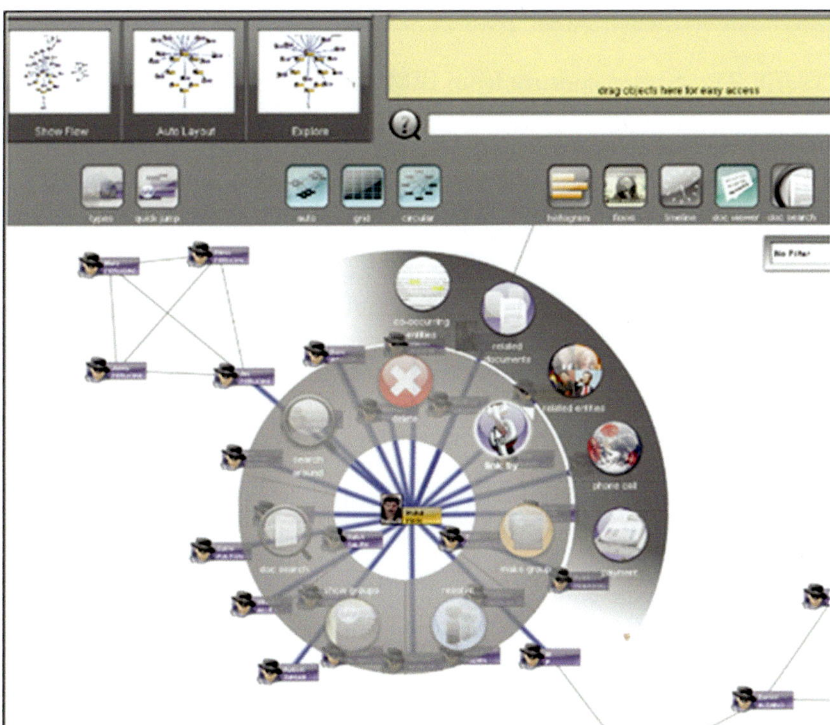

FIGURE 9.8 Palantir™ Gotham screen capture.

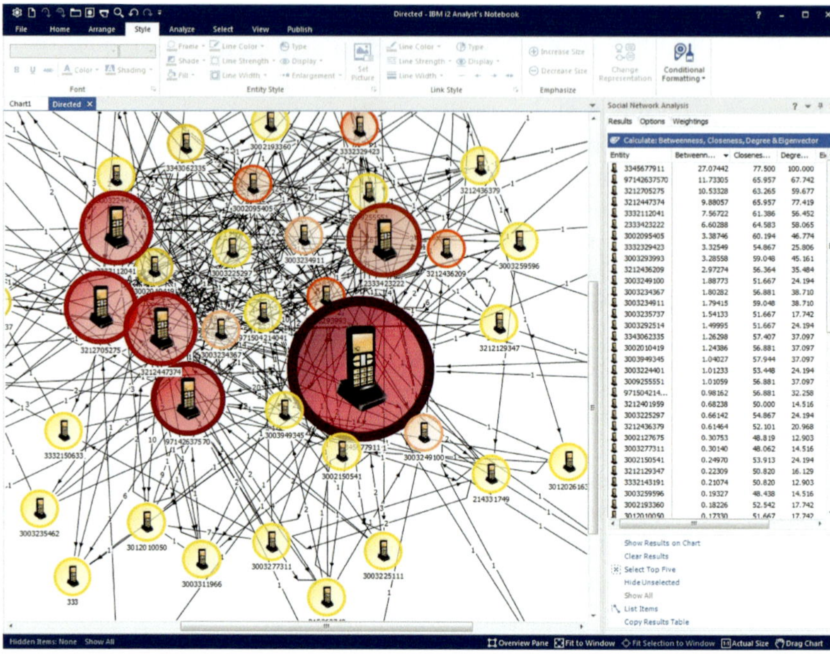

FIGURE 9.9 Screen capture from IBM's Analyst's Notebook™.

the National Security Agency (NSA), the Federal Bureau of Investigation (FBI), and IBM's Analyst's Notebook™ (Figure 9.9), widely utilized by the U.S. Army, have expanded the analyst's ability to access and analyze vast amounts of data.[13,14]

These platforms are more than just tools; they are force multipliers that enhance the capabilities of individual analysts. With the ability to query thousands of terabytes of data from their workstations, analysts can quickly sift through immense datasets to find the precise information needed to answer intelligence requirements. This capability not only speeds up the research process but also increases the accuracy and reliability of the analysis.

Once analysts have exhausted the available information resources at their disposal, they turn to collection managers to fulfill any remaining intelligence requirements. Collection managers then match these requirements against available collection assets and sources, orchestrating a coordinated effort to gather the necessary raw intelligence. This collaborative process between analysts and collection managers ensures that no stone is left unturned in the quest for actionable intelligence.

The Evolution of Intelligence Collection: Integrating Traditional and Modern Approaches

The evolution of intelligence collection reflects the broader shifts in technology and information management. While traditional methods laid the groundwork, modern tools have expanded the possibilities, allowing analysts to operate with unprecedented speed and precision. However, the principles of effective intelligence collection remain the same as in applied research: thorough study, meticulous organization, and a relentless pursuit of the information needed to protect national security.

As we look to the future, integrating artificial intelligence (AI) and machine learning (ML) into the collection process will further transform the field. These technologies promise to automate routine tasks, enhance pattern recognition, and predict emerging threats, allowing analysts to focus on higher-level analysis and strategic decision-making. The ongoing innovation in this area underscores the importance of collection management as the backbone of effective intelligence operations, ensuring that the correct information gets to the right people at the right time.

COLLECTION PLANNING: CRAFTING A STRATEGIC BLUEPRINT FOR INTELLIGENCE GATHERING

Effective collection planning is the cornerstone of successful intelligence operations. Despite the critical importance of this phase, many analysts, even seasoned professionals, often fall into the trap of approaching collection managers with vague requests like, "These are my gaps; how can you help?" Such an approach overlooks the need for a well-thought-out collection strategy that maximizes resources and increases the likelihood of gathering actionable intelligence.

A more strategic approach to collection planning involves systematically listing the expected data and identifying the most straightforward methods to obtain it. This begins by defining the target and understanding the associated activities—whether physical features, human interactions, or specific behaviors. For instance, if you need to confirm whether a particular individual resides at a specific address, you could explore several options: sending an anonymous package, making a phone call, or conducting 24-hour surveillance. Each method has pros and cons regarding cost, efficiency, and reliability.

The collaboration between the collection manager and the intelligence analyst is vital in this process. Together, they identify the most revealing activities that align with the intelligence requirements (IR). They must answer the key questions: "What exactly am I looking for, and how will I recognize it when I find it?" By working together to identify essential elements that are both reliable and valid, they can increase confidence in the intelligence gathered, ensuring that the collection plan is not just comprehensive but also strategically sound.

To better illustrate the collection planning process, let us perform a simplified exercise in collection planning.

- *Example: How to build a basic collection plan based on target-related activities*
- *Collection Task: You want to know if a person lives at a specific address*

The first step in planning a collection strategy is to first prepare a list of expected data (and collection mechanisms) associated with your target and determine the simplest to collect. The analyst (collaborating with the collection manager) determines the activity associated with desired data (or target), including physical features of terrain or objects, human contacts or associations, target behavior, or natural and man-made occurrences.

The collection activity associated with the target is that you need their "address," what the person "looks like," and you may also want to know "how their voice sounds."

- *Possible Collection Activities: To validate if they live at the address, one could (see Figure 9.10):*

- Have an inexpensive gift delivered anonymously by a messenger
- Call their home phone number, or even
- Set up 24-hour surveillance of the residence

FIGURE 9.10 Possible collection activities.

These approaches to collecting the information are all possible; some are more efficient than others, but none are foolproof.

Selecting Sensors and Sources: The Art of Precision Targeting

Selecting suitable sensors and sources is not just a task; it's a strategic decision that carries the weight of the entire intelligence operation. It requires a deep understanding of the target and the available collection tools. Several factors influence this selection process, each contributing to the effectiveness of the intelligence operation.[15]

What Worked in the Past

One of the primary considerations is past success. Historical data on what has worked in previous operations can guide decisions on which collection sources or methods are most likely to succeed. For example, if a particular sensor has reliably provided high-quality data on similar targets in the past, it should be prioritized.

Target Type

Another critical factor is the type of target. Large, fixed targets like industrial facilities or military installations can often be monitored using fewer resources, such as commercial satellite imagery. However, tracking a highly mobile individual, such as a lone terrorist in an urban environment, may require a combination of sensors and sources, including ground surveillance, UAVs, and human intelligence (HUMINT).

New Collection Technologies

Advancements in technology are not just tools, they are game-changers in the field of intelligence collection. Emerging tools like visual biometrics and GPS tracking have revolutionized intelligence collection, offering unprecedented precision and reliability. The collection plan should prioritize these cutting-edge technologies, especially when dealing with elusive or high-value targets.

Limitations on Collections: Navigating the Challenges

Despite the advancements in collection methods and technologies, several limitations can hinder the effectiveness of intelligence gathering. However, understanding these challenges is not a setback; it is a proactive step toward developing realistic and effective collection plans.

Too Many Requirements and Not Enough Collectors

One of the most significant limitations is the availability of collection assets. The demand for intelligence often outstrips the available resources, leading to difficult choices about prioritizing requirements. Constraints on time, money, and skilled professionals compound this scarcity. Cutting-edge sensors, for example, may only be available in limited quantities, with only a handful of operators and analysts qualified to use them effectively.

Too Much Data and Not Enough Analysts

Sensor data overload is another critical issue. The U.S. Military and Intelligence Community (IC) experienced this firsthand in Afghanistan and Iraq, where the volume of data streaming in from sensors far exceeded the capacity of analysts to process it. This deluge of information can lead to missed opportunities or delayed responses, highlighting the need for more efficient data management and analysis tools.

AUTHOR'S NOTE ON GPS TRACKING

- *GPS tracking is becoming increasingly common in law enforcement activities today.*
- *GPS-collected evidence was allowed and contributed to the successful conviction of Scott Peterson in his 2004 murder trial, in which Peterson was convicted of murdering his pregnant wife, Laci.*
- *GPS evidence showed that Peterson returned to the scene of the crime multiple times while under investigation.*
- *Prosecutors say the GPS evidence was circumstantial but indicates Peterson behaved as if he were guilty by driving to San Francisco Bay in January 2003, possibly fearing someone would find the bodies.*

Jurisdictional or Other Regulatory Constraints

Legal and regulatory constraints also significantly limit collection efforts. Authorization for certain collection types, such as wiretapping or surveillance, is tightly controlled by legal frameworks designed to protect privacy and civil liberties. Navigating these regulations requires a thorough understanding of the legal landscape and carefully balancing intelligence needs with ethical considerations.

Correct Data: Wrong Format

Finally, the usability of collected data is a crucial concern. Data that lacks proper formatting or essential metadata, such as time and location stamps, can be virtually useless. Ensuring that all collected data is in a usable format from the outset is critical to the success of any intelligence operation.

The Evolving Landscape of Intelligence Collection Planning

The collection process is an ever-evolving field shaped by technological advances, changing legal landscapes, and the dynamic nature of global threats. As we move forward, integrating artificial intelligence (AI) and machine learning (ML) into the collection process will further transform how intelligence is gathered and analyzed. These technologies promise to enhance the precision and efficiency of collection efforts, allowing for faster and more accurate intelligence production.[16]

COLLECTION SOURCES AND DISCIPLINES: THE BACKBONE OF INTELLIGENCE GATHERING

The journey from raw data to actionable intelligence is complex and multifaceted in the world of intelligence. While analysts can directly utilize some data, a significant portion must undergo rigorous processing and analysis before it becomes useful. This transformation is primarily facilitated by various intelligence disciplines, each specializing in a different aspect of data collection and processing.

Intelligence Disciplines: Transforming Raw Data into Usable Intelligence

Intelligence disciplines are the foundational elements of the collection process. They are specialized fields that collect data and refine it into a form that can be meaningfully analyzed. Here is an overview of the primary intelligence disciplines:

- **Human Intelligence (HUMINT)**: Involves information gathered by human operatives through interpersonal interactions. HUMINT is often the most in-depth intelligence source, offering insights that are difficult to obtain through other means. It includes intelligence gathered from prisoners, informants, refugees, and covert operatives.
- **Imagery Intelligence (IMINT)**: This type of intelligence relies on visual data captured by satellites, aerial reconnaissance, and drones. IMINT provides crucial information about physical objects and locations, making it a vital tool in military operations and strategic planning.
- **Measurement and Signature Intelligence (MASINT)**: Encompasses data collection from various sensor technologies that measure and identify specific characteristics of targets. MASINT subdisciplines include:
  - **Radar Intelligence (RADINT)**: Focuses on analyzing radar signals to gather information on objects and their movements.
  - **Acoustic Intelligence (ACOUSTINT)**: Involves collecting and analyzing sound signatures to identify and locate objects or activities.

- **Open-Source Intelligence (OSINT):** Gathers information from publicly available sources, such as news reports, academic papers, and social media. Due to the vast amount of online information, OSINT is increasingly valuable and is often the foundation for further analysis in other disciplines.
- **Signals Intelligence (SIGINT):** Involves intercepting communications and electronic signals. SIGINT is divided into:
  - **Electronic Intelligence (ELINT):** Focuses on non-communication signals, such as radar emissions, to gather information about electronic systems.
  - **Communications Intelligence (COMINT):** Centers on intercepting and analyzing voice and data communications.
  - **Cyber Intelligence (CYBINT):** Refers to the collection, analysis, and application of information related to cyber threats, vulnerabilities, and activities to protect national security, organizations, and individuals from cyberattacks and digital espionage.
- **Technical Intelligence (TECHINT):** This involves analyzing captured enemy equipment and materials to assess their capabilities and vulnerabilities. TECHINT provides critical insights during conflicts, enabling forces to counteract enemy technology.[17]

Raw data collected by these disciplines undergo rigorous processing before becoming actionable intelligence. This process ensures the information is accurate, relevant, and ready for analysis.

Sources of Intelligence: The Building Blocks of Analysis

Intelligence analysts draw on various sources to build hypotheses and generate Intelligence Requirements (IRs). According to Jerome Clauser and Sandra Weir, four general categories of information sources underpin intelligence gathering: people, physical objects, emanations, and records. These sources provide the raw material that analysts use to develop a comprehensive understanding of their targets.[18]

- **People:** Human sources are invaluable in intelligence gathering, often providing timely and accurate information that might not be documented elsewhere. HUMINT relies heavily on interpersonal communication and can include information from experts, eyewitnesses, or individuals with direct knowledge of a situation. The insights gained from human sources are often more nuanced and contextually rich than data obtained from other sources.

- **Physical Objects:** Physical objects provide tangible evidence that corroborates or refutes information gathered from human sources. For example, satellite imagery (IMINT) offers a bird's-eye view of military installations or other points of interest, providing crucial context for understanding a situation. During the Gulf War and subsequent conflicts, IMINT was pivotal in supporting combat operations by offering real-time visual intelligence.

- **Emanations:** Emanations refer to the data collected from emissions, such as electronic signals or acoustic signatures. These sources are particularly useful in technical and scientific analysis. For example, MASINT can detect and analyze the unique signatures of various materials, while SIGINT provides insights into the operations of electronic systems through intercepted signals. The ability to analyze emanations is critical in identifying and tracking targets that might otherwise remain undetected.

- **Documents/Records:** Written records, whether electronic, databases, or archived files, are a rich intelligence source. These records can provide historical context, verify facts, and offer detailed information that might be overlooked in real-time analysis. Open-source intelligence (OSINT) leverages publicly available documents to create a foundational layer of understanding that informs more classified or sensitive intelligence operations.

Special Sources: The Highly Classified Edge of Intelligence Collection

In addition to the standard sources, intelligence agencies have access to "special sources," which are highly restricted and often classified. These special sources include:

- **Espionage/HUMINT:** Information obtained through covert operations and espionage activities. This source is often the most sensitive and closely guarded.
- **Intercepted Communications/SIGINT:** Data derived from intercepting enemy communications, which can reveal intentions, plans, and capabilities.
- **Spy Satellite Imagery/IMINT:** High-resolution images captured by classified satellites, offering unparalleled detail and accuracy.

Due to their sensitive nature, these special sources are subject to strict classification and compartmentalization. This can sometimes lead to information being stovepiped—isolated within specific departments or agencies, limiting its accessibility to the broader Intelligence Community.

However, the fundamental principles of collection planning, sensor selection, and understanding the limitations of collections remain as crucial as ever. By combining these timeless strategies with modern tools, intelligence professionals can continue to provide the critical insights needed to safeguard national security.

COLLECTION OPERATIONS: THE HEARTBEAT OF INTELLIGENCE GATHERING

Once collection requirements are defined and strategies are selected, the next critical step in the intelligence process is conducting collection operations. This phase involves not only the selection of appropriate resources to gather intelligence but also the exploitation of the collected data for further analysis. These tasks, often performed by specialists within the Intelligence Community (IC), are central to transforming raw data into actionable intelligence. In isolated field operations, a single individual or a small team may manage all aspects of collection management, demonstrating the flexibility and adaptability required in diverse operational environments.

The success of collection operations hinges on strategically applying key concepts: Tipping and Cueing, Redundancy, Mix, and Integration. These principles guide the development of a collection strategy that maximizes the effectiveness of available resources.

Tipping and Cueing: Precision Targeting through Sensor Synergy

Tipping and Cueing involve the strategic use of multiple sensor systems, where one system's data guides the deployment of another, more precise sensor. This approach allows for the efficient identification and targeting of specific threats. For example, consider the challenge of locating a low-profile watercraft at sea (see Figure 9.11). A broad-area surveillance system, like surface-level radar, might first sweep the suspected area. If the radar detects potential targets, it "tips" off a more accurate sensor, like an unmanned aerial vehicle (UAV), to conduct a closer, more detailed inspection. This layered approach enhances the likelihood of identifying the target while minimizing resource expenditure. Tipping and Cueing are especially valuable in complex operational environments where the probability of detection must be maximized with limited resources.[19]

Redundancy: Ensuring Reliability through Multiple Channels

Redundancy is the practice of using multiple identical collection assets to monitor the same target. This strategy increases the likelihood of success,

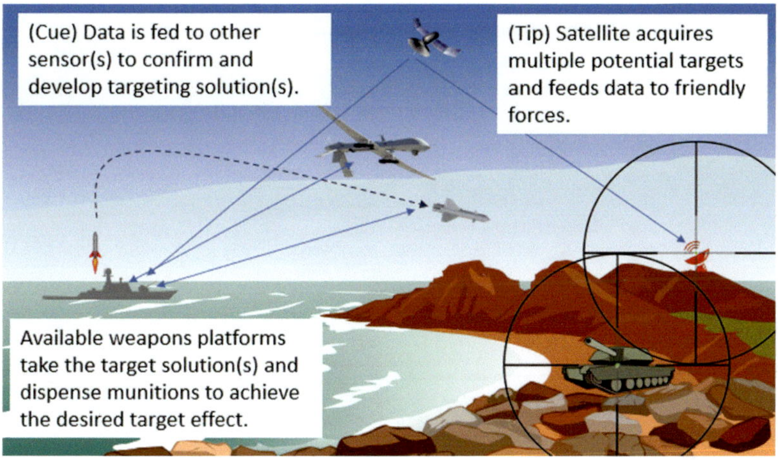

FIGURE 9.11 Surface craft radar tipping a UAV sensor as to the location of a distant watercraft.

mainly when dealing with high-priority targets with unacceptable risk of failure. For instance, deploying several listening devices across different locations, such as a suspect's home, office, and vehicle, ensures that critical communications are captured, even if one device fails or is compromised. Redundant collection provides a safety net, reducing the chances of missing essential information due to equipment malfunction, operator error, or enemy countermeasures.[20]

Mix: Enhancing Accuracy with Diverse Collection Assets

Mix refers to the deliberate combination of different collection assets from various disciplines to comprehensively cover a target. By integrating different types of sensors, intelligence operations can cross-verify data, reduce the risk of deception, and ensure more accurate reporting. For example, in a scenario where a UAV captures thermal imagery of suspected drug production sites in a jungle, ground reconnaissance might be used to confirm the nature of the hot spots detected. This approach ensures that innocent activities, such as villagers cooking meals, are not mistaken for illicit operations. A well-planned sensor mix enhances the overall accuracy and reliability of the intelligence collected.[21]

Integration: Streamlining Resources for Maximum Efficiency

Integration involves efficiently managing collection resources by incorporating new requirements into existing or planned missions (see Figure 9.12). This strategy helps avoid under-utilizing capable collectors and ensures that all available assets are used to their full potential. During

FIGURE 9.12 Visualization of integrated collection assets (shutterstock.com).

periods of high collection capacity, integrating additional tasks into ongoing operations can help address unfulfilled intelligence requirements. The collection manager ensures that the Intelligence Community remains agile and responsive to emerging threats by reallocating excess resources to critical tasks. Integration is a crucial factor in maintaining the efficiency of intelligence operations, particularly when resources are stretched thin.[22]

Small Element Collection Management Operations: Agile and Efficient Intelligence Gathering

Small, multidisciplinary intelligence teams, such as UAV operation cells, often manage multiple phases of the intelligence process simultaneously. These teams benefit from reduced bureaucracy and greater efficiency as they handle tasking, collection, processing, exploitation, and dissemination (TCPED) within a single unit. The compact nature of these teams allows for quicker decision-making. It reduces the risk of communication errors or delays, as the collected information does not need to leave the unit for additional external processing.

However, these small teams also face unique challenges. Cross-training personnel in multiple disciplines requires significant investment in both time and resources. Additionally, the scope of their operations is often limited by the sensors and sources available to them. For example, a UAV operations cell's analytical output is constrained by the capabilities of the sensors on the UAV platform and the available communication links with other intelligence assets.

Despite these challenges, small intelligence elements are crucial in delivering high-priority, actionable intelligence to decision-makers in real-time. As the volume of data within the IC continues to grow, the ability of these teams to manage the entire intelligence cycle efficiently becomes increasingly important. The agility and adaptability of small collection teams make them indispensable in modern intelligence operations.[23]

The Evolving Landscape of Collection Operations

Collection operations are the lifeblood of the intelligence cycle, transforming raw data into insights that drive decision-making. Intelligence organizations can optimize their collection efforts by leveraging strategies such as tipping and cueing, redundancy, mixing, and integration, ensuring practicality and efficiency. As technology and global threats evolve, so must the strategies employed in collection operations. The ability to adapt and innovate in this domain will remain a key determinant of success in the ever-changing landscape of intelligence gathering.

PRACTICAL EXERCISE: DEVELOPING AN OPEN-SOURCE COLLECTION PLAN

To provide a realistic but unclassified example, the text uses the Internet as an "open-source data source, which is also commonly used by the intelligence community." Therefore, OSINT will be used exclusively to develop a collection plan for demonstration purposes. See the following scenario for an example of constructing a simplified OSINT collection plan.

> ***Example: Open-Source Collection Plan***
>
> *Scenario: Recent media reports indicate that ISIS/ISIL is using "X" (formerly Twitter) to promote riots and terror-related activities. DHS officials have raised concerns about the possibility of ISIS/ISIL planning, coordinating, or even instigating terror acts or social unrest in the U.S., as shown in Figure 9.13 and Figure 9.14.*
>
> *You have been tasked to do an OSINT analysis of the following IR: "Are terrorist organizations (specifically ISIL) using social networks (specifically the "X" platform, known formerly as "Twitter") to plan or encourage terrorism in the United States?"*
>
> *Instructions: Develop a collection plan describing how to identify, collect on, and validate this IR.*

Author's Notes on How Terrorist Groups Exploit Social Media Platforms:

Terrorist organizations have increasingly leveraged social media platforms such as Twitter (now X), Facebook, YouTube, WhatsApp, and Instagram to advance their agendas. These platforms, designed for connectivity and engagement, offer unique features that terrorists exploit for propaganda, recruitment, communication, fundraising, and operational planning.

FIGURE 9.13 Why terrorists love social media.

FIGURE 9.14 Example 2, Jihadist posting on X.

Simplified Open-Source Data Collection Plan Worksheet

Select indicators and information you will collect and for each one, identify the data collection methods you will most likely use and the schedule for your data collection (see Table 9.1).

Information Requirement

Are terrorist organizations (specifically ISIL, aka ISIS) using social networks (specifically X [formerly Twitter]) to plan or encourage terrorism in the United States?

TABLE 9.1 Simplified Open-Source Data Collection Plan

Information/Data	*Indicator(s)*	*Data Collection Method*	*How Will Data Be Validated?*
Identify the information/data you are looking for and write it below	*Identify which indicator(s) to be measured to find the desired information/data, and write them below*	*Identify which type of OSINT data collection method will be conducted (e.g. search engine, social network search, etc.)*	*Describe the validation methodology*
ISIL-related threating posts on X	• Positive validated returns for ISIL threats on the U.S. • Determine baseline • Determine trend	**Topsy.com:** Social Media Analytics online application. Allows search by keyword, time, and place, set alerts, and analyze sentiment for every tweet ever made	Cross-reference results using "socialmention .com" and random Google searches

Collection Planning Steps

1. *Analyze IR: "What am I looking for, and how will I recognize it if I see it?"*
    - *e.g., Threatening posts on X, a keyword search for ISIS/ISIL using phrasing from previous posts, etc.*
2. *Do I already have the answer: Yes/No. "No." Look to see if the answer has already been generated.*
    - *If it has, the analyst must only validate that it remains accurate and current.*
    - *If it checks out, then the information is distributed to the end-user.*
3. *Prepare a list of expected data and collection mechanisms associated with your IR and determine what would be the simplest to collect. e.g., associated icons, Jihadist flags, collection mechanism: "tweetbinder.com," etc.*
4. *Determine collection strategy:*
    - *What has worked in the past?*
    - *What collection mechanisms are new and promising?*
    - *What is available?*
5. *What are the processing and validation requirements?*
    - *e.g., Process to determine baseline activity, analyze for trends, validate results using "socialmention.com," etc.*
6. *Assign and schedule resources.*

*Note: Since the "simplified" example noted only used one collection mechanism/platform, there was no "Tipping and Cueing, Redundancy, Mix, or Integration" of the collection mechanism/platforms. However, there are other readily available online social media analytics applications. These social media analytic applications could be applied to the example task in parallel to provide Tipping and Cueing, Redundancy, Mix or Integration, and likely higher product confidence levels. Some social media analytic applications that could have been used are Social Analytics (**SOCAnalytics**), **Rival IQ**, **SproutSocial.com**, **Google Analytics**, etc.*

CHAPTER SUMMARY

This chapter explored the critical role of the collection process in intelligence analysis, emphasizing that the foundation of actionable intelligence lies in gathering relevant, accurate, and timely data. The collection process starts with defining collection requirements and involves collaboration between analysts and collection managers to ensure that the correct data is obtained through various intelligence disciplines. Collection management serves as the nerve center, coordinating, acquiring, and validating information from diverse sources and disciplines such as HUMINT, SIGINT, IMINT, and OSINT.

You learned that traditional intelligence-gathering methods, like the "analyst's shoebox," have evolved with technological advancements, giving rise to sophisticated tools and platforms that enable analysts to process vast amounts of data efficiently. Modern techniques leverage cutting-edge technologies, including artificial intelligence and machine learning, to enhance data collection, analysis, and predictive capabilities. These sophisticated digital tools included Palantir™ and IBM's Analyst's Notebook™. Additionally, it discusses the selection of collection strategies, including tipping and cueing, redundancy, and mix, which help optimize the efficiency and accuracy of collection operations. The chapter also introduces emerging challenges, such as sensor data overload and legal limitations, while emphasizing the importance of adapting to new technologies, including artificial intelligence and machine learning.

Small, multidisciplinary intelligence teams demonstrate agility and efficiency by managing multiple phases of the intelligence cycle, though they also encounter challenges related to resource availability and expertise. The evolving landscape of intelligence collection underscores the necessity for continuous adaptation and innovation to address emerging threats and leverage new technologies effectively.

Finally, after defining the collection requirements and selecting collection strategies, the intelligence organization needs to choose a process for selecting resources to collect and then exploit the collected data for further analysis. These activities are referred to as collection operations. Whether it is an individual or an IC collection staffing element, the responsible collection element develops the collection strategy taking into account the following concepts:

- Tipping and Cueing
- Redundancy
- Mix
- Integration[24]

Key Concepts Covered

1. **Explain** how collection supports requirements and reduces key intelligence gaps.
2. **Distinguish** major collection disciplines (e.g., HUMINT, SIGINT, GEOINT/IMINT, MASINT, OSINT) and when each is most appropriate.

3. **Describe** how collection plans translate questions into tasks, timelines, and reporting expectations.
4. **Identify** common collection risks (bias, duplication, deception, legal/ethical constraints, timeliness).
5. **Describe** feedback loops that refine collection based on analytic findings and changing conditions.

Learning Objectives Accomplished

1. **Explain** the intelligence collection process and its role in transforming raw data into actionable intelligence.
2. **Understand** the critical role of the collection process in transforming raw data into actionable intelligence.
3. **Describe** the functions and importance of collection management within intelligence operations.
4. **Analyze** historical intelligence failures caused by inadequate collection processes.
5. **Differentiate** between various intelligence collection disciplines and their applications.
6. **Assess** the impact of emerging technologies on intelligence collection.
7. **Develop** effective collection plans by applying strategic concepts such as tipping and cueing, redundancy, mix, and integration.
8. **Identify and evaluate** various intelligence disciplines and sources, including their applications and limitations.
9. **Assess** common challenges and limitations in the collection process and propose mitigation strategies.
10. **Apply** open-source intelligence (OSINT) information to construct efficient collection plans.
11. **List** new technologies for enhancing intelligence gathering and analysis efficiency, speed, and accuracy.

Practical Application

- Convert a vague requirement into three specific, answerable collection questions.
- Build a mini "collection matrix" that maps questions to sources, indicators, and expected reporting.
- Run a quick "collection sanity check" to detect redundancy, gaps, and unrealistic timelines.
- Write a short collection request/tasking note that specifies: who/what/when/where, priority, and deliverable.
- Create a one-paragraph collection assessment identifying what you have, what you lack, and what you need next.

Reflection Questions

1. What did you assume about the target environment that could be wrong, and how would that misdirect collection?
2. Which collection discipline felt most persuasive to you, and how could that preference create blind spots?
3. How would you defend your collection choices if resources were cut by 30%?
4. What indicators would tell you that an adversary is trying to manipulate your collection?
5. What would "good enough" collection look like when time is limited?

Collection is where good questions become real evidence—keep practicing how to ask for what you truly need, not just what is easy to obtain.

GLOSSARY OF TERMS

Here is a glossary of key terms introduced and discussed in Chapter 9 to enhance your understanding of the material:

Collection Management: The process of planning, organizing, and directing intelligence collection operations.

Cyber Intelligence (CYBINT): Intelligence gathered from online data, hacking activities, and digital footprints.

HUMINT (Human Intelligence): Intelligence gathered from human sources.

IMINT (Imagery Intelligence): Intelligence derived from satellite and aerial imagery.

Integration: Coordinating multiple intelligence disciplines to maximize collection effectiveness.

Mix: Refers to combining different collection assets and disciplines to cover the same target, enhancing data accuracy, reducing the risk of deception, and providing comprehensive intelligence through cross-verification.

OSINT (Open-Source Intelligence): Information collected from publicly available sources.

Redundancy: Employing multiple collection assets to increase reliability.

SIGINT (Signals Intelligence): Intelligence collected from intercepted communications and electronic signals.

Stovepiping: The practice of isolating intelligence information within agencies limiting cross-agency collaboration.

Tipping and Cueing: The process of using one collection method to guide another more precise method.

This glossary serves as a quick reference for understanding key terms and concepts from the chapter. Feel free to revisit it as you progress through the material!

NOTES

1. Jeffrey T. Richelson, *Sword and Shield: Soviet Intelligence and Security Apparatus*, Cambridge, MA: Ballinger Publishing, 1986.
2. Robert Chesney and Danielle K. Citron, 'Deep Fakes: A Looming Challenge for National Security', *California Law Review*, 107(6), 1753–1819, 2019.
3. Office of the Director of National Intelligence (ODNI), *Artificial Intelligence & Intelligence Analysis Report*, 2021.
4. A. Singhal, 'Machine Learning for Signals Intelligence: A Case Study of NSA Operations', *MIT Technology Review*, 2020.
5. National Security Agency (NSA), *Machine Learning in Modern Intelligence Operations*, 2022.
6. A. Zegart, *Spies, Lies, and Algorithms: The History and Future of American Intelligence*, Princeton University Press, 2022.
7. National Geospatial-Intelligence Agency (NGA), *Big Data in GEOINT Analysis*, 2023.
8. T. Rid, *Cyber War Will Not Take Place*, Oxford University Press, 2021.
9. UK GCHQ, *Cyber Intelligence: Countering Terrorism in the Digital Age*, 2022.
10. National Institute of Standards and Technology (NIST), *Post-Quantum Cryptography and Intelligence Operations*, 2023.
11. RAND Corporation, *Quantum Computing and the Future of SIGINT*, 2023.
12. Department of the Army, *U.S. Army Field Manual 2-0, Intelligence Operations*, 2010.
13. Wikipedia, Palantir Technologies, Retrieved August 2024, https://en.wikipedia.org/wiki/Palantir_Technologies.
14. A. S. Hulnick, *Keeping Us Safe: Secret Intelligence and Homeland Security*, Praeger Security International, 2006.
15. R. M. Clark, *Intelligence Analysis: A Target-Centric Approach* (5th ed.), CQ Press, 2019.
16. A. S. Hulnick, *Keeping Us Safe: Secret Intelligence and Homeland Security*, Praeger Security International, 2006.
17. Department of the Army, *U.S. Army Field Manual 2-0, Intelligence Operations*, 2010.
18. Jerome Clauser and Sandra Weir, *Intelligence Research Methodology: A Study of the Collection, Analysis, and Utility of Intelligence*, Springfield, VA: National Technical Information Service, 1976.
19. Robert M. Clark, *Intelligence Collection*, Washington, DC: CQ Press, 2014.
20. Arthur S. Hulnick, 'What's Wrong with the Intelligence Cycle?' *Intelligence and National Security*, 21(6), 959–997, December 2006.
21. Mark M. Lowenthal, *Intelligence: From Secrets to Policy*, Washington, DC: CQ Press, 2017.
22. Abram N. Shulsky and Gary J. Schmitt, *Silent Warfare: Understanding the World of Intelligence,* Washington, DC: Potomac Books, Inc., 2002.
23. Department of the Army, *U.S. Army Field Manual 2-0, Intelligence Operations*, 2010.
24. U.S. Department of the Army, *FM 34-2 Collection Management and Synchronization Planning*, 1994.

CHAPTER 10

The Art and Science of Analytical Tradecraft

INTRODUCTION

In the shadowy intelligence world, "tradecraft" has long been synonymous with espionage, conjuring images of covert exchanges, dead drops, and microdots. Historically, it described spies' clandestine techniques to gather and transmit secrets. However, as the global landscape of threats and intelligence has evolved, so has tradecraft's meaning. Today, "Analytical Tradecraft" is the backbone of modern intelligence work, encompassing specialized methods designed to decipher complex information and turn raw data into actionable insight.

Analytical tradecraft operates in plain sight, unlike covert espionage techniques, yet its methods are just as critical. It equips analysts with the tools to navigate an overwhelming flood of information, discern subtle patterns in chaos, and unmask deceptive tactics. More importantly, it ensures that intelligence products provide clear, precise, and timely answers to decision-makers, often when those answers are most elusive (see Figure 10.1).

The Intelligence Community's (IC) efforts to standardize these practices took a significant leap forward in 2007. The Intelligence Community Directive (ICD) 203 codified rigorous, unbiased, and transparent analysis standards. This directive set the benchmark for analytical integrity and catalyzed a transformation within the IC to refine and enhance analytical methods.[1]

However, analytical tradecraft is not just about adhering to standards; it is about adaptability in the face of ever-evolving threats. Analysts must continually refine their techniques in a world where adversaries are increasingly sophisticated and information is weaponized. The intelligence failures of the past have driven a relentless pursuit of innovation, pushing the community to develop new tools, frameworks, and

DOI: 10.4324/9781003561712-10

FIGURE 10.1 Concepts of analytical tradecraft.

methodologies to better support a diverse range of intelligence consumers, from military leaders to policymakers.[2]

This chapter delves into the IC's journey toward establishing analytical tradecraft as a foundational element of intelligence analysis. It explores the standards that guide the process, the cutting-edge techniques analysts employ, and the real-world challenges that make these methods indispensable. Whether predicting the next geopolitical shift or identifying a cyber threat hidden in plain sight, applying analytical tradecraft has never been more crucial or more complex.

ANALYTICAL METHODS AND TECHNIQUES: CRAFTING INTELLIGENCE FROM CHAOS

By the time an intelligence analyst reaches the point of analyzing collected data, they have already traversed a complex journey. From defining the intelligence question to developing a comprehensive collection strategy and finally gathering and filtering relevant information, each step is critical. But now, the real challenge begins: turning fragmented

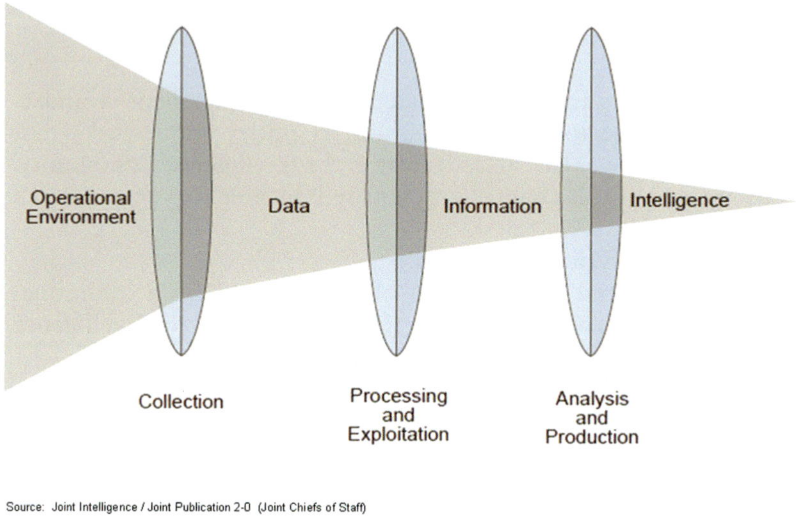

FIGURE 10.2 Relationship of data, information, and intelligence (Department of Defense).

and often incomplete data into a meaningful intelligence assessment. The question that arises is, "How do I craft a reliable, actionable intelligence assessment?" See Figure 10.2.

Analysis in the intelligence world is rarely straightforward. Unlike academic research, where data often aligns neatly to support a hypothesis, intelligence analysis resembles assembling a 10,000-piece jigsaw puzzle, where many pieces are missing and others are damaged. The image on the puzzle box is unclear. Therefore, the analyst must sift through diverse sources, decipher complex information, and, often using technical tools, extract meaning from the chaos. It is a rigorous intellectual exercise that demands a methodical approach, creativity, and critical thinking.

The ultimate objective of analysis is to synthesize collected data and generate an intelligence product that answers critical questions, provides context, and supports decision-makers. This chapter provides the mental framework you need to approach this daunting task. Mental readiness is not just important; it is essential to success. Intelligence analysis requires more than just skills; it requires a mindset geared toward evaluating ambiguity, managing uncertainty, and thinking critically about information.

LESSON LEARNING OBJECTIVES: THE ART AND SCIENCE OF ANALYTICAL TRADECRAFT

These objectives aim to equip students with a comprehensive understanding of the tools, methods, and cognitive frameworks that define modern analytical tradecraft in the Intelligence Community.

By the end of this chapter, students will be able to:

1. **Define Analytical Tradecraft:**
    - Understand the evolution of "tradecraft" from traditional espionage to modern analytical techniques in the Intelligence Community (IC).
    - Explain the significance of analytical tradecraft in transforming raw data into actionable intelligence.
2. **Explain the Impact of Intelligence Community Directive (ICD) 203:**
    - Identify the key components of ICD 203 and describe its role in setting the standards for unbiased and transparent analysis in the Intelligence Community.
3. **Describe the Role of Structured Analytical Techniques (SATs):**
    - List and explain the primary SATs, including the Analysis of Competing Hypotheses (ACH), Red Team Analysis, Devil's Advocacy, and others.
    - Illustrate how SATs help mitigate cognitive biases and improve the reliability of intelligence assessments.
4. **Apply Critical Thinking and Metacognition to Intelligence Analysis:**
    - Understand the concept of metacognition in the Framework for Analytic Cognition (FAC) and its importance in identifying and addressing biases during the analytical process.
    - Develop strategies for engaging in critical thinking to assess ambiguous or incomplete information effectively.
5. **Assess Various Analytical Methods and Techniques:**
    - Compare different analytical techniques such as pattern recognition, timeline analysis, social network analysis, and geospatial analysis.
    - Evaluate when and how to apply these techniques to make sense of complex intelligence data.
6. **Explore the Use of Contrarian and Imaginative Thinking Techniques:**
    - Understand the importance of contrarian techniques, such as Devil's Advocacy and Team A/Team B Analysis, in challenging assumptions and preventing groupthink.

- Recognize the value of imaginative thinking techniques like Alternative Futures Analysis in preparing for high-impact, low-probability scenarios.

7. **Synthesize Analytical Tradecraft into Actionable Intelligence Products:**
   - Develop an understanding of how analytical tradecraft is applied to create intelligence products that provide clear, precise, and timely information to decision-makers.
   - Demonstrate the ability to synthesize disparate data into a coherent and actionable intelligence assessment.
8. **Identify Real-World Applications of Analytical Tradecraft:**
   - Analyze how modern intelligence analysts use tradecraft to address contemporary threats, such as cyber warfare, disinformation campaigns, and geopolitical shifts.
   - Provide examples of how SATs and other analytical methods are applied in real-world intelligence operations to ensure accurate, actionable insights.

THE ART OF THINKING CRITICALLY: A LEGACY OF INTELLIGENCE ANALYSIS

The study of intelligence analysis is deeply rooted in history. Sherman Kent, a Yale historian and one of the foremost pioneers of modern intelligence analysis, famously outlined two key stages of analysis: *Critical evaluation of the data* and *Finding inherent meaning in the evaluated data.*[3]

Kent's framework remains a cornerstone of intelligence work, but in today's overwhelming data volumes and increasingly subtle threats, extracting meaning from information has grown exponentially more complex. While still valuable, traditional intelligence analysis methods are no longer sufficient in a world where data streams from myriad sources—from satellites to social media—adversaries use sophisticated techniques to obfuscate their intentions.

To meet these challenges, the Intelligence Community has developed and embraced Structured Analytical Techniques (SATs), a suite of methods designed to bring rigor and discipline to the analytical process. SATs are tools that help analysts manage uncertainty, challenge their assumptions, and systematically approach complex intelligence problems. They serve as cognitive frameworks that guide analysts through the maze of fragmented data and help them avoid the common pitfalls of bias, tunnel vision, and oversimplification.

INTRODUCING THE POWER OF STRUCTURED ANALYTIC TECHNIQUES (SATs)

SATs enable analysts to think critically about the information they interpret. By formalizing the analysis process, SATs reduce the risk of cognitive biases, such as confirmation bias, where an analyst might inadvertently seek out information that supports their initial hypothesis while ignoring conflicting evidence.[4] SATs also encourage creative thinking, allowing analysts to explore alternative scenarios and challenge conventional wisdom. This creativity is particularly valuable when dealing with complex or novel threats, such as cyber warfare or disinformation campaigns.[5]

A few key SATs that are regularly employed in intelligence analysis that one may already be familiar with (and will be addressed in detail later) include:

- **Analysis of Competing Hypotheses (ACH):** This technique helps analysts consider multiple explanations for a given dataset and assess which is most likely based on available evidence.[6]
- **Red Team Analysis:** This technique enables analysts to challenge their assumptions and explore alternative strategies or intentions that the adversary might employ by adopting the adversary's perspective.[7]
- **Devil's Advocacy:** A structured critique of prevailing assumptions or conclusions, devil's advocacy ensures that alternative viewpoints are considered and potential flaws in the analysis are uncovered.[8]

The role of SATs extends beyond mere data evaluation. They provide analysts with a structured approach to managing complexity, improving the reliability of their assessments, and ensuring that intelligence products are as unbiased and accurate as possible.

FRAMEWORK FOR ANALYTIC COGNITION

Understanding the cognitive processes involved in analysis is as important as understanding the data. The Framework for Analytic Cognition (FAC) highlights the importance of metacognition, the awareness of one's thinking processes, and its impact on the quality of analysis. Analysts must constantly question their thought processes, identify potential biases, and remain open to new information and perspectives.[9]

In subsequent chapters, you will explore additional techniques and methods designed to help you organize your analysis, test hypotheses, and derive meaning from seemingly chaotic data. But at the core of every successful analysis is the ability to challenge your thinking, engage with uncertainty, and approach every intelligence question rigorously and with imagination.

> ***ANALYTICAL TRADECRAFT TIPS***
>
> - *First, identify the relevant and diagnostic information acquired through open source and clandestine means.*
> - *Then choose an appropriate SAT that adequately interprets gathered information and considers a range of alternative explanations and outcomes to ensure potentially relevant hypotheses are NOT dismissed and supporting information opportunities to warn of those that may be potentially missed.*
> - *Use diagnostic techniques to actively review mindsets' accuracy by applying structured analytic techniques to make those mental models more explicit and expose key assumptions.*
> - *Use contrarian techniques to challenge all assumptions and current thinking by adding diverse knowledge and beliefs.*
> - *Use imaginative thinking techniques to develop new insights and different perspectives and/or develop alternative outcomes or predict future events.*

The Analytical Toolbox for Modern Threats

This chapter introduces the critical role that Structured Analytical Techniques (SATs) play in intelligence analysis. These tools help analysts refine their thinking, manage uncertainty, and extract meaningful insights from incomplete or ambiguous data. The Intelligence Community's reliance on these structured techniques grows as global threats become more multifaceted and deceptive.

In the end, the practice of intelligence analysis is a blend of art and science, a constant balancing act between creativity and rigor. By mastering the cognitive frameworks and structured techniques underpinning modern analysis, you will be equipped to navigate the ever-evolving landscape of global intelligence.

STRUCTURED ANALYTIC TECHNIQUES: BRINGING RIGOR TO INTELLIGENCE ANALYSIS

The debate over the value and effectiveness of Structured Analytic Techniques (SATs) is as old as the techniques themselves. Analysts and scholars alike have questioned their role in intelligence analysis, while others see them as an essential part of modern intelligence tradecraft. Despite the discourse, there has been little systematic research on SATs' application, leaving the field divided on how extensively they should be used. Yet, as threats evolve and information flows become more complex, a growing chorus of voices within the Intelligence Community (IC) advocates for their broader adoption.

The Current State: Intuitive vs. Structured Analysis

Unfortunately, the most common method of intelligence analysis remains the intuitive approach, often described as "read a bunch of stuff, think about it for a bit, and write something down." While this approach has produced countless intelligence assessments, its heavy reliance on individual judgment and experience leaves it vulnerable to cognitive biases and analytical blind spots.[10] Even those familiar with the SATs admit that traditional approaches, such as the "CIA method of analysis," which involves quickly reading through available material, thinking critically, and delivering a concise conclusion, still dominate the field.

This intuitive method has roots in historiographical approaches that focus heavily on descriptive analysis. While this method captures a broad overview, it risks overlooking subtle patterns or alternative explanations. As global threats grow more complex and nuanced, relying solely on intuition may no longer suffice.

Why Use SATs?

SATs offer a solution to the inherent limitations of intuitive analysis. Their defining feature is their ability to externalize analytical thinking, breaking down complex problems into discrete steps that others can examine, review, and critique. This process increases transparency and allows for a more collaborative and rigorous examination of the data. Importantly, SATs do not require advanced technical training. They are designed to be accessible to analysts across all levels of expertise, making them a powerful tool for both new and seasoned analysts alike.[11]

Key Benefits of SATs

The benefits of using SATs include the following:

- **Mitigating Cognitive Biases:** SATs help counteract common biases like confirmation bias and anchoring, ensuring that preconceptions do not sway the analysis.[12]
- **Creating an "Audit Trail":** One of the major advantages of SATs is the ability to create an analytic audit trail. This documentation provides a clear path from raw data to final conclusions, allowing others to trace how judgments were made.[13]
- **Enabling Collaboration:** SATs provide a structured framework for analysts to collaborate, share insights, and challenge each other's assumptions productively.[14]

These benefits are invaluable in the modern intelligence landscape, where threats are rapidly evolving, and the stakes are high.

SAT Groupings: A Toolbox for Analysis

Given the diversity of intelligence challenges, no single SAT can address every analytical problem. Instead, SATs are categorized into four primary tradecraft groupings: **Pattern Recognition, Diagnostic, Contrarian, and Imaginative Techniques**. These categories encompass a wide range of methods, each suited to different types of analysis. Notably, many techniques span multiple categories, and analysts should feel empowered to choose the ones that best fit their task.

While SATs do not guarantee perfect accuracy or precision, they do enhance intelligence assessments' sophistication, transparency, and credibility. As intelligence expert Richards Heuer has noted, "analysis can be improved," and SATs are one of the most effective ways to do so.[15]

PATTERN RECOGNITION TECHNIQUES: FINDING CLARITY IN COMPLEXITY

Pattern recognition techniques are designed to help analysts detect meaningful trends, relationships, or structures within large datasets. In an era of constant information overload, these techniques help make sense of disparate data points and identify emerging patterns that might otherwise be missed.

These techniques are widely used in the Intelligence Community, business sector, and criminal forensics, highlighting their versatility. Some of the most used pattern recognition techniques include:

- **Classic Pattern Recognition:** Identifying recurring patterns or anomalies in data based on historical precedents.[16]

- **Social Network Analysis:** Involves mapping and analyzing the relationships between individuals or entities to uncover networks of influence or communication.[17]
- **Trend Analysis:** Examining data over time to identify significant changes or trends that might indicate future developments.[18]
- **Five-Forces Analysis:** Popular in business intelligence, this technique assesses competitive forces that shape industries and markets, but it can also be adapted for geopolitical analysis.[19]
- **Strength, Weakness, Opportunity, Threat (SWOT) Analysis:** A method for assessing the strategic position of a situation or organization by identifying internal and external factors.[20]
- **Geospatial Analysis:** The use of geographic data to identify spatial patterns and relationships, often employed in military and counterterrorism operations.[21]
- **Timeline Analysis:** Organizing events chronologically to understand causal relationships and predict future events.[22]
- **Cost-Benefit Analysis (CBA):** This method weighs the potential costs and benefits of a decision or action and is frequently used in policy analysis.[23]
- **Sorting:** A basic technique that categorizes information to reveal hidden structures or associations.
- **Event Trees and Fault Trees:** Graphical methods used to map out possible events leading to success or failure in a system, helping to assess risk and outcomes.[24]

Each technique helps analysts organize data in ways that allow for deeper insights and more actionable intelligence.

Leveraging SATs for Better Analysis

As intelligence analysis becomes more complex, analysts must move beyond purely intuitive approaches and embrace structured techniques that improve their work process and outcomes. SATs provide a range of tools designed to help analysts think more rigorously, collaborate more effectively, and draw more transparent and defensible conclusions. While no method is a panacea, SATs undoubtedly improve the quality and reliability of intelligence analysis.

Pattern Recognition: Unlocking Hidden Structures

Pattern recognition involves arranging and analyzing data to uncover relationships, trends, or recurring behaviors that may not be immediately apparent. Whether predicting insurgent attacks or identifying long-term criminal behaviors, pattern recognition enables analysts to see beyond the noise and find meaningful insights that drive action.

When to Use

In the U.S. Military, pattern analysis is critical for anticipating potential threats by observing events over time in specific geographic locations. For example, analysts might track roadside bombings along a supply route, noting similarities in timing, location, or methods. These patterns can help predict where future incidents are likely to occur, allowing military planners to mitigate risks. The coordinates register and pattern-analysis plot sheet are standard tools for this process, which help visualize spatial and temporal data.[25] See Figure 10.3 for an example of a completed pattern-analysis plot sheet.[26]

> ***SAT TIPS***
>
> - *There is NO magic formula for always making the right analytic judgment*
> - *However, SATs are well-established procedures for reducing the frequency and severity of analytical errors*
> - *SATs enable collaboration by:*
>
> *Documenting and externalizing analysis to allow a thought exchange process*
>
> *Decomposing analysis into steps for external review by other knowledgeable analysts*

Beyond the battlefield, pattern recognition is applied in criminal forensics, particularly in bloodstain pattern analysis. In crime scene investigations, analysts study bloodstain shapes, sizes, and trajectories to determine how a violent event unfolds. The behavior of blood droplets, influenced by variables like height, velocity, and the type of surface, creates patterns that can help reconstruct the sequence of events.[27] Whether used in military or criminal contexts, pattern recognition turns fragmented data into a coherent narrative, guiding decision-makers toward informed actions. Figure 10.4 demonstrates a pattern analysis of blood drops, illustrating critical aspects like impact angles, velocity, and directionality of blood spatter.

Social Network Analysis: Mapping the Web of Influence

Social Network Analysis (SNA) is a powerful tool for understanding the relationships and interactions within a group. By mapping how individuals, organizations, or entities connect, SNA reveals hidden structures of influence, power, and communication.

When to Use

SNA is invaluable for answering the question, "Who knows whom?" and how these relationships impact behavior and decision-making. Intelligence analysts often use SNA to model informal communication networks within organizations, including terrorist groups, criminal

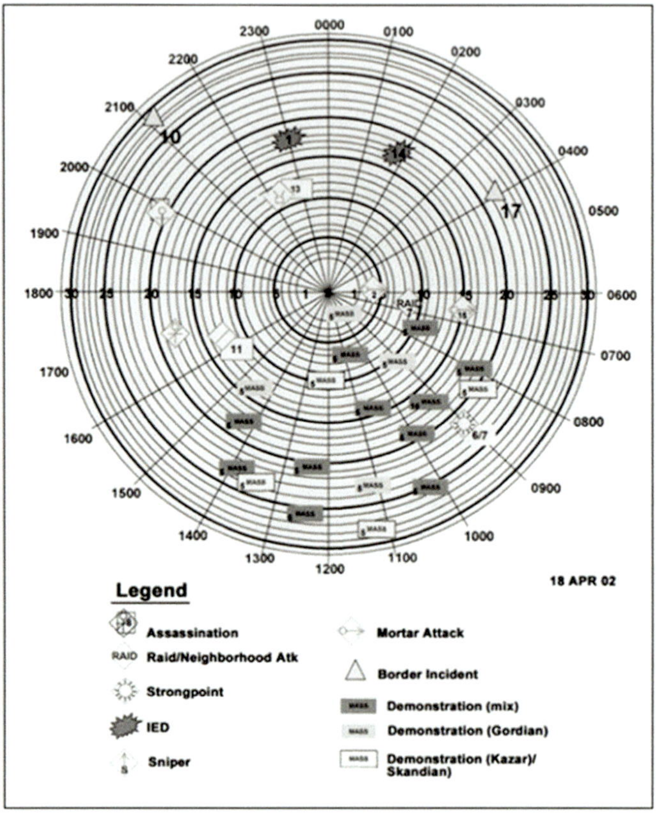

FIGURE 10.3 Pattern-analysis plot sheet (Department of Defense, FM 3-24.2, Tactics in Counterinsurgency).

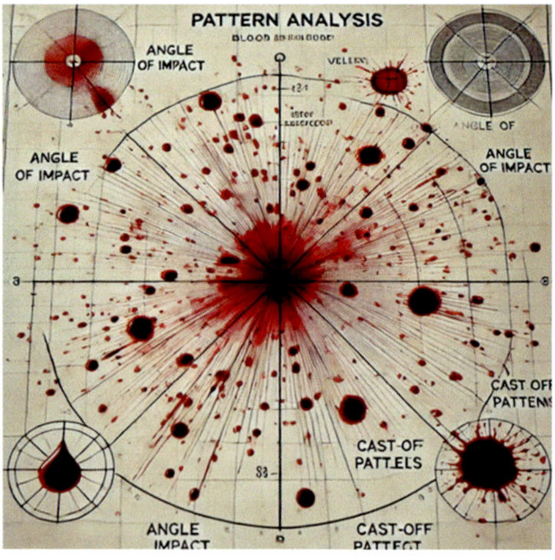

FIGURE 10.4 Blood spatter analysis.

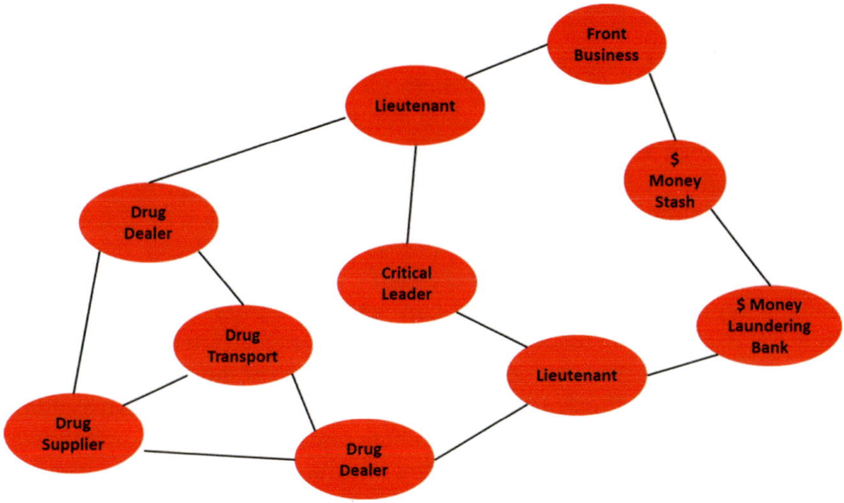

FIGURE 10.5 Social network analysis of a criminal organization network (money laundering and drug money flow) (Department of Defense).

organizations, or corporate environments. By visualizing these networks, analysts can identify key players, such as the most influential leaders or the critical communication nodes.[28]

For example, SNA has been used to analyze terrorist networks, revealing how loosely connected cells operate and communicate. Such analysis helps security agencies determine where to focus efforts to disrupt operations. The insight gained from SNA also allows for more strategic interventions by predicting how altering relationships through arrests might shift the network dynamics.[29] SNA has also become a cornerstone of modern crime analysis as a tool for understanding current interactions and anticipating future behaviors. See Figure 10.5, which represents a criminal organization's network, showing the flow of money laundering and drug money. It illustrates the connections between crime leaders, lieutenants, drug dealers, laundering entities (such as banks and front businesses), and the flow of drugs and money within the organization. The structure highlights how different entities work together to facilitate illicit activities.

Trend Analysis: Seeing the Big Picture in Shifting Landscapes

Trend analysis examines changes over time, allowing analysts to identify long-term movements or cyclical patterns in data. It is used across various fields, from military strategy to business intelligence; it helps anticipate future developments by studying past and present trends.

When to Use

Trend analysis is especially effective when part of a broader analytical approach. It includes several sub-methodologies, such as historical trend analysis, which examines past data for recurring trends, and content analysis, which explores the frequency and context of specific themes within a dataset. Another method, the Delphi process, involves gathering expert opinions to forecast future events, offering a mix of quantitative and qualitative insights.[30]

For instance, in 2012, the U.S.-led coalition in Afghanistan mistakenly reported a decline in Taliban attacks. Figure 10.6 erroneously shows a decrease in *Enemy-initiated attacks* in the latter part of 2011. Upon further analysis, trend data revealed no significant change from the previous year, illustrating how accurate trend analysis can prevent false narratives from emerging.[31] When paired with other techniques like pattern recognition or SNA, trend analysis provides critical insights that enhance the overall intelligence picture.

AUTHOR'S NOTE

Trend analysis, like all types of analysis, is susceptible to erroneous inputs and subsequent erroneous outputs.

I call into question the basis (rather than the data) of the "Enemy-Initiated Attacks" chart (Figure 10.6). Why use a drop in the number of Taliban-initiated attacks as a metric of success? Wouldn't the number of successful attacks be a better metric for attacks that cause coalition casualties? Would not five attacks, each of which caused casualties, deserve greater consideration than 50 ineffective attacks that caused zero casualties?

Analysts must consider the validity of the data they are collecting for trend analysis and ensure it truly measures what they want to measure.

One should observe that each of the pattern recognition techniques presented in this chapter are designed to arrange the data to aid the analyst's efforts to:

- *Interpret the information presented.*
- *Comprehend and express the meaning or significance of various experiences, situations, data, events, judgments, conventions, beliefs, rules, procedures, or criteria.*

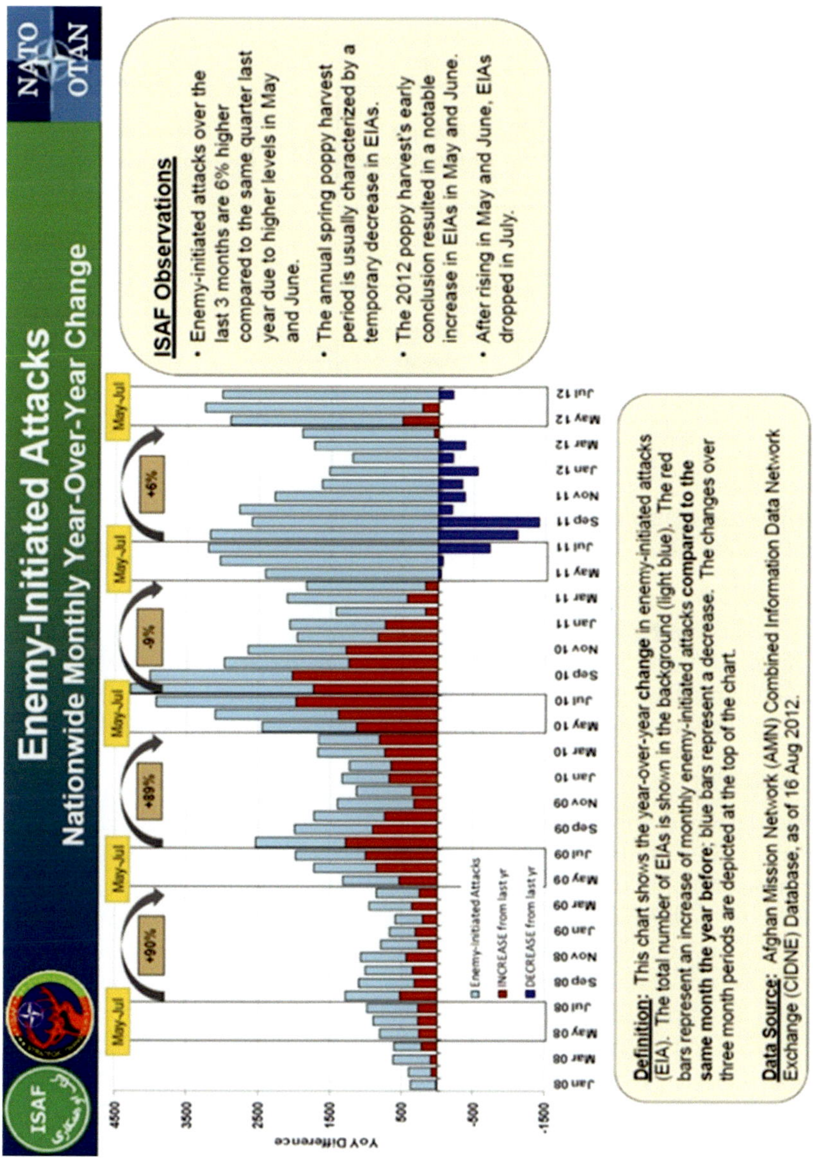

FIGURE 10.6 Enemy-initiated attacks, May–July 2008 to 2012 in Afghanistan.

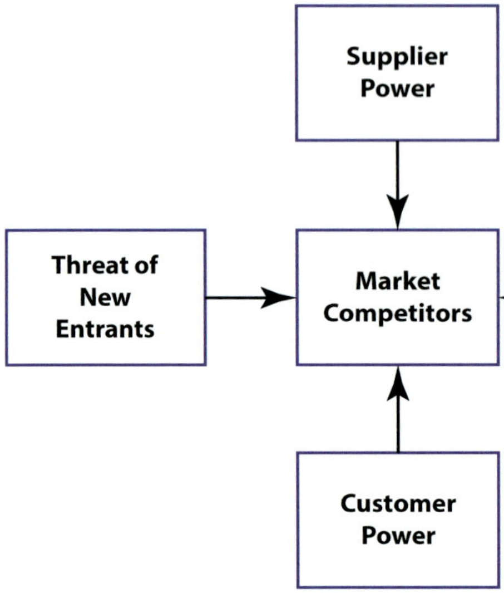

FIGURE 10.7 Five-Forces Analysis.

Five-Forces Analysis: Navigating Competitive and Conflict Environments

Developed by Harvard Business School Professor Michael E. Porter, the Five-Forces Analysis framework is a strategic tool designed initially for business but widely applicable to other fields, including intelligence and security. The model explains that five forces shape every market or industry, influencing its competitiveness and potential profitability.

When to Use

While designed for corporate strategy, Five-Forces Analysis is equally useful in the intelligence world, particularly when assessing competitive environments like criminal organizations, insurgent groups, or rival state actors. The five forces: Threat of New Entrants, Power of Suppliers, Power of Buyers, Threat of Substitutes, and Market Competitors, can be applied to understand the dynamics between rival groups.[32] See Figure 10.7 for a simplified depiction of a Five-Forces Analysis.

For example, intelligence analysts could use this model to assess how drug cartels compete for resources, control territory, or negotiate regional power. Analyzing the power of suppliers (e.g., access to narcotics), the threat of new entrants (e.g., rival gangs), and the influence of market competitors (e.g., other cartels) provides a comprehensive view of the conflict landscape.[33] Applying Porter's Five Forces in intelligence allows analysts to deconstruct competitive environments and predict future strategic moves.

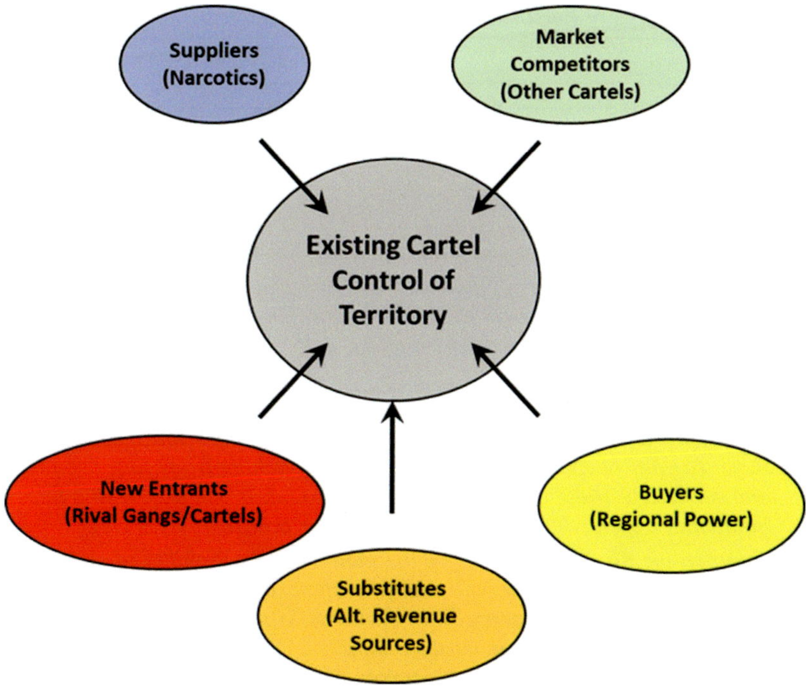

FIGURE 10.8 Example of a Five-Forces Analysis of drug cartel competition.

Example of a Five-Force Analysis of a Drug Cartel Competition

Figure 10.8 is a representation of a Five-Force Analysis focused on drug cartels competing for resources, control of territory, and negotiations with a regional power. Figure 10.8 shows the fundamental forces influencing the competition.

1. *Suppliers (**Access to Narcotics**): Cartels rely on access to narcotics as their primary resource.*
2. *Threat of New Entrants (Rival Gangs): Rival gangs threaten existing cartels by entering the market.*
3. *Market Competitors (Other Cartels): Competition among cartels over control of territory and resources.*
4. *Buyers (Regional Power Negotiations): Cartels may negotiate with regional powers, such as political or military authorities.*
5. *Substitutes (Other Sources of Revenue): Alternative revenue streams, such as arms trafficking, could influence the cartels' behavior (see Table 10.1).*

TABLE 10.1 Steps in Performing a Five-Forces Analysis

Method
Five-Forces Analysis assumes that five important forces determine competitive power in a business situation (or other competitive environments). These forces are as follows: 1. *Supplier Power: This assesses how easy it is for suppliers to raise prices. It is driven by the number of suppliers of each key input, the uniqueness of their product or service, their strength and control over you, the cost of switching from one to another, and so on. The fewer your supplier choices and the more you need suppliers' help, the more powerful your suppliers are.* 2. *Buyer Power: Here, you ask, "How easily can buyers drive prices down?" Again, this is driven by the number of buyers, the importance of each buyer to your business, the cost to them of switching from your products and services to those of someone else, and so on. If you deal with a few influential buyers, they can often dictate your terms.* 3. *Competitive Rivalry: This gauges the number and capability of your competitors. Suppose you have many competitors, and they offer equally attractive products and services. In that case, you will most likely have little power in the situation because suppliers and buyers will go elsewhere if they do not get a good deal from you. On the other hand, if no one else can do what you do, you can often have tremendous strength.* 4. *Threat of Substitution: This is affected by your customers' ability to find a different way of doing what you do. For example, if you supply a unique software product that automates an important process, people may substitute it by manually performing the process or outsourcing it. If substitution is easy and viable, then this weakens your power.* 5. *Threat of New Entry: Power is also affected by people's ability to enter your market. Suppose it costs little time or money to compete effectively in your market. In that case, if there are few economies of scale or little protection for your key technologies, new competitors can quickly enter your market and weaken your position. If you have strong and durable entry barriers, you can preserve a favorable position and take fair advantage of it.*

Integrating Analytical Techniques for Holistic Insights

While each technique—Pattern Recognition, Social Network Analysis, Trend Analysis, and Five-Forces Analysis—offers its own strengths, they are most effective when combined. Together, they provide a multidimensional view of complex environments, from uncovering hidden relationships to forecasting future developments. In a world where information and threats are increasingly complex, mastering these tools is essential for crafting accurate, actionable intelligence assessments.

FIGURE 10.9 SWOT matrix.

Strengths, Weaknesses, Opportunities, and Threats Analysis: A Strategic Snapshot

Strengths, Weaknesses, Opportunities, and Threats (SWOT) Analysis is a strategic planning tool used to evaluate an organization's internal strengths and weaknesses and external opportunities and threats. By organizing information into a SWOT matrix, analysts can focus on critical factors that influence a project, mission, or organization's success (see Figure 10.9). The technique encourages a balanced examination, helping strategists avoid focusing only on either strengths or weaknesses. Instead, it offers a holistic perspective on an entity's position within a dynamic environment (see Table 10.2).

When to Use

SWOT is particularly useful when an organization or team needs a quick, comprehensive evaluation of its current situation. Whether assessing a military strategy, a corporate initiative, or a government project, SWOT provides clarity by breaking down complex environments into manageable components. This clarity allows for informed decision-making and planning based on actionable insights.[34]

Geospatial Analysis: Mapping Intelligence with Precision

Geospatial Analysis involves gathering, displaying, and interpreting data related to physical locations on the Earth's surface. It integrates various data sources such as satellite imagery, GPS data, and historical records, making it a powerful tool for intelligence and military operations. This analysis reveals spatial patterns and relationships, enabling

TABLE 10.2 SWOT Analysis Matrix

	Method	
-	STRENGTHS *1.* *2.* *3.* …	WEAKNESSES *1.* *2.* *3.* …
OPPORTUNITIES *1.* *2.* *3.* …	*Opportunity/Strength (O/S) Strategies* *(Use the strengths to take advantage of opportunities)* *1.* *2.* …	*Opportunity/Weakness (O/W) Strategies* *(Overcome weaknesses by taking advantage of opportunities)* *1.* *2.* …
THREATS 1. 2. 3. …	*Threat/Strength (T/S) Strategies* *(Use strengths to avoid threats)* *1.* 2. 3. …	Threat/Weakness (T/W) Strategies *(Minimize weaknesses and avoid threats)* 1. 2. 3. …

Note: Remember that performing a SWOT aims to reveal positive forces that work together and potential problems that need to be recognized and possibly addressed.

decision-makers to visualize data in geographic contexts (see Figure 10.10).

When to Use

Geospatial analysis is essential in targeting operations, where understanding the physical environment is critical to success. Military strategists use this technique to track enemy movements, assess terrain, and forecast how weather or geography might influence an operation's outcome. In counterterrorism, it helps to identify networks of safe houses or track smuggling routes across borders. In disaster response, geospatial analysis provides real-time situational awareness by visualizing affected areas and allocating resources efficiently.[35] Analysts can produce detailed visual products that guide critical decisions by combining raw imagery, geospatial information, and intelligence data (see Figure 10.10).

Timeline Analysis: Understanding the Sequence of Events

Timeline Analysis allows analysts to chart events along a continuum, making it easier to understand the relationship between events over time

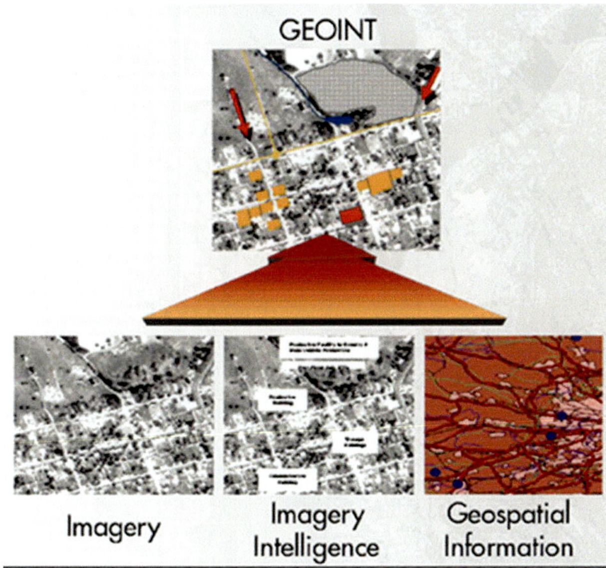

FIGURE 10.10 Geospatial information as a component of GEOINT (National Geospatial-Intelligence Agency).

more manageable. By visualizing occurrences sequentially, analysts can identify patterns, cause-and-effect relationships, and key moments that may have contributed to a particular outcome (see Figure 10.11).

When to Use

This technique is ideal for investigating complex incidents or forensics, where understanding how events unfold over time is crucial. For instance, in intelligence operations, tracking the movement of insurgent groups over a time period allows analysts to predict future actions or patterns. In political analysis, timelines can help map out the escalation of a conflict, illustrating key decision points that influenced its course.[36] Whether used in military, criminal, or policy contexts, timeline analysis offers a clear, chronological view that enhances situational awareness.

Cost-Benefit Analysis: Weighing Options for Optimal Outcomes

Cost-benefit analysis (CBA) compares the costs and benefits of different courses of action, projects, or policies. It is more than just a tool; it is a strategic framework that allows decision-makers to systematically weigh the pros and cons of any action, policy, project, or decision. By assigning value to tangible and intangible factors, CBA provides a structured

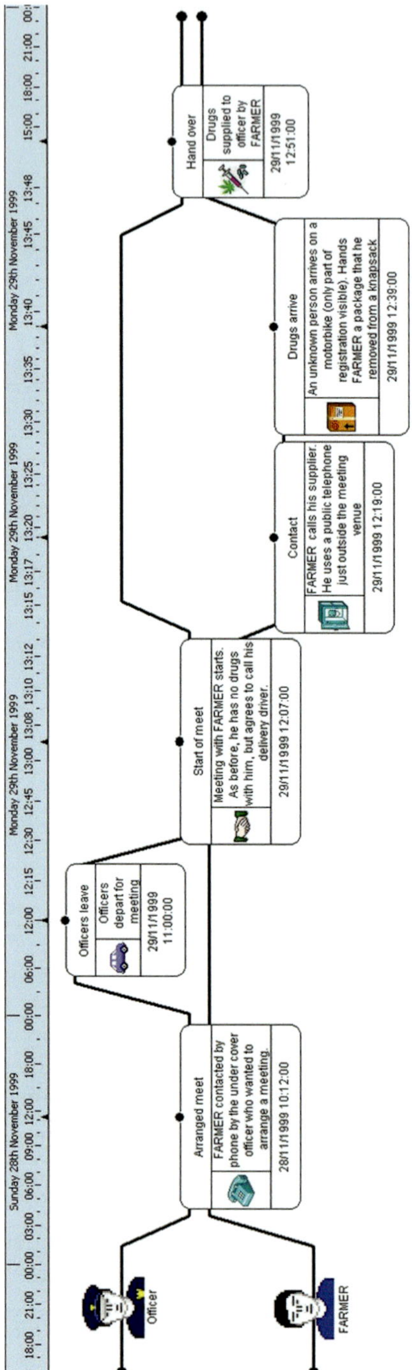

FIGURE 10.11 Example of timeline analysis (Analyst's Notebook).

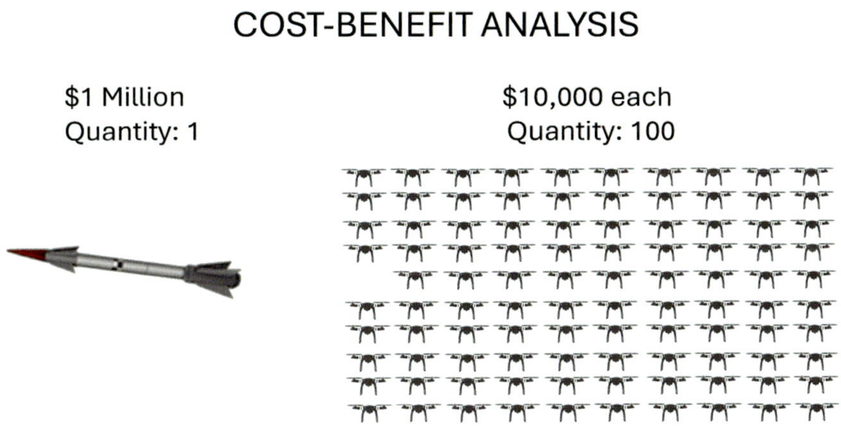

FIGURE 10.12 Simplified CBA for an expensive missile vs. cheap drones.

approach to decision-making, especially when resources are limited and trade-offs must be made. See Figure 10.12 for an oversimplified CBA for an expensive missile vs. a cheap drone. By examining tangible and intangible costs and benefits over a defined period, CBA provides a clear view of each option's value. Whether you are evaluating the feasibility of a new initiative or comparing competing alternatives, CBA transforms complexity into clarity.

When to Use

CBA is essential when analysts need to justify the feasibility or soundness of a decision or project. Governments, for example, use CBA in policy analysis to weigh the societal benefits of infrastructure projects, healthcare reforms, or defense spending. In military contexts, CBA can help commanders determine whether the potential benefits of an operation outweigh the associated risks, such as loss of life or financial costs. The process involves comparing labor, time, resources, and other costs against the expected benefits to ensure strategic and fiscally sound decisions.[37]

Public sector organizations rely on CBA to guide large-scale decisions, from building transportation infrastructure to shaping health, education, or environmental policies. CBA's power lies in its ability to make abstract outcomes (like improved quality of life) comparable to concrete costs (such as dollars or labor hours). It can be used across various fields, including defense, education, criminal justice, etc.[38]

Why Use CBA?

CBA serves two crucial purposes:

- To justify a decision's soundness – Is the investment worth the resources? Can it be justified financially or in terms of impact?
- To compare competing decisions or projects – When you need to decide between several options, CBA shows which would deliver the greatest return on investment, whether that is measured in dollars, time, or outcomes like improved public safety, lives saved, or cleaner air (see Table 10.3).

Example: Cost-Benefit Analysis for Missile vs. Drones

Scenario

Let us apply the 7-step Cost-Benefit Analysis (CBA) process to compare the $1 million missile vs. the $50 drone. This will follow the prior-structured approach to weigh tangible and intangible costs and benefits.

1. Define the Activity/Project/Policy

We are evaluating the decision to use a $1 million missile to destroy a $50 drone. This scenario occurs within the context of military defense, where the drone may pose some threat, such as gathering intelligence or delivering a payload. At the same time, the missile is a high-cost, high-capability asset. The analysis period will cover the immediate event (single missile launch) and consider longer-term impacts such as reputation, resource depletion, and opportunity costs.

2. List the Alternatives

Here are the alternatives for handling the $50 drone:

- *Option 1: Use the $1 million missile to destroy the drone.*
- *Option 2: Use electronic warfare (such as jamming or hacking) to disable the drone.*
- *Option 3: Deploy a lower-cost anti-aircraft missile (e.g., $20,000 short-range missile) or ground-based intercept system.*
- *Option 4: Deploy a small interceptor drone (~$10,000–$20,000) to neutralize the target.*
- *Option 5: Take no immediate action, allowing the drone to continue its mission, assuming it poses a low-level threat (e.g., reconnaissance only).*

TABLE 10.3 How to Perform a Cost-Benefit Analysis: Step-by-Step

Method
1. ***Define the Activity, Project, or Policy.*** *Start by identifying what you are evaluating. Whether it is a new public transit system, a defense project, or a criminal justice policy, clearly articulate the project scope and the time period over which the costs and benefits will be measured.*
2. ***List the Alternatives. Every Decision Has Alternatives.*** *Whether it is different policy options, alternative projects, or a "do nothing" scenario, list them out. Each alternative should be realistic and provide some contrast to the others in terms of cost or outcome. This step sets the stage for comparison.*
3. ***Identify Key Factors for Comparison.*** *What are the critical variables for each alternative? Is it the dollar amount, human lives affected, environmental impact, or future cost savings? Each factor should have a clear rationale behind its inclusion. For instance, if analyzing a healthcare policy, immediate financial costs, and long-term public health outcomes would be significant.*
4. ***Estimate Costs for Each Alternative.*** *Identify all associated costs, from initial capital outlays to ongoing maintenance or staffing needs. This might include labor hours, monetary expenditures, resource consumption, and intangible costs like time or societal disruption. Develop a mechanism to gather this data through internal accounting methods or external benchmarks.*
5. ***Estimate the Benefits Similarly.*** *Estimate the expected benefits for each option. These benefits could be monetary, like increased revenue or cost savings, but they could also be non-monetary: improved public safety, increased happiness or productivity, and enhanced quality of life. Benefits, such as improved organizational morale or environmental sustainability, can sometimes be indirect.*
6. ***Compare Costs vs. Benefits with All the Data Collected.*** *Now, compare the costs and benefits of each alternative. Array them side-by-side in a matrix or chart for easy comparison. Which alternative provides the highest benefit for the lowest price? And how much do the benefits outweigh the costs, if at all?*
7. ***Make a Final Recommendation Based on the Comparison.*** *Select the option that offers the best value, considering both quantitative and qualitative factors. Be sure to justify your choice by referencing the data and explaining how it aligns with broader goals, such as fiscal responsibility, public health, business opportunities, or environmental protection.*

Note: This is a simple step-by-step explanation of CBA. In reality, it will be significantly more complex.

3. Identify Key Factors for Comparison

To compare these alternatives, we will consider the following factors:

- *Monetary cost: Direct expenditure on equipment, maintenance, and operations.*
- *Effectiveness: The ability to neutralize the drone and ensure it does not complete its mission.*
- *Opportunity cost: The impact on future missions of using high-value assets (such as a $1 million missile).*
- *Reputation and strategic impact: How the decision affects public and military perception and potential political fallout.*
- *Risk of collateral damage: Especially relevant for high-power munitions in populated or sensitive areas.*
- *Deterrence value: The potential to deter future drone incursions or similar threats.*
- *Environmental or logistical costs: Long-term environmental damage or the logistical challenges of each option.*

4. Estimate Costs for Each Alternative

Option 1: $1 Million Missile

- *Monetary Cost: $1,000,000 for the missile, plus operational costs (fuel, personnel). Let us estimate an additional $10,000 in operational expenses.*
- *Opportunity Cost: Using a high-value missile could reduce the availability of this asset for more significant threats. There may also be a delay or cost associated with restocking the missile.*
- *Reputation Costs: Using such an expensive asset against a low-cost target could draw public or international criticism as excessive, though it demonstrates strong military capability.*

Option 2: Electronic Warfare

- *Monetary Cost: Deploying electronic warfare assets (jamming, hacking) may cost around $100,000.*
- *Effectiveness: High probability of success in neutralizing the drone's communications or disabling it entirely, depending on its technology.*
- *Reputation: Less public visibility but shows sophisticated, cost-efficient tactics.*

Option 3: Lower-Cost Anti-Aircraft Missile

- *Monetary Cost: A short-range missile costs approximately $20,000, with operational costs adding $5,000.*
- *Effectiveness: High likelihood of drone destruction without overkill.*
- *Reputation: A reasonable, proportional response, potentially positive both publicly and militarily.*

Option 4: Interceptor Drone

- *Monetary Cost: Deploying a drone interceptor would cost around $10,000–$20,000.*
- *Effectiveness: High probability of success, with the potential to capture the drone for intelligence gathering. Reusable asset for future threats.*
- *Reputation: Positive perception of innovation and efficiency.*

Option 5: Do Nothing

- *Monetary Cost: $0 in direct costs.*
- Effectiveness: *The drone may continue its mission and gather valuable intelligence or deploy a payload.*
- *Reputation: Perceived as inaction, signaling weakness or vulnerability to adversaries.*

5. Estimate the Benefits for Each Alternative

Option 1: $1 Million Missile

- *Benefit: Immediate, guaranteed destruction of the drone. Potential deterrence effect for future threats.*
- *Reputation Benefit: Demonstrates overwhelming military capability, which could deter adversaries.*

Option 2: Electronic Warfare

- *Benefit: Disables the drone without destruction, potentially recovering valuable intelligence or technology.*
- *Reputation Benefit: Showcases the use of advanced, cost-effective tactics without physical escalation.*

Option 3: Lower-Cost Anti-Aircraft Missile

- *Benefit: Drone destruction is likely at a fraction of the cost. Maintains high availability of critical, expensive assets for more significant threats.*
- *Reputation Benefit: Proportional military response, positive in both domestic and international perception.*

Option 4: Interceptor Drone

- *Benefit: The drone is neutralized and may even be captured intact for analysis. The interceptor drone can be reused.*
- *Reputation Benefit: Highlights technological innovation and efficiency, likely generating positive public perception.*

Option 5: Do Nothing

- *Benefit: Saves all resources but may lead to significant intelligence or physical risk if the drone gathers critical information or deploys a payload.*
- *Reputation: Major risk of signaling weakness*, **emboldening future adversaries.**

6. Compare Costs vs. Benefits

Here is a simple comparison of costs and benefits across all alternatives (see Table 10.4).

Option 6: Make a Final Recommendation

- *After evaluating all alternatives, the best recommendation would be to deploy a lower-cost anti-aircraft missile or an interceptor drone. Both options provide a cost-effective solution with high effectiveness while minimizing reputational and opportunity costs. The $1 million missile is overkill for such a tiny target, making it a less practical option unless the drone presents a much greater risk than currently known. Electronic warfare is also a viable option, mainly if intelligence collection is a priority, but it is less certain in terms of effectiveness.*
- *The final recommendation balances military efficiency, cost, and the need to deter future threats with minimal risk of collateral damage or international criticism.*

Final CBA Thoughts

CBA is not just a tool for intelligence analysis; it is a decision-making tool and a way to think critically about any weighty choice. In today's fast-paced world of constrained resources and high-stakes decisions, CBA empowers leaders to move forward confidently, knowing that a thoughtful and data-driven process supports their choices.

TABLE 10.4 Results of the CBA

Factor	*$1M Missile*	*Electronic Warfare*	*Low-Cost Missile*	*Interceptor Drone*	*Do Nothing*
Monetary Cost	$1,010,000	$100,000	$25,000	$10,000–$20,000	$0
Effectiveness	Very High	High	High	High	None
Opportunity Cost	High	Low	Low	Low	N/A
Reputation Cost	Risk of Overkill	Efficient and Positive	Proportional and Positive	Innovative and Positive	Negative (perceived inaction)
Collateral Risk	Moderate (depending on area)	None	Low	Very Low	None
Deterrence	High	Moderate	Moderate	Moderate	Low

FIGURE 10.13 Soldiers sorting information (Department of Defense).

By breaking complex problems down into measurable components, CBA allows us to make informed decisions that balance the present and future, ensuring the most significant impact for the lowest cost.

Sorting: Organizing Data for Maximum Insight

Sorting is a foundational technique for arranging and categorizing information to reveal insights and facilitate analysis. The purpose of sorting information is to optimize its usefulness for specific tasks. By grouping data based on shared characteristics, such as category, size, time, or geographic location, analysts can optimize their ability to extract meaning from large datasets (see Figure 10.13).

When to Use

Sorting is especially valuable when analysts face overwhelming volumes of data, a common challenge in intelligence work. For example, sorting intelligence reports by location or event type in counterterrorism can reveal hidden connections between disparate activities. In cybersecurity, sorting threat data by source or severity helps identify attack patterns. Whether the dataset is large or small, sorting helps analysts focus on the most critical information, enabling them to form conclusions more efficiently.[39]

Example: Sorting Intel Data in Counterinsurgency in Urban Operations

Scenario

A military intelligence unit is tasked with supporting a counterinsurgency operation in a densely populated urban area. Intelligence analysts face an overwhelming volume of data from various sources, including human intelligence (HUMINT) reports, signals intelligence (SIGINT), drone footage, intercepted communications, and social media activity. The goal is to identify patterns of insurgent activity, locate safe houses, and prevent imminent attacks.

Problem

The sheer amount of raw intelligence creates information overload. Without organization, it is nearly impossible to detect hidden patterns or critical information, such as the location of insurgent cells or planned attack timing. Analysts need to quickly make sense of the information to provide actionable insights to commanders on the ground.

Sorting Method

To manage this influx of data, intelligence analysts apply sorting to categorize the information based on key shared characteristics, such as:

- **Location:** Analysts group intelligence by geographic areas (e.g., neighborhoods, districts) where insurgent activities are reported. Sorting by location helps them identify clusters of activity or specific regions where insurgents are concentrating their efforts.
- **Event Type:** Reports are sorted based on the nature of events (e.g., IED attacks, arms smuggling, recruitment efforts). This reveals patterns, such as a spike in certain types of attacks, enabling analysts to predict future operations.
- **Time:** Sorting by time helps create a timeline of insurgent actions. This is especially useful to identify when attacks are likely to occur based on historical patterns or recent surges in activity.
- **Insurgent Affiliation:** By categorizing reports according to the insurgent groups or factions involved, analysts can discern which groups are most active and where their influence is growing. This helps prioritize targeting and resource allocation.

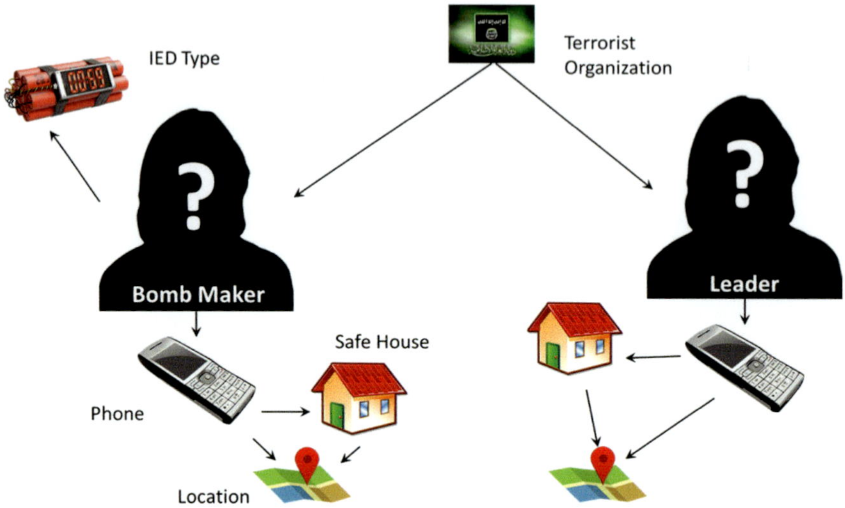

FIGURE 10.14 Network drawing of terrorist affiliations obtained from sorting intel data.

Analysis

After sorting, analysts notice that most insurgent attacks in one district occur after midnight, often following communications between specific phone numbers traced to known insurgent leaders. They also find that certain safe houses in the western part of the city serve as hubs for arms smuggling, which is corroborated by multiple HUMINT and SIGINT reports. These insights allow the intelligence team to brief commanders with actionable data, recommending increased patrols in specific areas during critical time windows (see Figure 10.14).

Outcome

The intelligence unit successfully identifies key insurgent safe houses and disrupts arms smuggling operations thanks to the sorting process. By narrowing their focus, analysts also provide commanders with accurate predictions about insurgent activity, leading to several preemptive strikes and the capture of key insurgent leaders. This significantly weakens the insurgents' operational capabilities and improves the overall security situation in the urban area.

Summary

In this military intelligence scenario, sorting helped analysts manage large volumes of data, turning chaos into order. By organizing information by location, event type, time, and affiliation, they extracted critical insights, optimized decision-making, and more effectively supported counterinsurgency efforts.

Event Trees and Fault Trees: Mapping Events and Their Outcomes

Event trees and fault trees are graphical techniques used to map the sequence of events and explore potential outcomes based on conditional probabilities. While they are often confused, the two serve different purposes: Event trees focus on the logical sequence of events and possible outcomes; at the same time, fault trees concentrate more on identifying system failures and their underlying causes[40] (see Figure 10.15 and Figure 10.16).

Event Tree Analysis

Event tree analysis (ETA) is a forward-looking, inductive method used to model the possible outcomes of an initial "initiating event" (such as a

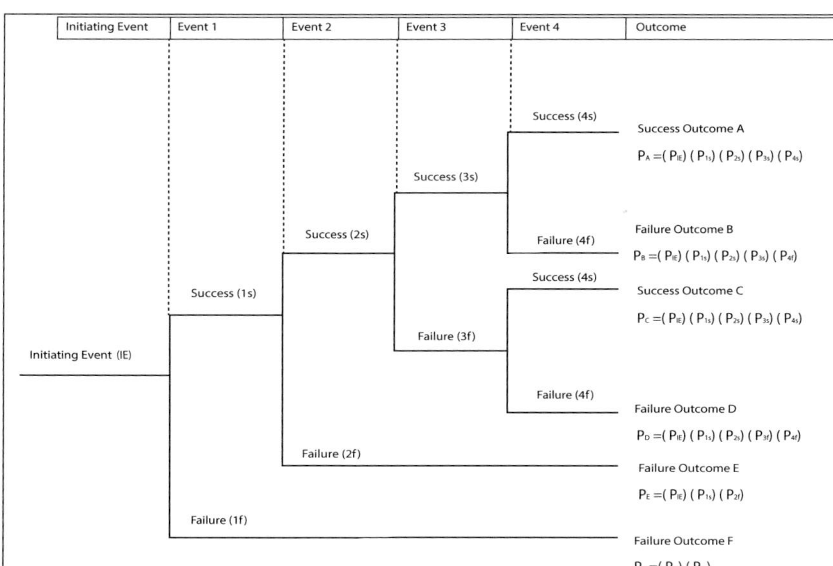

FIGURE 10.15 Example of event tree analysis.

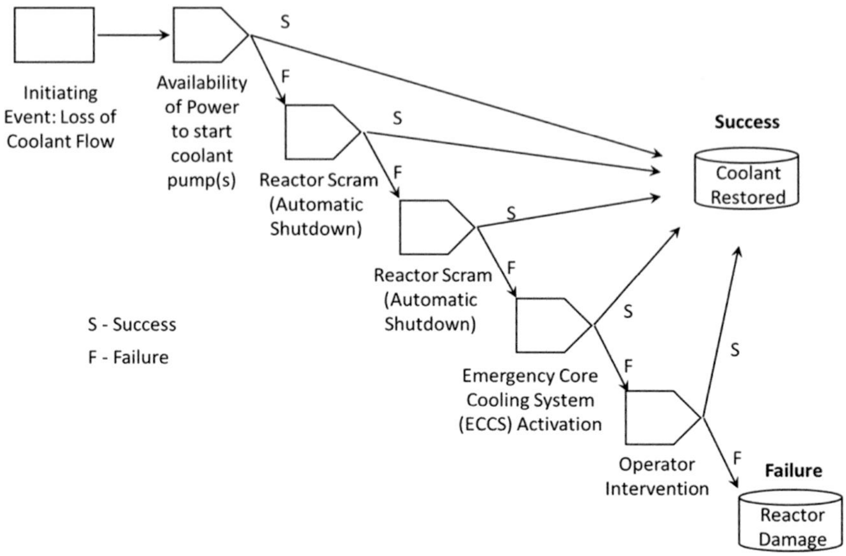

FIGURE 10.16 Event tree for a reactor meltdown.

failure or hazard) and trace how different systems or processes respond to this event.

ETA focuses on sequences of events and is used to analyze the success or failure of safety systems that mitigate risk after an initiating event.

Each branch of the event tree represents a different outcome, and the tree shows all possible paths to success/failure and their consequences.

When Is ETA Best Utilized?

- **Accident Scenario Modeling:** ETA is best used when you want to model how a system responds to a failure and what the possible outcomes could be, such as in the aviation, nuclear power, or chemical industries.
- **Assessing Safety Systems:** This is particularly useful for evaluating how well safety measures, such as backup systems, emergency shutdowns, or operator interventions, mitigate risk after an incident occurs.
- **Risk Management:** ETA is ideal for understanding how various combinations of system successes and failures can affect overall safety or risk (see Table 10.5).

Fault Tree Analysis

Fault tree analysis (FTA) is a deductive, top-down approach that starts with an undesired "top event" (such as a system failure or accident) and

TABLE 10.5 Event Tree Step-by-Step Process

Method
1. **Define the Initiating Event:** *The initiating event is the starting point of the analysis. In this case, it is the failure of the main coolant system.*
2. **Identify the Safety Systems:** *Determine what systems are designed to prevent the event's progression. For this scenario:* • *Backup coolant system* • *Automatic reactor shutdown system* • *Manual intervention by operators*
3. **List the Possible Outcomes for Each System:** *Each safety system can function successfully or fail. This creates branches in the event tree for each possible outcome.*
4. **Determine the Consequences:** *For each combination of system success or failure, identify the potential consequence, which ranges from no significant impact to a catastrophic event.*
5. **Build the Event Tree:** *Using the initiating event as the trunk, create branches for each safety system, representing success and failure. The branches continue for each subsequent system.*
6. **Analyze the Outcomes:** *Review the event tree branches to understand the likelihood and severity of various consequences.*

works backward to find all possible root causes or combinations of failures that could lead to that event.

FTA uses logical gates (like AND, OR gates) to model the interaction between different causes and helps identify the weakest links in the system that could lead to failure.

When Is FTA Best Utilized?

- **Failure Cause Analysis:** FTA is useful when you want to trace the causes of a specific undesired event and break it down into its contributing factors. This helps in the understanding of the failure mechanism.
- **System Reliability Assessment:** It is best for identifying vulnerabilities or "single points of failure" within complex systems, often used in the design phase of engineering projects (e.g., aerospace, automotive).
- **Problem Diagnosis:** FTA is excellent for diagnosing and preventing failures by helping to isolate root causes that, if addressed, could prevent future occurrences of the failure (see Table 10.6).

TABLE 10.6 Fault Tree Step-by-Step Process

Method
1. ***Create the Top Event:*** *Start by writing down the top event. Some examples include a network/security breach at a government facility, a power plant unexpectedly going offline, a commercial jet crash, or an operational security breach.*
2. ***Add Main Categories Using OR Gates:*** *Beneath the top event (security breach), use OR gates to represent what could happen due to any one of the following:* • ***Unauthorized Entry*** • ***System Compromise*** • ***Physical Security Lapse***
• *For a power plant unexpectedly going offline:* – ***Equipment Failure*** *(e.g., a key piece of plant equipment, such as a turbine, generator, or transformer experiences a mechanical or electrical failure)* – ***Grid Instability or Overload*** *(e.g., sudden grid disturbances, such as fluctuations in voltage or frequency, can cause the plant to trip offline to protect the equipment)* – ***Operator Error or Human Intervention*** *(e.g., human error during operation, maintenance, or system control can unintentionally lead to the plant going offline)*
• *For a commercial jet crash:* – **Mechanical Failure** – **Pilot Error** – **Severe Weather Conditions**
• *For a breach of operational security:* – ***Insider Threat:*** *(e.g., an employee or authorized individual deliberately or inadvertently compromises the security system)* – ***Unauthorized Access:*** *(e.g., a failure in physical or digital access control mechanisms that allows unauthorized individuals to enter restricted areas or systems)* – ***System Vulnerability Exploitation:*** *(e.g., exploitation of unpatched software vulnerabilities or misconfigured network systems by external attackers)*
3. ***Add Subcauses and Break Each Category into Specific Causes:*** • *Use an OR gate to represent that it could happen due to, e.g., human error (under security breach), could be a lack of security oversight, or possible improper ID verification.* • *Continue breaking down each cause into more specific events.*
4. ***Draw the Fault Tree:*** *Use software (e.g., PowerPoint™, Lucidchart™) or draw by hand to arrange the fault tree visually. Note: be sure to properly use OR gates to show that an event can happen if any input cause occurs. Basic events (circles) for events like "Failed ID verification" that are not broken down further. Use undeveloped events (diamonds) if you cannot further analyze a cause.*

Note: The completed fault tree will show the top event at the top, leading down to the categories and further breaking down each category into more specific subcauses. Use OR gates, basic events, and undeveloped events where appropriate.

PRACTICAL EXERCISE: CREATING A FAULT TREE CHART FOR A NETWORK SECURITY BREACH

This exercise allows students to create a fault tree analysis from scratch, helping them understand how security failures can have multiple potential causes and how to represent them visually using standardized symbols.

This exercise demonstrates the importance of analyzing systems (military, government, or private industry), particularly physical and cybersecurity measures and operational vulnerabilities, such as power outages. The facility can significantly reduce the risk of future breaches by identifying and addressing weaknesses in backup systems, door lock protocols, and network security.

Logic Symbols

Specific elements (symbols) are included for a more straightforward representation to properly recreate the fault tree with standardized fault tree symbols like AND gates, OR gates, basic events, undeveloped events, and other recognized symbols used in fault tree analysis.

Here is an explanation of the symbols:

- *OR Gate*: Output occurs if any input event happens.
- *AND Gate*: Output occurs only if all input events happen.
- *Basic Event (Circle)*: Initiating event not broken down further.
- *Undeveloped Event (Diamond)*: Event that could occur but is not further developed due to a lack of information or significance (see Figure 10.17).

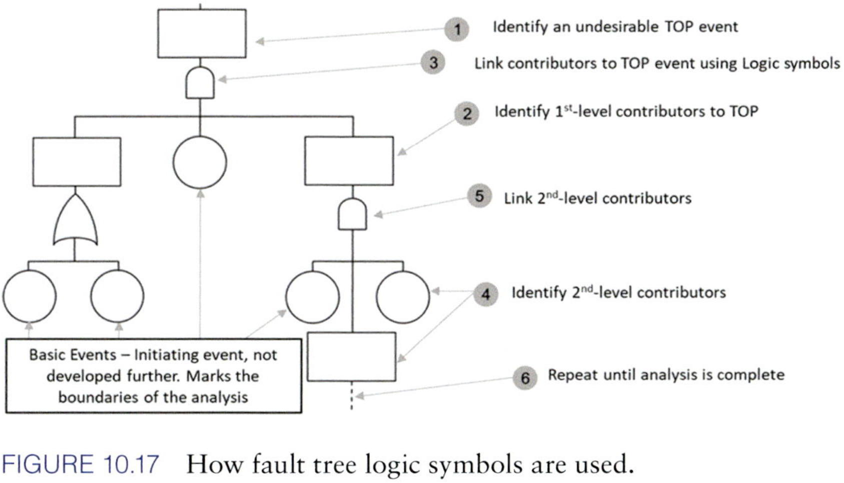

FIGURE 10.17 How fault tree logic symbols are used.

Objective

Students will learn how to construct a fault tree chart step by step using a network security breach scenario in a government facility. The exercise will guide them in identifying causes and using standardized symbols such as AND gates, OR gates, and basic events to create a visual fault tree.

Scenario

A government facility experienced a security breach. The objective is to analyze and represent the possible root causes of the breach using a fault tree.

Incident Summary

On the night of September 15, 2024, a security breach occurred at the (Fictitious Government Facility) during off-day shift hours. The breach involved the following critical failures:

1. Power failure disables physical security systems, including cameras and alarms.
2. Door lock malfunction, allowing unauthorized entry into a secure facility area.
3. An infected USB device, introduced by an intruder, compromises sensitive network systems.

This report outlines the sequence of events, contributing factors, and recommendations for corrective action to prevent future incidents (see Table 10.7).

Incident Analysis

1. **Power Failure (Physical Security System Failure)**
   - The external power failure triggered a shutdown of the facility's electronic security measures, including cameras, alarms, and door locks.
   - Because the generator's auto start had been disabled, the backup power systems failed to engage immediately, leaving the facility vulnerable for over an hour.
   - Alarms in the control room alerted security personnel to the power outage, but due to miscommunication and delays in technical response, security measures could not be restored quickly.
   - Manual security protocols were insufficient, as security guards were unprepared for an extended power outage scenario, leaving several access points vulnerable.

TABLE 10.7 Timeline of Events Provided by Security Personnel

Time	*Event Description*
22:35	***Power Failure:*** *External power loss affects the facility. Backup power systems fail to activate automatically, leading to a total shutdown of critical physical security systems (alarms, surveillance cameras, and electronic locks). The facility is left in a vulnerable state for over an hour.*
22:50	***Control Room Alarm:*** *The control room receives a "Loss of Power" alarm from the backup power generator system. Control room staff attempts to reboot the system but fails, delaying communication with external maintenance teams.*
23:00	***Security Staff Report:*** *Security personnel report that the electronic door locks are malfunctioning. Manual lock procedures have been initiated, but due to the power outage, electronic logs of door access are unavailable.*
23:45	***Unauthorized Entry:*** *An unidentified person dressed as a maintenance worker is observed entering the facility through an electronically malfunctioning door. The camera system has a separate power system but does not record the incident. Security guards fail to physically monitor the area because of understaffing during the night shift.*
23:55	***Suspicious USB Activity:*** *An intruder introduces an infected USB drive into Server Rack D4 in Server Room #1. This triggers an automatic malware injection into the network, compromising sensitive data. The breach goes unnoticed until later.*
00:15	***Security Responds:*** *A security patrol team notices an unauthorized individual in a restricted area. The intruder flees before being apprehended. The control room is notified, and an internal investigation begins.*
00:45	***Power Restored:*** *Maintenance personnel discovered the backup generator's auto-start switch had been placed in the "OFF" position. The generator was manually started, and power was restored to the facility, but the damage had already occurred. Cameras and door lock logs were reviewed but showed no footage or digital evidence during the blackout period.*
01:10	***Server Room Compromise Detected:*** *IT staff detected abnormal network activity. An infected USB drive was used, resulting in the malware's injection into the system. Sensitive data might have been accessed. IT immediately isolated the compromised system.*
01:30	***Police Report Filed:*** *Local law enforcement is contacted to investigate the breach. A detailed incident report is submitted, and security footage leading up to the power failure is handed over.*
02:00	***Security Lockdown:*** *The facility is placed on heightened alert. Additional security staff is called in for the investigation, and security protocols are reviewed. The south-side generator room door latch was discovered to have adhesive tape on the outer door, preventing it from latching properly.*
02:30	***Security Hands the Intruder over to the Police:*** *The police physically search the intruder, find a driver's license, and determine that the culprit is a data center employee who was recently reprimanded for being in a secure area without authorization.*

2. **Door Lock Malfunction (Unauthorized Entry)**
   - The power failure led to a malfunction in the electronic door locks, which allowed unauthorized access to restricted areas.
   - Security staff did not perform routine physical patrols during the breach due to short-staffing on the night shift.
   - The intruder could gain access through a malfunctioning door without triggering any alarm due to the lack of power.
   - A review of security procedures showed that manual locking procedures had not been adequately implemented or followed, which might have deterred unauthorized entry.

3. **Infected USB Device (Malware Injection)**
   1. After gaining access, the intruder entered the control room and inserted an infected USB device into a workstation.
   2. The USB drive contained malware, which compromised sensitive data on the network.
   3. Security staff initially did not notice the malicious activity until IT staff detected anomalous behavior in the system.
   4. An investigation revealed that the malware allowed the attacker to access confidential files and potentially compromise several secure systems.
   5. Network isolation procedures were implemented, but only after the breach had occurred, minimizing the scope of the attack but not preventing it.

Statements from Personnel

1. **Control Room Operator Statement**
   At around 22:50, we received an alarm from the backup generator system, indicating a total power failure. We tried rebooting the systems, but the cameras and electronic door locks were down. We contacted maintenance, but there was no immediate response. We manually initiated the door lock override but couldn't monitor all entry points due to the system failure.

2. **Security Staff (Patrol) Statement**
   We noticed someone moving in the restricted area outside the generator room around 23:45, but by the time we responded, the individual had already accessed the building. The south-side generator door lock had been tampered with. The interior door electronic locks were not functioning, and it was difficult to track movement because of the power outage. We called for backup and secured the area as soon as possible.

3. IT Department Statement

At around 01:10, we saw unusual network activity from one of the server racks. Upon inspection, we found an infected USB drive in the server rack D4 in Server RM #1, which had initiated a malware attack. We isolated the affected systems, but sensitive data may have been compromised.

Alarms Received

- **22:50**: "Loss of Power" alarm from the backup power system.
- **23:55**: Suspicious network activity triggered by malware detection (logged by IT monitoring systems).

Police Report Summary

The police report indicates that an individual posing as a maintenance worker entered the facility during the blackout period. The lack of surveillance and operational door locks allowed access to sensitive areas. Introducing the USB drive suggests deliberate actions to compromise the facility's network systems. Local law enforcement is investigating the incident, and additional security measures are recommended. The suspect is in police custody and is not cooperating with investigators (see Table 10.8).

Table 10.8 outlines various analytical issues/problems along with the most appropriate analytical techniques that analysts can select to assist in resolving them.

Note: The "Timeline" technique is not designed as a stand-alone method but is most useful when combined with other analytical approaches.

Conclusion (Pattern Recognition Techniques)

Pattern recognition techniques give intelligence analysts powerful tools to distill clarity from complex and voluminous data. Analysts can identify hidden patterns, forecast potential threats, and understand intricate relationships within datasets by systematically applying methods such as social network analysis, trend analysis, and geospatial analysis. These techniques are crucial for illuminating what might otherwise remain obscured. Pattern recognition techniques also possess a versatility that can be used across various domains, from military operations to criminal forensics and business intelligence.

Moreover, integrating pattern recognition with other structured analytical techniques, like SWOT Analysis and Cost-Benefit Analysis,

TABLE 10.8 Analytical Issues/Problems vs. Appropriate Diagnostic Techniques Matrix

Analysis Issue/Problem \ Analytical Technique	Trend Analysis*	(SWOT) Strengths, Weaknesses, Opportunities, and Threats	Five Forces Analysis	Social Network Analysis	Classic Pattern Recognition	Geospatial Analysis*	Timeline Analysis	Cost Benefit Analysis (CBA)	Sorting	Event Trees and Fault Trees
Tactical and Strategic Operations Planning and Assessment	X	X	X	X	X	X	X	X	X	X
Current situation in a short period of time		X				X				
Political (or other competitive) environment surrounding a government (or criminal/terror) organizational entity		X	X					X		X
Modeling organizational communication patterns				X						
Determining event patterns and predict potential hazards	X				X	X	X	X		
Understanding cause and effect and identifying patterns							X			X
Performing targeting analysis					X	X				
Determining soundness of a decision		X						X		
Providing a basis for comparing projects/decisions		X						X		
When absorbing and evaluating a large amount of data									X	
Tracking events to monitor and evaluate changes	X									
Weighing validity of sources/information	X	X	X	X	X	X	X	X	X	X
Checking/rechecking key assumptions		X	X					X		

enables a more holistic and rigorous approach to intelligence work. This combination allows for a deeper understanding of the dynamics at play, leading to more informed decision-making and strategic planning. As intelligence challenges grow in complexity, effectively utilizing these pattern recognition techniques becomes increasingly vital for transforming data into actionable intelligence and maintaining a strategic advantage in ever-evolving environments.

DIAGNOSTIC TECHNIQUES IN INTELLIGENCE ANALYSIS

Diagnostic techniques in intelligence analysis are tools used to make analytic arguments, assumptions, and intelligence gaps more transparent. These techniques encourage analysts to critically assess the basis of their judgments, with the goal of enhancing objectivity and mitigating bias. The four key diagnostic techniques commonly employed to challenge and validate an analyst's mindset include:

- Key Assumptions Check
- Quality of Information Check
- Indicators or Signposts of Change
- Analysis of Competing Hypotheses (ACH)

Key Assumptions Check

The Key Assumptions Check aims to systematically review the assumptions underpinning key judgments, aiming to make both stated and unstated premises explicit. A key assumption is a foundational hypothesis that is accepted as accurate and forms the basis of the analysis.

> ***Examples:***
>
> *In military analysis, assumptions about the operational environment (e.g., desert conditions) shape the interpretation of military capabilities. Historically, the U.S. analysis of Soviet-Warsaw Pact operations against NATO had to "assume" a level of non-Soviet Warsaw Pact reliability (e.g., would these forces fight?). In this case, there was a high degree of uncertainty. Depending on the level of reliability one assumed, the analyst could arrive at very different conclusions about a potential Soviet offensive operation.*
>
> *Similarly, economic analysts might assume political stability in a foreign country when assessing potential reforms without considering how fluctuations in this stability might alter outcomes. The goal of this technique is not to dismiss key assumptions but to scrutinize them, identifying the conditions that warrant reevaluation.*
>
> *The goal of this technique is not to dismiss key assumptions but to scrutinize them, identifying the conditions that warrant reevaluation. Likewise, political analysts reviewing a developing country's domestic stability might unconsciously assume stable oil prices when this fundamental determinant of economic performance and underlying social peace might fluctuate.*
>
> *These examples highlight that analysts often rely on stated and unstated assumptions to conduct their analysis. The goal is not to undermine or abandon key assumptions but to make them explicit and identify what information or developments would demand reassessment.*[41]

When to Use

A Key Assumptions Check is most effective at the outset of an analytic project. It ensures that the analytical foundation is sound by revealing hidden or unexamined assumptions. Periodic reassessments throughout the analysis process can help avoid errors caused by reliance on outdated or inaccurate assumptions.

Reassessing assumptions may also be valuable before finalizing judgments to ensure the assessment does not rest on flawed premises. Identifying hidden assumptions can be one of the most difficult challenges an analyst faces, as they are ideas often held subconsciously to be accurate; therefore, they are seldom examined and rarely challenged[42] (see Table 10.9).

Quality of Information Check

The Quality of Information Check is a critical technique for evaluating the completeness, accuracy, and reliability of the sources that inform intelligence analysis. This process is not a one-time effort but an ongoing,

TABLE 10.9 Steps Involved in the Key Assumptions Check

Method	*Questions to Ask*
Checking for key assumptions requires analysts to consider how their analysis depends on the validity of certain premises, which they do not routinely question or believe to be in doubt. A four-step process will help analysts: 1. ***Review:*** *Write down the current analytic line or hypothesis.* 2. ***List Assumptions:*** *Identify all explicit and implicit assumptions that support the analysis.* 3. ***Challenge Assumptions:*** *Question why each assumption must be accurate and whether it holds under all conditions.* 4. ***Refine Assumptions:*** *Narrow down to those assumptions that must be true for the analysis to hold and consider what developments might undermine them.*	***Key questions to ask during this process include:*** • *How confident are we that this assumption is correct?* • *What would change our confidence level?* • *What information could disprove this assumption?* • *Could this assumption have been valid in the past but no longer applicable?* • *If the assumption proves wrong, would it significantly alter the analytic line? If so, how?* • *Has this process identified new factors that need further analysis?*

dynamic approach to ensure that analytic judgments are based on sound information.

When to Use

Assessing the validity of sources is fundamental to rigorous critical thinking. The confidence in an analytic judgment should be directly tied to the trustworthiness of the underlying information. Intelligence analysis is highly vulnerable to becoming anchored to weak or outdated information if source reliability is not continually scrutinized. This makes the quality of information check a necessary, ongoing process.

While multiple sources enhance an analysis, quantity should never be mistaken for quality. A thorough examination of information sources is essential to avoiding analytic errors. Analysts must periodically reassess the strength and relevance of their information, especially before making significant assessments. This ensures that past caveats or uncertainties are not overlooked and that new developments are integrated into the broader context of an evolving intelligence picture.

Analysts should collectively or individually review the information base whenever a critical analysis is conducted. This process helps them refresh their understanding of the intelligence reporting's origins, strengths, and limitations, which underpin their judgments. By recognizing the circumstances in which critical information was gathered, analysts can more accurately assess its validity and set an appropriate confidence level in the final intelligence product[43] (see Table 10.10).

Indicators or Signposts of Change: A Dynamic Tool for Intelligence Analysis

The Indicators or Signposts of Change technique is a structured, proactive method for systematically monitoring observable events or trends to track developments, identify emerging patterns, and anticipate unexpected changes. By periodically reviewing a carefully curated list of indicators, analysts can assess the evolution of critical issues and ensure early detection of environmental shifts, whether economic, military, political, or societal.

When to Use

An analyst or team can create a list of indicators reflecting the observable events or variables one would expect to see if a particular situation unfolds. This may involve tracking economic reforms, military advancements, political instability, democratization, or other evolving situations. Depending on the issue's complexity, identifying and selecting critical indicators may take only a few hours or require several days of in-depth analysis.

TABLE 10.10 Steps Involved in a Quality of Information Check

Method
1. *An analyst or a team might begin a "quality of information" check by developing a database in which information is stored according to source type and date, with additional notations indicating strengths or weaknesses in those sources. Ideally, analysts would have a retrieval and search capability on the database so that periodic reviews are less labor intensive and result in a more complete review of all sources used in past analyses. Analysts will need as much background information on sources as possible for the information review to be fully effective. Knowing the circumstances in which reporting was obtained is often critical to understanding its validity. With the data in hand, analysts can then:*
2. *Review systematically all sources for accuracy.*
3. *Identify information sources that appear most critical or compelling.*
4. *Check for sufficient and strong corroboration of critical reporting.*
5. *Reexamine previously dismissed information in light of new facts or circumstances that cast it in a different light.*
6. *Ensure that any recalled reporting is identified and adequately flagged for other analysts; analysis based on recalled reporting should also be reviewed to determine if the reporting was essential to the judgments made.*
7. *Consider whether ambiguous information has been interpreted and caveated correctly.*
8. *Indicate a level of confidence analysts can place in sources likely to figure in future analytic assessments.*

This method is particularly useful when analysts need to monitor a situation over time. It can also enhance other structured analytic techniques by helping assess mounting evidence supporting or against a hypothesis, potential scenario, or low-probability event.

When facing divergent views on an issue, the Indicators or Signposts method can serve as a neutral framework, helping to shift focus toward a shared set of objective criteria. This approach depersonalizes the debate and helps clarify the core areas of substantive disagreement. Once all parties agree on the key indicators, they can assess ongoing developments more clearly and resolve differences based on concrete evidence rather than subjective interpretations.

In an era of rapid change and complex challenges, the Indicators or Signposts of Change technique empowers analysts to stay ahead of the curve, making it an indispensable tool in modern intelligence analysis[44] (see Table 10.11).

TABLE 10.11 Process of Developing Indicators or Signposts of Change

Method
Whether used alone or in combination with other structured analyses, the process is the same: 1. *Identify a set of competing hypotheses or scenarios.* 2. *Create separate lists of potential activities, statements, or events expected for each hypothesis or scenario.* 3. *Regularly review and update the indicator lists to see which are changing.* 4. *Identify the most likely or correct hypotheses or scenarios based on the number of changed indicators observed.*

Note: Developing two lists of indicators for each hypothesis or scenario may prove helpful in distinguishing between indicators that a development is or is not emerging. This is particularly useful in a "What If?" analysis when it is essential to make a case that a particular event is unlikely to happen.

Analysis of Competing Hypotheses (ACH): A Systematic Approach to Objectivity

The Analysis of Competing Hypotheses (ACH) technique is a structured method designed to identify and evaluate multiple possible explanations (hypotheses) for a given situation by focusing on disconfirming rather than confirming evidence. By systematically testing hypotheses against all available information, ACH helps reduce bias, avoids premature conclusions, and increases the overall rigor of the analytical process.

When to Use

ACH is particularly effective when dealing with complex issues that involve large volumes of data and when it is critical to ensure objectivity. While individual analysts can apply ACH, the technique yields the best results in a collaborative setting where a small team can challenge each other's evaluations. This method is ideal for:

- **Controversial or complex issues**, where analysts must maintain a clear record of their thought process.
- **Situations involving denial and deception**, where the possibility of misleading evidence needs to be considered carefully.
- **Analytical transparency**, allowing other analysts or policymakers to review the reasoning behind a given judgment and identify areas of agreement or disagreement.

ACH is also valuable when working under tight timeframes. Developing a fundamental ACH matrix with alternative hypotheses and loading data into the framework can be completed in a day or less. However, a more in-depth re-examination may take longer if the dataset needs to be revisited (see Table 10.12).

ACH is essential for intelligence analysts, particularly in complex or high-stakes situations where objectivity, transparency, and rigor are critical. By focusing on disproving rather than confirming hypotheses, ACH encourages analysts to remain open-minded, reduces cognitive bias, and ensures that conclusions are based on a comprehensive and impartial assessment of the evidence. This process helps identify the most likely explanation and ensures that less likely hypotheses are not prematurely discarded, offering a more robust and nuanced understanding of the issue at hand.

Ultimately, ACH provides a framework that can withstand external scrutiny and serves as a transparent record of the analytical process, which is essential for building confidence in the resulting judgments and decisions.

Conclusion (Diagnostic Techniques in Intelligence Analysis)

In conclusion, diagnostic techniques such as Key Assumptions Check, Quality of Information Check, Indicators or Signposts of Change, and Analysis of Competing Hypotheses (ACH) are essential tools that enhance intelligence analysis's rigor, transparency, and objectivity. By systematically reviewing assumptions, evaluating the credibility of information, monitoring key indicators, and testing multiple hypotheses, analysts can avoid common pitfalls like cognitive biases, overreliance on flawed assumptions, or anchoring on unreliable data. These techniques ensure that analytic processes remain adaptable, evidence-based, and capable of adjusting to new developments or shifts in the intelligence landscape.

Moreover, these methods foster a culture of critical thinking within intelligence teams. By incorporating structured checks and ongoing reassessment, analysts can more effectively challenge entrenched viewpoints and improve the robustness of their conclusions. This approach leads to more accurate intelligence assessments and builds the foundation for strategic decisions that can withstand scrutiny and respond dynamically to changing circumstances. Ultimately, using diagnostic techniques strengthens the overall integrity of intelligence analysis, supporting more informed and objective decision-making in complex and evolving environments.

Table 10.13 outlines various analytical issues/problems and the more appropriate diagnostic techniques analysts can select to assist in resolving them.

TABLE 10.12 Steps Involved in Performing an Analysis of Competing Hypotheses

Method
ACH ensures that all reasonable hypotheses are considered, that evidence is weighed equally, and that analysts avoid the natural tendency to favor a single explanation too soon. The process is structured around the following key steps:

1. ***Identify All Possible Hypotheses:*** *Start by brainstorming among analysts from diverse backgrounds to ensure a wide range of potential explanations are considered. This helps prevent narrow thinking and ensures that no critical hypotheses are overlooked.*
2. ***List Relevant Evidence:*** *Compile all relevant evidence and arguments related to the hypotheses. The goal is to include both supporting and opposing information without bias.*
3. ***Create a Hypotheses-Evidence Matrix:*** *Build a matrix with hypotheses listed across the top and individual pieces of evidence listed down the side. This matrix allows analysts to visually compare how each piece of evidence aligns with or contradicts each hypothesis.*
4. ***Evaluate Each Piece of Evidence:*** *For each hypothesis, assess whether each piece of evidence is:*
   - *Consistent: Supports the hypothesis.*
   - *Inconsistent: Contradicts the hypothesis.*
   - *Not Applicable: Irrelevant to the hypothesis.*
5. ***Refine the Matrix and Reassess Hypotheses:*** *As evidence is evaluated, analysts may need to refine the matrix by adding new hypotheses or adjusting existing ones. This iterative step helps ensure that the analysis remains flexible and comprehensive.*
6. ***Focus on Disproving Hypotheses:*** *ACH differs from traditional approaches by prioritizing disproving hypotheses rather than attempting to confirm a favored one. This method helps guard against confirmation bias and encourages a more objective analysis.*
7. ***Tally Consistent and Inconsistent Evidence:*** *Summarize the evidence consistent or inconsistent with each hypothesis. Hypotheses with the most inconsistent evidence should be discarded first, leaving those with the fewest contradictions for further scrutiny.*
8. ***Analyze Sensitivity to Key Evidence:*** *Identify any critical evidence that disproportionately impacts the analysis. If this crucial evidence turns out to be wrong or misleading, how would it affect the conclusions? This step is vital in cases where deception or unreliable data is a concern.*
9. ***Identify Missing or Expected Evidence:*** *Ask what evidence should be present if a hypothesis were true but is not. This can help detect gaps in the analysis and highlight potential efforts at denial and deception.*
10. ***Report Conclusions Transparently:*** *Document all findings, including solid and weak hypotheses. Even weaker hypotheses should be noted and monitored, as future evidence may shift their relevance. The final analysis should be clear about the relative likelihood of each hypothesis.*
11. ***Monitor Indicators for Future Developments:*** *Establish indicators that signal each hypothesis's confirmation or refutation. Monitor these indicators over time to stay aware of new developments that could alter the original conclusions. This step ensures the analysis is dynamic and responsive to evolving data.*

Note: As the matrix is refined, each piece of evidence's "diagnostic value" becomes clear. Evidence that supports only one hypothesis has high diagnostic value, helping to differentiate between explanations. In contrast, evidence that supports multiple hypotheses is less helpful in distinguishing between them and should be regarded as having lower diagnostic value. This distinction ensures that the analysis focuses on the most informative evidence.

TABLE 10.13 Analytical Issues/Problems vs. Appropriate Diagnostic Techniques Matrix

Analysis Issue/Problem \ Analytical Technique	Key Assumptions Check	Quality of Information Check*	Indicators or Signposts of Change	Analysis of Competing
Tactical and Strategic Operations Planning and Assessment	X	X	X	X
Current situation in a short period of time		X		
Political (or other competitive) environment surrounding a government (or criminal/terror) organizational entity	X	X		
Modeling organizational communication patterns		X	X	
Determining event patterns and predict potential hazards		X	X	
Understanding cause and effect and identifying patterns	X	X		
Performing targeting analysis	X	X		
Determining soundness of a decision	X	X		
Providing a basis for comparing projects/decisions		X		
When absorbing and evaluating a large amount of data		X		X
Tracking events to monitor and evaluate changes		X	X	
Weighing validity of sources/information	X	X	X	X
Checking/rechecking key assumptions	X	X	X	X
Challenging mind-sets with two existing dominant views		X		
Recognizing impact of seemingly low probability events		X		
Challenging an analytic consensus or a key assumption	X	X		X
Challenging a strong mind-set that an event will NOT happen or confidently made forecast may NOT be justified	X	X		
Stimulating new thinking on a problem/issue		X		
Identifying all the critical, external factors that could influence how a particular situation will develop	X	X	X	
Trying to see a situation from perspective of another individual or group	X	X		
Situation is viewed as "too complex" or the outcomes as "too uncertain" to trust a single outcome assessment	X	X	X	

Note: These techniques are not necessarily designed to be used alone. They are generally most useful when combined with other analytical approaches.

CONTRARIAN TECHNIQUES: CHALLENGING ASSUMPTIONS TO STRENGTHEN ANALYSIS

Contrarian techniques are critical tools in intelligence analysis that help challenge entrenched thinking and broaden the analytical perspective. By introducing diverse viewpoints and examining alternative explanations, these methods help reduce the risk of groupthink, challenge biases, and uncover hidden assumptions. Four commonly used contrarian techniques are:

- Devil's Advocacy
- Team A/Team B
- High-Impact/Low-Probability Analysis
- "What If?" Analysis

Devil's Advocacy: A Structured Challenge to Consensus

The Devil's Advocacy technique challenges a firmly held view or consensus by rigorously developing the best possible case for an alternative explanation. This method creates a structured environment where dissenting views are encouraged and essential for ensuring the resilience of the prevailing analytic conclusion (see Table 10.14).

When to Use

Devil's Advocacy is particularly effective when there is a robust analytic consensus on a critical issue, especially one with high stakes, and getting it wrong is not an option. Analysts can reaffirm their confidence in the existing analysis by rigorously testing the dominant view or uncovering alternative explanations that warrant further investigation. This technique is especially valuable when:

- Analysts have developed a strong mindset after working on an issue for an extended period.
- There is uncertainty or doubt surrounding a key assumption in the analysis.
- A manager designates an analyst to challenge the consensus to ensure robustness and avoid blind spots.

Sometimes, the Devil's Advocacy process will lead to a formal alternative analysis, presenting the arguments and data supporting a contrary hypothesis. In others, it may reinforce the prevailing view, having passed a rigorous test of its assumptions and evidence. Either way, Devil's Advocacy ensures that the analytic process remains resilient, transparent, and objective.[45]

TABLE 10.14 Steps Involved in Performing a Devil's Advocacy Assessment

Method
To perform the Devil's Advocacy process, one would follow these steps: 1. ***Outline the Current Analytic View:*** *Start by clearly stating the dominant judgment or consensus, including the key assumptions and evidence supporting this view. This sets the foundation for challenging the analysis.* 2. ***Identify Vulnerable Assumptions:*** *Select one or more explicit or implicit assumptions that appear most susceptible to challenge. These assumptions often underpin the analytic framework and can be the weakest link.* 3. ***Examine the Evidence:*** *Critically review the evidence used to support the current view. Assess whether any information is of questionable validity, if there's potential for deception, or if significant gaps in knowledge exist.* 4. ***Highlight Contradictory Evidence:*** *Identify any data or information that could support an alternative hypothesis or contradict the prevailing thinking. This helps build a credible case for the alternative view.* 5. ***Expose Flaws or Gaps:*** *Present findings that reveal flawed assumptions, unreliable evidence, or possible deception. This step is crucial for illustrating the weaknesses in the current consensus and validating the need for an alternative explanation.* 6. ***Develop a Contrarian Case:*** *If significant flaws are uncovered, consider drafting a separate contrarian analysis that lays out the arguments and evidence supporting an alternative conclusion. This ensures that all possibilities are explored in depth.* 7. ***Clarify the Purpose of the Exercise:*** *Clearly label any products generated as part of a "Devil's Advocate" effort to avoid confusion with the official analytic position. Transparency is key to distinguishing between the contrarian view and the current consensus.*

This technique helps safeguard against complacency, ensuring that intelligence assessments are accurate and robust enough to withstand scrutiny.

If this issue has been ongoing for an extended period, it is probably wise to assume that a strong mindset exists that deserves the closer scrutiny provided by Devil's Advocacy.[46]

Team A/Team B Exercise: Enhancing Analytical Rigor

The Team A/Team B exercise is a structured approach that fosters competitive analysis by developing and testing competing hypotheses on a given issue. This method is designed to improve objectivity, reduce bias, and deepen understanding of complex topics by forcing analysts to comprehensively argue different sides of an issue.

When to Use

A Team A/Team B approach differs from Devil's Advocacy, which aims to challenge a single dominant mindset. Team A/Team B recognizes that there may be competing and possibly equally strong mindsets on an issue that needs to be clarified. Sometimes, analysts confuse the two techniques by drafting a Team B exercise, which is a Devil's Advocacy exercise.

Suppose there are at least two competing views within an analytic cell or perhaps competing opinions within the policymaking community on a critical issue. In that case, Team A/Team B analysis can be the appropriate technique. Developing a full-blown Team A/Team B exercise requires a significant commitment of analytic time and resources, so consideration should be given to whether the analytic issue merits this kind of attention.

Some situations that warrant Team A/Team B analysis are a long-standing policy issue, a critical decision with far-reaching implications, or a dispute within the analytic community that has obstructed effective cross-agency cooperation. These would be grounds for using Team A/Team B. If those circumstances exist, analysts must review all the data to develop alternative papers that capture the essential differences between the two viewpoints[47] (see Table 10.15).

High-Impact/Low-Probability Analysis: Preparing for the Unexpected

High-Impact/Low-Probability (HILP) Analysis is a strategic tool for considering the potential impact of seemingly unlikely events that could have profound policy consequences. This technique encourages analysts to think beyond conventional expectations and anticipate the possible occurrence of rare but transformative events.

When to Use

HILP analysis is instrumental when analysts and policymakers are overly confident that a specific event is unlikely. This method pushes them to consider what might happen if the event did occur despite its low probability. By addressing the "what if," analysts can better prepare for unexpected scenarios, such as the fall of the Shah of Iran, the collapse of the Soviet Union, or the reunification of Germany, events that, though unlikely, had immense global repercussions[48] (see Table 10.16).

Using HILP analysis, intelligence analysts can proactively prepare for improbable but high-stakes events, offering valuable foresight in an unpredictable world.

TABLE 10.15 Team A/Team B Exercise Procedural Steps

Method
Process: 1. ***Identify Competing Hypotheses:*** *Begin by outlining two or more competing viewpoints or hypotheses regarding a particular issue. These could range from geopolitical strategies to differing military, economic, or social development forecasts.* 2. ***Form Teams:*** *Designate teams or individual analysts to represent each hypothesis, encouraging them to build the strongest case for their assigned position. This step promotes thorough analysis and forces participants to consider all angles.* 3. ***Review and Analyze Data:*** *Each team reviews all available information that supports their respective hypothesis. Teams should also identify gaps or missing data that, if obtained, could strengthen their argument.* 4. ***Construct Arguments:*** *Teams structure their case by explicitly presenting key assumptions, supporting evidence, and logic. Every argument should be rooted in sound reasoning and clearly acknowledge uncertainties or vulnerabilities.*
Presentation and Evaluation: 1. ***Oral Presentation:*** *Organize a structured session where teams present their findings and challenge the opposing team's arguments. Depending on the context, this can be either a formal debate or a more informal brainstorming session.* 2. ***Peer Review:*** *Assemble a neutral panel of peers to act as an independent jury. The jury will critically evaluate each argument, questioning teams on their assumptions, evidence, and conclusions.* 3. ***Rebuttal and Critique:*** *Teams should be allowed to rebut the opposing side's critique and further defend their own position. This back-and-forth exchange sharpens both sides of the argument and often reveals hidden insights.* 4. ***Jury Deliberation:*** *After the debate, the jury considers the strength of each argument and provides recommendations for further research, analysis, or data collection.*

"What If?" Analysis: Challenging Assumptions

"What If?" analysis assumes that an event has a potential (negative or positive) impact and explains how it might occur.

When to Use

Use What If? analysis when analysts or policymakers are overly confident about a particular forecast and have not fully considered alternative outcomes. This method helps to uncover hidden vulnerabilities and overlooked possibilities that may disrupt conventional thinking. "What if" analysis is another contrarian technique for challenging a strong mindset

TABLE 10.16 Process Steps Associated with HILP

Method
1. ***Define the High-Impact Outcome:*** *Start by clearly articulating the unlikely but potentially significant outcome. This outcome justifies considering the event despite its low probability.*
2. ***Develop Plausible Pathways:*** *Create one or more plausible pathways that could lead to a low-probability outcome. These pathways help identify potential triggers and allow for later monitoring of indicators.*
3. ***Identify Triggers or Momentum Shifts:*** *Include possible triggers, such as natural disasters, sudden leadership changes, or economic shocks, that could set the scenario in motion. Drawing on historical parallels or experiences from other regions can add realism to these scenarios.*
4. ***Collaborate with Diverse Analysts:*** *Involve analysts with a wide range of expertise to brainstorm triggers and events that may have been overlooked. This enhances the quality of the scenarios and ensures a broader perspective.*
5. ***Monitor Indicators:*** *Once the pathways are identified, determine a set of observable indicators to track over time. Monitoring these indicators will provide early warning signs that the scenario may be starting to unfold.*
6. ***Consider Mitigating Factors:*** *Analyze potential factors that could deflect the event or lead to a positive outcome instead of a negative one. This step ensures that the analysis is comprehensive and accounts for both risks and opportunities.*

that an event will not happen or that a confidently made forecast may not be entirely justified. It is like a High-Impact/Low-Probability analysis. Still, it does not dwell on the event's consequences as much as it accepts its significance and directly explains how it might occur[49] (see Table 10.17).

What If? analysis is a valuable tool for challenging overconfidence and encouraging analysts to explore alternative outcomes. Pushing the boundaries of conventional thinking ensures that intelligence assessments remain adaptable and responsive to emerging risks.

The following figure outlines various analytical issues and problems and the more appropriate contrarian techniques analysts can select to assist in resolving them (see Table 10.18).

Conclusion (Contrarian Techniques)

In conclusion, contrarian techniques are indispensable tools in intelligence analysis. They provide structured ways to challenge assumptions, test competing viewpoints, and explore alternative scenarios. Techniques

TABLE 10.17 The Process Steps Involved with "What If?" Analysis

Method
Like other contrarian methods, "What If?" analysis must begin by stating clearly the conventional analytic line and then pausing to consider what alternative outcomes are too important to dismiss, even if unlikely. Brainstorming over a few days or weeks can develop one or more plausible scenarios by which the unlikely event occurs: 1. ***State the Conventional View:*** *Outline the accepted analytic consensus or forecast. This provides the baseline for exploring alternative scenarios.* 2. ***Assume the Event Has Occurred:*** *Imagine that the unlikely event has already occurred. This mental exercise forces analysts to shift their focus from whether the event could happen to how it might happen.* 3. ***Identify Triggering Events:*** *Postulate potential triggers, such as a leader's death, a financial crisis, or a natural disaster, that could set the scenario in motion. These triggers make the scenario more plausible by providing a logical starting point.* 4. ***Work Backward:*** *Think backward from the assumed event to identify the chain of developments that would lead to the outcome. This helps clarify each scenario stage and ensures the analysis is grounded in reality.* 5. ***Develop Multiple Pathways:*** *Identify several plausible pathways or scenarios that could lead to the unlikely event. This broadens the scope of the analysis and allows for a more thorough exploration of possibilities.* 6. ***Generate Observable Indicators:*** *For each scenario, develop a set of observable indicators that would signal the event is beginning to unfold. Monitoring these indicators ensures the analysis remains forward-looking and actionable.* 7. ***Consider the Impacts:*** *Analyze each scenario's potential positive and negative consequences. Understanding the scope of these impacts helps prioritize which scenarios warrant further monitoring.* 8. ***Ongoing Monitoring:*** *Periodically review the indicators to assess whether any scenario is beginning to materialize. This continuous monitoring helps maintain situational awareness and supports timely decision-making.*

such as Devil's Advocacy and Team A/Team B exercises foster analytical rigor by promoting dissent and encouraging a comprehensive examination of different perspectives. High-Impact/Low-Probability and "What If?" analyses push analysts to consider unlikely but potentially transformative events, ensuring preparedness for unexpected developments.

These methods enhance the quality of intelligence assessments by uncovering blind spots, reducing the risk of groupthink, and promoting open-mindedness. By integrating contrarian techniques into the analytical process, intelligence professionals can strengthen their conclusions,

TABLE 10.18 Analytical Issues/Problems vs. Appropriate Diagnostic Techniques Matrix

Analysis Issue/Problem \ Analytical Technique	Devil' s Advocacy	Team A/Team B	High-Impact/Low-Probability Analysis	*What If?* Analysis
Tactical and Strategic Operations Planning and Assessment	X	X	X	X
Weighing validity of sources/information	X	X	X	X
Checking/rechecking key assumptions	X	X	X	X
Challenging mind-sets with two existing dominant views		X		
Recognizing impact of seemingly low probability events			X	
Challenging a strong mind-set that an event will NOT happen or confidently made forecast may NOT be justified				X

making them more resilient and adaptive to evolving circumstances. Ultimately, contrarian thinking is essential for producing robust, well-rounded intelligence that can withstand scrutiny and support sound decision-making in uncertain environments.

IMAGINATIVE THINKING TECHNIQUES

Imaginative thinking techniques are essential tools in intelligence analysis for generating new insights, developing alternative perspectives, and forecasting potential outcomes in uncertain situations. These methods foster creative thinking and break down entrenched mindsets, allowing analysts to consider a broader range of possibilities. The following are four of the most used imaginative thinking techniques used by the Intelligence Community:

- Brainstorming
- Outside-In Thinking
- Red Team Analysis
- Alternative Futures Analysis

Brainstorming

Brainstorming is an unrestrained group process to generate fresh ideas, hypotheses, or concepts by encouraging free-flowing discussion and collaboration.

When to Use

Brainstorming can be employed at the outset of a project to generate a wide array of hypotheses, perspectives, or approaches to an issue. It is a

FIGURE 10.18 Brainstorming sessions can take many forms. Here General Darryl Williams (right center), commander of U.S. Army Europe and Africa and commander of NATO's Allied Land Command discusses mission command execution with senior officers from NATO HQ Allied Rapid Reaction Corps during Steadfast Jupiter 23, October 18, 2023 (U.S. Army/Kyle Larsen).

highly versatile tool that can complement other structured analytic techniques and is particularly useful when analysts need to overcome mental blocks or expand the scope of their analysis (see Figure 10.18).

Brainstorming usually involves a group of analysts discussing a common challenge, allowing participants to build upon each other's ideas. While individuals can brainstorm independently, group brainstorming benefits from diverse perspectives, often leading to more innovative and robust ideas. However, individual brainstorming can avoid the social pressures or biases that may arise in a group setting[50] (see Table 10.19).

Outside-In Thinking

Outside-In thinking involves identifying external forces and trends that could indirectly shape an issue, expanding the scope of consideration beyond immediate, internal factors.

When to Use

This technique is especially useful when conceptualizing an analytic project. It helps analysts identify key external drivers and social,

TABLE 10.19 Process Steps Involved in Brainstorming

Method
Effective brainstorming should follow a structured approach to ensure productivity despite its open-ended nature. Paradoxically, brainstorming should be a very structured process to be most productive. An unconstrained, informal discussion might produce some fascinating ideas, but a more systematic process is usually the most effective way to break down mindsets and deliver new insights. In particular, the process involves a divergent thinking phase to generate and collect new ideas and insights, followed by a convergent phase in which ideas are grouped and organized around key concepts.

Some simple rules to be followed include but are not limited to:

- *Never censor an analyst's ideas, no matter how unconventional they might sound.*
- *Find out what prompted the thought, as it might contain the seeds of an important connection between the topic and an unstated assumption.*
- *Give yourself enough time to do brainstorming correctly. It usually takes one hour to set the "rules" of the game, get the group comfortable, and exhaust the conventional wisdom on the topic. Only then will the genuinely creative ideas begin to emerge.*
- *Involve at least one "outsider" in the process. The outsider should be someone who does not share the same educational background, culture, technical knowledge, or mindset as the core group but has some familiarity with the topic.*

The process typically includes two phases.

Divergent Thinking Phase:

1. *Distribute Post-it notes to participants and pose a central "focal question." (Typically, 10–12 people work best.)*
2. *Pose the problem in terms of a "focal question." Display it in one sentence on a large easel or whiteboard. Encourage participants to write down responses without restrictions.*
3. *Stick the notes to a wall, treating all ideas equally and avoiding judgment or censorship.*
4. *Continue collecting ideas until pauses in the conversation suggest conventional thinking is exhausted.*

Convergent Thinking Phase:

1. *Ask the participants to rearrange the notes on the wall according to their commonalities or similar concepts as a group. No talking is permitted. Some notes may be moved several times as they begin to cluster. Copying some notes is permitted to allow ideas to be included in more than one group.*
2. *Select a word or phrase that characterizes each grouping or cluster once all the notes have been arranged.*
3. *Identify any outlier ideas that are worthy of further exploration.*
4. *Use a voting process to prioritize areas for further analysis, guiding the next steps. Instruct each participant to select one or two areas that deserve the most attention. Tabulate the votes.*
5. *Set the brainstorming group's priorities based on the voting and decide on the next steps for analysis*

technological, economic, environmental, and political factors that could impact the issue at hand. It is beneficial when working on large-scale projects or developing databases requiring a comprehensive view of all relevant categories to avoid missing critical variables. It works well for a group of analysts responsible for a range of functional and regional issues. When assembling an extensive database that must identify a number of information categories or database fields, this technique can aid in visualizing the entire set of categories that might be needed in a research effort.

Often, analysts realize too late that some additional information categories will be required and then must review all previous files and recode the data. With a modest amount of effort, "Outside-In Thinking" can reduce the risk of missing essential variables early in the analytic process[51,52] (see Table 10.20).

Red Team Analysis

Red Team analysis (see Figure 10.19) is designed to simulate how an adversary might think, aiming to anticipate potential behaviors by stepping into the shoes of the opposing side. Red Team analysis is complicated. Developing a team of qualified experts who think like the adversary requires significant time. The team must distance itself from the regular analysis and work as though living in the target's world. Analysts cannot behave or think like the enemy without a comprehensive understanding of the foreign group's culture, operational environment, and personal history. Analysts can never truly escape their own experiences and mindsets, but this technique can at least prevent them from falling into mirror-imaging unconsciously.

TABLE 10.20 Process Steps Involved in Outside-In Thinking

Method
The process begins by developing a generic description of the problem or the phenomenon under study. Once this has been completed, analysts should: 1. *List key external forces that may influence the issue, focusing on factors (social, technological, economic, environmental, and political) beyond the actors' control.* 2. *Consider elements that can be influenced, such as policy actions or market dynamics.* 3. *Assess how these forces could impact the issue, ensuring no critical variables are overlooked.* 4. *Determine whether these forces impact the particular issue based on the available evidence and, if so, how they impact it.*

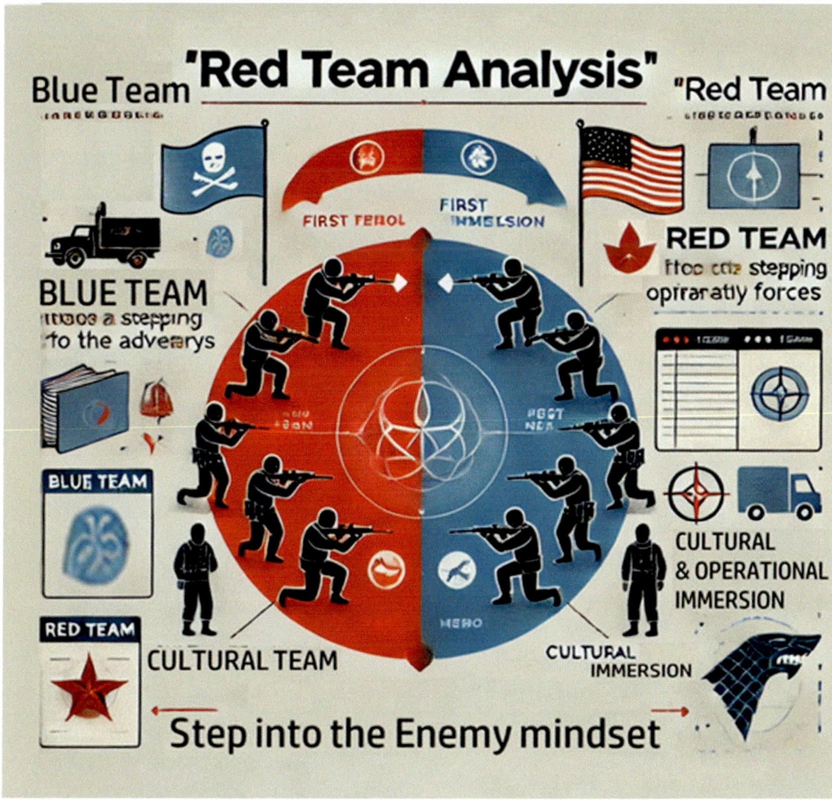

FIGURE 10.19 Red Team analysis conceptual diagram.

The novel feature of Red Team analysis is its presentation. Some examples of these differing features are:

- The analysis is often in a first-person format, drafted as memos to or from a leader or group.
- Red Team analysis avoids using caveats or qualifications. It assumes that the recipient understands that the approach aims to provoke or challenge the conventional understanding of an adversary's thoughts. Such analytical assessments are rarely coordinated among other experts and do not purport to represent the consensus view on an issue.

When to Use

Traditional analysis sometimes assumes that foreign leaders or groups will behave "rationally" and act as the analysts would if faced with the same threats or opportunities. History has shown that foreign leaders often respond differently to events because of different cultural, organizational, or personal experiences. This technique is beneficial when analysts face the risk of mirror-imaging, unconsciously projecting their artistic, organizational, or personal biases onto an adversary. Red Team Analysis is valuable in predicting how foreign leaders or groups, influenced by different experiences and worldviews, might respond to events.

One should be aware that Red Team analysis does not plot out all possible courses of action but seeks to give a prediction based on the target's special personal, organizational, or cultural experiences[53] (see Table 10.21).

> ***AUTHOR'S NOTE***
>
> - *The team should include individuals who understand the language and those who have experienced the culture, share the ethnic background, or have worked in a similar operational environment.*
> - *Once the team is established and separated from traditional analysis, it should put itself in the adversary's circumstances and react to external stimuli as the target would.*
> - *"First-person" questions that the adversary might ask include: "How would I perceive incoming information?" "What would my concerns be?" "To whom would I seek an opinion?"*
> - *The more these assessments align with the target's cultural and personal norms, the more they can provide a unique perspective on the analytic problem.*

Alternative Futures Analysis

Alternative Futures Analysis systematically explores multiple

TABLE 10.21 Process Steps Involved in Red Team Analysis

Method
1. *Build a team of experts familiar with the adversary's cultural, operational, and personal context. For issues that lend themselves to Red Team analysis, the analytical lead needs to build a team of experts with in-depth knowledge of the operating environment, the target's personality, and the thinking style used. This first step will likely prove to be the most difficult.*
2. *The team should work from the adversary's perspective, asking first-person questions about how the target perceives information or reacts to stimuli.*
3. *Draft "first-person" memos or policy papers from the adversary's perspective, simulating decisions or recommendations.*
4. *Ensure the analysis reflects the target's cultural or organizational norms.*

ways a situation could develop, focusing on high complexity and uncertainty (see Figure 10.20).

When to Use

AFA (often called "scenarios") is most useful when a situation is viewed as too complex or the outcomes are too uncertain to trust a single outcome assessment.

This technique is valuable when the situation is too uncertain or complex to rely on a single outcome assessment. It helps policymakers and analysts prepare for a range of possible futures rather than betting on one definitive prediction. Imaginative contrarian techniques, which seek to challenge high-confidence judgments, contrast by embracing uncertainty and complexity to explore diverse outcomes.

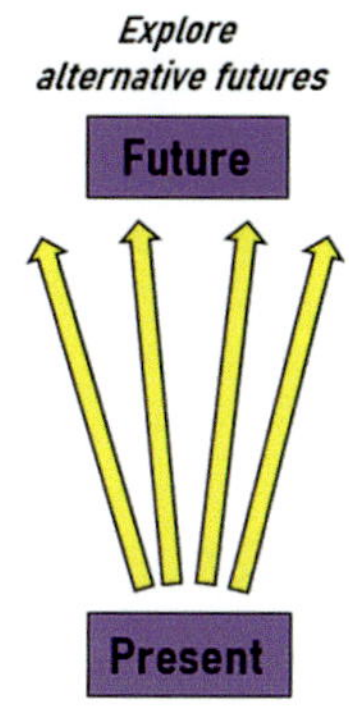

FIGURE 10.20 Alternative futures analysis.

First, analysts must recognize the high uncertainty surrounding the topic in question. Second, they, and often their customers, realize they must consider a wide range of factors that might bear on the question. Third, they are prepared to explore a range of outcomes and are not wedded to any preconceived result. Depending on how elaborate the future project is, the effort can amount to a considerable investment in time, analytic resources, and money. A team of analysts can spend several hours or days organizing, brainstorming, and developing multiple futures. Alternatively, a larger-scale effort may involve organizing a multiday workshop that gathers participants, including outside experts. Such an undertaking typically requires the distinct skills of trained scenario-development facilitators and appropriate conferencing facilities.

This technique contrasts sharply with contrarian techniques, which attempt to challenge analysts' high confidence and relative certainty about an event or trend. Instead, multiple futures development is a divergent thinking technique that uses a situation's complexity and uncertainty to describe multiple outcomes or futures that the analyst and policymaker should consider rather than predict one outcome.[54]

AUTHOR'S NOTE

- *The brainstorming session should be held by both internal and external experts.*
- *It is unlikely to achieve unanimity, so select the two most critical and uncertain forces by group consensus.*

- *The endpoints for each factor should be the most relevant; e.g., if economic growth were the most critical, uncertain force, the endpoints could be "fast" and "slow" or "transformative" and "stabilizing" depending on the type of issue addressed (see Table 10.22).*

Participants, especially policymakers, can then consider how current decisions or strategies would fare in each of the four worlds and identify alternative policies that might work better in all or specific futures.

Example of Alternative Futures

For example, a brainstorming session on potential terrorist attacks might identify the sophistication of weapons and the intended impact as two key uncertainties. These variables could form the axes of a futures matrix, allowing analysts to explore different combinations, from low-sophistication and selective attacks to high-sophistication and widespread impacts. The resulting quadrants would help analysts and policymakers prepare for various scenarios, ranging from cyberattacks on infrastructure to targeting critical social systems like healthcare (see Figure 10.21).

TABLE 10.22 Process Steps Involved in Alternative Futures Analysis

Method
Although there are a variety of ways to develop alternative futures, the most common approach used in both the public and private sectors involves the following steps: 1. *Develop a "focal issue" by consulting experts to frame the general topic.* 2. *Brainstorm forces and factors that could affect the focal issue.* 3. *Select the two most critical and uncertain factors and use them to create axes with endpoints.* 4. *Cross the axes to form a matrix with four quadrants representing alternative futures.* 5. *Develop narratives or "stories" for each future and identify potential indicators or signposts.* 6. *Use these futures to assess how current policies or strategies would perform in each scenario, considering alternative approaches for flexibility and preparedness.*

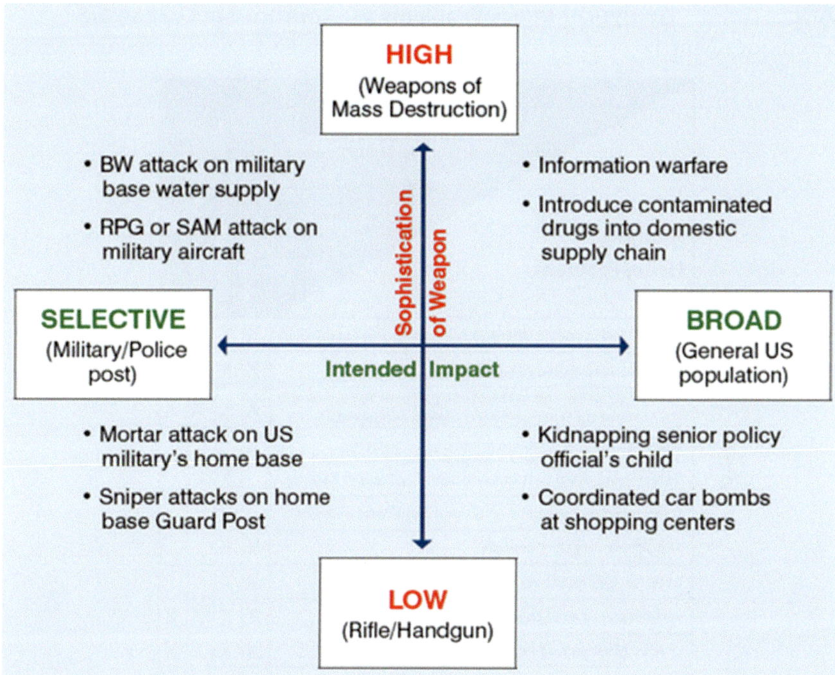

FIGURE 10.21 Example illustration of alternative futures analysis.

Conclusion (Imaginative Thinking Techniques)

Imaginative thinking techniques are critical for intelligence analysis in scenarios where conventional thinking falls short. These methods foster creativity, expand the scope of analysis, and help analysts anticipate a broader range of outcomes. By systematically applying techniques like Brainstorming, Outside-In Thinking, Red Team Analysis, and Alternative Futures Analysis, analysts can generate more innovative and flexible responses to complex global challenges (see Table 10.23).

Table 10.23 outlines various analytical issues/problems and the more appropriate imaginative techniques that analysts can select from to assist in resolving the issue.

Choosing a Suitable Structured Analytic Technique

Many classifications of Structured Analytic Techniques (SATs) have been done. For example, Richards Heuer describes eight types: Decomposition and Visualization, Idea Generation, Scenarios and Indicators, Hypothesis Generation and Testing, Assessment of Cause and Effect, Challenge Analysis, Conflict Management, and Decision

TABLE 10.23 Analytical Issues/Problems vs. Appropriate Diagnostic Techniques Matrix

Analysis Issue/Problem \ Analytical Technique	Brainstorming	Outside-In Thinking	Red Team Analysis	Alternative Futures Analysis
Tactical and Strategic Operations Planning and Assessment	X	X	X	X
Current situation in a short period of time	X	X	X	
Political (or other competitive) environment surrounding a government (or criminal/terror) organizational entity	X	X	X	X
Modeling organizational communication patterns	X			
Determining event patterns and predict potential hazards		X		
Understanding cause and effect and identifying patterns		X		
Performing targeting analysis	X	X		
Determining soundness of a decision	X	X		
Weighing validity of sources/information	X	X	X	X
Checking/rechecking key assumptions	X	X	X	X
Challenging mind-sets with two existing dominant views	X	X		
Recognizing impact of seemingly low probability events	X	X		
Challenging an analytic consensus or a key assumption	X	X		
Challenging a strong mind-set that an event will NOT happen or confidently made forecast may NOT be justified	X	X		
Stimulating new thinking on a problem/issue	X	X		
Identifying all the critical, external factors that could influence how a particular situation will develop		X		
Trying to see a situation from perspective of another individual or group			X	
Situation is viewed as "too complex" or the outcomes as "too uncertain" to trust a single outcome assessment				X

Support. Heuer's recent book, *Structured Analytic Techniques for Intelligence Analysis*, describes 50 techniques.[55]

A sampling of SATs from the intelligence literature (i.e., DIA, CIA courses, and others) are grouped into four general categories: pattern recognition, diagnostic, contrarian, and imaginative.

Of course, there is no direct one-for-one mapping of the cognitive factors and the SATs. In addition, many SATs address multiple aspects of thinking; some are designed for individual use and some for group use. However, the text contains numerous matrix tables identifying the more appropriate techniques for analytical issues/problems.

Selecting the appropriate Structured Analytic Technique (SAT) is critical for producing a high-quality intelligence analysis. As intelligence problems vary widely, analysts must first assess the nature of the issue. For example, is the issue concerned with forecasting future developments, understanding current dynamics, or evaluating past events? If the intelligence problem relates to future predictions, how far into the future are we projecting? Is it a matter of days, months, years, or even decades? These temporal factors directly influence the appropriate choice of SAT.

Additionally, some intelligence problems focus on specific actors' actions, decisions, and intentions, whether individuals, groups, nation-states, or international organizations. The nature of these actors and the geopolitical or strategic context they operate within can shape which SATs will provide the most valuable insights. For instance, structured techniques like *Red Team Analysis* might be better suited for issues involving adversarial intent, while *Scenario Analysis* could be ideal for long-term strategic forecasting.

However, understanding the nature of the intelligence issue alone is insufficient for SAT selection. Analysts must also consider the cognitive challenges they are addressing. Different SATs are designed to mitigate various cognitive biases and enhance certain types of thinking, diagnostic, creative, or evaluative. For example, techniques like *Analysis of Competing Hypotheses (ACH)* are intended to aid in diagnostic reasoning by systematically evaluating alternative explanations, reducing the likelihood of confirmation bias. On the other hand, creative techniques like *Morphological Analysis* help explore a wide range of possible outcomes in complex, uncertain environments, encouraging divergent thinking.

The key to choosing an appropriate SAT is understanding the problem's structure and the type of cognitive support required. Analysts must ask themselves: Does the SAT help in isolating and interpreting specific data points (data-focused techniques), aggregating large amounts of information (holistic techniques), or both? Furthermore, is the SAT aimed at enhancing critical thinking, broadening perspectives, or challenging existing assumptions? Analysts can optimize their approach and deliver more robust, well-reasoned intelligence by aligning the SAT with the problem's nature and the analysis's cognitive needs.

For further reading on the relationship between SATs and cognitive biases in intelligence analysis, see Heuer and Pherson's *Structured Analytic Techniques for Intelligence Analysis* (2021), a foundational resource for understanding the application and selection of SATs in modern intelligence work.

CHAPTER SUMMARY

This chapter has traced the evolution of analytical tradecraft from its origins in covert espionage to its modern role as a cornerstone of intelligence analysis. We explored a range of structured analytical techniques—from ACH and Red Team Analysis to Alternative Futures Analysis—designed to help analysts organize complex data, challenge assumptions, and mitigate cognitive biases. With a renewed focus on transparency and rigor, modern analytical tradecraft empowers analysts to produce intelligence that is not only more reliable but also creatively adaptable to an ever-changing threat landscape. The integration of case studies, interactive flowcharts, and reflective exercises further ensures that the concepts learned are both practical and enduring.[56,57,58]

Key Concepts Covered

1. **Analytical Tradecraft:** Intelligence analysis relies on disciplined methods that transform raw information into reliable assessments. Analytical tradecraft provides the framework for conducting rigorous and transparent analysis.
2. **Structured Analytic Techniques (SATs):** SATs help analysts organize information, challenge assumptions, and explore alternative explanations in complex intelligence problems.
3. **Pattern Recognition Techniques:** Methods such as geospatial analysis, trend analysis, and social network analysis help identify relationships and patterns within large datasets.
4. **Diagnostic Techniques:** Tools such as Analysis of Competing Hypotheses, Indicators and Signposts, and Quality of Information Checks test evidence and evaluate competing explanations.
5. **Contrarian Techniques:** Techniques like Devil's Advocacy and Team A/Team B analysis introduce structured dissent and help reduce the risk of groupthink.
6. **Imaginative Thinking Techniques:** Brainstorming, Red Team Analysis, and Alternative Futures Analysis encourage creative thinking and help analysts anticipate emerging threats.
7. **Choosing Appropriate SATs:** Analysts must select techniques that match the intelligence problem, time constraints, and available information.
8. **Analytic Integrity:** Applying structured methods strengthens transparency, credibility, and analytic rigor consistent with standards outlined in Office of the Director of National Intelligence analytic tradecraft guidance.

Learning Objectives Accomplished

1. **Define** analytical tradecraft.
2. **Explain** the impact of Intelligence Community Directive (ICD) 203.
3. **Describe** the role of Structured Analytical Techniques (SATs).
4. **Apply** critical thinking and metacognition to intelligence analysis.
5. **Assess** various analytical methods and techniques.
6. **Explore** the use of contrarian and imaginative thinking techniques.
7. **Synthesize** analytical tradecraft into actionable intelligence products.
8. **Identify** real-world applications of analytical tradecraft.

Practical Application

You were introduced to practical scenarios demonstrating how analytical tradecraft supports intelligence operations, including:

- Using pattern recognition techniques to detect insurgent attack trends.
- Applying ACH and other diagnostic techniques to test competing explanations for adversary activity.
- Conducting Devil's Advocacy exercises to challenge dominant analytic judgments.
- Using Red Team analysis to understand adversary decision-making.
- Exploring Alternative Futures to anticipate geopolitical or technological disruptions.

Reflection Questions

1. Why is it important for intelligence analysts to use Structured Analytic Techniques rather than relying solely on intuition?
2. Which SAT category do you think is most useful when evaluating uncertain intelligence information? Why?
3. How can contrarian techniques improve the quality of intelligence assessments?

Thank you for your continued effort in mastering the craft of intelligence analysis. The techniques introduced in this chapter will serve as essential tools as you continue developing your analytical expertise.

GLOSSARY OF TERMS

Here is a glossary of key terms introduced and discussed in Chapter 10 to enhance your understanding of the material:

Alternative Futures Analysis: A scenario-building technique that explores multiple potential outcomes in an uncertain environment.
Analysis of Competing Hypotheses (ACH): A technique that evaluates multiple hypotheses by seeking evidence that disproves each one.
Analytical Tradecraft: The set of methods and tools used to transform raw data into actionable intelligence.
Diagnostic Techniques: Methods used to evaluate the quality and reliability of the information and the analytical process.
Key Assumptions Check: A process to identify, examine, and challenge the underlying assumptions of an analysis.
Metacognition: The awareness and evaluation of one's own thinking processes. Metacognition is crucial for identifying biases in analysis.
Red Team Analysis: A contrarian method where analysts simulate an adversary's perspective to challenge prevailing assumptions.
Structured Analytical Techniques (SATs): Systematic methods (such as ACH, SWOT, and Red Team Analysis) designed to improve the objectivity and rigor of intelligence analysis.

This glossary serves as a quick reference for understanding key terms and concepts from the chapter. Feel free to revisit it as you progress through the material!

NOTES

1. Office of the Director of National Intelligence, *Analytic Standards: Intelligence Community Directive 203 (ICD 203)*, 21 June 2007.
2. U.S. Government, 'Commission on the Intelligence Capabilities of the United States Regarding Weapons of Mass Destruction', Retrieved 23 October 2023, http://govinfo.library.unt.edu/wmd/about.html.
3. Sherman Kent, *Strategic Intelligence for American World Policy*, Princeton University Press, 1949.
4. Richards J. Heuer, Jr., *Psychology of Intelligence Analysis*, Center for the Study of Intelligence, 1999.
5. Jennifer E. Sims and Burton Gerber, *Transforming U.S. Intelligence*, Georgetown University Press, 2005.
6. Central Intelligence Agency, *A Tradecraft Primer: Structured Analytic Techniques for Improving Intelligence Analysis*, 2009.
7. Richards J. Heuer, Jr. and Randolph H. Pherson, *Structured Analytic Techniques for Intelligence Analysis* (3rd ed.), CQ Press, 2021.

8. U.S. Government Accountability Office, *Avoiding Surprise in an Era of Global Technology Advances (GAO-07-454)*, 2007.
9. Richards J. Heuer, Jr. and Randolph H. Pherson, *Structured Analytic Techniques for Intelligence Analysis* (3rd ed.), CQ Press, 2021.
10. Richards J. Heuer, Jr. and Randolph H. Pherson, *Structured Analytic Techniques for Intelligence Analysis* (3rd ed.), CQ Press, 2021.
11. CQ Press, Robert M. Clark, *Intelligence Analysis: A Target-Centric Approach*, 2019.
12. Farrar, Straus and Giroux, Daniel Kahneman, *Thinking, Fast and Slow*, 2011.
13. U.S. Government, Central Intelligence Agency (CIA*), A Tradecraft Primer: Structured Analytic Techniques for Improving Intelligence Analysis*, March 2009.
14. Georgetown University Press, Jennifer E. Sims, and Burton Gerber, *Transforming U.S. Intelligence*, 2005.
15. Richards J. Heuer, Jr. and Randolph H. Pherson, *Structured Analytic Techniques for Intelligence Analysis* (3rd ed.), CQ Press, 2021.
16. Charles H. Martin, *Introduction to Pattern Recognition: A MATLAB Approach*, Academic Press, 2020.
17. Kathleen M. Carley, *Dynamic Network Analysis*, Carnegie Mellon University Press, 2003.
18. Joseph E. Inikori, *The Atlantic Slave Trade: Effects on Economies, Societies and Peoples in Africa, the Americas, and Europe*, Duke University Press, 1992.
19. Michael E. Porter, *Competitive Strategy: Techniques for Analyzing Industries and Competitors*, Free Press, 1980.
20. Albert S. Humphrey, *SWOT Analysis for Management Consulting*, SRI International, 1960.
21. Mark Monmonier, *How to Lie with Maps*, University of Chicago Press, 2018.
22. Douglas W. Hubbard, *The Failure of Risk Management: Why It's Broken and How to Fix It*, Wiley, 2009.
23. Charles L. Schultze, *The Politics and Economics of Public Spending*, Brookings Institution Press, 1968.
24. Eric J. McNulty, and Leonard J. Marcus, *You're It: Crisis, Change, and How to Lead When It Matters Most*, Public Affairs, 2019.
25. U.S. Department of the Army, *Military Decision-Making Process (FM 6-0)*, 2015.
26. U.S. Department of the Army, *Tactics in Counterinsurgency, (FM 3-24.2)*, 2009.
27. Stuart H. James, Paul E. Kish and T. Paulette Sutton, *Principles of Bloodstain Pattern Analysis: Theory and Practice*, CRC Press, 2005.
28. Jennifer Golbeck, *Analyzing the Social Web*, Morgan Kaufmann, 2013.
29. Matthew D. Lanfear et al., *Social Network Analysis in Law Enforcement and Counterterrorism*, RAND Corporation, 2017.
30. Harold A. Linstone and Murray Turoff, *The Delphi Method: Techniques and Applications*, Addison-Wesley, 1975.
31. CBS News, *Coalition in Afghanistan Revises 2012 Attack Data*, February 2013.
32. Michael E. Porter, *Competitive Strategy: Techniques for Analyzing Industries and Competitors*, Free Press, 1980.
33. Vanda Felbab-Brown, *Narco Noir: Mexico's Cartels, Cops, and Corruption*, Brookings Institution Press, 2019.
34. Albert S. Humphrey, *SWOT Analysis for Management Consulting*, SRI International, 1960.
35. Mark Monmonier, *How to Lie with Maps*, University of Chicago Press, 2018.
36. Brian J. Reiser et al., *Explanation and Model-Based Learning*, Rutgers University Press, 2002.

37. Richard O. Zerbe and Allen S. Bellas, *A Primer for Benefit-Cost Analysis*, Edward Elgar Publishing, 2006.
38. E. Pate, K. J. Wheaton, E. E. Mosco and D. E. Chido, eds., *The Analyst's Cookbook* (Vol. I), Mercyhurst College Institute of Intelligence Studies Press, 2006.
39. Jennifer E. Sims and Burton Gerber, *Transforming U.S. Intelligence*, Georgetown University Press, 2005.
40. Defense Intelligence Agency (DIA), Anonymous, *A Tradecraft Primer: Basic Structured Analytic Techniques* (2nd ed.), 2009.
41. U.S. Government, Central Intelligence Agency (CIA), *A Tradecraft Primer: Structured Analytic Techniques for Improving Intelligence Analysis*, March 2009.
42. U.S. Government, Central Intelligence Agency (CIA), *A Tradecraft Primer: Structured Analytic Techniques for Improving Intelligence Analysis*, March 2009.
43. U.S. Government, Central Intelligence Agency (CIA), *A Tradecraft Primer: Structured Analytic Techniques for Improving Intelligence Analysis*, March 2009.
44. U.S. Government, Central Intelligence Agency (CIA), *A Tradecraft Primer: Structured Analytic Techniques for Improving Intelligence Analysis*, March 2009.
45. U.S. Government, Central Intelligence Agency (CIA), *A Tradecraft Primer: Structured Analytic Techniques for Improving Intelligence Analysis*, March 2009.
46. U.S. Government, Central Intelligence Agency (CIA), *A Tradecraft Primer: Structured Analytic Techniques for Improving Intelligence Analysis*, March 2009.
47. U.S. Government, Central Intelligence Agency (CIA), *A Tradecraft Primer: Structured Analytic Techniques for Improving Intelligence Analysis*, March 2009.
48. U.S. Government, Central Intelligence Agency (CIA), *A Tradecraft Primer: Structured Analytic Techniques for Improving Intelligence Analysis*, March 2009.
49. U.S. Government, Central Intelligence Agency (CIA), *A Tradecraft Primer: Structured Analytic Techniques for Improving Intelligence Analysis*, March 2009.
50. U.S. Government, Central Intelligence Agency (CIA), *A Tradecraft Primer: Structured Analytic Techniques for Improving Intelligence Analysis*, March 2009.
51. Richards J. Heuer, Jr. and Randolph H. Pherson, *Structured Analytic Techniques for Intelligence Analysis* (3rd ed.), CQ Press, 2021.
52. K. H. Pherson and R. H. Pherson, *Critical Thinking for Strategic Intelligence*, Thousand Oaks, CA: Sage Publications, 2012.
53. U.S. Government, Central Intelligence Agency (CIA), *A Tradecraft Primer: Structured Analytic Techniques for Improving Intelligence Analysis*, March 2009.
54. U.S. Government, Central Intelligence Agency (CIA), *A Tradecraft Primer: Structured Analytic Techniques for Improving Intelligence Analysis*, March 2009.
55. Richards J. Heuer, Jr. and Randolph H. Pherson, *Structured Analytic Techniques for Intelligence Analysis* (3rd ed.), CQ Press, 2021.
56. Richards J. Heuer, Jr., *Psychology of Intelligence Analysis,* Center for the Study of Intelligence, 1999.
57. Richards J. Heuer, Jr. and Randolph H. Pherson, *Structured Analytic Techniques for Intelligence Analysis* (3rd ed.), CQ Press, 2021.
58. M. M. Lowenthal, *Intelligence: From Secrets to Policy* (8th ed.), CQ Press, 2019.

CHAPTER 11

Navigating Cognitive Traps in Intelligence Analysis

INTRODUCTION

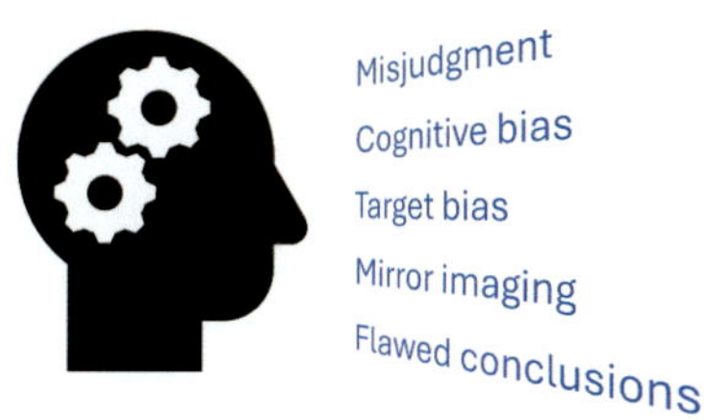

FIGURE 11.1 Common cognitive traps.

In the world of intelligence analysis, the greatest enemy is often not a foreign adversary but the analyst's own mind. Throughout history, critical intelligence failures, such as the misjudgment of Japan's intentions before Pearl Harbor or the erroneous assessments of Iraq's weapons of mass destruction, can be traced back to cognitive biases distorting perception, reasoning, and judgment. These "cognitive traps" operate beneath the surface of awareness, subtly shaping an analyst's interpretation of facts and leading to flawed conclusions.[1–3]

Imagine an intelligence analyst evaluating a potential security threat (see Figure 11.1). If the analyst unconsciously assumes the adversary will act in a way familiar to them, an error known as mirror-imaging, they might completely misinterpret the adversary's strategy. Similarly, an overreliance on past intelligence patterns could blind them to novel threats, a phenomenon known as target fixation. When these biases go unchecked, the consequences can be dire.

This chapter explores the most common cognitive traps that hinder intelligence professionals and provides actionable strategies to recognize

DOI: 10.4324/9781003561712-11

and counteract them. Analysts can minimize these biases and sharpen their assessments through structured analytic techniques (SATs), critical questioning, and peer reviews. By understanding how cognitive traps work and proactively mitigating them, intelligence professionals can ensure their conclusions are based on evidence rather than subconscious distortions. The ability to navigate these mental minefields may mean the difference between national security success and catastrophic failure.

LEARNING OBJECTIVES

By the end of this chapter, learners will be able to:

1. **Define and identify** key cognitive biases that affect intelligence analysis.
2. **Analyze real-world intelligence failures** through the lens of cognitive traps.
3. **Apply structured analytic techniques (SATs)** to counteract biases in intelligence assessments.
4. **Evaluate different perspectives and alternative hypotheses** to enhance objectivity.
5. **Develop critical thinking strategies** to recognize and mitigate biases in real-time analysis.

NAVIGATING BIASES IN INTELLIGENCE ANALYSIS: A NEW PERSPECTIVE

Biases in intelligence analysis are not just theoretical pitfalls; they are real and pervasive obstacles that can misdirect even the most seasoned analysts. To navigate this treacherous terrain, it is critical to understand the different categories of cognitive traps and to develop strategies to combat them effectively. From the subtle influence of personal experience to the overwhelming power of organizational culture, analysts must be constantly vigilant to prevent bias from leading their assessments astray.

CATEGORIES OF BIAS

Cognitive biases in intelligence analysis can be classified into several major categories, though the list is far from exhaustive. The most common include:

- Personality Bias
- Confirmation Bias

- Target Fixation
- Improper Use of Analogy
- Organizational Culture Bias

Each of these biases nudges the analyst away from objectivity and toward subjectivity. However, recognizing these traps is the first step toward mitigating their impact on analysis, empowering you to take control of your objectivity.[4]

TIPS FOR AVOIDING COGNITIVE TRAPS

1. *Cognitive traps such as personality bias, confirmation bias, target fixation, improper use of analogy (or model), and organizational culture feed analytical bias and create bad analyses.*
2. *Most of these traps can be recognized, mitigated, or avoided entirely by use of one or more of the following:*
   - *Structured analytical techniques (SATs)*
   - *Recognizing the pattern of the trap through critical questioning*
   - *Properly framing the problem*
   - *Leveraging other perspectives and using peer reviews*

The Trap of Personality Bias: Mirror-Imaging

One of the most insidious forms of bias stems from the analyst's personality, particularly the tendency to assume that others think and behave in the same way they do. This phenomenon, known as *mirror-imaging*, can be dangerous. When an analyst unconsciously asks, "How would I do this?" they often filter incoming data through their personal perspective, focusing on information that aligns with how they would act while ignoring data that contradicts this view.

As discussed in the previous chapter, experienced analysts use structured analytic techniques (SATs) to identify and correct for personal biases. Techniques like the Analysis of Competing Hypotheses (ACH) and Red Teaming, an analytical technique where teams are tasked with challenging assumptions, are invaluable tools in preventing the trap of mirror-imaging. These structured techniques provide a solid framework for analysis, instilling confidence and reassurance in the analysis process. Moreover, peer reviews, particularly by colleagues from diverse backgrounds, can add an extra layer of scrutiny, preventing bias from going unnoticed.

Confirmation Bias: The Filter of Belief

We all tend to seek information confirming our beliefs while disregarding evidence contradicting them. This is known as confirmation bias, which can be disastrous in intelligence analysis. Whether tuning into our favorite news channel or selectively recalling data that supports our analysis, this bias works silently to reinforce our preconceived notions.

For intelligence analysts, the consequences of confirmation bias can lead to tunnel vision, where critical evidence is overlooked. Studies from the 1960s, such as those by psychologist Peter Wason, demonstrated how humans naturally gravitate toward confirming their beliefs rather than challenging them.[5]

To counter this, analysts are encouraged to actively disconfirm their hypotheses, an intellectual exercise that involves searching for information that could disprove their initial assessment method, for doing so is the devil's advocate technique where analysts adopt an opposing viewpoint and rigorously search for evidence that refutes their working theory. A MITRE Corporation study has shown that using a particular SAT, Analysis of Competing Hypotheses (ACH), to mitigate the effects of confirmation bias is particularly effective.[6] Structured approaches like ACH have been proven highly effective in mitigating confirmation bias. These SATs force analysts to weigh competing hypotheses objectively based on the available evidence.[7] For more information on ACH, see Chapter 10. Later in the chapter, more information is provided on techniques to avoid cognitive traps.

Target Fixation: When Focus becomes a Hazard

Target fixation occurs when analysts become so focused on a single hypothesis or piece of evidence that they lose sight of the broader picture. In aviation, pilots can fixate so intently on hitting their target that they crash into it. In intelligence analysis, the consequences of such fixation are equally dire: essential pieces of information can be disregarded, and flawed assessments may be made in haste.

Some infamous examples of target fixation might include, "Terrorists only hijack planes; they don't fly them into buildings" or "All snipers are lone adult white male gunmen." Neither of these statements is accurate, and even if these assumptions are statistically supportable as "more likely" than not, they should be tested against available evidence and validated before analysts inadvertently discount viable leads and reports. Target fixation occurred in the lead-up to the 9/11 attacks, where the assumption that "Terrorists only hijack planes ..." led to a misinterpretation of vital intelligence (see Figure 11.2).

Criminal investigators often try to place suspects at the scene of a crime. They do this by checking to see if a potential suspect has a reasonable and verifiable alibi for a crime, such as being incarcerated at the time of the crime; failing that, they move on to other persons of interest.

To prevent target fixation, intelligence analysts or criminal investigators should develop tests to continuously validate their hypotheses. Analysts must routinely validate their hypotheses by conducting *alternative analysis* exercises that vet all available evidence rather than cherry-picking the data that fits their assumptions.

Conducting alternative analysis exercises, where divergent viewpoints are explored and divergent explanations are entertained, is a structured approach to mitigating analytical bias. This helps to broaden their perspective and reduces the risk of missing critical clues.

> ***AUTHOR'S NOTE***
>
> ***Target Fixation*** *– Refers to a concept where an individual's extreme concentration or focus on a single task or goal becomes so intense that it creates negative consequences, essentially turning their focus into a danger.*
>
> ***Key Aspects of Target Fixation***
>
> - ***Excessive Narrowing:*** *Occurs when one's focus becomes so laser-like that it eliminates peripheral awareness, potentially overlooking essential details or risks.*
> - ***Tunnel Vision:*** *Similar to the visual phenomenon where someone is so fixated on a single point that they lose sight of the surrounding area, metaphorically applied to mental focus.*
> - ***Ignoring Context:*** *Due to their singular focus, overly-focused individuals might neglect the broader context or potential negative implications of their actions.*

The Danger of Inappropriate Analogies

Using analogies can be a helpful way to frame a problem or predict behavior, but when misapplied, they become a significant cognitive trap. The brain loves patterns and often forces an analogy even when the comparison is weak or inapplicable. Misapplied analogies can cause analysts to overestimate the similarities between two situations, leading to flawed conclusions.

A stark example of this occurred after the Oklahoma City bombing. On 19 April 1995, Timothy McVeigh parked a rented Ryder truck in front of the Alfred P. Murrah Federal Building in downtown Oklahoma City. Moments later, a third of the building had been reduced to rubble. Dozens of cars were incinerated, and more than 300 nearby buildings were damaged or destroyed.

In the wake of the earlier World Trade Center bombing (1993), the media and law enforcement initially suspected Middle Eastern terrorists. This assumption was based on a faulty analogy between the two events, ultimately delaying Timothy McVeigh's identification as the perpetrator.

However, FBI analysts identified the rear axle of the Ryder truck from the vehicle identification number and traced it to a body shop in Junction City, Kansas. Employees at the shop helped the FBI quickly put together a composite drawing of the man who had rented the van (see Figure 11.3). Agents showed the drawing around town, and local hotel employees supplied a name: Tim McVeigh.[8]

FIGURE 11.2 9/11: An example of target fixation.

To avoid the inappropriate analogy trap, analysts must remain aware of their knowledge gaps and be willing to admit uncertainty. Organizational cultures that penalize ambiguity may push analysts toward "safe" conclusions based on familiar analogies. However, a more rigorous approach, where assumptions are continuously tested and challenged, can prevent these missteps.

AUTHOR'S NOTE

Showing that a suspect cannot be placed at the scene of the crime does not necessarily exonerate them from any involvement in the crime:

- *Organized crime or drug cartel murders are most often perpetrated by assailants who are paid killers, as opposed to the individual who ordered the homicide.*
- *Similarly, it has been shown that arsonists may have no personal connection with the fires they start. Instead, they are paid by third parties to collect fraudulent insurance claims or for other nefarious reasons. An example of such a case occurred in Russellville, Indiana, whereby Christina Snyder allegedly approached her neighbor and propositioned her with a $5,000 payoff if she would help burn down her house. The neighbor declined and reported Snyder to the police. The claim would have paid out $80,000.*

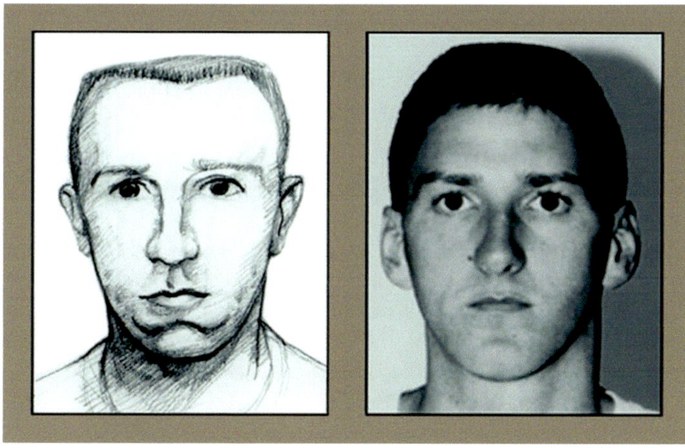

FIGURE 11.3 FBI composite and actual photo of Timothy McVeigh (FBI).

Groupthink and Organizational Culture

One of the most overlooked biases in intelligence analysis is the role of organizational culture. Groupthink, first defined by psychologist Irving Janis in the 1970s, occurs when the pressure to conform within a group stifles creativity and independent thought. This can be particularly dangerous in intelligence organizations, where hierarchies are prevalent. Analysts may suppress their unique insights if they conflict with the prevailing narrative[9] (see Figure 11.4).

FIGURE 11.4 Illustration of groupthink in organizational cultures (www.shutterstock.com).

Organizations must foster an environment where dissent is tolerated and encouraged to combat groupthink. Techniques like structured debate and devil's advocacy can create a culture of constructive disagreement where alternative viewpoints are explored and validated.

Example of Groupthink:

To better illustrate the point, let us look at a hypothetical situation. Imagine yourself to be the lone analyst in a county sheriff's office along the U.S./Canada international border. You have collected significant evidence from multiple sources that terror networks are smuggling arms across the border, specifically through your county.

You have forwarded your analysis to leadership, and a copy has been sent to the FBI. The FBI reviews your analysis and does not concur with your assessment. What might be your response?

Understandably, your report might better fit conventional paradigms and be more eagerly accepted if your assessment cited "local criminal groups" and "terror networks" or if your location was along the U.S./Mexico border, where previous reporting reflects an ongoing international terror presence. Unfortunately, neither is the case nor does the potential for ridicule and professional embarrassment exist for you and your department. What should you do? Should you retract your report and apologize? Maybe you should somehow modify your assessment to make it more palatable to outside organizations. Perhaps you should look for supporting data to prove your point better.

The most appropriate response would be to continue to collect evidence without bias, which either objectively or definitively proves or denies your assessment (see Figure 11.5).

AVOIDING COGNITIVE TRAPS: A DYNAMIC AND HOLISTIC APPROACH

Mitigating bias in intelligence analysis is not a one-size-fits-all solution. It requires a dynamic, multifaceted approach that blends structured analytic techniques (SATs) with an ongoing commitment to critical thinking and reflection. SATs are invaluable and provide a structured roadmap that helps analysts navigate the complex world of data interpretation and hypothesis testing. However, SATs alone cannot fully shield analysts from cognitive traps. Analysts must also cultivate an awareness of their own thinking, actively seek opposing viewpoints, and leverage the insights of diverse peers.

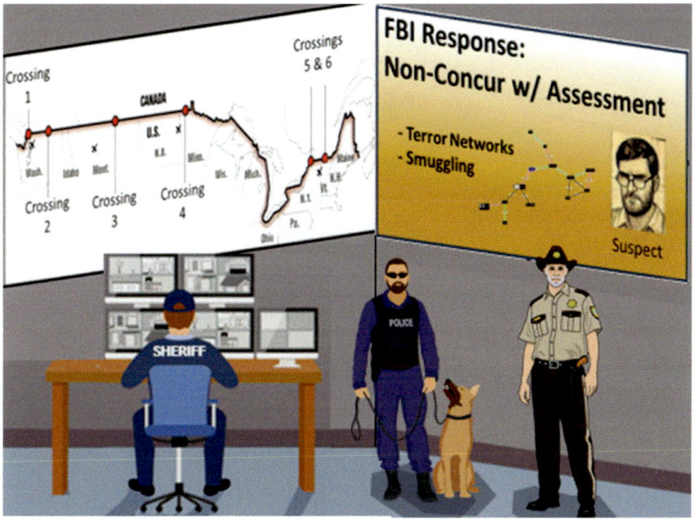

FIGURE 11.5 Example of groupthink.

Biases are inherent in human cognition and do not have to dictate intelligence outcomes. With the right mindset and toolkit, analysts can recognize and counteract the biases that threaten objective analysis, leading to more accurate and reliable assessments (see Figure 11.6).

Following are some of the key techniques for avoiding cognitive traps:

- **Pattern Recognition**
- **Properly Framing the Problem**
- **Leveraging Other Perspectives**
- **Structured Analytic Techniques (SATs)**

Recognizing Patterns: Learning from Past Mistakes

Pattern recognition is at the heart of intelligence analysis, but is also a double-edged sword. The brain's tendency to look for familiar patterns can lead to both insights and cognitive traps. To avoid falling into old traps, analysts must ask themselves: "What cognitive biases have I fallen prey to in the past?" and "Am I seeing these patterns now?"

While this might seem obvious, failing to learn from past cognitive errors aligns with Einstein's famous definition of insanity: *doing the same thing repeatedly and expecting different results*. The risk here is not only repeating mistakes but also failing to evolve one's thinking in

FIGURE 11.6 Conceptual illustration of avoiding cognitive traps.

response to new information or challenges. For example, after a terror attack is labeled as an "Islamist extremist" act by the media, an analyst should ask: "Does all evidence support this assertion, or am I being influenced by previous patterns?"

History is full of examples of mistaken pattern recognition. In their heyday, the infamous James-Younger Gang in the Old West was credited with committing dozens of robberies. However, historians generally agree that there were only 20 robberies (10 banks, seven trains, and three stagecoaches). However, not all historians agree, so the total may be as low as seventeen. So, why are there discrepancies (see Figure 11.7)?

Criminals and adversaries also exploit patterns in our thinking. These Old West robbers exploited the notoriety of the James-Younger Gang to prevent lawmen from following their trails. Similarly, Osama bin Laden used human couriers instead of digital communications, knowing the U.S. Intelligence Community's focus on signal intelligence (SIGINT). Human traffickers often exploit U.S. Border Patrol shifts, predictable patterns of law enforcement operations.

If specific cues or prompts automatically generate labels like terrorist acts, drug crimes, or gang-related violence, is there a chance criminals and terrorists may be using some of the signals and cues analysts and investigators use to analyze crime and acts of terror?

FIGURE 11.7 Wanted poster of the James-Younger Gang.

For example, authorities now believe Tamerlan Tsarnaev (the Boston Marathon Bomber) may have been responsible for a triple homicide in 2011, which at the time was labeled as a "drug-related" killing because thousands of dollars' worth of marijuana and money were left covering the mutilated bodies, and the case was never closed. However, forensic evidence connected Tsarnaev to the scene of the killings and that their cell phone records placed them in the area.[10]

These examples demonstrate how essential it is for analysts to challenge their assumptions and continuously evaluate the patterns they rely on. This is necessary to prevent adversaries from manipulating and exploiting intelligence operations.

FIGURE 11.8 Example of framing.

Properly Framing Problems: A Critical First Step

Framing is a powerful tool for making sense of complex problems, but it can also be a source of bias if done carelessly. Framing essentially refers to how analysts define and contextualize a problem; issues arise when done too hastily or improperly. When humans frame problems, they use mental shortcuts based on personal experiences, emotions, and values, which can skew the analysis from the outset (see Figure 11.8).

For example, consider walking into a room and seeing a lion's head mounted on the wall. Most people would immediately think it is a trophy. But if that lion's head suddenly moved and growled, would you still think it is a trophy, or would you now believe it is real? The initial frame (trophy) persists even when new evidence challenges it. In intelligence, this is known as the Law of Primacy, where the first impression often remains the strongest, even when additional information contradicts it.

In intelligence analysis, framing errors can have severe consequences. Analysts must carefully frame problems from the outset, ensuring they are considering all relevant perspectives and not falling into preexisting cognitive traps. Collaborating with colleagues from different backgrounds or conducting peer reviews can provide fresh perspectives, helping to reframe problems in ways that might avoid bias. For example, an analyst transitioning from a high-tempo environment, such as a terrorism watch desk, to a slower-paced office may initially misframe intelligence problems as requiring urgent action. Over time, they must adjust to a more thorough and deliberate analytical approach.

Leveraging Other Perspectives: The Key to Objectivity

No two analysts will see the same problem precisely the same way. This diversity of thought is invaluable, yet many analysts fail to leverage it effectively. By working collaboratively and incorporating different viewpoints, analysts can paint a fuller, more accurate picture of a situation.

> ***AUTHOR'S NOTE***
>
> - *Collaborative efforts should be formed from analysts with diverse perspectives (e.g., HUMINT, Geospatial, and a SIGINT Analyst)*
> - *Independent critical peer reviews also benefit from diversity of perspective (e.g., If a junior team made up of HUMINT, Geospatial, and SIGINT analysts produced an intel product, the critical peer review might best be performed by a senior MASINT analyst)*

Consider the analogy of a can of soda placed on a table. Each person's description will vary from different angles (or perspectives), above or below, or from the side, listening, or by touch; yet all perspectives are equally valid. Only by combining these perspectives does a complete and accurate picture emerge. Intelligence analysis works similarly. Early collaboration among analysts, where different perspectives are actively sought, can help mitigate the risks of personal bias or tunnel vision (see Figure 11.9).

Although peer reviews are helpful, they are not a substitute for early collaboration. Ideally, analysts should involve multiple perspectives throughout the analysis process, not just at the final review stage. This approach encourages the cross-pollination of ideas and helps prevent cognitive traps from taking hold.

Structured Analytic Techniques: Powerful Tools for Bias Mitigation

Structured Analytic Techniques (SATs) are a suite of methods designed to help analysts think more rigorously and mitigate cognitive biases. These techniques, including Analysis of Competing Hypotheses (ACH), Red Teaming, and Devil's Advocacy, enforce discipline in the analytical process, reducing the likelihood of falling into cognitive traps like confirmation bias or mirror-imaging.[11]

While SATs are critical, they should be used in combination with other techniques discussed earlier, such as framing, leveraging perspectives, and continuous self-reflection. A holistic approach that combines

FIGURE 11.9 Leveraging differing perspectives to provide a more complete picture.

these tools ensures a robust analysis that can withstand scrutiny from both internal and external reviews.

Example of Cognitive Bias:

Scenario
First, consider George, a 29-year-old married and outgoing man. Years ago, during George's college days, he was very involved in animal rights causes and participated in People for the Ethical Treatment of Animals (PETA) protests.

Which is more probable about George's occupation today?

a. *George is a stockbroker;*
b. *George is a veterinarian;*
c. *George is a large animal veterinarian full-time, but remains very active in the animal rights movement.*

What is your answer? (a) or (b) or (c)? And, in what precise order?

- *Example Solution: The best answer is "(a)" first (most likely), "(b)" next, and then "(c)," in that order.*

Supporting Information:

- *According to the Financial Industry Regulatory Authority (FINRA), there were 643,298 active brokers in the U.S. as of October 2015. This high-paying career in most states only requires one of two specific qualification tests and no college or other academic requirements to be eligible.*

- *According to the U.S. Bureau of Labor Statistics' Employment Projections program, there were 78,300 veterinarians in the U.S. as of October 2014. Veterinarian medicine is a highly competitive and generally well-compensated profession that requires a doctorate-level graduate degree, which is only available at roughly 30 universities in the U.S.*

***Note*: The number of large animal veterinarians would be less than the total number of veterinarians because it is a subset of the total.**

Alternate Solution: "(a)" or "(b)", then "(c)", in that order. Just in case you did not intuitively understand, there is a surplus of stockbrokers in America (see Figure 11.10).

The key: If you ranked c) as more probable than a) or b), you are very wrong ... and very likely to have answered the question the same as most of humanity.

Most people tend to rank (c) before (a) or (b) the first time they encounter this particular question, and it reflects a very pervasive cognitive bias, technically called a "conjunction fallacy." (Definition: A fallacy that occurs when specific conditions are assumed to be more probable than a single general one.)

Observing from a strictly statistical perspective, it is more probable that George is a stockbroker or veterinarian of any kind than that he is likely to be both a large animal veterinarian full-time and active in the animal rights movement, which is a subset of the category of all veterinarians.

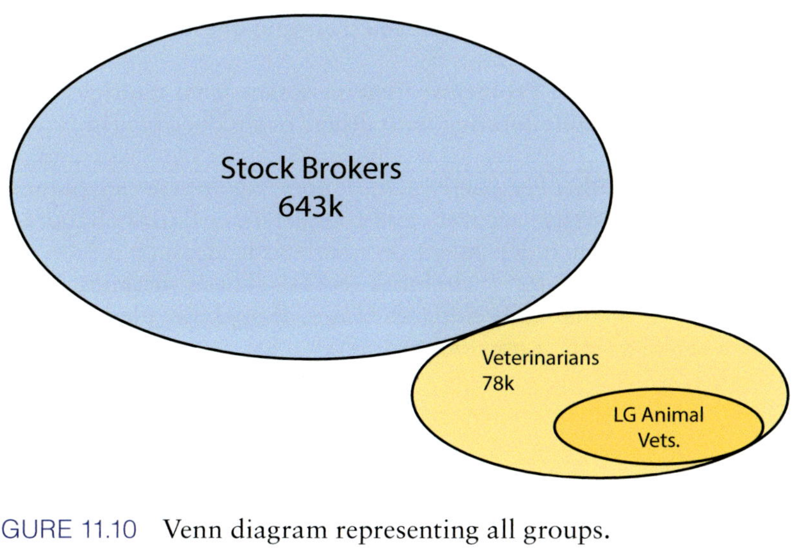

FIGURE 11.10 Venn diagram representing all groups.

CHAPTER SUMMARY: COGNITIVE TRAPS IN INTELLIGENCE ANALYSIS

This chapter explores various cognitive biases, or "traps," that impact intelligence analysts and other professionals. While psychologists have identified over 100 cognitive biases, the chapter focuses on a few common ones that significantly influence intelligence analysis. Recognizing these biases is critical for analysts to mitigate their effects and improve judgment.

Common Cognitive Biases

1. **Personality Bias (Mirror-Imaging):** Analysts often assume that foreign actors think and behave as they would, leading to faulty assessments.
2. **Confirmation Bias:** Individuals tend to seek, remember, and prioritize information that aligns with their preexisting beliefs while disregarding contradictory evidence.
3. **Target Fixation:** Focusing too narrowly on a specific idea or objective can cause analysts to miss broader patterns or critical threats.
4. **Wrong Analogy:** Using inappropriate analogies or models can lead to misinterpretations, especially when applied without sufficient supporting evidence.
5. **Organizational Culture:** Groupthink can suppress critical perspectives, leading to flawed or biased intelligence assessments.

Avoiding Cognitive Traps

- **Recognizing Patterns:** Analysts should critically assess whether they are repeating past cognitive errors and question underlying assumptions in their analysis.
- **Properly Framing Problems:** Viewing issues from multiple perspectives and collaborating with others can reduce bias in problem framing.
- **Leveraging Other Perspectives:** Incorporating diverse viewpoints enhances analytical accuracy and completeness. Early collaboration followed by independent peer reviews is ideal.
- **Structured Analytic Techniques (SATs):** These methods help analysts systematically mitigate biases, though detailed discussion is covered in a previous chapter.

While completely eliminating cognitive biases is unrealistic, being aware of them and adopting structured techniques can significantly improve intelligence analysis and decision-making.

Key Concepts Covered

1. **Cognitive Bias in Intelligence Analysis:** Analysts are vulnerable to systematic thinking errors that can distort the interpretation of information.
2. **Common Cognitive Biases:** Biases such as confirmation bias, anchoring bias, mirror imaging, and availability bias frequently influence analytic judgments.
3. **Groupthink:** Organizational pressures may discourage dissenting opinions and lead to flawed consensus judgments.
4. **Analytical Mindsets:** Awareness of cognitive biases helps analysts maintain intellectual humility and critical thinking.
5. **Mitigation Strategies:** Structured Analytic Techniques help counter cognitive bias by introducing systematic evaluation of evidence.
6. **Critical Thinking Discipline:** Effective analysts continuously question assumptions and evaluate the strength of evidence.
7. **Analytic Integrity Standards:** Recognizing cognitive traps supports the objectivity and intellectual honesty emphasized in ICD 203 analytic standards.

Learning Objectives Accomplished

1. **Define and identify** key cognitive biases that affect intelligence analysis.
2. **Analyze** real-world intelligence failures through the lens of cognitive traps.
3. **Apply** Structured Analytic Techniques (SATs) to counteract biases in intelligence assessments.
4. **Evaluate** different perspectives and alternative hypotheses to enhance objectivity.
5. **Develop** critical thinking strategies to recognize and mitigate biases in real-time analysis.

Practical Application

You explored real-world examples illustrating how cognitive bias can affect analysis, including:

- Analysts anchoring on early intelligence reports during a developing crisis.
- Intelligence teams overlooking alternative explanations due to confirmation bias.

- Groupthink influencing strategic assessments within large organizations.
- Applying structured techniques to challenge assumptions and improve analytic rigor.

Reflection Questions

1. Which cognitive bias do you believe presents the greatest risk to intelligence analysts? Why?
2. How can analysts recognize when their thinking may be influenced by bias?
3. What role do Structured Analytic Techniques play in mitigating cognitive traps?

By recognizing and managing cognitive bias, analysts strengthen their ability to deliver objective and credible intelligence assessments.

GLOSSARY OF TERMS

Here is a glossary of key terms introduced and discussed in Chapter 11 to enhance your understanding of the material:

Confirmation Bias: The tendency to seek out information that confirms preexisting beliefs while ignoring contradictory evidence.
Groupthink: The tendency for a group to conform to a single viewpoint, suppressing dissent and alternative perspectives.
Mirror-Imaging: Assuming an adversary will act or think as the analyst would.
Structured Analytic Techniques (SATs): Methods such as Red Teaming and Analysis of Competing Hypotheses (ACH) used to mitigate cognitive bias.
Target Fixation: The phenomenon where analysts focus so narrowly on one hypothesis that they ignore alternative possibilities.

This glossary serves as a quick reference for understanding key terms and concepts from the chapter. Feel free to revisit it as you progress through the material!

NOTES

1. Richards J. Heuer Jr., *Psychology of Intelligence Analysis*, Pherson Associates LLC, 2007.
2. P. E. Tetlock and D. Gardner, *Superforecasting: The Art and Science of Prediction*, Crown, 2015.

3. Richards J. Heuer Jr, *Psychology of Intelligence Analysis*, CIA Center for the Study of Intelligence, 1999.
4. Richards J. Heuer Jr., *Psychology of Intelligence Analysis*, Pherson Associates LLC, 2007.
5. Peter C. Wason, 'On the Failure to Eliminate Hypotheses in Conceptual Task', *Quarterly Journal of Experimental Psychology*, 12(3), 129–140, 1960.
6. MITRE Corporation, *Confirmation Bias in Complex Analyses* (MITRE Technical Report, MTR 04B0000017), 2004.
7. Peter O. Gray and David F. Bjorklund, *Psychology* (7th ed.), Worth Publishers, 2014.
8. U.S. Federal Bureau of Investigation, *The Oklahoma City Bombing*, Retrieved March 2025, https://www.fbi.gov/history/famous-cases/oklahoma-city-bombing.
9. Irving L. Janis, *Victims of Groupthink: A Psychological Study of Foreign-Policy Decisions and Fiascoes*, Houghton Mifflin, 1972.
10. Michele McPhee, 'Boston Bomb Suspect Eyed in Connection to 2011 Triple Murder', *ABC News*, 22 April 2013.
11. National Intelligence University, *Structured Analytic Techniques in Intelligence Analysis*, 2015.

CHAPTER 12

Probability Estimation and the Visualization of Data

INTRODUCTION

Why Use Probability Estimation over Intuition? Even in today's data-driven world, some intelligence analysts and criminal investigators rely heavily on "gut instincts." While intuition can sometimes guide successful outcomes, it often lacks the rigor and accountability needed in professional environments. Relying solely on instincts becomes especially problematic when briefing intelligence assessments to decision-makers or prosecuting criminal cases in court. In contrast, probability estimation provides a framework to reduce guesswork, introduce objectivity, and ensure that assessments are transparent, reproducible, and analytically sound.

Imagine you are an intelligence analyst tasked with assessing the likelihood of a potential terrorist attack on a foreign embassy. Your team has gathered scattered intelligence, some from reliable sources, others unverified. Decision-makers are awaiting your assessment. If you rely solely on intuition, your report may be inconsistent, subjective, and difficult to justify. However, you can provide a structured, transparent, and defensible assessment using probability estimation.

Probability estimation is more than just a mathematical concept; it is a critical tool that intelligence analysts, law enforcement officers, and policymakers use to make informed decisions. Whether predicting future security threats, evaluating the credibility of a source, or solving criminal cases, probability provides a systematic way to navigate uncertainty.

Despite its potential value, probability estimation has historically been underutilized in intelligence and law enforcement communities. The chapter explores the fundamentals of probability estimation and

DOI: 10.4324/9781003561712-12

data visualization, illustrating their practical applications in evaluating intelligence reports, solving crimes, and informing public policy. By the end of this chapter, you will understand why probability estimation and data visualization are indispensable for making sound, data-driven decisions.

Despite their growing importance, probability estimation and data visualization are not exact sciences, and until recently, their usage lacked consistency across the U.S. Intelligence Community (IC). This chapter introduces probability estimation and data visualization concepts, explores their applications, and highlights tools similar to those reportedly used by the Department of Homeland Security (DHS).

This chapter does not delve deeply into advanced statistical methods but instead aims to familiarize you with the math concepts underpinning probability. It also demonstrates its impact in criminal and intelligence contexts and provides tools to enhance analytical estimations.

LEARNING OBJECTIVES

By the end of this lesson, learners should be able to:

1. **Define** probability and its significance in intelligence analysis.
2. **Differentiate** between theoretical and experimental probability.
3. **Apply** the concepts of conditional probability in assessing intelligence scenarios.
4. **Interpret** the ODNI Directive 203 Probability Terminology Chart and NATO Source Reliability/Credibility Assessment Matrix.
5. **Explain** the concept of risk assessment and its application in analyzing terrorist threats.
6. **Utilize** tools like probability trees and event trees for analytical assessments.
7. **Evaluate** probability's historical and contemporary applications in intelligence and law enforcement contexts.
8. **Understand** the role of probability in criminal justice policy and resource allocation.
9. **Perform** basic probability calculations, including normal distribution and standard deviation analysis.
10. **Visualize** and analyze datasets to support decision-making in intelligence analysis.

ANALYTICAL APPLICATIONS TO PROBABILITY

From Assessments to Actionable Insights

Analysts use probability estimates to convey their confidence levels in intelligence findings, including sources' reliability and data's accuracy. These estimates are integral in crafting criminal profiles, shaping intelligence products, and guiding stakeholders' decision-making.

For example, criminologists use empirical datasets to assess crime patterns and predict future behavior. Intelligence analysts apply probabilities to convey uncertainty when complete raw data is lacking. This enables assessments that avoid vague descriptors like "slam dunk" or "no-brainer" and instead adhere to structured frameworks, such as the Office of the Director of National Intelligence (ODNI) Directive 203 standards.

Standardizing Probability Terminology

The ODNI provides a standardized scale to align probability language with numerical ranges, ensuring consistency across the IC. Table 12.1 illustrates these terms.

This framework helps avoid overconfidence in assessments while offering transparency to stakeholders. For example, labeling a threat as "likely" (55–80%) ensures users understand the degree of certainty involved.

RELIABILITY AND CREDIBILITY OF SOURCES

Assessing Sources: The NATO System

In addition to event probabilities, analysts estimate the reliability of information sources. A widely adopted system used by NATO and many Western military and intelligence organizations, it employs a 6x6 matrix that evaluates a source's reliability against the credibility of its information (see Table 12.2).

Therefore, if you received a report from a field informant with a rating of "A-2," it would be reasonable to assess the information as having a high probability (80–95%) of being true.

To provide some historical context of how probability is assessed and the associated problems with the calculation process, let us look at the attack on Pearl Harbor on 7 December 1941. According to diplomatic documents belonging to the American ambassador to Japan, Joseph Grew, it was discovered sometime after World War II that Grew had received intelligence that Japan was planning to attack Pearl

TABLE 12.1 ODNI Directive 203, Analytic Standard, Likelihood or Probability Terminology[1]

Almost No Chance	*Very Unlikely*	*Unlikely*	*Roughly Even Chance*	*Likely*	*Very Likely*	*Almost Certain*
Remote	Highly Improbable	Improbable	Roughly Even Odds	Probable	Highly Probable	Nearly Certain
1–5%	5–20%	20–45%	45–55%	55–80%	80–95%	95–99%

TABLE 12.2 NATO Source Reliability/Credibility Assessment Chart

Source Reliability	*Credibility of Information*
A: Completely reliable	1: Confirmed by other sources
B: Usually reliable	2: Probably true
C: Fairly reliable	3: Possibly true
D: Not usually reliable	4: Doubtful
E: Unreliable	5: Improbable
F: Reliability unknown	6: Cannot be judged

Harbor. Grew received this intelligence from the Peruvian ambassador, who reportedly received it from his chef. The information was dated 27 January 1941, nearly a year before the attack. Ambassador Grew passed this information back to Washington, D.C.; supposedly, Grew's comments on the information indicated that he thought the information to be unlikely at best.

Using this case as an example, an analyst receiving this information could easily assign a rating of "F-6" to this report based upon the lack of corroborating information and no previous reporting from the source (the Peruvian ambassador's chef) to assess the source's reliability.

CRIME PROBABILITIES

How Probability Helps Solve Crime

Probability does not solve crimes in isolation, though, along with other investigative methods, it can be a powerful tool for focusing investigations. For example, in the case of serial killer Robert Lee Yates, a combination of probability-based insights and hard evidence, such as DNA analysis, ultimately secured his conviction. Key evidence included:

- Traffic records: Linked Yates's car to a crime scene.
- DNA evidence: Elevated the probability of Yates's guilt to near-certainty.

Integrating probability with investigative tools like forensics and data analytics underscores its value in modern criminal investigations.

ASSESSMENT PROBABILITY

Previously, we discussed IC efforts to normalize the reporting of assessment analytical uncertainty using the standard that the Office of the Director of National Intelligence (ODNI) set forth.

Table 12.1 aids in standardizing assessment results. Granted, it is not perfect or precise; its variability fluctuates in a bell-curve fashion from 5% to 25% from one extreme to the other.

In probability theory, the normal distribution is a widespread probability distribution (see Figure 12.1). Normal distributions are important in statistics and are often used in the natural and social sciences to represent real-valued random variables whose distributions are unknown. The chapter will cover normal distribution calculations and how to use the results.

SIMPLE INFERENCE

This is the most straightforward manner of inference using one known event, "A," and one dependent variable event, "B." You can express it in terms of an "if" or "then" statement, such as: if "A" occurs, then "B" occurs with some estimated likelihood. Simple inference, or probability, refers to the likelihood that a specific event will occur, expressed as a value between 0 and 1. There are two categories of simple probabilities: theoretical and experimental; analysts use both.

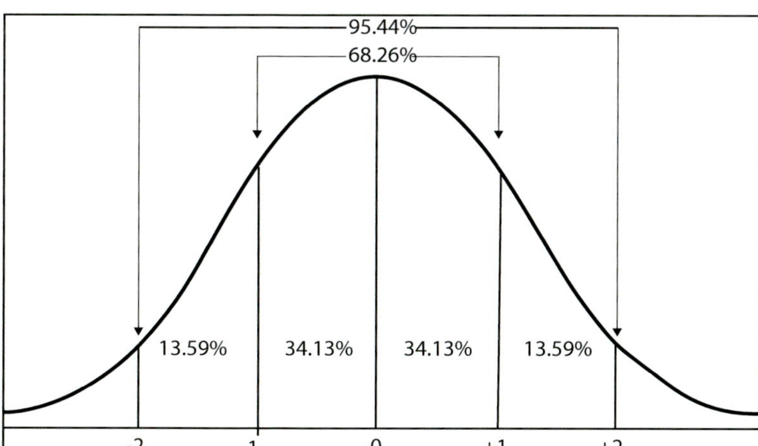

FIGURE 12.1 Normal distribution, "bell curve."

THEORETICAL PROBABILITY

Theoretical probability is the calculated probability. If every event is equally likely, it is the ratio of the number of ways the event can occur to the total number of possible outcomes. It can be expressed mathematically as:

$$\textit{Theoretical probability} = \frac{\textit{Number of ways to get what you want (or favorable outcomes)}}{\textit{Total number of possible outcomes}}$$

> *Example:*
>
> *There are eight prisoners of war (POWs) with actionable information. Therefore, the number of favorable outcomes equals eight. There are a total of 20 prisoners who were captured in the group. Thus, the total outcomes are 20. Therefore, the probability equation would be*
>
> $$\frac{8}{20} = \frac{2}{5}$$
>
> *In other words, you would have a 2/5 chance (or 40%), at random, of interrogating any of the POWs in the group, and that POW would have the desired actionable information you seek.*

The probability of whether a POW has the "pertinent" (or desired) information is built into the military's interrogation screening process[2] *(see Table 12.3 and Table 12.4).*

TABLE 12.3 Source Screening Codes

CODE	COOPERATION LEVEL
1	Responds to direct questions.
2	Responds hesitantly to questioning.
3	Does not respond to questioning.
	KNOWLEDGEABILITY LEVEL
A	Very likely to possess PIR information.
B	Might have IR information.
C	Does not appear to have pertinent information.

TABLE 12.4 Interrogation Priorities by Screening Category

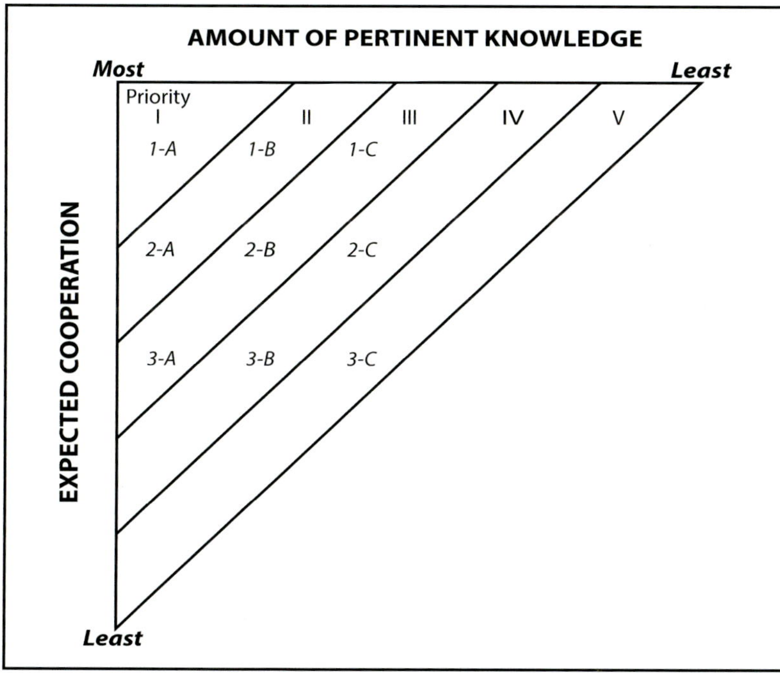

AUTHOR'S NOTE

In Human Collection Operations, there is a basic concept involved: Look for information where it is most likely to be found.

An interrogator or a covert operative who spends all their time interviewing people who have little or no chance of possessing the information pertinent to the mission is wasting their time. Therefore, screening operations are essential to increasing the chances of success.

The example provided is the U.S. Army's process of POW screening operations. By concentrating their efforts on priority "1-A" candidates and utilizing the "1-B" and "2-A" candidates to validate what they learn from the "1-As," they make the most efficient use of their time.

Experimental Probability

Experimental probability is the probability based on data collected from experimentation. It can be expressed mathematically as:

$$Experimental\ probability = \frac{Number\ of\ times\ the\ event\ occurred}{Total\ number\ of\ outcomes}$$

Conditional Probability

Conditional probability is one of probability theory's most fundamental and critical concepts. That said, conditional probabilities can also be perfidious and require careful analysis and interpretation.

To explain the concept of conditional probability, let's consider the events "A" and "B." If the event of interest is "A" and the event "B" is a recognized or expected outcome, "the conditional probability of *A* given *B*," or "the probability of *A* under the circumstance *B*," is usually written as $P(A|B)$ (in other terms: "Probability" of "A" given "B" has taken place).

CALCULATING RISK OF TERRORIST ATTACK

A Structured Approach to Risk Analysis

The risk of a terrorist attack is a key focus of intelligence analysis. Risk can be systematically assessed using the equation:

$$Risk = Consequence \times Vulnerability \times Threat$$[3]

This equation allows analysts to break down complex scenarios into measurable components. Consequence evaluates the attack's impact, vulnerability assesses the target's susceptibility, and threat considers the attacker's intent and capabilities. While the model simplifies analysis, real-world applications often require nuanced, multifactor assessments considering geopolitical, cultural, and historical contexts.

Extending this train of thought and laying it out mathematically, the

$$Risk\ of\ Attack\ [P(A)] = Consequences\ [P(C)] \times Vulnerability\ [P(V)] \times Threat\ [P(T)]$$

The following sections discuss probability calculations of "risk of attack" from a historical and a more contemporary perspective.

Historical Application: Pearl Harbor

The Pearl Harbor attack illustrates how miscalculations of risk can have dire consequences. Despite the critical importance of losing the Pacific Fleet and the vulnerability of a confined harbor, the threat was viewed as minimal. U.S. planners believed Japan lacked the capacity for a large-scale, long-distance naval assault. However, Japan's meticulously planned operation, which assembled aircraft carriers and supporting vessels, proved these assumptions wrong.

Naval operational planners at the time correctly observed that there were no Japanese-held land-based airfields capable of reaching Pearl Harbor. Consequently, the only reasonable attack vector remaining was from the sea. Naval analysts would realistically conclude that a substantial sea-based airstrike capability (including multiple carriers and their support auxiliaries) would need to traverse thousands of miles of open sea undetected to execute a successful attack (see Figure 12.2).

Assembling and moving such a large naval force, comprising six carriers, two battleships, three cruisers, nine destroyers, and various support vessels and submarines, without detection is considered highly unlikely. Unfortunately for the U.S. Navy, that was precisely what Japan intended to do.

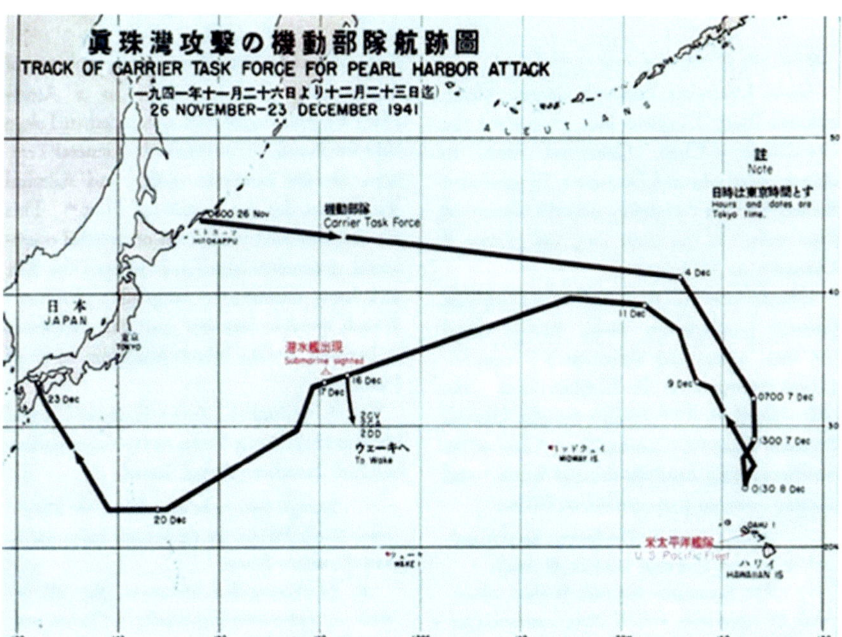

FIGURE 12.2 Japanese naval task force route to and from Pearl Harbor.

This failure highlights the risks of underestimating an adversary's innovative capabilities and the need to reassess threat factors based on new intelligence. Pearl Harbor stands as a cautionary tale for contemporary risk assessments, emphasizing the importance of challenging entrenched assumptions.

More Contemporary Applications: Estimating Terrorist Attack Risk

Modern terrorist organizations, unlike state actors, often target symbolic locations that have high visibility and emotional impact, or isolated and accessible military targets, for propaganda purposes. When assessing the consequences, terrorists evaluate the potential psychological and economic effects. For instance, a World Cup event offers global visibility, potential for mass casualties, and significant political implications, making it a high-consequence target.

Conversely, an abandoned soccer stadium holds little strategic or symbolic value, diminishing its attractiveness.

Vulnerability is another critical factor. "Soft targets" (e.g., schools or public gatherings) are often preferred over heavily guarded sites like military bases. Attacks on soft targets, such as the 2002 Chechen Moscow theater siege or the 2004 Beslan school massacre, are easier to execute and instill significant fear, as shown in Figure 12.3.

Propaganda targets may involve videotaping kinetic strikes against Western military forces to encourage the recruitment of terrorist fighters. An attack on a vehicle convoy illustrates to potential recruits that

FIGURE 12.3 2002 Moscow theater siege.

the enemy can be harmed, even if it involves only a single vehicle. Lastly, risk assesses the attacker's capabilities and intent. Pre-9/11 analysts dismissed the possibility of a large-scale attack on U.S. soil due to logistical challenges. However, 9/11 demonstrated how terrorists could exploit unconventional means, transforming civilian aircraft into weapons to carry out devastating attacks. This adaptability highlights the necessity of continuously updating threat models based on evolving tactics and capabilities.

Estimating the risk of a terrorist attack is a complex, multidisciplinary process that incorporates various quantitative and qualitative methodologies. It involves assessing the likelihood of an attack, its potential impact, and the target's vulnerability. Following is a breakdown of how the risk assessment process is carried out.

Risk Assessment Framework

Terror attack risk is often calculated using the previously introduced equation:

$$Risk = Consequence \times Vulnerability \times Threat$$ [4]

Each component is analyzed separately.

Consequence Analysis – Evaluates the potential impact of an attack:

- Human Impact: Casualties, injuries, psychological effects.
- Economic Damage: Recovery costs, business disruptions, and infrastructure damage.
- Reputational/Strategic Impact: Loss of public trust, geopolitical implications.

Vulnerability Analysis – Identifies weaknesses in a target's defenses that could be exploited:

- Physical Security: Access control, surveillance systems, perimeter defenses.
- Cybersecurity: Protection of critical digital infrastructure.
- Operational Processes: Emergency response plans and personnel training.

Threat Analysis – Determines the likelihood of a terrorist attack based on:

- Historical Data: Patterns of past attacks in similar contexts.

- Intelligence Reports: Information on active groups, capabilities, and intents.
- Trends and Emerging Threats: Technological advancements (e.g., cyberterrorism), ideological shifts, or regional instability.

This structured approach ensures a thorough understanding of risks, facilitating effective planning and mitigation.

> ***AUTHOR'S NOTE: SOURCES FOR FURTHER RESEARCH***
>
> - *Government Publications: Reports by DHS, FBI, and international organizations like INTERPOL*
> - *Academic Journals: Articles in terrorism studies, criminology, and security studies*
> - *Think Tanks: RAND Corporation, Center for Strategic and International Studies (CSIS)*
> - *Risk Management Standards: ISO 31000 (Risk Management) and ISO 28000 (Supply Chain Security)*

Probability in Solving Crimes

The Role of Probability in Criminal Investigations

Just as intelligence analysis has progressed, so too has criminal analysis. Crime scene forensics, recorded media (e.g., audio tapes and videos), biometrics, DNA analysis, ballistics, and other analytical techniques have transformed the courtroom. Statistical analysis may influence a jury, but solid and irrefutable evidence remains the most effective method for convicting a criminal.

But can probability solve crimes? The answer is "yes." However, it is usually not the only tool used, nor should it be. It is best employed to focus the investigation and can likely lead to a conviction when combined with other solid evidence. So, how can probability solve a crime?

Probability enhances crime-solving by concentrating investigations and reinforcing evidentiary arguments. While probability alone cannot solve crimes, it serves as a powerful tool for securing convictions when paired with physical evidence. Take, for instance, the case of Robert Lee Yates, a serial killer who operated in Spokane, Washington, during the late 1990s.

Example Scenario:

The Case of Robert Lee Yates (also known as the Spokane Serial Killer and the Grocery Bag Killer)

In the late 1990s, Spokane, Washington, was haunted by a serial killer who eluded police for years, targeting prostitutes working in the city's Skid Row area. To combat this threat, a task force was established at a cost exceeding two million dollars. After three years of investigation, they uncovered several similar DNA traces at the crime scenes, obtained a description of a white male in his 30s or 40s, and received reports of a 1977 white Corvette spotted in the area following some of the murders. Among the hundreds of suspects examined by this police task force, Robert Lee Yates Jr. (see Figure 12.4) stood out in connection with the serial killings of 18 prostitutes across Spokane and Tacoma.

Traffic records of a 1977 white Corvette that received a citation in the area revealed a name. This name, combined with a DNA test and further questioning, led to the arrest and conviction of Yates for 13 murders dating back to 1990.

At the time of Yates's arrest, he no longer owned the Corvette. The vehicle needed to be located, and a search warrant was executed to link the car to Jennifer Joseph, a 16-year-old prostitute whose body was found on a farm northeast of Spokane in 1997. The traffic ticket tied Yates to the vehicle and to the area at the time of the murders, but that was circumstantial at best and could easily be discredited in a court of law. The DNA evidence of Jennifer Joseph's blood pushed the probability into "the millions" that this was the vehicle involved in the murder, tipping the scales.

FIGURE 12.4 The Spokane serial killer.

As an afterthought, Yates served in the military for 18 years and was stationed in various military posts in the United States and overseas in Germany and later Somalia. According to court documents, Yates hired prostitutes during his two tours in Germany. Based on Yates's preference for killing prostitutes, there is an argument to be made that there are murder victims in other locations. Considering this information, now consider the probability that Yates hunted elsewhere.

Whether there are other victims or not, German police are investigating whether Yates might be involved in the murders of as many as 26 women in that country. Perhaps the "high probability" of association applied to DNA evidence will close some cold cases in other countries and locales.

SYNOPSIS OF CASE STUDY RESULTS: ROBERT LEE YATES

- *DNA evidence linked Yates to multiple murders.*
- *Traffic citations tied Yates's 1977 Corvette vehicle to crime scenes.*
- *Probability assessment elevated the likelihood of Yates's guilt, turning circumstantial evidence into a compelling narrative.*

Forensic advances such as DNA analysis have revolutionized crime-solving. In Yates's case, the DNA match placed the probability of guilt in the millions-to-one range, tipping the scales in court. This example demonstrates how probability can clarify complex investigations and lead to convictions.

Just as in the purer forms of intelligence analysis, criminal analysis falls short of perfection, and the results must be expressed as probabilities. However, that does not imply that probability calculations are without value when analyzing aggregate crime data or individual crimes. We will look at areas where probability plays a significant role in solving crimes and driving law enforcement and criminal justice policy.

PROBABILITY AND LAW ENFORCEMENT POLICY

Probability and statistics are crucial tools in modern law enforcement. They support efforts to identify suspects, guide investigations, secure convictions, and deter criminal behavior. Data from the National Highway Traffic Safety Administration (NHTSA) illustrates the persistent issue of impaired driving. For example, NHTSA estimates that over two million individuals with three or more drunk driving convictions will operate vehicles during the holiday season (Thanksgiving to New Year's Day). Tragically, approximately 1,500 people are killed in drunk-driving crashes during this period annually (NHTSA, 2023).

Deterrence Factors: A study on high-risk drivers for impaired or intoxicated driving reveals that the key deterrence factors include the perception of the likelihood of being stopped or arrested, supporting political calls for deterrence laws (NHTSA, 2020). Research indicated that high-risk drivers' decisions to drive under the influence are strongly influenced by their perceptions of the likelihood of being stopped or arrested. While all states have impaired driving laws, evidence of their effectiveness in preventing high-risk behaviors is mixed.[5] However, studies support the value of high-visibility enforcement campaigns, public education, and media outreach. For instance, initiatives like the NHTSA's "Drive Sober or Get Pulled Over" campaign combine public awareness with increased law enforcement visibility to reduce impaired driving incidents. These campaigns have successfully altered public perceptions and behaviors[6] (see Figure 12.5 and Figure 12.6).

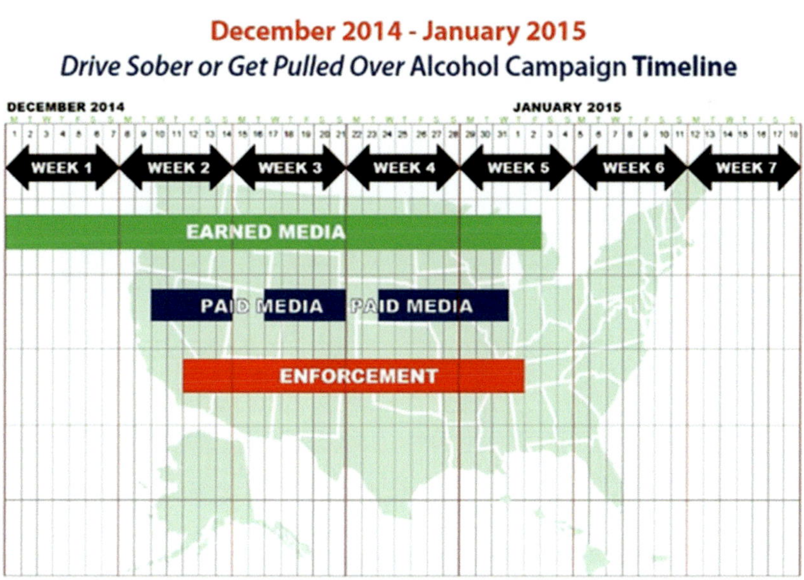

FIGURE 12.5 From the NHSTA 2015 pre-holiday campaign (National Highway Traffic Safety Administration [NHTSA]).

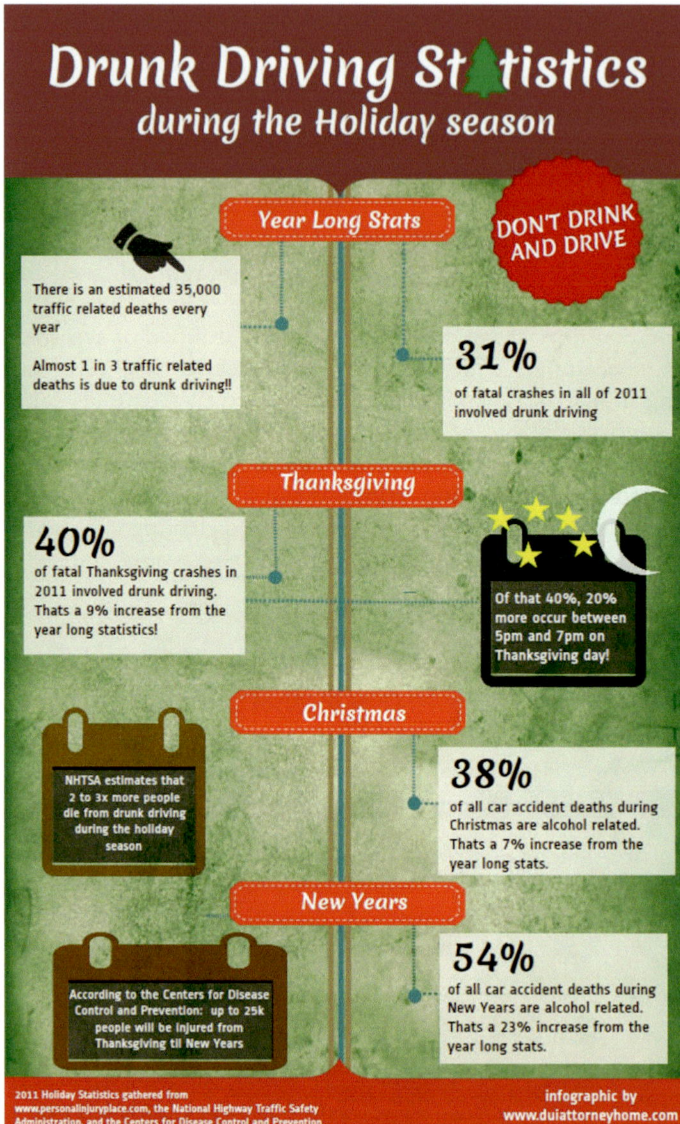

FIGURE 12.6 From the NHSTA 2011 pre-holiday campaign (National Highway Traffic Safety Administration [NHTSA]).

Probability in Criminal Justice Policy

Probability also shapes criminal justice policies, such as mandatory sentencing laws. In the 1990s, most U.S. states adopted "three-strike laws" to incapacitate repeat offenders. Typically, these laws mandate life imprisonment after three felony convictions, often including at least one violent offense, such as murder, sexual assault, or aggravated robbery.

Critics argue that these laws contribute significantly to the rise in incarceration rates. Between 1980 and 2013, the U.S. prison population experienced substantial growth, coinciding with the adoption of these policies. However, the relationship between incarceration and crime reduction is complex. Studies suggest that while increased incarceration accounts for a portion of the decline in crime rates, its overall impact is limited. For example, between 1992 and 1997, incarceration accounted for only 25% of the decline in crime, with other factors, such as improved policing strategies, economic growth, and community-based programs, playing more significant roles.[7]

These findings prompt significant questions: What are the cost-benefits of continuing to rely on incarceration? Does expanding prison populations yield diminishing returns in terms of public safety? With constrained budgets and rising incarceration costs, policymakers must explore alternative strategies to enhance community safety more effectively (see Figure 12.7).

Coinciding with the rise in incarceration rates, there has been a reduction in violent and property crimes.

Several recent studies argue that increased incarceration rates have some impact on reducing crime rates, but the scope of that impact is limited[8] (see Figure 12.8).

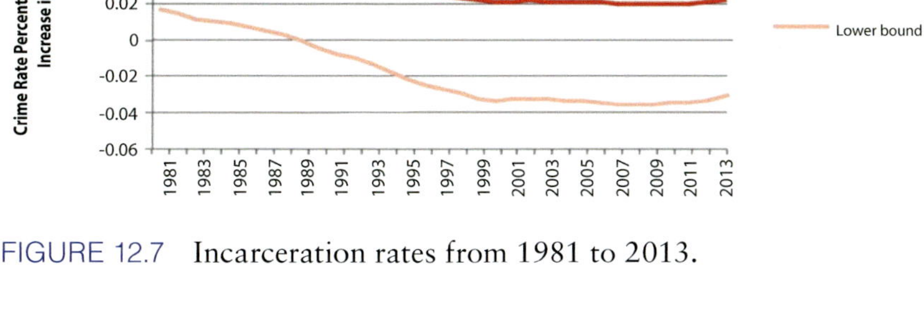

FIGURE 12.7 Incarceration rates from 1981 to 2013.

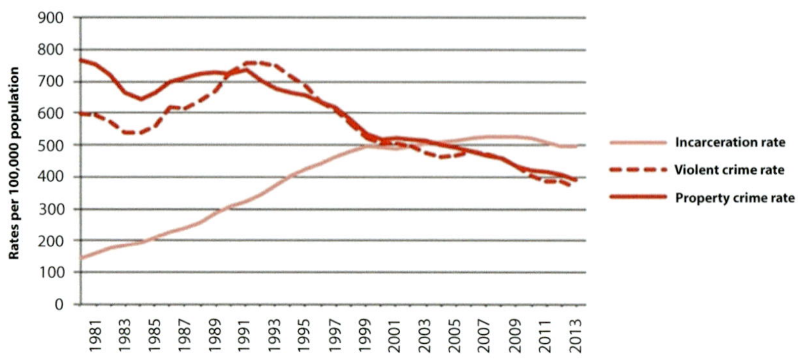

FIGURE 12.8 Crime percentage decrease from a 1% increase in imprisonment.

When the precipitous drop in crime between 1992 and 1997 was examined, imprisonment accounted for only 25% of that reduction, with the remainder attributed to factors other than incarceration.[9] As a result, pundits contend that incarceration may not be the most effective way to increase public safety.

This presents a developing societal issue in a period of limited funding for new prisons and the ever-rising cost of incarceration. *What are the cost-benefit implications of continued growth in incarceration? Does it prevent considerably fewer, if any, crimes? If so, what is the cost to taxpayers?*

TOOLS FOR CALCULATING PROBABILITY

Complex events, such as large-scale terror attacks or public safety crises, require detailed probability assessments. Breaking these events into components using structured tools can help estimate their likelihood. This section discusses two widely used tools: event trees and probability trees. Both are integral to risk analysis and resource allocation strategies within agencies such as the Department of Homeland Security (DHS).

Event Trees

Event trees utilize Boolean logic to analyze the progression of an event over time, visually mapping subsequent events and their corresponding outcomes. This approach provides a systematic framework to assess risks, such as those associated with terrorism. For example, DHS uses

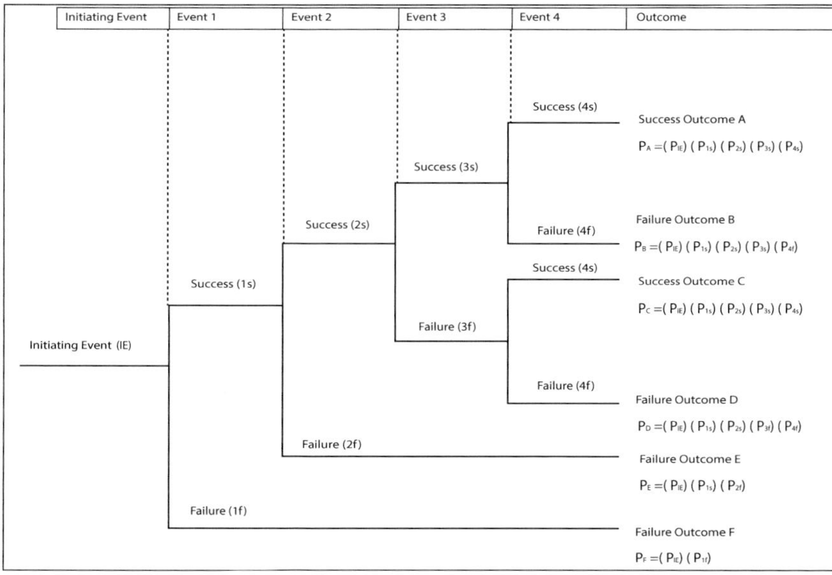

FIGURE 12.9 Event tree.

event trees to evaluate potential attack scenarios, incorporating initiating events, response actions, and cascading consequences. By segmenting the analysis, event trees enable the prioritization of risks and the effective allocation of resources (see Figure 12.9).

Probability Trees

Probability trees extend the functionality of event trees by including numerical probabilities at each branch, representing the likelihood of sequential events. These diagrams enable analysts to calculate the overall probability of various outcomes and assess alternative actions. For instance, in terrorism risk analysis, a probability tree might model an attacker's decision-making process, assigning probability values to different choices and estimating the chances of success. Probability trees comprehensively view risks and decision impacts by incorporating mitigating actions and potential outcomes. This process prioritizes managing the most significant risks over attempting to protect everything.[10] Event and probability trees can be used to model uncertain events and estimate their likelihood (see Figure 12.10).

Both tools are critical in DHS's shift toward risk-based resource allocation, focusing on addressing the highest-priority threats. A recent RAND Corporation study highlighted the effectiveness of these

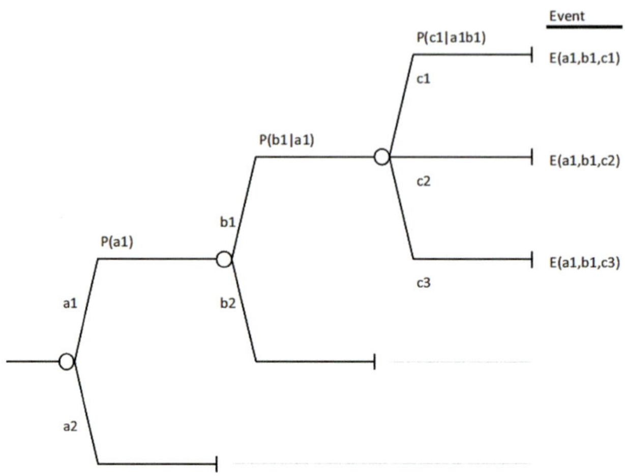

FIGURE 12.10 Probability tree.

methods in structuring complex analyses and enhancing decision-making in national security contexts.[11]

Probability and statistical tools are indispensable in modern intelligence and law enforcement strategies. By integrating these methodologies into policy-making and operational decision-making, agencies can enhance public safety outcomes, optimize resource utilization, and adapt to evolving threats. As challenges grow more complex, the continued refinement and application of probabilistic tools will remain essential to effective intelligence analysis.

Probability Tree Example

The probability tree is a branched diagram that represents multiple sequential events and their calculated probability distribution or density, using Excel.

As mentioned in the introduction, this chapter is not a higher math course that teaches statistics in extreme detail. Still, some basic concepts and calculations are necessary to understand the collected datasets.

> **AUTHOR'S NOTE**
>
> *There are many spreadsheet and statistical software tools available today and this should not be considered an endorsement of the Microsoft Excel product. However, most college students are at least familiar with Excel and therefore Excel is considered the best choice to present the information in this section.*

One conceptual method is a probability distribution. A probability distribution describes the proportion of a population having a specific range of values (or density) for a particular attribute. Analysts and researchers use this calculation to visualize and better understand datasets. In this section, you will use MS Excel software as a convenient calculation tool to visualize a global terror dataset.

VISUALIZING THE DATA

Often, plotting datasets on a chart helps us better understand the data and the underlying problem (or problems) they represent. Intelligence analysts rely on visualizing data to transform raw information into actionable insights, but without proper visualization, they risk misinterpreting patterns, overlooking critical details, or drawing flawed conclusions. The following seven reasons, along with their detailed explanations, demonstrate why data visualization is crucial, starting with the pitfall of misinterpreting natural (norm-referenced) trends as evidence for erroneous suspicions. Additional key reasons follow, each illustrated with real-world examples. The reasons are as follows:

- Avoiding Misinterpretation of Natural Trends as Suspicious Patterns
- Identifying Hidden Patterns and Anomalies
- Enhancing Communication and Decision-Making
- Contextualizing Data over Time and Space
- Reducing Cognitive Overload and Bias
- Enabling Predictive Analysis
- Facilitating Cross-Disciplinary Collaboration

1. Avoiding Misinterpretation of Natural Trends as Suspicious Patterns

Analysts often work with vast datasets, where natural variations, such as seasonal fluctuations or statistical noise, can mimic trends that align with preconceived hypotheses. Without visualization tools (e.g., graphs, heatmaps), they might mistake these norms for anomalies, leading to false positives or wasted resources.

- **Why It Matters:** Raw data in tables or logs obscures context. However, visuals like time-series plots or scatter charts reveal whether a spike is an outlier or part of a baseline. Misreading natural trends as threats can escalate tensions or misdirect policy, especially in counterterrorism or geopolitical analysis.[12]

- **Real-World Example:** In 2016, U.S. intelligence tracked a surge in encrypted communications from a Middle Eastern region, initially suspecting an imminent IS attack. Analysts later visualized the data against historical norms, revealing that it aligned with Ramadan, a period of naturally heightened online activity among Muslim communities, thereby avoiding a costly overreaction, as per declassified reports cited in *Foreign Policy* (2017). Without visualization, the spike could have fueled a flawed hypothesis of coordinated terror.[13,14]

2. Identifying Hidden Patterns and Anomalies

Visualization reveals relationships or irregularities that tabular data may conceal, allowing analysts to identify genuine threats or opportunities that are obscured by complexity.

- **Why It Matters:** Terrorist networks, financial flows, or cyber threats often leave subtle traces across datasets, such as phone records and travel logs. Maps, network diagrams, or cluster analyses can highlight connections, such as a sudden convergence of operatives, that raw numbers may miss.[15]
- **Real-World Example:** The 9/11 Commission Report (2004) noted that pre-attack intelligence failed to visualize call patterns between hijackers and Al-Qaeda affiliates. Post-event network visualizations revealed clear links (e.g., Khalid al-Mihdhar's calls to Yemen hubs), which, if revealed earlier, might have flagged the plot.[16] This spurred the development of modern tools, such as Palantir, for link analysis (see Figure 12.11).

3. Enhancing Communication and Decision-Making

Visuals distill complex data into formats (e.g., charts, dashboards) that policymakers or field operatives can quickly grasp, bridging the gap between analysts and decision-makers.

- **Why It Matters:** Intelligence often informs urgent action (e.g., drone strikes or sanctions). A table of 10,000 rows will not sway a general or senator, but a map showing attack clusters or a graph of rising casualties can drive consensus and clarity.[17]
- **Real-World Example:** During the 2014 IS caliphate surge, CENTCOM used heatmaps of IS-controlled territory to brief the Obama administration, per the *Washington Post*. These visuals showing Mosul's fall and supply line choke points directly shaped airstrike strategies, proving more persuasive than raw casualty stats[18] (see Figure 12.12).

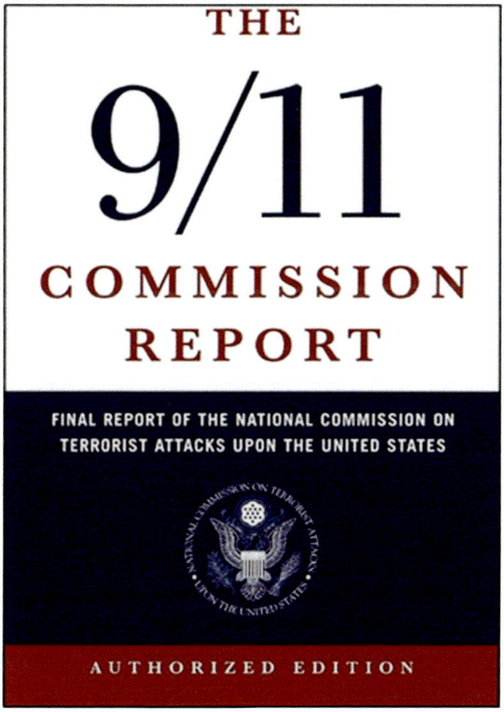

FIGURE 12.11 The 9/11 Commission Report cover.

4. Contextualizing Data over Time and Space

Visualizing data across timelines or geographies provides context, revealing trends or shifts that static numbers cannot, thereby preventing analysts from overemphasizing isolated events.

- **Why It Matters:** A single data point (e.g., 266 attacks in Burkina Faso in 2019) lacks meaning without context; did the number spike or decline? Maps indicate whether violence tends to cluster near borders or cities, informing resource allocation[19,20] (see Figure 12.13).
- **Real-World Example:** In 2023, GTI data revealed 260 attacks in Burkina Faso. Visualizing this on a timeline (a 27% drop from 2019 to 2020) and a map (concentration in the Sahel) clarifies JNIM's (Jama'at Nusrat al-Islam wal-Muslimin's) persistent threat, despite fewer incidents, according to the Vision of Humanity organization and GTI data. Raw counts alone might have suggested a decline, misguided aid, or a shifting military focus[21] (see Figure 12.14).

FIGURE 12.12 CENTCOM heatmap of IS-controlled territory.

5. Reducing Cognitive Overload and Bias

Human brains struggle to process large datasets without aids—visualization simplifies this process, curbing errors caused by fatigue or confirmation bias, where analysts tend to see what they expect.

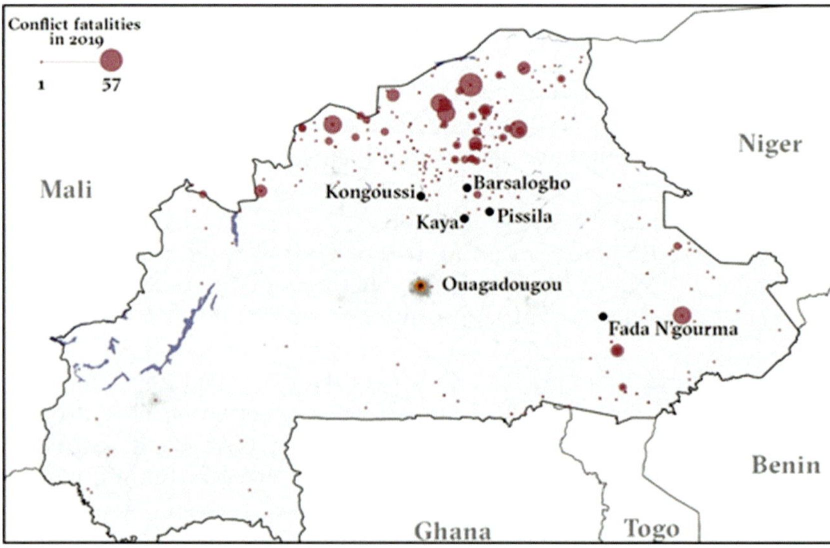

FIGURE 12.13 Terror attacks in Burkina Faso.

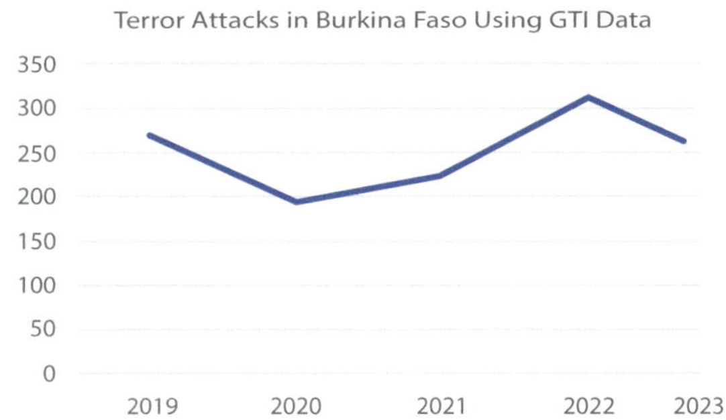

FIGURE 12.14 Terror attack timeline.

- **Why It Matters:** Analysts juggling thousands of signals (e.g., SIGINT, HUMINT) can miss critical shifts or overemphasize data fitting their suspicions. Bar charts, pie graphs, or Sankey diagrams alleviate mental strain, allowing patterns to emerge objectively[22] (see Figure 12.15).
- **Real-World Example:** The CIA's 2002 Iraq WMD analysis infamously misjudged aluminum tubes as nuclear evidence. Raw procurement data was not visualized against industrial norms; however, later scatter plots showed that it fit legitimate uses (e.g., rockets), as reported by the Iraq Survey Group (2004) (see Figure 12.16). Visualization may have mitigated the bias toward Saddam's nuclear threat.[23]

6. Enabling Predictive Analysis

Visual tools, such as regression lines or heatmaps, help analysts forecast trends, identifying potential hotspots or escalation risks before they materialize.

- **Why It Matters:** Proactive intelligence (e.g., predicting ISK's next Afghan target) relies on identifying precursors, such as recruitment spikes and the flow of weapons. Visuals make these projections tangible and testable[24] (see Figure 12.17).
- **Real-World Example:** In 2015, Europol visualized IS-inspired lone-wolf attack patterns (e.g., Paris, 130 deaths) against social media radicalization spikes, predicting a wave in Germany. This led to preemptive arrests in Berlin, per the *Guardian* (2016), averting a plotted attack.[25]

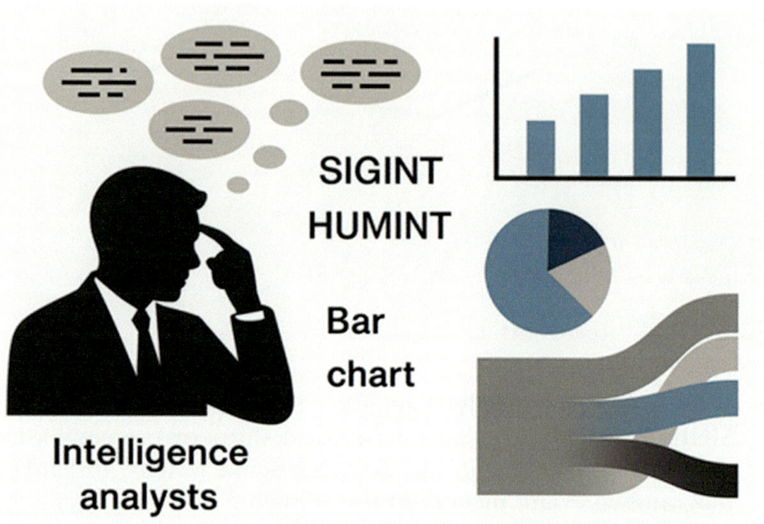

FIGURE 12.15 Visualizing information overload.

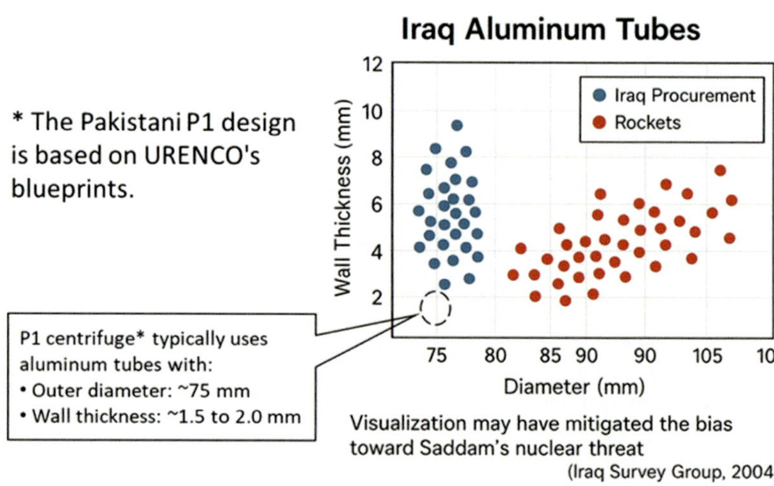

FIGURE 12.16 Visualization of the aluminum tube data.

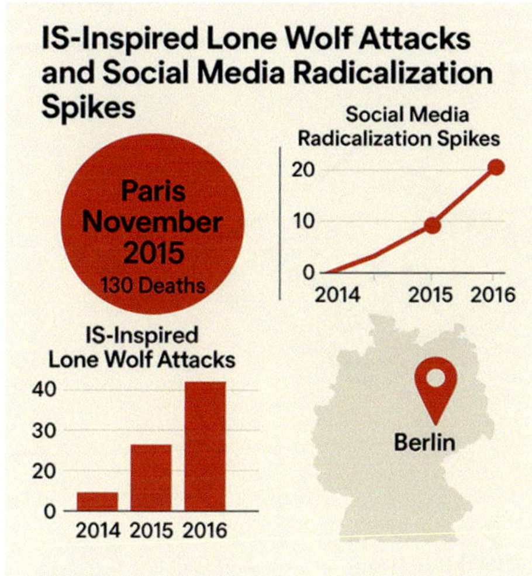

FIGURE 12.17 Predicting IS lone-wolf attacks.

7. Facilitating Cross-Disciplinary Collaboration

Visualizations standardize data interpretation across teams, encompassing analysts, linguists, and engineers, ensuring a shared understanding despite diverse expertise.

- **Why It Matters:** Intelligence is multidisciplinary; a linguist might miss a financial trend that a visualization reveals to an economist. Unified visuals align efforts, which is crucial in joint operations such as counterterrorism campaigns.
- **Real-World Example:** The 2011 bin Laden raid (Operation Neptune Spear) used geospatial visualizations of Abbottabad compound movements, integrating NSA signals and CIA HUMINT. Per Zero Dark Thirty accounts and declassified briefs, these maps unified SEALs, analysts, and commanders, ensuring precision (see Figure 12.18).

Visualization is indispensable for intelligence analysts because it counters misinterpretations (e.g., Ramadan spikes), unearths hidden threats (e.g., 9/11 links), and drives actionable decisions (e.g., IS airstrikes). It contextualizes (Burkina Faso's Sahel focus), reduces bias (Iraq WMD), predicts risks (Europol arrests), and fosters collaboration (bin Laden raid). Real-world failures, such as pre-9/11 oversights or WMD errors, underscore the cost of neglecting it, while successes highlight its power

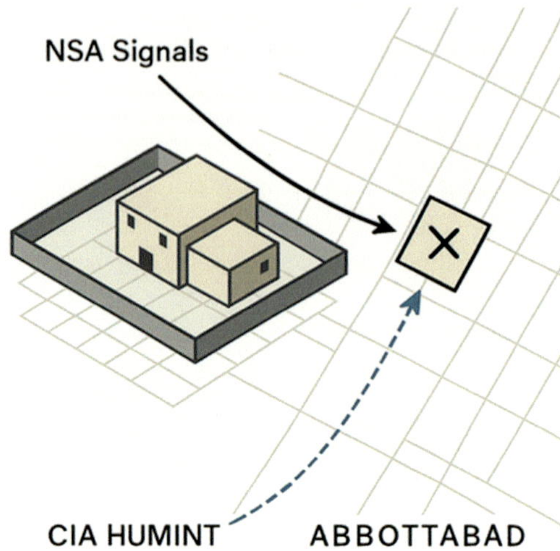

FIGURE 12.18 Simplified illustration of cross-disciplinary collaboration.

to transform data into clarity. Tools like maps, graphs, and dashboards are not just aids; they are the lens through which modern intelligence avoids chaos and finds truth.

Statistical Terminology and Concepts

Rarely will one find data spread across populations or geographical areas in a homogeneous format. Most datasets contain values near the average (or mean); some have values farther away from the average, and some are exceptionally distant.

The *standard deviation* of a dataset measures the data's spread (or deviation) from its mean. For this discussion, we refer to large datasets (in the hundreds or thousands), without digits beyond the decimal point. Normal distributions usually contain roughly 68% of a sample within one standard deviation of the mean and 95% within two standard deviations.

The *z-value* is the distance between a particular data point and the mean, expressed in terms of standard deviations.

Before we start the exercise, we also need to cover three other terms: mean, mode, and median.

- The "mean" is the average of the dataset.
- The "mode" is the number that occurs most frequently (with the highest frequency) in the dataset.
- The "median" is the number in the middle of the dataset.

Normal Distribution

In several cases, the data tends to cluster around a central value with no bias to the left or right, and it approaches a "Normal Distribution," as shown in Figure 12.19.

Many things found in nature and made by man closely follow a Normal Distribution; examples include:

- Zebra stripes
- People's height
- Measurement errors
- Blood pressure
- Test scores
- Financial and sales data

> ***POTENTIAL PITFALLS OF PROBABILITY AND STATISTICS AND HOW TO AVOID THEM***
>
> ***Potential Misuses:***
>
> - *Manipulating scale to change the appearance of the distribution of data*
> - *Eliminating high/low data points for a more coherent presentation*
> - *Inappropriately focusing on certain variables to the exclusion of other variables*
> - *Presenting correlation as causation*
>
> ***Measures to Avoid the Pitfalls:***
>
> - *Testing results for reliability and validity*
> - *Testing for statistical significance*
> - *Critically reading statistical results*

Simply stated, data is considered to be "normally distributed" when it symmetrically clusters around a central data point, with 50% of the values being less than the mean and 50% being greater than the mean; and the mean, mode, and median are equal.

Normal distributions are important in statistics and probability calculations. Understanding whether data is normally distributed or not is essential because if the data is treated as normal when it is not, significant errors can be introduced into the analysis.

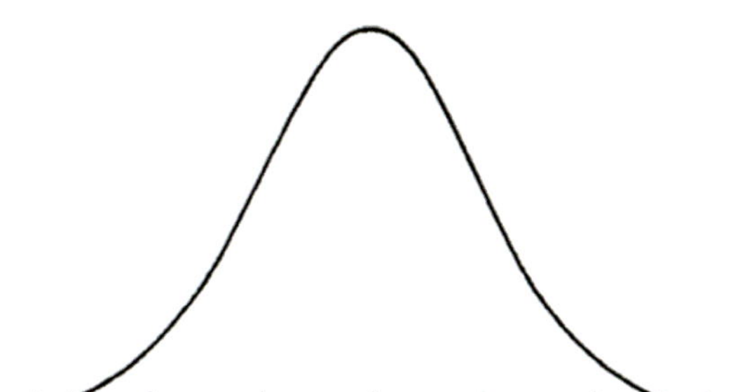

FIGURE 12.19 The "normal" distribution curve.

PRACTICAL EXERCISE: VISUALIZING DATA HANDOUT

This exercise helps students understand one method of visualizing data and determining whether the data is considered "normal" to determine analytical probabilities.

The practical exercise is a learning activity designed to help understand methods of visualizing data and determine whether a dataset is considered "normal." To begin, you will need additional data beyond what is partially presented in Figure 12.21. The instructor will provide this data as part of a Practical Exercise.

> *AUTHOR'S NOTE*
>
> *Before you can do most statistical data calculations using Excel, you must activate the Excel "Analysis ToolPak" add-in by:*
>
> 1. *Clicking on the FILE tab, and choose "Options"*
> 2. *An "Excel Options" dialog box appears; choose "Add-Ins" from the list, check to ensure "Excel Add-Ins" is displayed in the "Manage" window, and Click on the GO button*
> 3. *An "add-Ins dialog box appears. Click the check box for "Analysis ToolPak" and Click the OK button*

Load the Analysis ToolPak

The Analysis ToolPak is a Microsoft Excel add-in program that is available when you install Microsoft Office or Excel. However, you need to load it first to use it in Excel.

1. Click the **File** tab, and then click **Options**.
2. Click **Add-Ins**, then select Excel Add-ins in the Manage box.
3. Click **Go**.
4. In the **Add-Ins available** box, select the **Analysis ToolPak** check box, and then click **OK**.
5. If **Analysis ToolPak** is not listed in the **Add-Ins available** box, click **Browse** to locate it.
    - If you get prompted that the Analysis ToolPak is not currently installed on your computer, click **Yes** to install it.
6. After loading the Analysis ToolPak, the Data Analysis command becomes available in the **Analysis** group on the **Data** tab (see Figure 12.20).
7. Click on **"Data Analysis"** in the **Analysis** section of the toolbar.

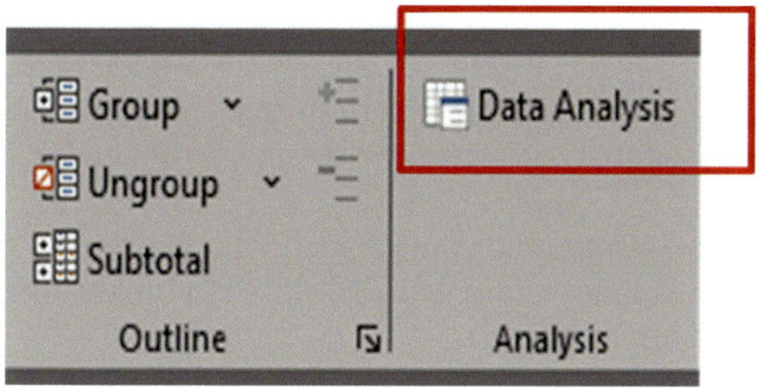

FIGURE 12.20 Data analysis tool.

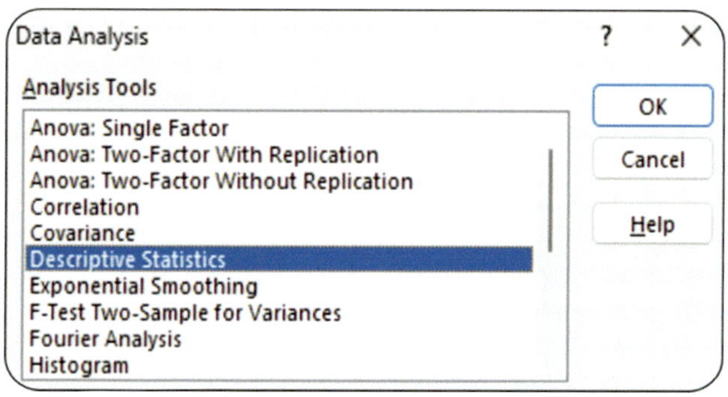

FIGURE 12.21 Data analysis dialog box.

8. Scroll down the list to "Descriptive Statistics" and click on it (see Figure 12.21).

Scenario and Raw Data

> ***AUTHOR'S NOTE***
>
> *The Descriptive Statistics analysis tool generates a report of univariate (i.e., data with only one variable) statistics for data within the input range, providing information about the central tendency and variability of your data.*

Here, we will visualize the data to determine if it can be considered normal, allowing us to calculate probabilities. There are multiple correct ways to visualize data. Some are very intensive and require multiple data samples. This exercise illustrates the process of visualizing a dataset using MS Excel. This process will be found helpful for intelligence analysis or any analytical or research process.

The exercise is done using MS Excel. Although other, more robust statistical calculation software packages are available (e.g., IBM's SPSS, MINITAB, Prism), we are using Excel simply because it is widely accessible. Also, most statistical software packages can import data from Excel.

This exercise is completed using Excel, which is part of the Microsoft 365 application. The steps may vary slightly if you are using a different version of Microsoft Excel.

This lesson will not teach how to use normal distributions to calculate probabilities. That will be covered in a more advanced lesson later. Here, we will only visualize the data to determine if it can be considered "normal." There are multiple correct ways to obtain this data, some requiring multiple steps to find each factor we are looking for.

Note: The facilitator must provide the complete raw data to input into the Excel file. Figure 12.22 only has an excerpt from the data file.

	A	B
1	Pakistan	490
2	Burkina Faso	258
3	Syria	224
4	Somalia	193
5	Mali	150
6	Nigeria	100
7	Niger	80
8	Afghanistan	70
9	Israel	50
10	Cameroon	40
11	Myanmar	30
12	Iraq	25
13	Democratic Republic of the Congo	20
14	India	15
15	Mozambique	10
16	Colombia	8
17	Kenya	5
18	Philippines	5
19	Chile	1

FIGURE 12.22 Raw sample dataset.

Generating Descriptive Statistics

In this step, we will generate some descriptive statistics for our dataset.

1. Open Excel and create a new, blank spreadsheet.
2. Copy the first two columns of the raw sample dataset to the blank sheet on the left side of the page (start in cell "B:1").
3. Click in the open cell to the right of the data (I chose "D:6").
4. Click the Data Analysis icon in the toolbar (located on the **Data** tab), and the Data Analysis dialog box appears (see Figure 12.21).
5. Select **Descriptive Statistics** from the list and click **OK.**
6. The **Descriptive Statistics** dialog box appears on the screen (see Figure 12.23).
7. In the **Input Range:** box, type "$B$1:$B$195" to select the dataset, and in the Output Range: box, type "$C$6".
8. Ensure **Columns, Summary Statistics,** and **Confidence Level for the Mean:** check boxes have been checked as shown in Figure 12.23 and click **OK.**

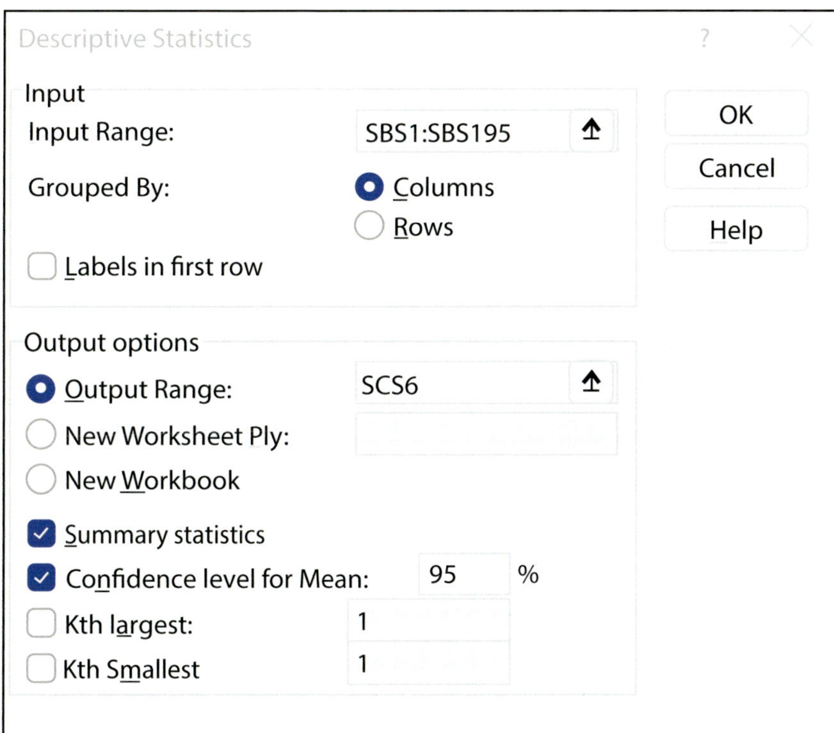

FIGURE 12.23 Descriptive statistics dialog box.

Column1	
Mean	9.1
Standard Error	3.4
Median	0.0
Mode	0.0
Standard Deviation	47.0
Sample Variance	2207.3
Kurtosis	63.6
Skewness	7.4
Range	490.0
Minimum	0.0
Maximum	490.0
Sum	1774.0
Count	195.0
Confidence Level (95.0%)	6.6

FIGURE 12.24 Descriptive statistics.

- In cell "C6", a set of descriptive statistical information appears (see Figure 12.24).
- Should your generated descriptive statistics not look like Figure 12.24 *(e.g., several digits past the decimal point are present, "9.0974358974359....),* then select the right-hand column of data, it should be column "D", right click, and select **Format Cells ...** and format the cells as a number with "1" decimal place. *(Note: In this exercise, we aim to understand concepts, rather than strive for precision.)*

Creating Bins

AUTHOR'S NOTE

The Descriptive Statistics analysis tool generates a report of univariate statistics (data with only one variable) for the data in the input range, providing information about the central tendency and variability of your data.

The next step in visualizing the data requires setting up some "bins." In statistics, data is usually sorted in one way or another. You might sort the data into classes, categories, ranges, or by placement on the number line. A bin is a way of sorting data for a histogram. We will sort our data based on intervals using the standard deviation determined from our calculated descriptive statistics. This interval will be utilized across the entire data range of 490.

Bins
0
47
94
141
188
235
282
329
376
423
470

FIGURE 12.25 Bins.

We will create several bins, starting at one end of our range, labeled "0," and ending at the other, labeled "490." Each bin will be separated by the value of the standard deviation we just calculated, which is 47. We do this by entering "0" in a cell and then entering "47" in the cell directly beneath it. Repeat the process until a column reaches the end of the data range, 490. (*Note: 47 does not divide evenly into 490, so we will stop at 470; see Figure 12.25. I started my bin data column in cell "F14."*)

Creating a Histogram Table

The next step is to create a histogram table. A histogram table contains the data used to construct a diagram whose area is proportional to the frequency of a variable and equal to the values associated with the bin (or class) interval.

1. Click on the **Data Analysis** icon in the toolbar (Data Tab, on the Analysis section of the toolbar), and the Data Analysis dialog box will appear (see Figure 12.21).
2. Select **Histogram** from the list and Click **OK**.
3. The **Histogram** dialog box appears on the screen (see Figure 12.26).
4. In the **Input Range:** box, type "\$B\$1:\$B\$195" to select the dataset, and in the **Output Range:** box, type "\$H\$23". *(Note: This is an arbitrarily selected location to place the histogram data table, which is about to be created.)*
5. In the **Bin Range:** box, type "\$F\$15:\$F\$25." *(Note: This is the area of the spreadsheet where you created the column of bin data.)*
6. Select the check boxes for **Labels** and **Pareto (sorted histogram)**.
7. Click **OK** (see Figure 12.27). (*Note: A Histogram data table appears with the upper left corner anchored in cell "H23."*)

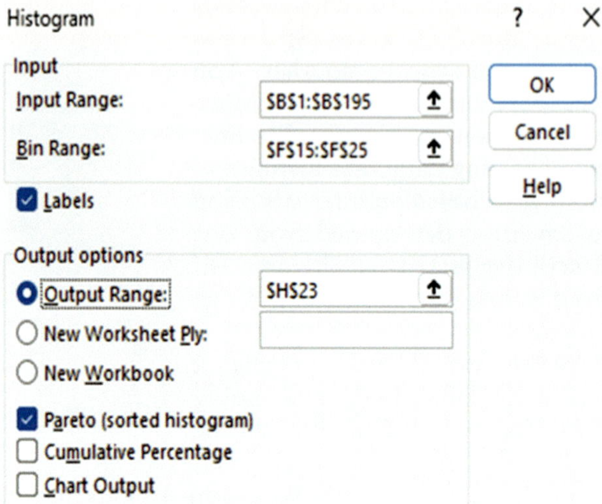

FIGURE 12.26 Histogram dialog box.

0	Frequency	0	Frequency
47	186	47	186
94	3	94	3
141	1	235	2
188	1	141	1
235	2	188	1
282	1	282	1
329	0	329	0
376	0	376	0
423	0	423	0
470	0	470	0
More	0	More	0

FIGURE 12.27 Histogram data table.

Creating a Chart to Visualize the Sorted Data

The histogram data table you created provides the necessary data to create a diagram that displays (or visualizes) the data.

To select all the data in the histogram data table,

1. Go to MS Excel and left click in the upper-left cell, directly below the word "Bin" (cell F15), and drag to the lower-right cell, right of the cell containing the value "0" in the second column (cell G25) (see Figure 12.27).
2. With the data selected, click the **Insert** tab of the toolbar. Next, choose **Recommended Charts** from the Charts section of the MS Excel Ribbon (see Figure 12.28).

   *Note: The **Insert Chart** dialog box appears (see Figure 12.29).*

3. On the **Insert Chart** dialog box, first click **All Charts** tab, next click the **X Y (Scatter)** icon (8th item in the left-side list), and last click on the Scatter with Straight Lines and Markers icon as shown in Figure 12.29.

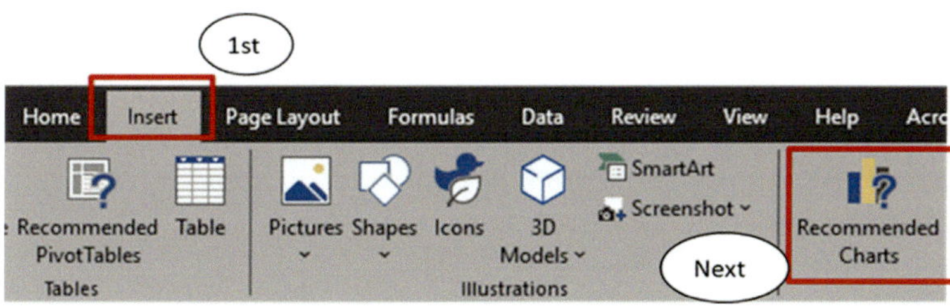

FIGURE 12.28 MS Excel insert tab and tool ribbon.

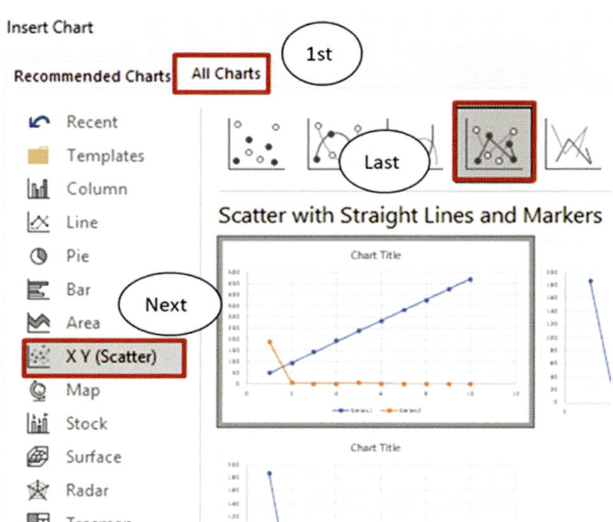

FIGURE 12.29 Insert chart dialog box.

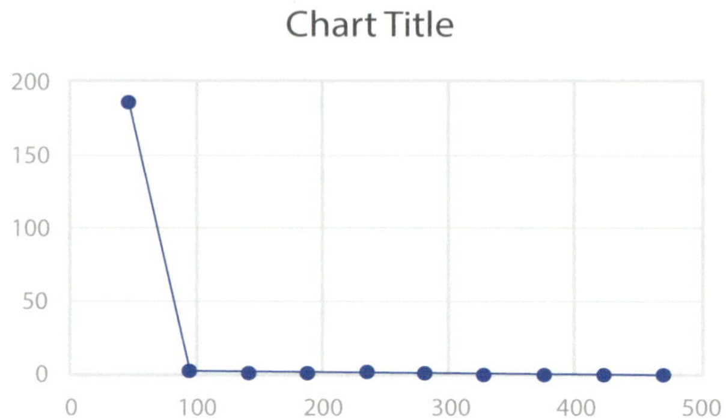

FIGURE 12.30 Visualized data chart. *Note*: The chart appears in the middle of the Excel spreadsheet. It will likely have to be moved and resized to fit the page. A figure showing the end state of all MS Excel data visualization steps is shown following. See Figure 12.31.

4. Then click **OK** (lower right-hand corner of the dialog box. A chart very similar to the one in Figure 12.30 appears.

Discussion of the Visualized Data

As mentioned earlier in the chapter, analysts often work with vast datasets, where natural variations, such as seasonal fluctuations or statistical noise, can mimic trends that align with preconceived hypotheses. Without visualization tools (e.g., graphs, heatmaps), they might mistake these norms for anomalies, leading to false positives, wasted resources, and potentially poor political and military decisions.

Raw data in tables or logs may obscure proper context. However, visuals like scatter charts reveal whether a trend line is a significant indicator, an outlier, or part of a natural baseline. Misreading normal trends as threats can escalate tensions or misdirect policy, especially in counterterrorism or geopolitical analysis.

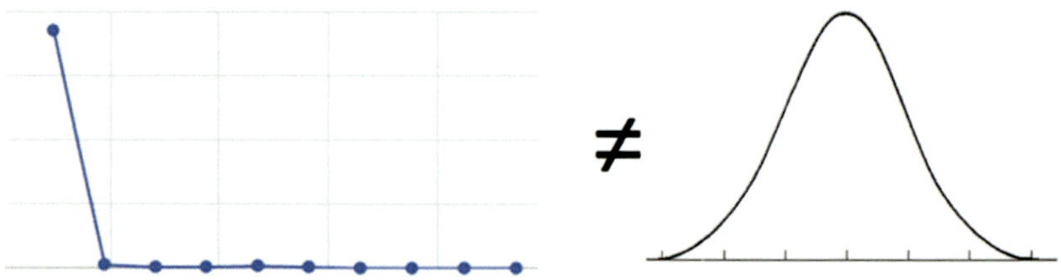

FIGURE 12.31 Final visualized data figure.

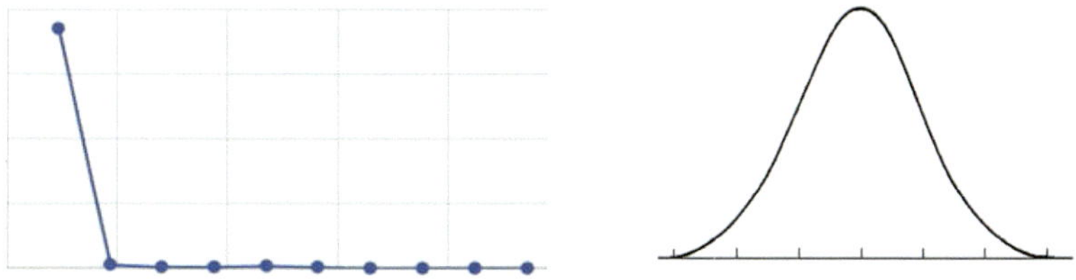

FIGURE 12.32 *Not* a normalized shape.

Question:

1. Can the data associated with this data be considered "Normal?"

Note: The Final Chart does *not* have a normalized shape (see Figure 12.32).

Now that we have determined our dataset does not represent a normal reference (bell) curve, take a moment to examine the data further. Recall the countries with the eight highest number of terror attacks? Refer to Table 12.5. Notice where they fall on the visualized data chart (see Figure 12.33).

Examining Figure 12.31, Figure 12.34, and Figure 12.35, several noteworthy points become clearer. Notice that the data is seriously skewed to the left, with no terror attacks reported in 176 countries.

Question:

2. Looking at Figure 12.34, in 2023, where (in what continents) are most terror attacks happening?

TABLE 12.5 2023 Top 8 Terrorism Countries

Country	*Total Attacks*
Pakistan	490
Burkina Faso	258
Syria	224
Somalia	193
Mali	150
Nigeria	100
Niger	80
Afghanistan	70
All Others	209

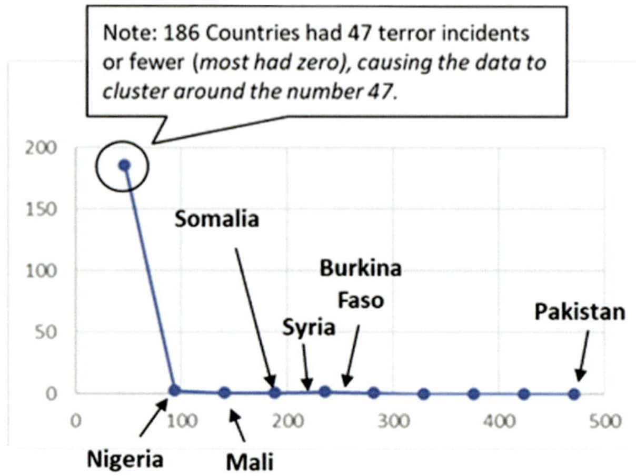

FIGURE 12.33 Terrorism worldwide 2023.

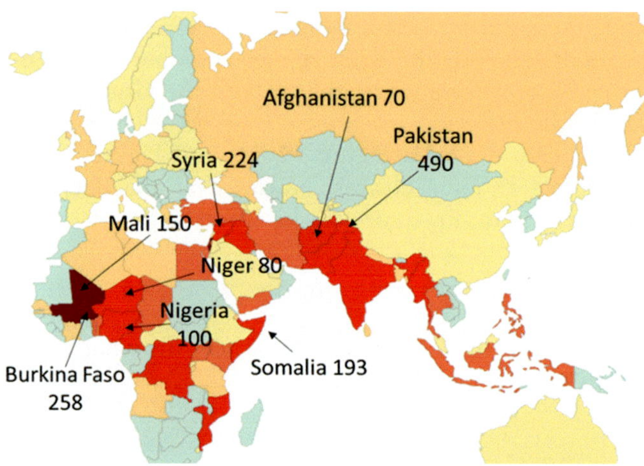

FIGURE 12.34 Countries with high levels of terror incidents.

Now, let us visualize the data differently, by organizing some of the same data into a figure and re-examining the top eight countries with the most terrorist incidents, according to the WTI.

For brevity's sake, we are taking the eight countries listed in Table 12.5 and placing them in Figure 12.35. Notice some cells are shaded to assist your observations.

Note: The Global Terrorism Index (GTI) data can be found at URL: https://www.visionofhumanity.org/maps/global-terrorism-index/#/

Countries with the Most Terror Incidents and Their Terror Groups

Country	Top 3 Terror Groups (2023)	Religious Affiliation
Pakistan	Tehrik-e-Taliban Pakistan (TTP)	Sunni Islam, Deobandi sect
	Balochistan Liberation Army (BLA)	None (Secular/Nationalist)
	Islamic State – Khorasan Province (ISK)	Sunni Islam, Salafi-Jihadist
Burkina Faso	Jama'at Nusrat al-Islam wal-Muslimin (JNIM)	Sunni Islam, Al-Qaeda-aligned Jihadism
	Islamic State – Sahel (IS-Sahel)	Sunni Islam, Salafi-Jihadist
	Ansaroul Islam	Sunni Islam, Jihadist with local roots
Syria	Islamic State (IS)	Sunni Islam, Salafi-Jihadist
	Hayat Tahrir al-Sham (HTS)	Sunni Islam, Al-Qaeda-aligned Jihadism
	Hurras al-Din	Sunni Islam, Al-Qaeda-aligned Jihadism
Somalia	Al-Shabaab	Sunni Islam, Al-Qaeda-aligned Jihadism
	Islamic State – Somalia (IS-Somalia)	Sunni Islam, Salafi-Jihadist
	Other Militias	None or Varied
Mali	Jama'at Nusrat al-Islam wal-Muslimin (JNIM)	Sunni Islam, Al-Qaeda-aligned Jihadism
	Islamic State – Sahel (IS-Sahel)	Sunni Islam, Salafi-Jihadist
	Ansar Dine	Sunni Islam, Jihadist with Tuareg ties
Nigeria	Islamic State West Africa Province (ISWAP)	Sunni Islam, Salafi-Jihadist
	Boko Haram (Jama'atu Ahl as-Sunnah lid-Da'wah wa'l-Jihad, JASDJ)	Sunni Islam, Jihadist with local roots
	Indigenous People of Biafra (IPOB)	None (Secular/Nationalist)
Niger	Islamic State – Sahel (IS-Sahel, formerly ISGS)	Sunni Islam, Salafi-Jihadist
	Jama'at Nusrat al-Islam wal-Muslimin (JNIM)	Sunni Islam, Al-Qaeda-aligned Jihadism
	Boko Haram	Sunni Islam, Jihadist with local roots
Afghanistan	Islamic State – Khorasan Province (ISK)	Sunni Islam, Salafi-Jihadist
	Tehrik-e-Taliban Pakistan (TTP)	Sunni Islam, Deobandi sect
	Al-Qaeda	Sunni Islam, Jihadist

Legend

Groups with multiple, former, weak, or no ties to any religious group.

Islamic State

Tehrik-e-Taliban Pakistan (TTP)

Al-Qaeda

FIGURE 12.35 Countries with the most terror incidents and their terror groups.

Figure 12.35 is an analysis and critical evaluation of Table 12.5 listing the countries with the most terrorist incidents in 2023 and their top terrorist groups, followed by a comprehensive list of anti-terror observations identified from the data. The table includes eight countries: Pakistan, Burkina Faso, Syria, Somalia, Mali, Nigeria, Niger, and Afghanistan, along with their top three terrorist groups and their religious affiliations.

The observations focus on patterns, affiliations, and implications for counterterrorism efforts, supported by explanations and critical insights. Since Figure 12.35 is the primary source provided (noted as based on the "WTI dataset"), citations beyond the figure itself are not included, but assumptions about its reliability are addressed.

Note: This objective analysis includes both positive and negative criticisms.

Analysis and Critical Evaluation

Figure 12.35 underscores countries experiencing significant terrorist activity in 2023, emphasizing the top three terrorist groups per country and their religious or ideological affiliations. The data shows a strong presence of religiously motivated groups, especially those associated with Sunni Islam, along with a smaller representation of secular or nationalist groups. Two major transnational terrorist networks, the Islamic State (IS) and Al-Qaeda, prevail on the list, with their affiliates appearing in multiple countries. The analysis uncovers patterns in religious affiliations, group prevalence, regional concentrations, and operational characteristics, while critically assessing the data's scope and limitations. Key points of critical analytical evaluation:

- **Scope Limitation:** The figure only lists the top three groups per country, potentially omitting other active groups or those with fewer but more severe incidents.
- **Data Specificity:** The absence of incident counts or impact metrics (e.g., casualties, economic damage) limits the ability to assess each group's relative threat beyond their presence.
- **Reliability:** The "WTI dataset" is referenced, but without further details on its methodology or sources, its accuracy is assumed rather than verified.
- **Affiliation Nuances:** Religious affiliations are simplified (e.g., "Sunni Islam, Salafi-Jihadist"), which may overlook internal ideological differences or local contextual factors.

AUTHOR'S NOTE: KEY METRICS DRIVING IS TO FIRST PLACE

- *Deaths: IS's lethality surged from 1,600 deaths in 2013 (GTI 2014) to over 6,000 annually in 2014–2015, whereas Al-Qaeda peaked at 4,400 in 2007 (post-9/11 decline). By 2015, IS accounted for 38% of global terror deaths (GTI 2016), while Al-Qaeda had significantly fewer.*

- *Incidents: IS carried out 607 attacks in 2014 (GTI 2015), compared to Al-Qaeda's 200–300 across affiliates, with the gap widening in 2015 as IS exceeded 1,000 incidents.*
- *Territory and Influence: IS's caliphate (2014–2019) highlighted Al-Qaeda's absence of centralized control after the Afghanistan invasion (2001). IS's propaganda attracted over 30,000 foreign fighters by 2015, according to UN estimates, surpassing Al-Qaeda's recruitment efforts.*
- *Bin Laden's Death (May 2, 2011): Al-Qaeda's decline quickened after this event, with Zawahiri unable to match IS's charisma or operational tempo, as noted in posts on X and analyses in publications like* Foreign Affairs.
- *Mid-2014: IS's declaration of a caliphate and the capture of Mosul represented both a symbolic and operational shift, overshadowing Al-Qaeda's decentralized model. The GTI 2015 indicates IS as the deadliest group that year.*
- *Mid-2015: IS's global attacks (e.g., Paris) and the growth of its affiliates solidified its status. Al-Qaeda's last significant peak occurred in 2007–2008, during the Iraq insurgency, and by 2015, it had diminished into a shadow of its former self, according to GTI trends.*

Question:

3. Who is the most common terror group in the table? Who is the second most common?

Some Anti-Terror Observations

To aid with the discussion, here are some observations (from an anti-terrorism perspective), each explained in detail with supporting evidence from the table and critical insights for counterterrorism implications.

Note: Any events that took place after 2023 are not included. This was done because the 2024 terrorism data was not complete or available at the time of publishing.

1. Sunni Islam Is the Most Common Religious Affiliation among Terrorist Groups

    - **Evidence:** Of the 24 terrorist groups listed across the eight countries, 20 are affiliated with Sunni Islam. This includes groups like Tehrik-e-Taliban Pakistan (TTP, Deobandi sect), Islamic State affiliates (Salafi-Jihadist), and

Al-Qaeda-aligned groups (e.g., JNIM, HTS). Only four groups: the Baluchistan Liberation Army (BLA) in Pakistan, the Indigenous People of Biafra (IPOB) in Nigeria, "Other Militias" in Somalia, and none in other countries, lack a Sunni Islam affiliation, and these are secular/nationalist or have varied/unspecified affiliations.

- **Explanation:** Sunni Islam's dominance reflects the ideological influence of Salafi-Jihadism and Al-Qaeda-aligned Jihadism, which have historically mobilized followers in conflict zones. Notably, no Shia Islam-affiliated groups or groups from other religions (e.g., Christianity, Hinduism) appear, possibly due to the Sunni-majority populations or socio-political conditions in these countries.
- **Critical Insight:** The **absence of Shia or other religious groups** may indicate a selection bias in the data or a focus on regions where Sunni extremism thrives. Counterterrorism strategies should prioritize understanding Sunni Jihadist ideologies while investigating whether other affiliations are underrepresented.

2. The Islamic State (IS) and Its Affiliates Are Present in All Eight Countries

- **Evidence:** IS or its regional affiliates appear in every country: ISK in Pakistan and Afghanistan; IS-Sahel in Burkina Faso, Mali, and Niger; IS in Syria; IS-Somalia in Somalia; and ISWA in Nigeria. In four countries (Syria, Nigeria, Mali, Burkina Faso), IS affiliates are among the top-listed groups, with IS itself topping Syria's list and ISWA leading in Nigeria.
- **Explanation:** IS's widespread presence demonstrates its successful franchise model, adapting to local contexts while maintaining a cohesive Salafi-Jihadist ideology. Its affiliates often compete with or complement other groups, such as Al-Qaeda affiliates, in these regions.
- **Critical Insight:** IS's ubiquity suggests it will remain a primary global terror threat in 2023 despite losing territorial control in Syria/Iraq by 2019. Anti-terror efforts must address IS's decentralized structure, targeting recruitment and propaganda networks across borders. However, Figure 12.35 lacks data on incident frequency, so IS's prominence in presence may not equate to dominance in impact.

3. Al-Qaeda and Its Affiliates Are Active in Six of Eight Countries

- **Evidence:** Al-Qaeda or its affiliates are present in Burkina Faso (JNIM), Syria (HTS, Hurras al-Din), Somalia (Al-Shabaab), Mali (JNIM), Niger (JNIM), and Afghanistan (Al-Qaeda). Only Pakistan and Nigeria lack direct Al-Qaeda affiliates among their top three, though TTP in Pakistan has historical ties to Al-Qaeda.
- **Explanation:** Al-Qaeda's network remains resilient, leveraging alliances with local groups to sustain influence. Its absence in two countries does not negate its broader regional impact, as groups like TTP may still align informally.
- **Critical Insight:** While IS affiliates appear in all eight countries, Al-Qaeda's presence in six suggests a competitive dynamic. Historical claims (e.g., IS surpassing Al-Qaeda around 2014) are not directly testable here, as the table (Figure 12.35) lacks longitudinal data. Counterterrorism must target both networks, recognizing their overlapping yet distinct operational styles—IS's high-profile attacks vs. Al-Qaeda's long-term insurgency focus.

4. Some Terrorist Groups Operate Transnationally across Borders

- **Evidence:** IS-Sahel operates in Burkina Faso, Mali, and Niger; JNIM is active in the same three countries; Boko Haram spans Nigeria and Niger; and TTP is listed in both Pakistan and Afghanistan. These groups exploit porous borders and regional instability.
- **Explanation:** Transnational operations indicate strong coordination, shared resources, or ideological alignment, particularly in Africa's Sahel region (IS-Sahel, JNIM) and South Asia (TTP). This amplifies their threat beyond national boundaries.
- **Critical Insight:** Regional cooperation is essential for counterterrorism, as unilateral efforts may fail against groups with cross-border safe havens. The table's (Figure 12.35) focus on top groups may underrepresent smaller transnational actors, necessitating broader intelligence sharing.

5. Secular or Nationalist Groups Contribute to Terrorism, Though Less Prevalent

- **Evidence:** BLA in Pakistan (secular/nationalist) and IPOB in Nigeria (secular/nationalist) are listed, alongside Somalia's

"Other Militias" with no clear religious affiliation. These groups contrast with the Sunni Islam majority, with BLA ranking second in Pakistan.

- **Explanation:** These groups reflect political, ethnic, or separatist grievances (e.g., Baloch independence, Biafran separatism) rather than religious ideology, showing terrorism's multifaceted drivers.
- **Critical Insight:** While less common, secular groups complicate counterterrorism, requiring strategies beyond religious deradicalization—e.g., addressing governance or ethnic tensions. Their lower prevalence may reflect the table's focus on religiously motivated threats.

6. Terrorism Is Concentrated in Specific Regions

- **Evidence:** Five of eight countries are in Africa (Burkina Faso, Somalia, Mali, Nigeria, Niger), two in South Asia (Pakistan, Afghanistan), and one in the Middle East (Syria). This clusters terrorist activity in the Sahel, Horn of Africa, and South Asia.
- **Explanation:** Regional factors like weak governance, poverty, and ongoing conflicts (e.g., Syrian civil war, Sahel insurgencies) create environments conducive to terrorism. The African concentration is striking, with overlapping IS and Al-Qaeda affiliates.
- **Critical Insight:** Counterterrorism should prioritize regional stabilization, but the table's (Figure 12.35) selection of "most incidents" countries may be biased toward these regions, potentially overlooking emerging threats elsewhere (e.g., Southeast Asia).

7. Variations within Sunni Islam Reflect Ideological Diversity

- **Evidence:** Sunni-affiliated groups include Deobandi (TTP), Salafi-Jihadist (IS affiliates), Al-Qaeda-aligned Jihadism (JNIM, HTS), and locally rooted Jihadism (Ansaroul Islam, Boko Haram). These distinctions shape their goals and tactics.
- **Explanation:** The diversity within Sunni Islam—e.g., Deobandi's South Asian roots vs. Salafi-Jihadism's global ambitions—highlights how local and international ideologies intersect in terrorism.

- **Critical Insight:** Counterterrorism must tailor responses to these nuances, as a one-size-fits-all approach to "Sunni extremism" may miss group-specific motivations or alliances.

CRITICAL EVALUATION SUMMARY

Figure 12.35 provides a snapshot of terrorist activity in 2023, emphasizing Sunni Islam's dominance, IS's widespread reach, and Al-Qaeda's persistent influence. However, its limitations, lack of incident data, focus on top groups, and simplified affiliations restrict a full threat assessment. Assuming the WTI dataset is reliable, these observations align with known trends (e.g., IS's franchise growth, Sahel instability). Still, counterterrorism strategies should supplement this data with incident-specific metrics and broader regional analysis to avoid overgeneralization.

Conclusion

At this point, the group's observations and discussions should reveal a complex terrorism landscape in 2023, dominated by Sunni Jihadist groups (notably IS and Al-Qaeda affiliates) yet diversified by secular actors and regional dynamics. Effective anti-terror measures must address ideological drivers, transnational networks, and local grievances, while adapting to the data gaps through comprehensive intelligence and cooperation.

CHAPTER SUMMARY

Probability estimation is a fundamental tool for intelligence analysts and law enforcement professionals. Unlike intuition, which can be subjective and inconsistent, probability provides a structured framework for making objective, transparent, and reproducible assessments. This lesson has covered the critical role of probability in crafting intelligence products, assessing risks, solving crimes, and shaping policy decisions.

Key Concepts

1. Why Probability Matters
   - Probability estimation ensures rigor and accountability in intelligence analysis, enhancing the clarity and credibility of assessments presented to decision-makers.
2. Types of Probability
   - Theoretical Probability: Based on logical calculations.
   - Experimental Probability: Derived from observed data.

3. Conditional Probability
   - Examines the likelihood of an event occurring, given that another event has already taken place (e.g., P(A|B)).
4. Standardization and Frameworks
   - The ODNI Probability Terminology Chart ensures consistent communication of likelihoods.
   - The NATO Source Reliability Matrix evaluates the trustworthiness of sources and their information, which is essential for assessing the validity of intelligence.
5. Applications in Risk Assessment
   - The formula Risk = Consequence × Vulnerability × Threat breaks down complex risks into manageable components.
   - Tools like event and probability trees support systematic analysis and resource prioritization.
6. Case Studies
   - The Pearl Harbor attack highlighted the dangers of flawed risk assessments, which can occur when adversaries are underestimated.
   - The Robert Lee Yates case demonstrated the synergy between probability-based insights and hard evidence, such as DNA, in solving crimes.
7. Probability and Policy
   - Probability underpins critical policy decisions, such as allocating resources for terrorism prevention and shaping criminal justice strategies like mandatory sentencing laws.
8. Statistical Tools and Concepts
   - Analysts utilize tools such as the normal distribution, standard deviation, and z-values to analyze large datasets.
   - Visual tools, such as charts and probability trees, help translate data into actionable insights.

Takeaways

Probability estimation transforms data into actionable insights, enabling analysts to navigate uncertainty, prioritize risks, and make informed decisions. By combining probability with tools like event trees, standard terminology, and data visualization techniques, intelligence and law enforcement professionals can enhance operational effectiveness and policy outcomes. This lesson highlights the importance of applying these methods to complex real-world scenarios, ranging from crime investigations to national security risk assessments.

Key Concepts Covered

1. **Probability Estimation:** Intelligence analysts must assess the likelihood of events using structured probability frameworks.
2. **Analytic Confidence:** Probability judgments should be paired with clear confidence levels based on evidence quality.
3. **Quantitative and Qualitative Judgments:** Analysts often combine numerical probability estimates with expert judgment.
4. **Visualization Techniques:** Charts, graphs, and geospatial displays help communicate complex analytical findings effectively.
5. **Data Interpretation:** Visualization tools reveal patterns and relationships that may not be apparent in raw data.
6. **Decision Support:** Clear probability estimates help decision-makers understand uncertainty and risk.
7. **Analytic Standards:** Expressing uncertainty clearly aligns with analytic tradecraft principles promoted by Office of the Director of National Intelligence.

Learning Objectives Accomplished

1. **Define** probability and its significance in intelligence analysis.
2. **Differentiate** between theoretical and experimental probability.
3. **Apply** the concepts of conditional probability in assessing intelligence scenarios.
4. **Interpret** the ODNI Directive 203 Probability Terminology Chart and NATO Source Reliability/Credibility Assessment Matrix.
5. **Explain** the concept of risk assessment and its application in analyzing terrorist threats.
6. **Utilize** tools like probability trees and event trees for analytical assessments.
7. **Evaluate** probability's historical and contemporary applications in intelligence and law enforcement contexts.
8. **Understand** the role of probability in criminal justice policy and resource allocation.
9. **Perform** basic probability calculations, including normal distribution and standard deviation analysis.
10. **Visualize** and analyze datasets to support decision-making in intelligence analysis.

Practical Application

You explored analytical examples including:

- Estimating the probability of insurgent attacks based on historical data.

- Using geospatial heat maps to visualize crime patterns.
- Presenting probability assessments in intelligence briefings.
- Using visual analytics to support strategic decision-making.

Reflection Questions

1. Why is it important for intelligence analysts to express uncertainty clearly?
2. How can visual data displays improve decision-maker understanding?
3. What risks arise when probability estimates are poorly communicated?

Clear probability estimates strengthen analytical credibility and support informed decision-making.

GLOSSARY OF TERMS

Here is a glossary of key terms introduced and discussed in Chapter 12 to enhance your understanding of the material:

Analytical Confidence: A qualitative judgment regarding the degree to which credible sources, sound reasoning, and reliable information support a judgment or conclusion.

Assessment Probability: An estimate of how likely a specific outcome is, expressed as a percentage or a verbal probability term, often aligned with standardized scales such as the ODNI Directive 203.

Bell Curve (Normal Distribution): A graphical representation of a normal distribution, which is symmetrical, shows that data near the mean are more frequent in occurrence.

Bin (in Statistics): A range of values used to group continuous data for visualization in histograms, aiding in the interpretation of distributions.

Conditional Probability: The probability of event A occurring given that event B has already occurred; expressed as $P(A|B)$.

Credibility of Information: A measure of the quality or truthfulness of the information provided, regardless of the source's reliability.

Event Tree: A visual analytical tool using Boolean logic that outlines potential event paths following an initiating incident is often used in risk assessment.

Experimental Probability: Probability is derived from actual data collected through observation or experimentation, and it is calculated as the number of successful outcomes divided by the number of trials.

Favorable Outcome: The desired result in a probability experiment is often used in theoretical probability calculations.

Histogram: A type of bar graph used to represent the distribution of a dataset, typically involving bins to group ranges of values.

NATO Source Reliability/Credibility Matrix: A 6x6 matrix was used to evaluate both the source's reliability and the information's credibility, providing a standardized rating (e.g., A-2).

Normal Distribution: A bell-shaped probability distribution where most occurrences cluster around the mean, with symmetrical tails on either side.

ODNI Directive 203: An Office of the Director of National Intelligence directive providing analytic standards, including standardized probability language for intelligence assessments.

Probability Tree: A diagram that maps out all possible outcomes of a sequence of events, and their associated probabilities helps calculate cumulative likelihoods.

Risk Assessment: The process of evaluating the probability and impact of an adverse event transpiring, typically using the formula: Risk = Consequence x Vulnerability x Threat.

Simple Inference: A direct relationship between two events (e.g., if A, then B), commonly used in basic probability analysis.

Source Reliability: An estimate of how trustworthy or consistent an information source has been in the past, rated on a scale (A–F) in NATO and IC systems.

Standard Deviation: A measure of the dispersion or spread in a data set indicates how much individual data points deviate from the mean.

Theoretical Probability: Probability is derived from a known set of possible outcomes, assuming all outcomes are equally likely.

Threat Analysis: An assessment of an adversary's or threat actor's intent and capabilities to carry out harmful actions.

Vulnerability Analysis: An evaluation of how susceptible a target is to potential threats based on physical, procedural, or systemic weaknesses.

Z-Value (Z-Score): The number of standard deviations a data point is from the mean is used to determine its relative position within a distribution.

This glossary serves as a quick reference for understanding key terms and concepts from the chapter. Feel free to revisit it as you progress through the material!

NOTES

1. Office of the Director of National Intelligence (ODNI), *Intelligence Community Directive #203, Analytic Standards*, 2015, http://www.dni.gov/files/documents/ICD/ICD%20203%20Analytic%20Standards.pdf.
2. Government Printing Office, *U.S. Army, Field Manual 2-22.3, Human Collection Operations*, Chapter 6, Screening, 2006.
3. Todd Sandler and Howard E. Lapan, 'The Calculus of Dissent: An Analysis of Terrorist's Choice of Targets', *Synthese*, 76, 245–261, 1988.
4. Todd Sandler and Howard E. Lapan, 'The Calculus of Dissent: An Analysis of Terrorist's Choice of Targets', *Synthese*, 76, 245–261, 1988.
5. Emily Smith, *MU Professor Recommends Changing Drivers' Perceptions of Law Enforcement to Deter Drinking and Driving*, University of Missouri, munews.missouri.edu/news-releases/2008/12-24-Richardson-drinkinganddriving.php
6. S. V. Masten and R. C. Peck, 'The Effectiveness of High-Visibility Enforcement Campaigns in Reducing Impaired Driving', *Traffic Injury Prevention,* 22(3), 1–8, 2021.
7. Bruce Western and Becky Pettit, 'Incarceration and Social Inequality', *Daedalus, Journal of the American Academy of Arts & Sciences*, 139(3), 8–19, 2010.
8. William Spelman, 'What Recent Studies Do (and Don't) Tell Us about Imprisonment and Crime', *Crime and Justice*, 27, 419, 2000.
9. William Spelman, 'Jobs or Jails? The Crime Drop in Texas', *Journal of Policy Analysis and Management*, 24, 133–165, 2000.
10. Barry Charles Ezell, Steven P. Bennett, Detlof von Winterfeldt, John Sokolowski and Andrew J. Collins, 'Probabilistic Risk Analysis and Terrorism Risk', *Risk Analysis*, 30(4), 575–591, 2010.
11. H. H. Willis, et al., *Risk-Based Resource Allocation at DHS*, RAND Corporation Report, 2024, Retrieved from rand.org.
12. Richards J. Heuer Jr., *Psychology of Intelligence Analysis*, CIA, Chapter 4, 1999.
13. Shane Harris, 'The Cyberwar against ISIS: How U.S. Hackers Took Down a Terror Network', *Wall Street Journal*, September 2016.
14. Institute for Economics & Peace. Global Terrorism Index (GTI) 2017, November 2017, Section 3.2, "Middle East and North Africa Trends," visionofhumanity.org, Retrieved April 2025.
15. W. J. Tolone et al., *Visual Analytics for Homeland Security*, IEEE Computer Society, 2008.
16. David Johnston and Douglas Jehl, 'Threats and Responses: Findings; Report Cites Lapses across Government and 2 Presidencies', *New York Times*, July 2004.
17. Robert M. Clark, *Intelligence Analysis: A Target-Centric Approach* (6th ed.), CQ Press, Chapter 9, 2019.
18. Greg Miller and Julie Tate, 'How the U.S. Military Targets the Islamic State', *Washington Post*, September 2014.
19. Robert M. Clark, *Geospatial Intelligence: Origins and Evolution*, Georgetown University Press, 2020.
20. The New Humanitarian Website, Retrieved March 2025, https://www.thenewhumanitarian.org/ar/media/89765.
21. Vision of Humanity, *Global Terrorism Index 2023: Burkina Faso*, March 2024.
22. Richards J. Heuer Jr., *Psychology of Intelligence Analysis*, CIA, Chapter 8, 1999.
23. Seymour M. Hersh, 'The Stovepipe', *New Yorker*, October 2003.
24. David Skillicorn, *Visualizing the Threat: Predictive Analytics in Counterterrorism*, Queen's University, 2015.
25. Kate Connolly, 'Three Suspected Isis Operatives Arrested at German Refugee Shelters', *The Guardian*, September 2016, Retrieved April 2025, https://www.theguardian.com/world/2016/sep/13/suspected-isis-operatives-arrested-germany-refugee-shelters.

CHAPTER 13

Crafting an Analytical Plan for Intelligence Operations

INTRODUCTION: FROM FOG TO FOCUS—WHY PLANNING DEFINES INTELLIGENCE SUCCESS

Imagine trying to assemble a puzzle without the picture on the box. Or all the puzzle pieces are different shades of the same color. You do not know what you are building, how the pieces fit, or what pieces might be missing (see Figure 13.1). That is the world of intelligence without an analytical plan.

In 2001, weeks before 9/11, U.S. intelligence agencies held information that, if connected and analyzed systematically, could have foreshadowed the attack. But that did not happen. Why? A lack of coherent analytical planning.

FIGURE 13.1 Assembling a puzzle, without the typical frames of reference, can be like the world of intelligence (www.shutterstock.com).

DOI: 10.4324/9781003561712-13

Whether tracking terrorist networks, mapping organized crime syndicates, or predicting market volatility, success does not come from sheer data but from shaping that data into a structured, actionable strategy. That is where an analytical plan becomes your compass. It aligns your purpose with process, connects fragmented knowledge, and transforms confusion into clarity.

Analytical planning bridges the gap between raw data and meaningful analysis. It involves defining the scope, developing questions, selecting methodologies, and determining resources. Most importantly, it ensures that the analysis is tailored to meet specific objectives and is usable within the given operational context.

In the realm of intelligence analysis, actionable insights rarely come by chance. A successful analytical outcome is not a product of luck or mere happenstance but the result of a well-structured analytical plan. Intelligence operations rely on meticulous planning to piece together vast and fragmented data into a coherent picture. Crafting such a plan is not optional; ensuring all efforts align toward understanding adversarial operations, intentions, and vulnerabilities is critical.

This chapter explores building that compass, from defining objectives to structuring timelines and resources, and how planning is the true engine behind meaningful intelligence.

Intelligence analysis is breaking down complex systems to understand their core mechanics. Much like mapping a criminal cartel or understanding the logistics of a terrorist network, the goal is to deconstruct the whole into its parts, examine interdependencies, and find exploitable weaknesses. This process forms the backbone of intelligence operations. A well-crafted analytical plan organizes this complexity into a systematic approach for transforming raw data into operational insights.

We will guide this journey with a relatable analogy: Building a shopping list. This analogy may seem simple, but it parallels the strategic thought process behind intelligence planning. Just as you do not walk into a grocery store without a clear list of your needs, you do not enter analysis without defining your objectives and resources. Success requires foresight, attention to detail, and connecting disparate pieces of information into a cohesive strategy, whether planning a small dinner or stocking up for a winter at a remote cabin.

The path to intelligence success begins with crafting a deliberate and well-thought-out analytical plan, ensuring each decision brings you one step closer to actionable intelligence.

LEARNING OBJECTIVES

By the end of this chapter, students will be able to:

1. **Define** the key components of an analytical plan and explain their interdependencies.
2. **Align** analytical plans with mission objectives across multiple intelligence sectors.
3. **Identify, prioritize, and justify** intelligence gaps using structured frameworks.
4. **Develop** actionable Priority Intelligence Requirements (PIRs) and Specific Information Requirements (SIRs).
5. **Apply** resource scheduling and project management concepts to analytical planning.
6. **Evaluate** data sources for relevance, accuracy, reliability, and ethical appropriateness.
7. **Anticipate and mitigate** planning pitfalls through reflection and the use of structured planning techniques.

DEFINING THE OBJECTIVES

The first step in creating an analytical plan is clearly defining the objectives (see Figure 13.2). These objectives should align with the needs of intelligence end-users, including military commanders, government officials, law enforcement agencies, and business leaders.

FIGURE 13.2 The intelligence analysis process flow.

The Initial Appraisal: Knowing Your "Knowns" and "Unknowns"

The first step in developing an analytical plan is to define your objectives. To do so, one must inventory what is already known and identify the critical intelligence gaps. This is your initial appraisal, a necessary process to confirm valid and uncertain information.

Case Study: Missteps in Pearl Harbor Intelligence

History has repeatedly demonstrated the importance of thoroughly reviewing initial assumptions. For instance, in the lead-up to the attack on Pearl Harbor, Japanese intelligence possessed accurate data on U.S. Military strength in the Pacific. However, their assessment of America's response capabilities was flawed. Despite knowing the vast superiority of U.S. industrial capabilities, they assumed that eliminating the Pacific fleet would force the U.S. into a quick peace, underestimating the resolve and recovery potential of the American public and military.

Had the Japanese taken more time to scrutinize their intelligence's limitations, they might have avoided such catastrophic strategic misjudgments. This highlights the importance of continuously revisiting the initial appraisal during intelligence operations (see Figure 13.3).

The Pearl Harbor miscalculation serves as a cautionary tale for modern analysts: never assume that what you think you know is complete or accurate without thorough vetting. In our shopping analogy, skipping this step would be akin to going to the store without first checking what supplies you already have at home; you risk buying unnecessary items or missing essential components.

Next, let us examine the limited nature of the information the Japanese had about U.S. Military capabilities before World War II. After the War, Japan General Staff Office Operations Bureau member and former Captain Shinobu Takayama recollected the following:

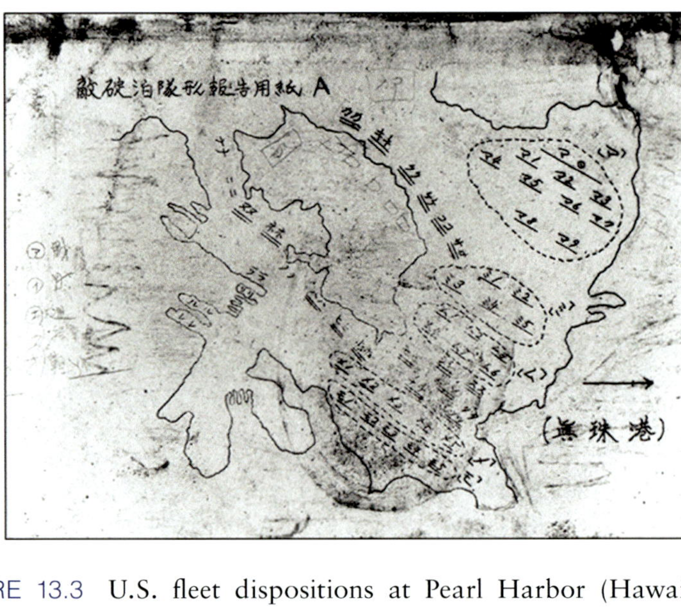

FIGURE 13.3 U.S. fleet dispositions at Pearl Harbor (Hawaii State Archives).

> As one responsible for operations, I should have more thoroughly investigated the situation regarding the U.S. and Great Britain, and of the U.S. in particular. I should have respected the opinions of the individuals in charge of U.S. and British intelligence within the General Staff office, as well as Japanese officers resident in other places such as those and other neutral countries.[1]

Japanese Intelligence utilized the news media to collect open-source information about the U.S. Military and assess the mood and morale of the American public. Several contemporary pieces of open-source information may have contributed to Japanese Intelligence's inaccurate assessment of American Military status and recuperative abilities.[2]

In the 1930s, the United States Navy and Army were starved of funding. This predicament would result in the United States entering the Pacific War with many obsolete warships, only six front-line aircraft carriers to deploy in the Pacific and Atlantic, and several obsolescent military aircraft.

U.S. newsreels of military training exercises depicted a poorly prepared U.S. Army (see Figure 13.4).

There was no U.S. Military draft, and in 1940, the combined total strength of all U.S. Military forces was only 458,365 personnel.[3] During

FIGURE 13.4 Excerpts from pre-WW II news (U.S. Army Archives).

the same timeframe, the Imperial Japanese Army numbered more than three times that number alone. During the 1930s, the United States entered a period of isolationism, characterized by a marked unwillingness to become involved in foreign issues that did not directly affect American national interests.

Historical records demonstrate that these data points were readily accessible to the public through multiple newspapers and other open media sources, and likely influenced the Japanese assessment. Had the Japanese exercised due diligence and vetted and discounted some of these misperceptions, they might have chosen a different course of action.

Using the "shopping list" analogy, suppose you went to the store without first looking in the cupboard to see what you were out of or what items you already had. You may end up buying unneeded items or not getting essential supplies. The results could be a failed dinner party, your family getting snowed in and starving, or both.

> *Example:*
>
> *In a military context, the objective may be to assess the potential for an adversary's future actions. For business, the goal might be to analyze market competition or anticipate economic trends. In either case, defining straightforward, actionable objectives will drive the rest of the analysis and ensure relevance (see Table 13.1).*
>
> *Key Questions to Consider:*
>
> - *What specific decision will this analysis inform?*
> - *What outcomes are stakeholders expecting from the analysis?*
> - *How will the intelligence products be used?*

Prioritizing Intelligence Gaps: Setting Intelligence Priorities

After vetting your knowns, the next step is identifying and prioritizing your intelligence gaps. Prioritization ensures that limited resources are directed toward the most critical gaps. In intelligence work, this is

TABLE 13.1 Defining Objectives Based on Intelligence Sectors

Sectors	***Objective Examples***
Military	*Assess adversary capabilities and intentions.*
Government	*Evaluate the impact of proposed legislation on national security.*
Law Enforcement	*Identify patterns in criminal activity across jurisdictions.*
Business	*Predict competitor movements in the marketplace.*

formalized into "priority intelligence requirements" (PIRs), which are designed to focus on the most pressing information needs.

The intelligence gaps are listed and prioritized once the "knowns" are vetted to an acceptable level. This is necessary because not all information is equal, and inadequate analysis and collection resources are seldom available to investigate all the identified gaps thoroughly. Analysts refer to these as "priority intelligence requirements." The United States Department of Defense (DoD) defines a priority intelligence requirement (PIR) as an intelligence requirement, which is stated as a priority for intelligence support, that the commander and staff need to understand the adversary or the environment.

There is no one hard-and-fast thumb rule for creating PIRs. PIRs and the supporting "specific information requirements" (SIRs) are based on the needs of the intelligence consumer. Each PIR generates multiple SIRs. SIRs contain the information required to answer all or part of an intelligence requirement. For example, the PIR: "Report all evidence of improvised explosive devices (IEDs) in the operational area" would generate the SIR: Report all evidence of IEDs in and around OBJ Mike, especially any areas of upturned earth, suspicious packages, suspicious debris in roadway or loose wires sticking out of ground.

In the military (division-level and below), PIRs are generally tied to the tactical mission or objective, and analysts work with commanders to determine what the PIRs should be. Above division (corps/theater-level), PIRs become more strategic.

AUTHOR'S NOTE

- *Some analysts would argue that "There is little need for SIRs because everybody already knows what to look for." However, this is rarely the case. The police patrolman and the common foot soldier often do not understand the PIR, nor do the analysts.*
- *Look at the PIR example provided: "Report all evidence of improvised explosive devices (IEDs) in the operational area."*
- *Now ask yourself, if you were the "guy on the ground," wouldn't you prefer the SIR: "Report all evidence of IEDs in and around OBJ Mike, especially any areas of upturned earth, suspicious packages, suspicious debris in the roadway or loose wires sticking out of the ground," rather than the PIR used in the example? Doesn't the SIR more clearly define exactly what you are looking for?*

Commanders/Leaders (e.g., military personnel, law enforcement officials, government officials, etc.):

- Focus on adversaries' capabilities and intentions (e.g., enemy combatants, criminals, and rogue states).
- Analyze the operational environment (e.g., battlefield, areas of jurisdiction, sovereign borders, etc.).
- Identify adversary centers of gravity and critical vulnerabilities (e.g., lines of communication, threat finance, and populace motivators).
- Monitor events in the joint force commander's area of interest (e.g., enemy, criminal, or rogue state activities).
- Support the planning and conduct of campaigns (e.g., invasion of an enemy homeland, disruption or destruction of a criminal cartel, destabilization, or overthrow of a rogue state, etc.).

Intelligence analysts review existing databases for potential answers to intelligence and information requirements. If the intelligence does not exist, the requestor issues a "request for information" (RFI). An RFI is a specific time-sensitive informal requirement for information or intelligence products, distinct from other, more standardized requirements or scheduled intelligence production. An RFI can lead to a production requirement. If possible, the request should be answered with the information already available. If the requested information is unavailable, outdated, or deemed unreliable, it may result in a collection requirement. Projected production requirements are typically expressed as analytic tasks and their corresponding subtasks.[4]

Revisiting our analogy, consider the "dinner party" as a tactical requirement and the "stocking up the mountain cabin" as a more strategic requirement. In this analogy, you have the benefit of being the analyst and one of the intelligence consumers. However, there are other consumers whose needs you should also take into account. Your spouse and another guest may provide input to help shape your dinner party collection plan. Your guests previously showered you with compliments for the rib-eye steaks you prepared. Your spouse, other family members, or anyone sharing the cabin with you may provide input on the mountain cabin. When considering intelligence priorities for the mountain cabin, be aware that one of your children suffers from diabetes, and there is no hardline telephone or cell phone coverage at the cabin. Review the analysis plan entries in the table below based on the provided scenario information.

Table 13.2 illustrates how intelligence priorities align with real-world decision-making, balancing immediate tactical needs and long-term strategic objectives.

- Items to note regarding Table 13.2: All items are based upon the needs of the consumer(s)
- More critical items have higher priority
- Answers to higher-priority intelligence gaps often affect lower-priority items, sometimes reducing or negating their importance
- Strategic items tend to have greater importance/significance and have to be considered over periods further into the future

Developing the Collection Plan

Any collection requirements generated should have supporting SIRs created to allow the allocation of the appropriate collection capabilities to satisfy them. Suppose the requestor (usually the analyst) does not provide SIRs. In that case, the collection manager should consult with the requestor to determine the activity indicators against which to focus collection capabilities so that appropriate SIRs can be developed.[5]

> ***TIPS FOR PRIORITIZING INTELLIGENCE GAPS***
>
> - *Do an initial assessment of "knowns" first.*
> - *List all your intelligence gaps, place them in matrix (as shown in the example).*
> - *Identify if there are both tactical and strategic considerations to account for.*
> - *Justify each intelligence gap and place the justification adjacent to the intelligence gap it is justifying.*

Chapter 9 covers the various aspects of collection planning in greater detail.

Allocating Resources and Schedule Development

Often, significant effort is put into the collection planning aspects of the Intelligence Cycle. However, planners generally provide little consideration to the allocation and scheduling of analytical resources as the information is collected. Typically, resources are assigned ad hoc as information is received from various sources and collection platforms.

Example:

(Note: All items in this exercise scenario are fictitious. Any resemblance to real people, living or dead, is unintended.)

You have a task to determine whether a particular criminal cartel, the Durango Drug Cartel, is acquiring the bomb-making skills of a

TABLE 13.2 Prioritizing Intelligence Gaps

Priority	*Tactical Requirement*	*Justification*	*Strategic Requirement*	*Justification*
1	*Ask the butcher for steak pricing/availability*	*High cost, essential item for success*	*Stock child's 90-day medication supply*	*Critical to health, no access to pharmacies*
2	*Consult guests on menu preferences*	*Tastes may have changed*	*Research satellite phones for emergencies*	*Critical communication if snowed in*
3	*Discuss dinner entertainment*	*Plan event logistics*	*Calculate non-perishable food needs*	*Sustained survival during isolation*

terror group, the Kraznovian Liberation Army (KLA), to wage war against a rival criminal organization. In your organization, there is a SIGINT analytical team with generic regional expertise for the subject area, an All-Source team with significant improvised explosive device (IED) experience, a third (HUMINT-based) team with subject matter expertise with the terror group, and another (Open-Source) team with expertise with criminal cartels in the region.

Collection requests were submitted to fill the following intelligence gaps:

- *Who are the bomb makers associated with the KLA? (HUMINT) What are their skill sets? (HUMINT and SIGINT) Have any of them come into the country? (HUMINT, SIGINT, and Database Search) Of the identified bomb makers, do any have known contacts in the region? (Police/Government Database Search, and HUMINT) What are their names/locations? (Open-Source and Police/Government Database Search)*
- *Which criminal cartels is the Durango Drug Cartel feuding with? (Open-Source and HUMINT) What is the status of the feud(s)? (Open-Source and HUMINT)*
- *Have bombs/IEDs been used by the Durango Drug Cartel in the past? (Open-Source and Police/Government Database Search) When? Where? What type(s)? (Open-Source and Police/Government Database Search)*

The application of project management principles has been advocated for in the open press for over ten years.[6] However, the practice is not widespread in the IC. Referring to the project management chart depicted in Figure 13.5, the Cartel Bomb Project, notice how basic

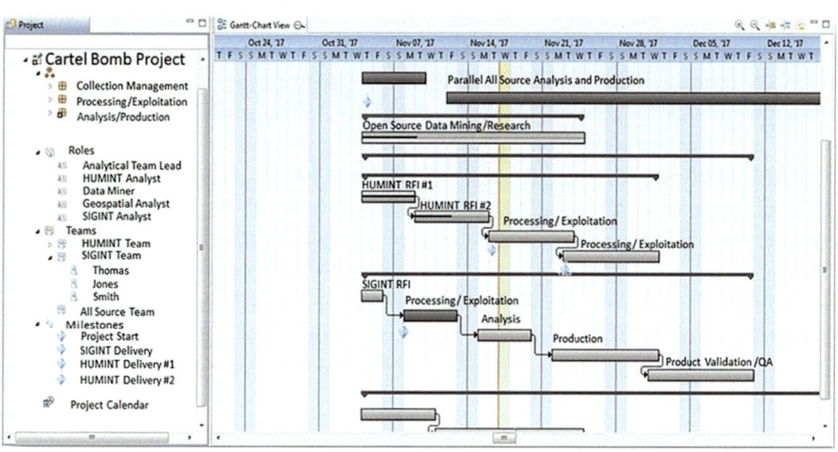

FIGURE 13.5 Cartel bomb project.

project management mechanisms streamline the analysis production cycle.

Breaking the intelligence production process into parts and knowing (or at least estimating) the performance periods for each step creates a work breakdown structure (WBS). Using the WBS and inputting project data into an off-the-shelf project management application enables a more efficient use of analysis and production resources.

The Gantt chart for the "Cartel Bomb Project" example illustrates how the allocation and scheduling of intelligence resources can be visualized. However, like any other non-intelligence project, no project plan is perfect, and schedules must be regularly monitored and adjusted to reflect unforeseen changes.

The processing/exploitation, analysis, and production aspects of the Intelligence Cycle also require careful planning. Flexibility in the planning process is imperative, as collection assets can fail, be routinely delayed, have their priorities changed, or miss their collection opportunities, necessitating rescheduling.

Processing and Exploitation

A significant percentage of U.S. intelligence resources (unlike Law Enforcement and Business Intelligence resources) is devoted to processing and exploiting raw data into a usable form for Intelligence analysis, which involves processing and exploitation that can include decoding messages, translating foreign media, interpreting imagery, manipulating data from one computer language to another for processing, storage, and retrieval; the list goes on and on. Each process requires time and resources, which must be factored into the planning process.

Collected, processed, and exploited information is fed via secure and, to varying degrees, classified computer networks to intelligence analysts from all sources related to their assigned areas. A step-by-step work breakdown should be performed to aid the planning process if one is not already available. The time intervals required for the processing and exploitation steps must be collected and updated periodically for each type of intelligence (e.g., SIGINT, IMINT, ELINT, etc.). These collection and processing times must also be adjusted for data volume and who is processing/exploiting the data. This information should then be tabulated and put into a project management format or work breakdown structure (WBS) by hand or using software. By going through these steps, one can better predict when the processed/exploited information will arrive for analysis.

TABLE 13.3 Types of Data Sources in Intelligence Sectors

Sector	*Data Sources*
Military	*HUMINT, SIGINT, OSINT, IMINT, GEOINT*
Government	*Classified sources, diplomatic cables, policy reports*
Law Enforcement	*Criminal databases, public safety reports, and digital surveillance*
Business	*Market research, financial statements, competitor analysis*

GATHERING AND EVALUATING INFORMATION

Information is the lifeblood of any analytical plan. Identifying credible sources, vetting information for accuracy, and maintaining awareness of potential biases are critical to successful intelligence analysis (see Table 13.3).

Importance of the Step

Gathering and evaluating information is one of the most critical steps in forming an analytical plan. The quality of your final analysis is directly tied to the quality and relevance of the data you collect. Information comes from diverse sources in intelligence work, whether for military, government, law enforcement, or business applications. Evaluating these sources for reliability and relevance ensures that your analysis is based on solid ground.

- **Military Application:** In combat operations, intelligence gathering encompasses data from human intelligence (HUMINT), signals intelligence (SIGINT), and open-source intelligence (OSINT). This is illustrated in Table 13.4.

TABLE 13.4 Military Intelligence Sources

Source	*Description*
HUMINT	*Information is gathered through interpersonal contact, such as interrogation, surveillance, or interviews.*
SIGINT	*Electronic data intercepted from communications or signals is often encrypted and requires complex decryption methods.*
OSINT	*Data from publicly available sources like media reports, public records, or academic publications.*
GEOINT	*Information derived from imagery and satellite data to assess physical locations and movements.*

TABLE 13.5 Government Intelligence Sources

Source	*Description*
Classified Intelligence	*These include intelligence gathered by national security agencies and protected by strict legal frameworks. Classified sources are paramount in government operations, particularly at the federal level.*
Policy Reports and Diplomatic Cables	*Government officials often rely on detailed policy reports, briefings from international embassies, and diplomatic communications.*
Public Data	*State-level operations may depend more on publicly available economic, health, and safety data relevant to local communities.*

Example:

During military operations, gathering real-time SIGINT from intercepted communications can be crucial for identifying enemy intentions and movements.

Government Application: Federal agencies depend significantly on data from classified sources, satellite imagery, and diplomatic channels, whereas state governments may prioritize public safety information and local trends (see Table 13.5).

Example:

A government agency tasked with predicting economic instability might analyze open-source economic trends and classified intelligence on foreign financial operations.

Law Enforcement Application: Data sources include criminal databases, informants, CCTV footage, and forensic evidence, as shown in Table 13.6.

TABLE 13.6 Law Enforcement Intelligence Sources

Source	*Description*
Criminal Databases	*Law enforcement agencies often use databases like the National Crime Information Center (NCIC) to gather data on criminal history, outstanding warrants, and missing persons.*
Forensic Evidence	*Physical evidence, such as DNA or fingerprints, can be gathered through forensics to solve cases or build a profile of criminal activity.*
Informants and Witnesses	*Human sources, such as informants or witnesses, provide crucial information in ongoing investigations.*
Surveillance Data	*Surveillance data includes CCTV footage, body camera recordings, and other digital surveillance records.*

TABLE 13.7 Business Intelligence Sources

Source	*Description*
Market Research	*Companies often gather data on consumer preferences, competitor actions, and market trends to stay competitive.*
Financial Reports	*These are essential for assessing competitors' financial health and forecasting future market behavior.*
Customer Data	*Information gathered from consumer behavior, feedback, and engagement with products or services is valuable for future business strategy.*
Supply Chain Data	*Understanding the flow of materials and goods can help identify vulnerabilities or opportunities for cost-saving improvements.*

Example:

In a multi-jurisdictional law enforcement case, gathering information from various criminal databases can reveal cross-state criminal activities by a single organization.

Business Application: Information can be gathered through financial reports, market analysis, customer feedback, and competitor activity in the corporate world (see Table 13.7).

Example:

A business may refine its product launch strategy by using customer data gathered from social media engagement and financial reports from competitors.

Evaluating Data Quality

Once information is collected, it is assessed for relevance, reliability, and validity. This process guarantees that only high-quality, pertinent data contributes to your analysis, as shown in Table 13.8.

- **Reliability:** Is the source trustworthy and consistent? Assessing a source's reliability ensures the data can be trusted. Sources with a history of providing accurate and consistent information are prioritized, while unverified or newly established sources are treated with caution.

Example:

In law enforcement, information from a long-standing informant with a proven track record of accuracy may be considered more reliable than data gathered from social media, which could be biased or misleading.

TABLE 13.8 The Information Evaluation Matrix

Criteria	*Description*	*Questions To Ask*
Relevance	*How applicable is this information to the objectives?*	*Does this data directly address the goals of the analysis?*
Reliability	*How trustworthy is the source of the information?*	*Has this source consistently provided accurate information in the past?*
Accuracy	*Does this information accurately reflect reality?*	*Can the data be verified with other sources?*
Timeliness	*Is this information up to date and applicable to the current situation?*	*How old is the information? Does it still reflect current conditions?*

Validity: Does the information accurately reflect the situation or subject of interest? Data accuracy refers to whether it correctly represents the reality of the analyzed situation. Cross-checking data from multiple sources helps verify its accuracy.

Example:

A business might cross-verify customer feedback with market trends to ensure that both sources reflect the same behavior patterns and confirm their accuracy.

Timeliness: Is the information current and relevant to the analysis timeframe? Intelligence is often time-sensitive, especially in fast-moving contexts like military operations or competitive business environments. Outdated information can lead to flawed analysis or missed opportunities.

Example:

During a law enforcement investigation into a potential terrorist threat, real-time social media monitoring may reveal essential leads that would be irrelevant if delayed by even a few hours.

Relevance: Does the information directly address the objectives of the analytical plan? The information's relevance is judged by how closely it addresses the specific objectives of the analytical plan. Information that does not directly contribute to the goal should be filtered out to avoid clutter.

Example:

News articles discussing unrelated political issues would be deemed irrelevant in a military analysis focused on assessing enemy capabilities.

Challenges in Gathering and Evaluating Information

While this step is crucial, it is also fraught with challenges. These challenges vary by sector, but all intelligence analysts must confront issues related to data overload, bias, and information gaps.

Data Overload

In the digital age, analysts are often inundated with vast amounts of information, making it difficult to understand what is relevant and valuable. The challenge lies in identifying critical insights from overwhelming amounts of data.

Bias

All information sources have inherent biases, whether from human intelligence (where sources may have personal agendas) or automated data (which may reflect algorithmic biases). Analysts must remain aware of these biases and account for them in their evaluations.

Information Gaps

Information gaps can be just as problematic as data overload. Incomplete or missing data creates uncertainty, which must be addressed by triangulating with other sources or acknowledging the limitations in the analysis.

Note: Table 13.8 provides sample questions to aid the analyst in evaluating the collected data.

Ethical and Legal Considerations in Information Gathering

Ethical and legal considerations must be paramount when gathering information in all intelligence sectors. Privacy rights, national security laws, and company policies often dictate what information can be legally collected and used in analysis (see Figure 13.6).

- **Military and Government:** Intelligence gathering is subject to national and international laws, including the Geneva Conventions and laws governing signals intelligence and surveillance.

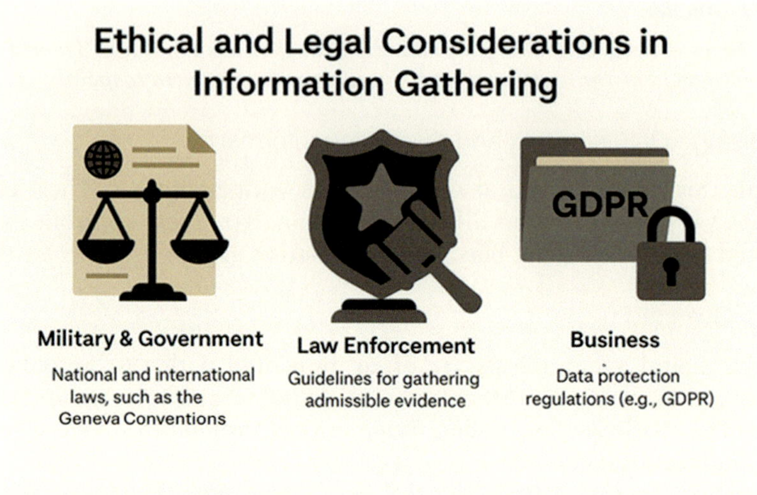

FIGURE 13.6 Ethical and legal considerations in information gathering.

- **Law Enforcement:** In many countries, law enforcement agencies must adhere to strict guidelines for gathering evidence to ensure it is admissible in court and does not infringe upon civil liberties.
- **Business:** Companies must adhere to regulations such as the General Data Protection Regulation (GDPR) in the European Union or the California Consumer Privacy Act (CCPA), which impose strict rules on collecting and handling personal data.

Example:

A business collecting customer data must ensure compliance with data protection laws, safeguard customer privacy, and avoid costly legal violations.

PRACTICAL EXERCISE: VETTING YOUR DATA

Information discrepancies are common in intelligence analysis. Learning to manage and resolve these discrepancies is essential to ensuring the accuracy and reliability of your assessments. This exercise underscores the importance of critically examining and verifying the "knowns" within intelligence data, highlighting the technical and strategic significance of vetting collected information.

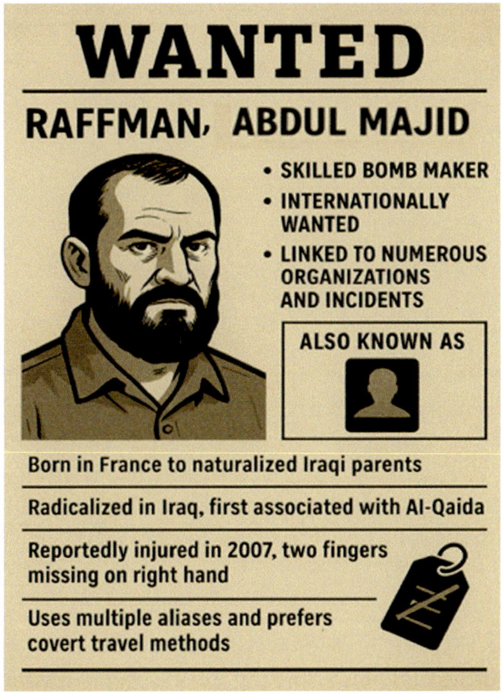

FIGURE 13.7 Abdul Majid Raffman.

Exercise Scenario

You are an intelligence analyst working for the Department of Homeland Security (DHS), tasked with identifying and locating terror threats to the United States and its citizens. Specifically, you are focused on finding a known terrorist reported to be traveling to America to attack a high-profile target. As shown in his wanted poster (Figure 13.7), your initial database search reveals the following details:

Subject Information

Subject Name: Abdul Majid Raffman
Aliases: "A J" Raffman
Age: 34
Height: 5'-10" / 178 cm
Weight: Approximately 200 lbs / 91 kgs
Eye Color: Brown
Complexion: Dark skin with severe acne scarring

Hair Color: Dark brown
Build: Average
Scars: Missing two fingers from the right hand (index and thumb)
Identifiers: DNA and fingerprints on file
Nationality: French
Photo(s): No photo available. Police artist drawing only

Background Information

Abdul Majid Raffman, a skilled bomb maker, is internationally wanted and linked to numerous organizations and incidents. He was born in France to naturalized Iraqi parents, radicalized in Iraq, and first associated with Al-Qaida. In recent years, Raffman has offered his services to various groups with no apparent ideological loyalty. Reportedly injured in 2007, losing two fingers on his right hand in a bomb-making accident, Raffman has continued to operate under multiple aliases and prefers covert travel methods.

New Data Findings

You conduct additional data mining routines on multiple intelligence and law enforcement databases. While most information aligns with your file, several discrepancies and new details emerge:

1. **Height:** 6' / 183 cm
2. **Eye color:** Conflicting reports of blue or sandy brown
3. **Scars:** Inconsistent reporting of missing fingers on the right hand
4. **Aliases:** New aliases "Raffles" and "Raj"
5. **Last known location:** Tripoli, Libya, one week ago, from a confidential informant with past reliable contact

Initial Appraisal

Using this scenario, evaluate the discrepancies, propose explanations for the inconsistencies, and recommend steps to reconcile these issues. Consider the following factors and questions:

Possible Causes of Discrepancies

- **Data Entry Errors:** Could different personnel or systems have made mistakes when recording physical descriptors, such as widespread fields like height and eye color?

- **Multiple Sources:** Have you considered that different agencies or informants may have reported conflicting details, possibly due to brief or indirect observations?
- **Cover Identity:** Raffman may use physical disguises or aliases, such as colored contact lenses or altered physical appearances, to obscure his identity.
- **Inconsistent Updates:** Could there be differences in database update frequency, leading to outdated or unsynchronized data points?

Steps to Address Discrepancies

- **Cross-Verification of Sources:** Determine the reliability and recency of each source contributing to the discrepancy, focusing on verified or highly rated sources over weaker, older reports.
- **Collaboration with Other Agencies:** Share the updated findings and request further information from agencies (such as INTERPOL or local law enforcement in France) to reconcile inconsistencies, especially regarding physical descriptors.
- **Additional Informant Contact:** Engage the confidential informant in Tripoli for further details, corroborating his location and whether he could confirm any recent changes in appearance or aliases.
- **Behavioral and Historical Analysis:** Review records for patterns in Raffman's use of aliases, disguises, and preferred travel methods to inform a more robust profile.

Discussion Prompt for Students

Reflect on the challenges and implications of data discrepancies in intelligence analysis. Discuss:

- The potential impact of minor inconsistencies on the overall assessment.
- Strategies for ensuring data accuracy when working with numerous or inconsistent data sources.
- Ethical considerations in data reconciliation, especially with sensitive or conflicting information.

Conclusion: The Vital Role of Data Validation in Intelligence Analysis

Gathering and evaluating information forms the backbone of any intelligence operation. Analysts can address data overload, bias, and intelligence gaps by practicing rigorous vetting, ensuring they develop an informed, balanced assessment. This exercise underscores the value of collaboration, consistency, and thoroughness in resolving discrepancies. By adhering to these standards, intelligence analysts create a foundation for sound, actionable intelligence, laying the groundwork for strategic, data-driven decision-making.

ANALYSIS PHASE

In the IC and law enforcement, intelligence analysts are generally assigned to a particular geographic or functional specialty (e.g., Southwest Asia, Counterterrorism, Counter-Narcotics). Most intelligence organizations do not allow analysts to work alone. The more established and better-funded organizations utilize an analytical grouping practice of peer review and oversight by more senior analysts.

Intelligence planners would use their familiarity with these analytical groups or teams and their understanding of the expected availability of information submitted for collection to make appropriate tasking decisions based on the group's analytical skill set and combined experience.

Returning to our "shopping list" analogy for analysis planning, visualize the shopping list as our list of RFIs. The various trips to the supermarket, sporting goods store, and other specialty shops to get food and supplies are the intelligence collection process. As the groceries and supplies are brought in, they must be handled, put away, stored, and refrigerated until needed (intelligence processing/exploitation).

Finally, the dinner party is held, and the mountain cabin vacation occurs (analytic production and dissemination).

Applying Analytical Techniques

Once data is gathered, various analytical techniques are applied to extract meaningful insights. Depending on the nature of the intelligence and the desired outcome, different sectors may require different approaches.

Common Analytical Techniques by Sector

1. **SWOT Analysis (Strengths, Weaknesses, Opportunities, Threats)**
   - **Application:** Primarily used in business and strategic military planning to assess internal and external factors. (Business/Military)

2. **Trend Analysis**
   - **Application:** Detect patterns over time, valuable in law enforcement to track crime waves or in business to anticipate market changes. (Law Enforcement/Business)

3. **Scenario Building and Wargaming**
   - **Application:** In military and government intelligence, scenario building helps predict adversary actions and prepares decision-makers for different future outcomes. (Military/Government)

4. **Red Teaming**
   - **Application:** Often used in military, government, and cybersecurity contexts to test plans by thinking like an adversary. (Military/Government/Business/Law Enforcement)
     Note: Cybersecurity crosses all sectors

5. **Link Analysis**
   - **Application:** This is particularly useful in law enforcement to uncover relationships between suspects, organizations, and activities. (Law Enforcement, Government)

TIPS FOR ANALYTICAL PLANNING

- *Use the "Shopping List" approach to visualize the planning process until the intelligence planning steps become more routine.*
- *Use the intelligence production cycle to provide your overall major process planning steps.*
- *Break down each major step into discrete subtasks for planning purposes and allocate time and resources to each subtask.*
- *You will never have enough collection resources, so prioritize your intelligence gaps.*
- *Use project management techniques for more complex intelligence production efforts.*

PRODUCTION AND DISSEMINATION

Once the analysis is completed, it must be reviewed and vetted. It is reviewed for completeness and accuracy by answering these two questions: "Did it answer the original question asked (RFI), and is the answer correct?"

Besides completeness and accuracy, the analysis results should be compared to previous results and the analysis of other outside groups. This vetting is not done to mimic others in the IC or participate in some

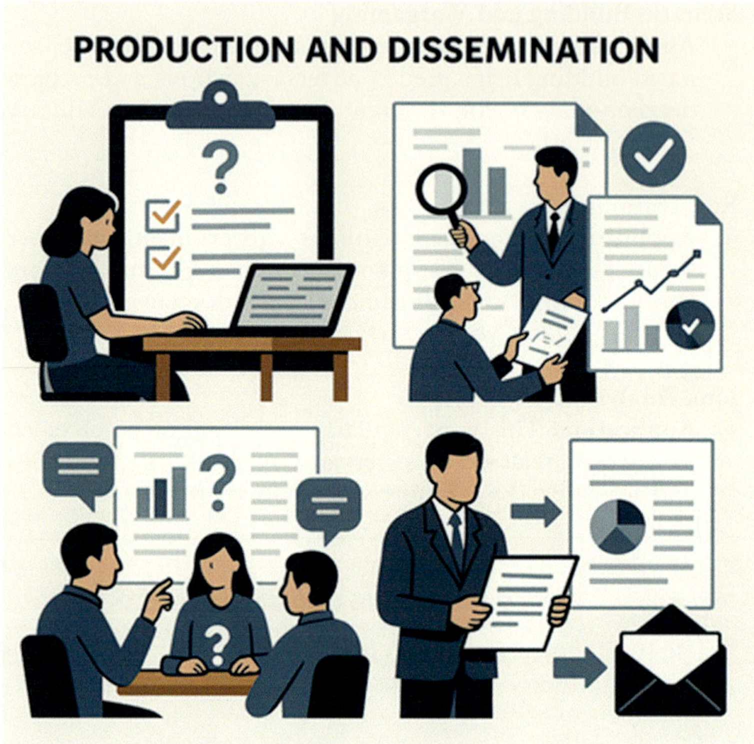

FIGURE 13.8 Production and dissemination.

form of "groupthink;" instead, it ensures nothing major was overlooked or misinterpreted. If significant discrepancies exist, new questions should be asked and satisfactorily resolved to ensure the conflicting intelligence results are erroneous and not your own (see Figure 13.8).

Once your team is satisfied with this analytical product review and vetting step, time and resources must also be allotted and planned for. The final product is disseminated to the intelligence consumer in a format that best communicates the requested information.

CHAPTER SUMMARY

In intelligence analysis, an analytical plan is essential for transforming raw data into actionable insights for decision-makers across various sectors, including military, government, law enforcement, and business. This chapter outlines a structured approach to designing and executing an effective analytical plan, ensuring that intelligence operations align with defined objectives and strategic needs.

Key Steps in Developing an Analytical Plan

1. **Defining Objectives:** An analytical plan begins by establishing clear objectives tailored to the needs of intelligence consumers, such as assessing adversary actions, predicting market trends, or understanding criminal activities. A well-defined objective keeps the analysis focused and relevant.
2. **Initial Appraisal:** Understanding "knowns" and identifying intelligence gaps is crucial. Using the Pearl Harbor case illustrates how an initial misjudgment in intelligence assessment can lead to strategic failures. A thorough initial appraisal mitigates the risk of basing decisions on incomplete information.
3. **Prioritizing Intelligence Gaps:** After vetting known data, intelligence gaps are prioritized based on urgency and importance, forming "Priority Intelligence Requirements" (PIRs). This step ensures that limited resources focus on addressing the most critical gaps.
4. **Collection Planning and Resource Allocation:** Developing a collection plan to fill intelligence gaps involves coordinating resources, identifying specific information requirements, and setting schedules. The process is illustrated through a fictitious analysis of a cartel-terror group, showing how SIGINT, HUMINT, and other intelligence sources collaborate.
5. **Data Gathering and Evaluation:** The chapter emphasizes the collection of high-quality data from diverse sources and its evaluation for reliability, relevance, accuracy, and timeliness. Different sectors utilize distinct intelligence sources, such as HUMINT and SIGINT in the military or criminal databases in law enforcement. A structured evaluation matrix aids analysts in assessing data quality.
6. **Ethical and Legal Considerations:** Intelligence gathering must adhere to ethical and legal standards, respecting the privacy rights of each sector and its corresponding regulatory requirements. The government, military, and business intelligence examples provided illustrate how legal frameworks impact data collection practices.
7. **Analysis Phase:** Analysts employ various techniques, such as SWOT analysis, trend analysis, and link analysis, tailored to sector needs. Collaborative analysis groups within intelligence organizations ensure that assessments benefit from diverse expertise, reducing errors and biases.
8. **Production and Dissemination:** Completed analyses undergo review for completeness, accuracy, and relevance before being disseminated to the intelligence consumer. This phase includes

rigorous vetting to ensure accuracy and alignment with previous findings, preventing significant discrepancies or oversights.

Challenges in Analytical Planning

- **Data Overload:** Managing the vast amounts of information available in the digital age.
- **Bias:** Accounting for biases in sources and algorithms.
- **Information Gaps:** Recognizing and addressing incomplete data.

A well-structured analytical plan is the cornerstone of successful intelligence analysis, bridging raw data and strategic insights. This chapter highlights how meticulous planning, clear objectives, prioritized intelligence needs, and ethical considerations create a robust framework for actionable intelligence, ultimately empowering informed decision-making across all sectors.

Key Concepts Covered

1. **Analytical Planning:** Effective intelligence analysis begins with a structured plan that aligns analytical tasks with intelligence requirements.
2. **Defining the Problem:** Clearly defining the intelligence question guides the entire analytical process.
3. **Information Requirements:** Analysts identify what information is needed to answer the intelligence question.
4. **Analytical Method Selection:** Selecting appropriate SATs ensures that the analysis is rigorous and structured.
5. **Managing Uncertainty:** Analytical plans must anticipate gaps in information and develop strategies to address them.
6. **Collaboration:** Analysts often coordinate with collectors, subject matter experts, and decision-makers during the planning process.

Learning Objectives Accomplished

1. **Define** the key components of an analytical plan and explain their interdependencies.
2. **Align** analytical plans with mission objectives across multiple intelligence sectors.
3. **Identify, prioritize, and justify** intelligence gaps using structured frameworks.
4. **Develop** actionable Priority Intelligence Requirements (PIRs) and Specific Information Requirements (SIRs).

5. **Apply** resource scheduling and project management concepts to analytical planning.
6. **Evaluate** data sources for relevance, accuracy, reliability, and ethical appropriateness.
7. **Anticipate and mitigate** planning pitfalls through reflection and the use of structured planning techniques.

Practical Application

You examined operational scenarios involving:

- Developing analytical plans for counterterrorism investigations.
- Defining intelligence questions related to geopolitical events.
- Selecting appropriate SATs to analyze complex intelligence problems.

Reflection Questions

1. Why is it important to define the intelligence question clearly before beginning analysis?
2. How can analytical planning improve the quality of intelligence products?
3. What challenges arise when analysts face significant intelligence gaps?

Strong analytical planning ensures that intelligence efforts remain focused, disciplined, and aligned with decision-maker needs.

GLOSSARY OF TERMS

Here is a glossary of key terms introduced and discussed in Chapter 13 to enhance your understanding of the material:

Accuracy: Refers to how correctly information reflects reality. Analysts confirm accuracy by cross-referencing multiple sources.

Actionable Intelligence: Insights that can be directly applied to decision-making or operations, often the end goal of analysis.

All-Source Analysis: An analytical approach that integrates information from various intelligence disciplines (e.g., HUMINT, SIGINT, OSINT).

Analytical Plan: A structured framework guiding the transformation of data into intelligence; includes objectives, methodologies, and resource allocation.

Bias: Systematic error introduced by personal, cultural, or methodological influences; a constant challenge in intelligence analysis.

Collection Plan: A structured approach for gathering intelligence to fill known gaps, aligning with PIRs and SIRs.

Data Overload: The challenge of managing excessive volumes of information, making it harder to identify relevant insights.

Evaluation Matrix: A structured tool used to assess information quality, typically using criteria like relevance, reliability, accuracy, and timeliness.

Exploitation (of data): The process of converting collected raw data into usable intelligence through translation, decoding, or formatting.

GEOINT (Geospatial Intelligence): Intelligence derived from imagery and geospatial information; often used to assess physical environments.

HUMINT (Human Intelligence): Information gathered from human sources through interviews, surveillance, or interrogation.

IMINT (Imagery Intelligence): Derived from analysis of photographic or satellite imagery to assess objects, locations, or events.

Information Gap: Areas where knowledge is missing or incomplete; these gaps drive the creation of PIRs.

Initial Appraisal: An early-stage process of assessing what is known and unknown, serving as the foundation for further planning.

Intelligence Consumer: The end-user of an intelligence product, such as a military commander, policymaker, or business executive.

Intelligence Cycle: The process of developing intelligence includes planning, collection, processing, analysis, and dissemination.

Link Analysis: A method used to identify relationships between entities, often visualized as networks; widely used in law enforcement and counterterrorism.

OSINT (Open-Source Intelligence): Information derived from publicly available sources such as news reports, academic publications, and social media.

PIR (Priority Intelligence Requirement): A top-level information need designated by a decision-maker; used to focus intelligence collection efforts.

Processing: The stage in the intelligence cycle where raw data is converted into a usable format, often involving technical procedures.

Production: The phase where intelligence findings are synthesized into a final product for dissemination to decision-makers.

Project Management (in analysis): Applying formal scheduling and resource allocation tools (e.g., Gantt charts, WBS) to improve analytical efficiency.

Red Teaming: An analytical technique where a group adopts an adversary's perspective to test vulnerabilities or challenge assumptions.
Relevance: Indicates how well a piece of information addresses the specific objectives of the analytical plan.
Reliability: Measures the consistency and trustworthiness of a source; critical in validating information.
RFI (Request for Information): A formal or informal inquiry for existing intelligence or data to support a current requirement.
Scenario Building: Analytical technique used to envision future events or conditions, helping prepare for uncertainty.
SIGINT (Signals Intelligence): Collected from intercepted communications or electronic signals, often encrypted and highly technical.
SIR (Specific Information Requirement): A more detailed subset of a PIR, identifying exactly what needs to be collected to satisfy a broader intelligence need.
Strategic Requirement: A long-term or high-impact intelligence need, often associated with broader national or organizational goals.
SWOT Analysis: A structured planning tool that assesses Strengths, Weaknesses, Opportunities, and Threats related to a scenario.
Tactical Requirement: A short-term or mission-specific intelligence need, often tied to immediate operations or events.
Timeliness: The extent to which information is current and applicable within the timeframe of the analysis.
Trend Analysis: An analytical method for identifying patterns over time; useful in forecasting and behavioral prediction.
Validation (of data): The process of confirming the quality, accuracy, and applicability of collected data before analysis.
Work Breakdown Structure (WBS): A project management tool that breaks a project into smaller tasks for better tracking and resource allocation.

This glossary serves as a quick reference for understanding key terms and concepts from the chapter. Feel free to revisit it as you progress through the material!

NOTES

1. Shinobu Takayama, *Sanbo Honbu Sakusenka [General Staff Office Operations Bureau]* (p. 355), Tokyo: Fuyo Shobo Publishing, 1985.
2. Kotani Ken, *Japanese Military Intelligence: "Why Is Intelligence Not Used?"* Tokyo: Kodansha, 2007.

3. U.S. World War II Museum, New Orleans, *US Forces by the Numbers*, Retrieved October 2024, http://www.nationalww2museum.org/learn/education/for-students/ww2-history/ww2-by-the-numbers/us-military.html.
4. U.S. DoD Joint Publication 3-0, Joint Operations, 2006.
5. U.S. DoD Joint Publication 2-0, Joint Intelligence, 2013.
6. Jerry H. Ratcliffe, *Strategic Thinking in Criminal Intelligence*, Federation Press, 2009.

CHAPTER 14

Preparing and Conducting Intelligence Briefings

INTRODUCTION

Preparing and delivering effective intelligence briefings is a critical responsibility for intelligence analysts. While this chapter emphasizes military intelligence briefings (see Figure 14.1), the techniques and principles discussed apply across vocations, including law enforcement and business environments. Mastering the art of briefing enhances professional credibility and ensures the clear and compelling transmission of information, especially in high-pressure scenarios. Successful briefings bridge the gap between complex analysis and actionable decision-making.

LEARNING OBJECTIVES

By the end of this lesson, learners will be able to:

1. **Explain** the purpose and value of intelligence briefings in various professional contexts.
2. **Identify** and mitigate stressors associated with public speaking.
3. **Describe** the key components of preparing and delivering an effective briefing.
4. **Differentiate** between information, decision, and mission briefings.
5. **Adapt** briefing content and style to the audience's expertise and needs.
6. **Demonstrate** ethical practices in presenting intelligence information.
7. **Use visual aids** effectively to complement verbal briefings.

DOI: 10.4324/9781003561712-14

FIGURE 14.1 Military intelligence briefing, an intelligence analyst gives the commander of 21st Theater Sustainment Command a terrain brief of Hohenfels Training Area on enemy activity (U.S. Army/Henry Chan).

THE PURPOSE AND VALUE OF BRIEFINGS

Intelligence briefings are a primary method of disseminating analyzed data to commanders or stakeholders, often called "customers." While written reports are essential, verbal briefings allow for interactive discussions, clarification of deductions, and sharing predictions. They also serve as updates for broader teams, fostering cross-functional communication during mission planning and execution.

Example:

In a military operation, a decision briefing may highlight the risks of weather conditions affecting air support, ensuring commanders are aware and can adapt accordingly. Similarly, in law enforcement, intelligence briefings might provide insights into crime patterns that guide patrol deployments or resource allocation. Briefings could present market trends and competitor analyses in business, helping executives make informed strategic decisions.

In the military context, briefings are integral to the "dissemination" phase of the intelligence cycle and are critical for mission analysis, as

FIGURE 14.2 Informal and formal military briefings (U.S. Department of Defense).

shown in Figure 14.2. Regular updates ensure that all sections, including operations, logistics, and intelligence, align effectively.[1] *Similarly, law enforcement agencies use briefings to coordinate interdepartmental actions, such as during large-scale investigations or tactical operations. In business, they are crucial in coordinating departments like marketing, operations, and finance before product launches or mergers.*

STRESS AND PUBLIC SPEAKING

Public speaking ranks as one of the most significant stressors for many individuals. Intelligence analysts, however, must regularly brief their command staff, sometimes multiple times a day. Adequate preparation and practice mitigate this stress, enabling analysts to deliver confident and professional briefings.

Techniques to Overcome Stress

- Practice deep breathing techniques to stay calm.
- Rehearse in front of a small group to build confidence.
- Focus on delivering clear, concise information rather than achieving perfection.

Example:

A law enforcement analyst preparing a briefing on gang activity can reduce stress by rehearsing with colleagues and ensuring all data is up to date. Similarly, a business analyst presenting quarterly financial data can build confidence by conducting mock presentations.

KEY COMPONENTS OF A BRIEFING

1. Preparation:

- **Thorough Research:** Collect data from reliable sources, verify accuracy, and distill it into concise points. Use current and relevant intelligence to support your conclusions.
- **Structured Organization:** Arrange information logically. For example, start with an overview, proceed with a detailed analysis, and conclude with recommendations.
- **Anticipate Questions:** Consider potential questions from your audience and prepare clear, evidence-based responses.
- **Practice Repeatedly:** Rehearse before peers or supervisors, focusing on clarity, timing, and confidence.

Illustration: For a briefing on cybersecurity threats, begin with global trends, narrow down to regional impacts, and conclude with specific vulnerabilities within the organization's systems. In a business context, this could translate to highlighting global supply chain disruptions and narrowing down to particular risks for the company's operations.

2. Delivery:

- **Engage Your Audience:** Make eye contact, modulate your tone, and use deliberate pauses to emphasize key points. Avoid monotonous delivery.[2]
- **Stay Focused:** Address the primary audience (e.g., the commander) and tailor your language to their level of expertise.
- **Clarity in Communication:** Avoid jargon or overly technical terms unless the audience is familiar with them. For a broader audience, replace terms like "SIGINT" with "signals intelligence."[3]

> ***PRACTICAL TIPS FOR ANALYSTS***
>
> - ***Practice:*** *Dedicate significant time to rehearsal, focusing on clarity and confidence.*
> - ***Body Positioning:*** *Face the audience and avoid turning your back. Use subtle movements to engage with slides without losing connection with the audience.*
> - ***Concluding Statements:*** *Always end with, "Pending your questions, this concludes my briefing." Pause briefly to allow for questions.*

Examples:

If briefing a mixed audience on terrorist networks, explain technical terms such as "network nodes" with broadly recognized analogies, e.g., "Think of nodes as communication hubs that connect various parts of the network." In a business briefing, "KPIs" could be explained as "key performance indicators that measure success" (see Figure 14.3).

ADDITIONAL BEST PRACTICES

- *Be concise but thorough. Avoid overloading slides with excessive text or data.*
- *Use visuals and analogies to make complex information more relatable.*
- *Monitor audience reactions to adjust pacing or clarify points as needed.*
- *Do not apologize for your pronunciation of names. Take your best shot and go with it.*

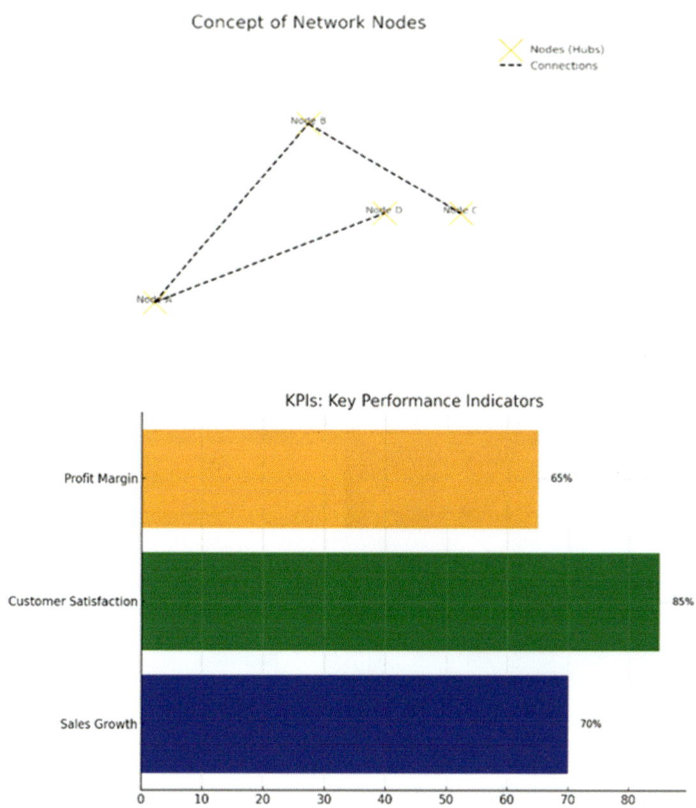

FIGURE 14.3 Examples of tailoring your briefing to your audience.

3. Slides and Visual Aids:

- **Concise Content:** Use bullet points to summarize data. Avoid cluttering slides with excessive text or visuals.
- **Visual Hierarchy:** Present information logically. For example, begin with a global perspective, transition to regional data, and conclude with specific details.
- **Design Standards:** Use consistent fonts, colors, and layouts. Ensure the text contrasts with the background for readability.
- **Interactive Visuals:** Incorporate maps, graphs, and images to complement your narrative. Highlight key elements with pointers or laser tools.[4]

Illustration: For a geographic briefing, begin with a world map, zoom into the region of interest, and conclude with tactical-level maps showing operational areas (see Figure 14.4). This might involve starting with industry-wide trends, narrowing to competitors, and presenting internal performance metrics in a business setting.

4. Audience Adaptation:

- Tailor the content to the audience's expertise and needs. High-ranking officials may prefer strategic insights, while field operatives require actionable intelligence.
- Respond to non-verbal cues, such as nods or confused expressions, and adjust your delivery accordingly.

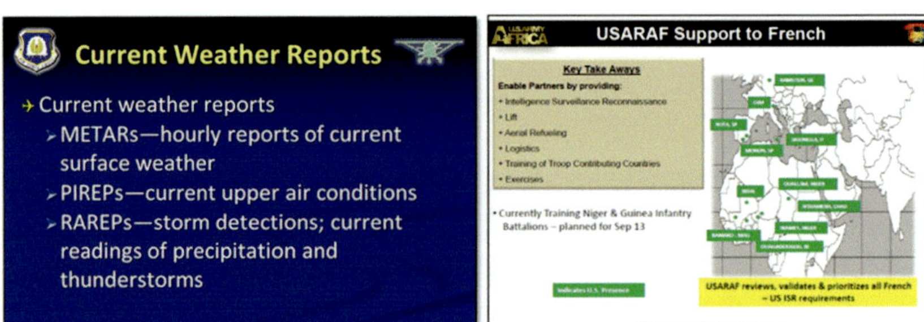

FIGURE 14.4 PowerPoint slides showing military-style briefing (U.S. Department of Defense).

Example:

A law enforcement analyst briefing a SWAT team might focus on actionable intelligence, such as suspect movements, while briefing senior officials on broader crime trends. In a business setting, executives might want high-level overviews, while department heads need specific action plans.

TYPES OF BRIEFINGS

There are three major types of intelligence briefings. They are informational, decision-making, and mission.

Information Briefings

Information briefings provide foundational knowledge on a specific area or topic, such as geography, technology, culture, or political dynamics. The purpose of information briefings is to provide foundational knowledge or updates on a specific topic, ensuring that the audience is well-informed. Unlike decision or mission briefings, these do not typically seek to elicit a decision or action but aim to build awareness or understanding. Their objectives include:

- **Educate the Audience:** Provide comprehensive, accurate, and up-to-date information on a subject.
- **Set Context:** Offer background knowledge or explain the significance of an issue, event, or development.
- **Facilitate Informed Discussions:** Ensure participants have a solid understanding of the topic to prepare them for subsequent discussions, decisions, or actions.
- **Highlight Key Developments:** Summarize recent events, trends, or changes in a field or area of interest.
- **Foster Awareness:** Ensure that all stakeholders share a common understanding of the subject matter.

Such briefings are critical for aligning participants, enabling informed participation, and supporting broader organizational objectives.

Example:

A military analyst briefing on the security environment in the South China Sea might discuss key players, maritime boundaries, and recent activities. A law enforcement analyst could present a community profile, including demographics and crime trends, before launching a neighborhood policing initiative, as illustrated in Figure 14.5. In business, this could involve a market analysis of a new region.

FIGURE 14.5 Intelligence briefing of the South China Sea (www.shutterstock.com).

Decision Briefings

Decision briefings present critical data for making specific operational decisions. The purpose of decision briefings is to present a specific issue, challenge, or opportunity to decision-makers and provide them with the information and options necessary to make an informed decision. These briefings aim to:

- **Present Critical Information:** Summarize relevant data, background, and context regarding the issue.
- **Propose Options:** Outline viable courses of action, including potential benefits, risks, and trade-offs for each option.
- **Facilitate Decision-Making:** Provide clarity and structure to assist decision-makers in evaluating alternatives.
- **Recommend Actions:** Often include a preferred course of action supported by rationale and evidence.
- **Highlight Implications:** Discuss the potential impacts of the decision, including financial, operational, or strategic consequences.
- **Address Concerns:** Allow decision-makers to ask questions, seek clarification, and raise any concerns before making a choice.
- **Establish Accountability:** Identify stakeholders responsible for implementing and monitoring the chosen decision.

Decision briefings are typically used in high-stakes or strategic scenarios, such as organizational planning, policy development, or crisis response, where clarity and alignment are critical for effective outcomes.[5]

> ***Example:***
> *Before a counterterrorism operation, an analyst might outline the likely locations of key targets and recommend courses of action. This could involve presenting tactical options for executing a high-risk warrant in law enforcement, as presented in Figure 14.6. In business, decision briefings might guide executives on whether to proceed with a merger or acquisition.*

Mission Briefings

Ensure all team members understand their roles and address any final concerns before the mission launch. The purpose of mission briefings is to ensure that all team members clearly understand their roles, responsibilities, and objectives before launching a mission or undertaking a significant task. These briefings also serve to:

- **Clarify Objectives:** Clearly define the mission goals and desired outcomes.

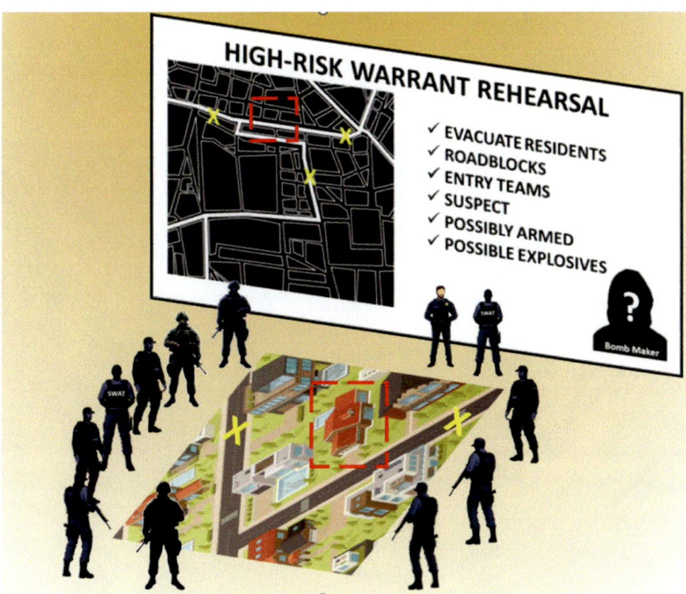

FIGURE 14.6 Law enforcement high-risk warrant briefing.

- **Assign Roles:** Specify the duties and responsibilities of each team member.
- **Enhance Coordination:** Ensure everyone understands how their tasks align with others and the overall mission.
- **Address Concerns:** Provide an opportunity to identify and resolve any last-minute issues or uncertainties.
- **Highlight Risks:** Communicate potential challenges, threats, or obstacles and outline mitigation strategies.
- **Reinforce Protocols:** Emphasize safety procedures, contingency plans, or standard operating guidelines.
- **Boost Team Confidence:** Instill confidence and foster a shared sense of purpose among participants.

In various contexts, such as corporate, military, or law enforcement settings, mission briefings help align all stakeholders and set the stage for a successful operation.

> ***Example:***
> *A business intelligence team might brief executives on market dynamics and potential risks before a large-scale corporate merger, as shown in Figure 14.7. In law enforcement, this could involve briefing officers on roles and safety protocols before a major operation.*

Ethical Considerations in Briefings

Integrity is paramount in intelligence briefings. Analysts must present objective, well-supported data, even when it conflicts with preferred

FIGURE 14.7 Business mission briefing (www.shutterstock.com).

narratives or expectations. Ethical briefing practices foster trust and credibility, essential qualities for effective decision-making.

Case Study: During the early phases of Operation Iraqi Freedom, analysts faced resistance when presenting predictions of insurgency. Ethical adherence to presenting factual data allowed commanders to adjust strategies despite initial reluctance to accept the analysis. Similarly, a law enforcement analyst presenting rising racial tensions in a community may face resistance but must ensure the data is accurately reported to guide policy changes. In business, presenting unfavorable market analyses is essential to prevent costly missteps.

AUTHOR'S NOTE

Although mission commanders, intelligence recipients, and customers should be familiar with simple geographical data, it is essential to relate this in briefings just in case (see Figure 14.8). For instance, it is easy to indicate bordering countries without seeming condescending and elementary. Commanders appreciate this as long as it is simple and to the point.

PRACTICAL EXERCISE: STUDENT GUIDE

Objective

Develop and refine briefing skills by preparing and delivering a country or area brief based on current international events. This exercise

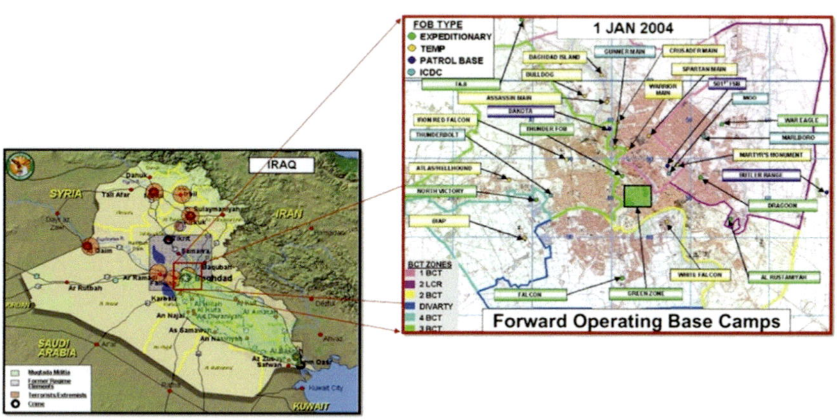

FIGURE 14.8 Effectively outlining maps, relevant regions, and directionality to the audience is essential to effective intelligence communication.

will simulate real-world briefing scenarios and emphasize collaboration, clear communication, and adaptability.

Instructions

1. Group Formation:
   - Form groups of 3–5 students. Each group will be assigned a current international event or topic.
2. Roles and Responsibilities:
   - Each group will create a briefing of no more than five slides.
   - Roles within the group (e.g., lead presenter, researcher, designer) will rotate with each update to ensure all members gain diverse experience.
3. Content Preparation:
   - Conduct thorough research on your assigned topic.
   - Summarize key points clearly and concisely.
   - Use visuals like maps, charts, or images to enhance your briefing.
4. Presentation Schedule:
   - **Week 1:** Deliver your initial brief to the class.
   - **Week 3:** Update your brief with the latest developments and deliver it again.
   - **Week 5:** Provide a final updated brief.
5. Feedback and Improvement:
   - After each presentation, classmates and the instructor will provide constructive feedback. Use this feedback to refine your delivery and content for subsequent presentations.
6. Expanded Collaboration (Optional):
   - Each group will represent a unique role (e.g., operations, logistics, or intelligence) to simulate cross-functional collaboration. Groups will coordinate and share insights to demonstrate interdepartmental communication.
7. Deliverables:
   - A five-slide briefing on your assigned topic.
   - Clear, concise verbal presentations with each member rotating as the lead presenter.
   - Participation in providing and receiving constructive feedback.

CHAPTER SUMMARY

Effective intelligence briefings are critical for bridging the gap between complex analyses and actionable decision-making. Briefings ensure stakeholders receive clear, concise, and actionable information in military, law enforcement, or business settings. This lesson explored the purpose, techniques, and types of intelligence briefings, emphasizing the importance of preparation, delivery, audience adaptation, and ethical considerations. Key takeaways include:

- **Purpose of Briefings:** Providing foundational knowledge, aiding decision-making, and preparing teams for missions.
- **Overcoming Stress:** Preparation, rehearsal, and focus help mitigate public speaking anxiety.
- **Components of a Briefing:** Preparation, structured delivery, use of visual aids, and tailoring content to the audience's needs.
- **Types of Briefings:**
  - **Information Briefings:** Provide background knowledge on topics.
  - **Decision Briefings:** Present critical data for informed decision-making.
  - **Mission Briefings:** Align team objectives, clarify roles, and address concerns.
- **Ethical Integrity:** Analysts must present objective, evidence-based information, even when it conflicts with expectations.

Through preparation, delivery, and ethical adherence, intelligence analysts can enhance their professional credibility and effectively communicate critical insights to stakeholders.

Key Concepts Covered

1. **Intelligence Communication:** Analysts must communicate findings clearly and concisely to decision-makers.
2. **Audience Awareness:** Intelligence products must be tailored to the knowledge and needs of the audience.
3. **Visual Communication:** Charts, maps, and graphics help convey complex information efficiently.
4. **Narrative Structure:** Effective briefings follow a logical structure that highlights key judgments and supporting evidence.
5. **Confidence and Uncertainty:** Analysts must clearly communicate both conclusions and the level of confidence behind them.
6. **Professional Delivery:** Strong presentation skills enhance credibility and ensure that intelligence insights are understood.

Learning Objectives Accomplished

1. **Explain** the purpose and value of intelligence briefings in various professional contexts.

2. **Identify** and mitigate stressors associated with public speaking.
3. **Describe** the key components of preparing and delivering an effective briefing.
4. **Differentiate** between information, decision, and mission briefings.
5. **Adapt** briefing content and style to the audience's expertise and needs.
6. **Demonstrate** ethical practices in presenting intelligence information.
7. **Use** visual aids effectively to complement verbal briefings.

Practical Application

You practiced techniques such as:

- Preparing briefing slides that summarize key intelligence judgments.
- Using maps and charts to illustrate complex analytical findings.
- Delivering concise verbal briefings to simulated decision-makers.

Reflection Questions

1. Why is audience awareness critical in intelligence briefings?
2. How can visual aids improve the effectiveness of a briefing?
3. What risks arise when analysts fail to communicate uncertainty clearly?

Effective communication ensures that intelligence insights influence real-world decision-making.

GLOSSARY OF TERMS

Here is a glossary of key terms introduced and discussed in Chapter 14 to enhance your understanding of the material. After each definition, additional *italicized* information provides further insight into the subject.

Analyst: A professional who collects, evaluates, and interprets data to produce insights for operational or strategic decision-making.
- *See: "Structured Analytic Techniques" by Richards Heuer.*

Audience Adaptation: Tailoring the briefing's content, language, and style to the specific audience's knowledge level, interests, and needs.
- *Rooted in communication theory and military presentation practices.*

Clarification of Deductions: The opportunity within briefings to explain how conclusions were drawn from data, enhancing transparency.
- *Integral to analytic tradecraft.*

Command Staff: Senior leaders directing missions or operations are the primary audience for military briefings.
- *Equivalent to C-suite executives in corporate contexts.*

Constructive Feedback: Targeted commentary used to improve future performance in briefings or presentations.
- *Foundational in adult learning theory and training exercises.*

Cross-Functional Communication: Collaboration between departments or disciplines (e.g., intelligence, logistics, operations) facilitated by briefings.
- *Critical in both interagency and corporate environments.*

Decision Briefing: A type of briefing designed to inform and support a decision-making process by presenting options, data, and recommended actions.
- *Similar to business case presentations.*

Dissemination: The phase of the intelligence cycle where findings are shared with decision-makers through reports or briefings.
- *Refer to the Intelligence Cycle in FM 2-0.*

Ethical Integrity: Commitment to presenting unbiased, evidence-based intelligence, even when politically or organizationally inconvenient.
- *Discussed in* The Psychology of Intelligence Analysis *by Heuer.*

Information Briefing: A presentation that provides context or background on a specific topic without prompting a decision or action.
- *See also: Education or Situational Awareness Briefings.*

Intelligence Briefing: A structured verbal presentation that communicates analyzed intelligence to decision-makers or stakeholders.
- *Common in military, law enforcement, and business intelligence contexts.*

Interactive Visuals: Dynamic elements like zoomable maps or highlighted graphics used during presentations to guide attention.
- *Used in geospatial and threat intelligence briefings.*

Key Performance Indicators (KPIs): Quantifiable metrics used to assess progress toward objectives; often explained in briefings to non-technical audiences.
- *Common in business and organizational strategy.*

Mission Briefing: An operational briefing given before a mission or task to clarify objectives, assign roles, and address concerns.
- *Standard in military planning and tactical operations.*

Non-Verbal Cues: Facial expressions, gestures, and body language from the audience provide feedback to the presenter.
- *See also: Nonverbal Communication studies by Mehrabian.*

Operational Environment: The conditions, forces, and variables affecting mission planning and execution. Often described in situational briefings.

- *Refer to Joint Publication 3-0 for further context.*

Public Speaking Anxiety: A psychological stressor affecting performance in oral presentations, common among analysts required to brief regularly.

- *See also: Glossophobia in psychology literature.*

Rehearsal: The process of practicing a briefing in advance improves delivery, timing, and response to questions.

- *Essential in reducing public speaking stress.*

Risk Mitigation Strategy: A plan included in decision or mission briefings that addresses how to reduce the likelihood or impact of identified threats.

- *Common in military operations and enterprise risk management.*

SIGINT (Signals Intelligence): Intelligence gathered from intercepted communications and electronic signals.

- *The technical term is often simplified in public-facing briefings.*

Stakeholder: Anyone with an interest in or influence on a decision, policy, or operation.

- *Examples include commanders, executives, and department heads.*

Strategic Insight: High-level analysis that informs long-term planning or policy decisions, usually aimed at senior leadership.

- *Contrast with tactical or operational intelligence.*

Structured Organization: The logical arrangement of information in a briefing (e.g., introduction, body, conclusion) supports comprehension and retention.

- *Based on principles of instructional design and briefing doctrine.*

Tactical-Level Map: A map that details a specific, actionable area of operation used in mission planning.

- *Often layered with real-time or geospatial data.*

Visual Aids: Supporting elements such as slides, maps, charts, and images used to enhance verbal briefings.

- *Refer to the guidance in* Designing Visual Language *by Kostelnick and Roberts.*

This glossary serves as a quick reference for understanding key terms and concepts from the chapter. Feel free to revisit it as you progress through the material!

NOTES

1. U.S. Military, *Joint Publication 2-0: Joint Intelligence*, 2010.
2. D. Carnegie, *How to Win Friends and Influence People* (Updated ed.), Simon & Schuster, 1936.
3. C. Heath and D. Heath, *Made to Stick: Why Some Ideas Survive and Others Die*, Random House, 2007.
4. N. Duarte, *Resonate: Present Visual Stories That Transform Audiences*, Wiley, 2010.
5. S. J. Gerras, *Critical Thinking for Strategic Leaders*, U.S. Army War College, 2010.

CHAPTER 15

Best Practices

INTRODUCTION

Imagine this: An intelligence report confidently states that a hostile nation possesses weapons of mass destruction. The world acts on that judgment—yet, the weapons are never found. This is not fiction. It is history.

Best practices in intelligence analysis were born out of such failures. The stakes are too high for guesswork or bias. Whether you are identifying terrorist threats, preventing cyberattacks, or tracking market shifts, how you analyze matters just as much as what you analyze (see Figure 15.1).

This chapter explores the Intelligence Community's gold standard, ICD 203, which outlines nine core analytic practices designed to elevate accuracy, transparency, and decision-making utility. These standards are not just for government use; they apply to law enforcement, business intelligence, and beyond.

Welcome to the blueprint for doing analysis right.

This chapter introduces the concept of "best practices" and identifies analytical methods and techniques recognized as standards within the Intelligence Community (IC). These practices are particularly relevant for Homeland Defense Intelligence Analysis. At its core, a "best practice" is a method or technique proven to achieve superior results, consistently outperforming alternative approaches.

DOI: 10.4324/9781003561712-15

FIGURE 15.1 The importance of best practices in analysis.

LEARNING OBJECTIVES

1. **Define** the concept of "best practices" in intelligence analysis and explain their significance.
2. **Identify** and apply the nine standards of ICD 203 to real-world scenarios.
3. **Evaluate** the quality and reliability of intelligence sources.
4. **Communicate** levels of uncertainty and confidence effectively.
5. **Construct** logical arguments and integrate alternative analysis techniques.
6. **Develop** visual aids that enhance analytic communication.

THE FOUNDATION OF BEST PRACTICES

Due to intelligence work's inherently secretive nature, observing and empirically measuring best practices presents unique challenges. Despite these difficulties, the Director of National Intelligence (DNI) established a framework to enhance the quality, relevance, and reliability of intelligence products. On June 21, 2007, ICD 203 was signed into effect, codifying nine analytical standards. These standards aim to mitigate errors, such as those seen in the flawed National Intelligence Estimate (NIE) on Iraqi weapons of mass destruction (WMD).

ANALYTICAL STANDARDS IN ICD 203

ICD 203 establishes nine analytical quality standards:

1. *Describing the Quality and Reliability of Underlying Sources*
2. *Caveats and Expressing Uncertainties or Confidence in Analytic Judgments*
3. *Distinguishing between Underlying Intelligence and Analysts' Assumptions and Judgments*
4. *Incorporating Alternative Analysis Where Appropriate*
5. *Demonstrating Customer Relevance and Addressing Implications*
6. *Using Logical Argumentation*
7. *Exhibiting Consistency of Analysis over Time or Highlighting Changes and Explaining Rationale*
8. *Making Accurate Judgments and Assessments*
9. *Incorporating Effective Visual Information Where Appropriate*

The following sections detail these standards, with examples from military intelligence, and how they might be applied to law enforcement and business.

ANALYTICAL BEST PRACTICES

1. Describing the Quality and Reliability of Underlying Sources

"How reliable is your intelligence source?" Failure to properly evaluate the quality or reliability of an intelligence source can negatively impact analytical conclusions and invalidate the final product entirely. Let us examine the reliability of a few intelligence disciplines, starting with IMINT. You have a picture. What more proof do you need? Pictures do not lie, right?—WRONG! Photographic evidence is not the only source that is suspect. Other disciplines also have their reliability shortfalls. HUMINT sources may lie or be mistaken. SIGINT can be misinterpreted or deliberately falsified. ELINT can be jammed or faked, and the list continues—the more sophisticated the adversary, the higher the possibility of deception.

Analysts generally receive some training to help them evaluate sources, spot errors, and recognize deception. Chapter 4, "Perception and Deception," discusses these concepts in more detail. Consistently assessing sources and validating collected information prevents flawed or deceptive information from being included in the assessment and allows analysts to identify intelligence gaps requiring additional collection efforts.

Since information is only as good as its source, evaluating the reliability of sources is essential to avoid flawed conclusions. Analysts must assess a source's placement, access, reliability, and historical performance.

Guidance to Better Describe the Quality and Credibility of Underlying Sources

By organizing and tying analytic judgments to the supporting data and intelligence, analysts create a pedigree of sorts for their assessments and associated findings. The more clearly organized and complete the judgment pedigree, the easier it is for peers and the analysis team supervision to review and spot bad data, analytical bias, errors, or adversarial deception. The following paragraph explains guidance and an example of how to build this judgment-source pedigree better.

> ***Example:***
> *The following provides a brief assessment of the quality and credibility of the underlying sources using an IMINT collection example. Military analysts apply this best practice by linking analytical judgments to specific supporting information and their respective sources. They include as much detail as feasible to describe the source's placement, access, reliability, and performance history. Analysts should also comment on the source's (or technical method's) susceptibility to deception, denial, or, in the case of HUMINT-provided information, the source's motivations or potential biases. Whenever possible, weighting factors should be associated with information that influences the product's assessment. Where practical, highlight specific prominent sources in the final assessment. Utilizing a Sources and Methods Summary Statement aids the consumer in understanding the number and types of sources used to develop the product. One or two sentences can indicate the number and types of relevant sources reviewed, how many supported the assessment findings, and how many conflicted (e.g., Assessment findings based on IMINT only). The imagery analysis package consists of 347 images of the designated collection area from 17 Predator sorties on different dates, nine-day collections, and eight nighttime collections (42% of the time, six nights, and one day); the target (terrorist HVT) was not spotted or positively identified in the imagery. (Analyst Comment: During the seven negative collection sorties, the target may have been away from the designated area, undercover and obscured, possibly sleeping. The IMINT data available cannot confirm if the HVT is regularly transiting in*

and out of the AOR or has made the area his permanent operational base. Additional intelligence is required to validate [or refute] the confidence level of the HVT's residence at over 58%.)

Applications

- **Military Intelligence:** Assess the credibility of SIGINT reports from a contested area to ensure strategic troop movements are based on verified intelligence (see Figure 15.2).
- **Law Enforcement:** Evaluate the reliability of informants' tips to prevent false arrests or wasted resources.
- **Business:** Vet market research sources to validate data on customer preferences or competitor strategies.

2. Caveats and Expressing Uncertainties or Confidence in Analytic Judgments

Accurately communicating uncertainty is vital. Communicating the degree of uncertainty is essential. Terms such as "likely" and "possible" should be quantified and contextualized. For example, an analysis might state, "There is a 70% likelihood that the adversary will launch a cyberattack within the next month." Analysts should:

- Use ICD 203's probability terminology.
- Identify gaps that could affect confidence levels.
- Quantify uncertainty where possible and explain its basis.

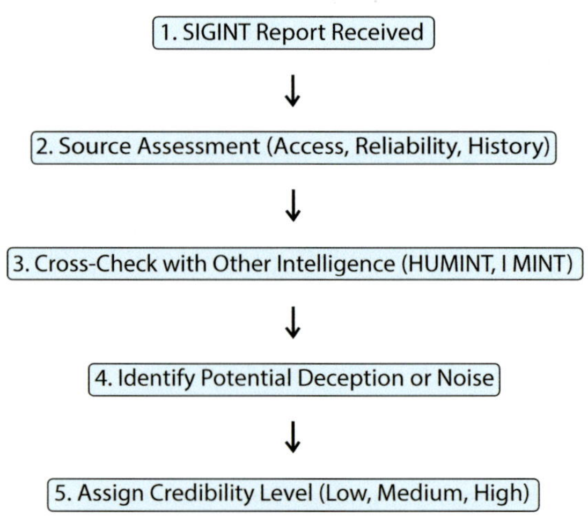

FIGURE 15.2 Assessing SIGINT credibility.

Guidance to Ensure Explanation and Expression of Uncertainties or Confidence in Analytic Judgments

Use the ICD 203 probability terminology to convey the assessment results' analytic certainty/uncertainty level. If there are significant uncertainties, to the extent possible, identify, quantify, and explain the rationale for the uncertainty (e.g., uncertainties exist due to generally reliable but conflicting HUMINT source reporting, significant intelligence gaps, etc.). To assist the consumer's understanding of the confidence level, they must identify confidence levels and their associated percentages in a table or legend for easy reference.

If intelligence gaps are identified that could meaningfully influence assessment findings, these should be communicated to the consumer. Additionally, further collection efforts should be initiated and findings reassessed as necessary. For example, when cloud cover limits visibility of the target area, this may reduce confidence in assessment results, prompting findings to be released as "preliminary." In such cases, a high-priority imagery collection request should be submitted, and the report will be updated and re-issued upon receipt of new imagery.

Applications

- **Military Intelligence:** Use probability ranges to forecast enemy actions, such as "There is a 70% probability of an attack within the next 48 hours."
- **Law Enforcement:** Express confidence levels when predicting crime hotspots using color codes based on historical data (see Figure 15.3).
- **Business:** Present uncertainty in market forecasts, clarifying potential economic or political disruptions.

3. Distinguishing between Underlying Intelligence and Analysts' Assumptions and Judgments

Assumptions must be explicitly identified and evaluated using structured analytic techniques (SATs). This transparency enables consumers to differentiate between factual intelligence and interpretive judgments.

An assumption is a proposition that analysts accept as a fact, forming the basis of the assessment. Utilizing SATs to evaluate and re-evaluate assumptions is valuable at any stage before finalizing a judgment, ensuring the assessment is not based on a faulty premise. Refer to Chapter 10 for more information on employing SATs to evaluate key analytical assumptions. By clearly stating the assumptions or judgments made by analysts, the cognitive processes of intelligence consumers concentrate

FIGURE 15.3 Fictitious hotspot map overlayed on a map of Houston, Texas.

on the supported facts and analytical judgments, allowing them to confidently accept or disregard assessments or judgments as appropriate.

Guidance on How to Properly Distinguish between Underlying Intelligence and Analytical Assumptions and Judgments

Identify any assumptions and judgments used. Segregate assumptions and judgments from underlying reporting, supporting data, and intelligence. Use analytical verbiage to state assumptions and judgments in the assessment findings, such as "consider," "assess," "calculate," "judge," "estimate," "determine," and "assume."

Applications

- **Military Intelligence:** Differentiate between confirmed intelligence and battlefield assumptions, such as enemy supply chain vulnerabilities.
- **Law Enforcement:** Clarify assumptions in profiling potential suspects vs. data-based evidence.
- **Business:** Clearly separate assumptions about market trends from empirical sales data in reports to stakeholders.

FIGURE 15.4 Business example distinguishing between underlying intelligence and analytical assumptions and judgments.

Example:

- *Empirical Sales Data: In Q2 2023, the company experienced a 15% increase in sales compared to Q2 2022, attributed to a marketing campaign targeting younger demographics (see Figure 15.4).*
- *Assumptions about Market Trends: The growth suggests a sustained trend of increasing demand among younger consumers, possibly indicating continued success if marketing efforts are maintained. However, this assumption does not account for potential economic downturns or competitor actions that may disrupt the trend.*
- *Contextual Risks: Data does not account for potential future economic downturns, competitor actions, or unforeseen market shifts.*

4. Incorporating Alternative Analysis Where Appropriate

To counteract cognitive biases and "groupthink," analysts should explore alternative hypotheses.

Guidance on How to Incorporate Alternative Analysis Where Appropriate

Analysts should incorporate insights from applying structured analytic techniques where time and resources are available. These techniques include, but are not limited to, analysis of competing hypotheses, argument mapping, and comparative analysis to decide if a potential alternative perspective or conclusion is more likely or trending toward higher probability. Using structured analysis to assess indicators and facts using a matrix or table where each column is a differing competing hypothesis aids in excluding most alternative hypotheses, thereby identifying the most likely hypothesis as the one with the smallest amount of contradicting evidence.

Table 15.1 displays a representative example of one method of comparing and scoring competing hypotheses. For more information on using SATs to incorporate alternative analysis, refer to Chapter 10.

> **AUTHOR'S NOTE**
>
> *Performing "Alternative Analysis of Competing Hypotheses" requires additional time and personnel. For example, if one has five competing hypotheses, you would potentially require five times the resources needed to develop one hypothesis fully. These additional resources are often difficult to obtain or may be completely unavailable due to competing mission priorities. Therefore, intelligence planners should be judicious in applying alternative analysis techniques.*

Applications

- **Military Intelligence:** Examine multiple hypotheses about adversary intentions, such as whether an increase in troop movement signifies an attack or routine drills (see Table 15.1).
- **Law Enforcement:** Use alternative analysis to evaluate multiple motives in a criminal investigation.
- **Business:** Explore alternative business strategies to adapt to disruptive technologies or shifting consumer demands.

5. **Demonstrating Customer Relevance and Addressing Implications**

Analytic products must answer the consumer's questions while addressing broader implications. For instance, assessing enemy troop movements should also discuss potential strategic impacts, such as risks to allied supply lines.

Guidance on Demonstrating Customer Relevance and Addressing Implications

A successful analyst "answers the question." However, best practice encourages the military analyst to go further. For example, when producing an analytic product that answers a question with limited scope

TABLE 15.1 Sample Alternative Hypotheses Table

Example of Alternative Hypothesis Matrix

Intelligence Requirement: Will Kraznovia retaliate for the U.S. bombing its Intelligence Headquarters?

Hypotheses:

H1: Kraznovia will publicly protest but will not retaliate.
H2: Kraznovia will publicly protest and sponsor a few low-level terrorist actions.
H3: Kraznovia will mount a major attack/terror action on an equivalent U.S. intelligence-related target.

	Reliability	Credibility	H1	H2	H3
E1: Kraznovian FM denounces U.S. attack at the UN	Medium	High	+	+	+
E2: Kraznovian President announces "he will not retaliate"	Medium	High	+	+	+
E3: Absence of terror retaliation after past U.S. attacks	Medium	Medium	+	+	-
E4: Assumption: Kraznovia would not want to provoke the U.S. further	N/A	N/A	+	+	-
E5: SIGINT chatter has increased between the Kraznovian government and field operatives	Medium	High	-	+	+
E6: Kraznovian embassies have higher security postures than before the HQ bombing	Medium	Medium	-	+	+
E7: Assumption: No retaliation would be perceived as a sign of weakness to the Kraznovian public/President's inner circle	N/A	N/A	-	+	+
E8: Assumption: No retaliation would be perceived as a sign of weakness to Kraznovian neighbors/adversaries	N/A	N/A	-	+	+

(e.g., Will the enemy attack Hill 293?), the analyst should fully answer the intelligence requirement (e.g., answer: The enemy will almost certainly attack Hill 293). See Figure 15.5 (upper half).

Then, the analyst would endeavor to provide added value (e.g., the enemy will most likely attack at night from the west using improved roads for armored vehicles and unimproved roads for lighter vehicles/dismounted troops to maximize the speed of advance of heavy armored forces). Additionally, the analyst includes any relevant near- and far-term

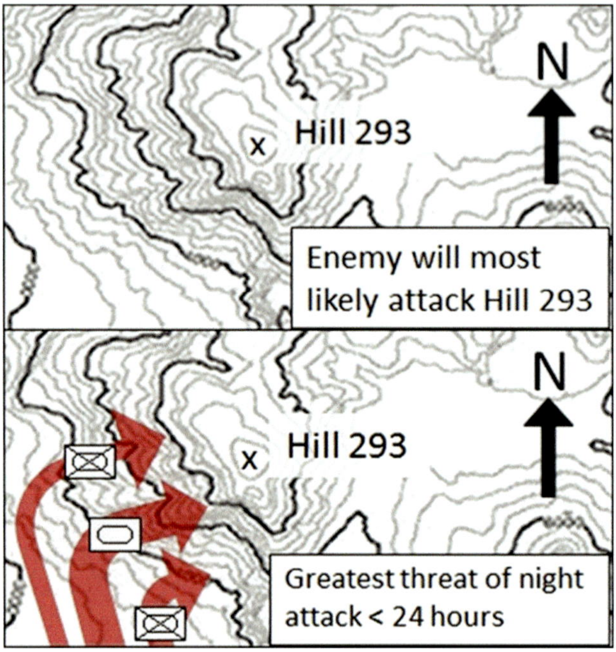

FIGURE 15.5 Success v. best practice.

implications (e.g., near-term, <24 hours, rapid assault from the west implies the enemy is prepared to take heavy casualties to sustain momentum and possibly take the initiative in this sector; a delayed assault, >24 hours, implies the enemy is consolidating forces, awaiting resupply and replacements and the main effort is likely in another sector). See Figure 15.5 (lower half).

As one can see, both responses "successfully" answer the intelligence consumer's question (e.g., "Will the enemy attack Hill 293?"). However, if the supporting data is available, the analyst should also provide other relevant information to aid the consumer's understanding of the problem and the associated near- and far-term implications, thereby painting a much fuller picture of the situation.

Applications

- **Military Intelligence**: Develop actionable assessments addressing specific mission needs, such as likely IED placement in a convoy route.
- **Law Enforcement**: Tailor reports to address community safety concerns, such as the potential escalation of gang activities.
- **Business:** Provide insights on how new regulations might impact product launches or market entry (see Figure 15.6).

6. Using Logical Argumentation

Analytic products should present a clear main analytic message upfront. Products containing multiple judgments should collectively have a main analytic message drawn from those judgments. All analytic judgments should be effectively supported by relevant intelligence information and coherent reasoning. Language and syntax should convey meaning unambiguously. Products should be internally consistent and acknowledge significant supporting and contrary information affecting judgments.[1]

Logical argumentation ensures coherence and credibility. A robust argument includes:

- Premises: Clearly stated evidence or reasoning.
- Inferences: Logical derivations from premises.
- Conclusions: Supported and clearly articulated outcomes.

Applications

- **Military Intelligence:** Use a logical framework to justify troop deployments based on enemy movement data.
- **Law Enforcement:** Build coherent arguments for search warrants based on collected evidence.
- **Business:** Justify investment in new markets with data-driven reasoning and clear conclusions.

Figure 15.6 presents a bar chart illustrating the impact of new regulations on various business aspects.

Insights:

- *Market Research: Scores decrease, indicating that regulations might reduce the feasibility of accurate or efficient market analysis.*
- *Compliance Costs: A significant increase, highlighting higher costs associated with adhering to new rules.*
- *Timeline Adjustments: Reduced scores suggest potential delays in product launches or market entry timelines.*
- *Competitor Impact: A score drop indicates that new regulations might affect competitive dynamics.*
- *Consumer Perception: There was a slight decrease, implying potential shifts in how consumers view the product under the new regulatory environment.*

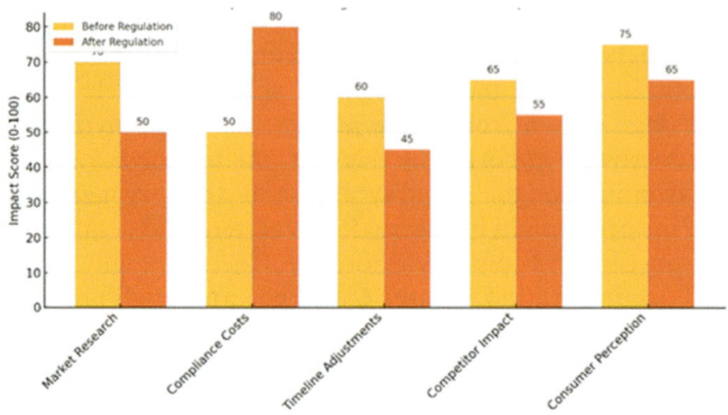

Above is a bar chart illustrating the impact of new regulations on various business aspects.

Insights:

Market Research: Scores decrease, indicating that regulations might reduce the feasibility of accurate or efficient market analysis.

Compliance Costs: A significant increase, highlighting higher costs associated with adhering to new rules.

Timeline Adjustments: Reduced scores suggest potential delays in product launches or market entry timelines.

Competitor Impact: A score drop indicates that new regulations might affect competitive dynamics.

Consumer Perception: There was a slight decrease, implying potential shifts in how consumers view the product under the new regulatory environment.

FIGURE 15.6 Insights on how new regulations might impact products.

Guidance on Using Logical Argumentation

A "logical argument" should consist of a series of related statements crafted to establish a straightforward proposition. A premise, inference, and conclusion should exist when making a logical argument. Refer to Figure 15.7 as each stage is discussed.

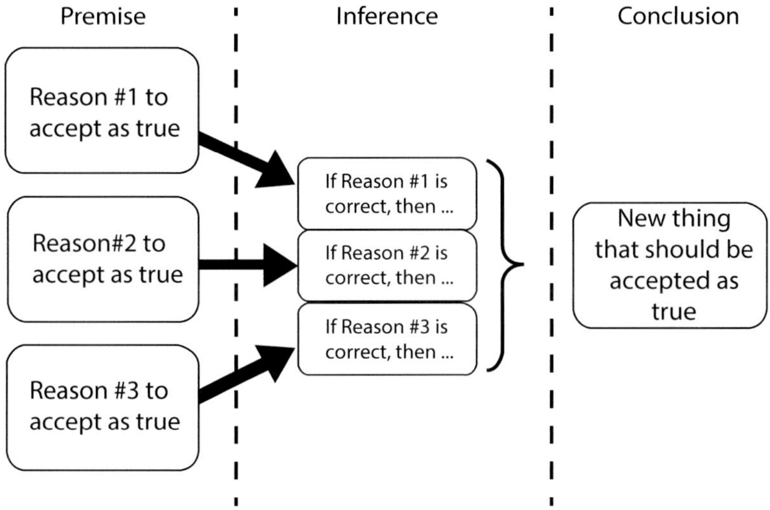

FIGURE 15.7 Logical argument.

Stage One: The Premise

Usually, more than one premise is needed to support an argument adequately. Premises need to be clear and succinct assertions. They should consist of evidence and logical reasoning and use supporting language to aid in identifying this as the "premise," such as "since," "because," or "if, then statements." Premises are the evidence (or basis) for accepting the argument and its conclusions.

The premise of the argument is bolded in the following examples:

- ***Since the volume of drug cartel-associated violence is significantly increasing****, one can logically expect it to spill outside the areas where it is presently reported.*
- ***Because the informant has reported with 100% reliability for three years****, he will likely report reliably in the near future.*
- ***If the enemy has advanced radar technology*** *and does not have a supporting R&D program, they likely got the technology from other sources.*

Stage Two: Inference

The premises of the argument are used to obtain further propositions. This process is known as inference. In inference, we start with one or more propositions that have been accepted. We then derive a new proposition. There are various forms of valid inference. The inference of the argument is bolded in the following examples:

- *Since the volume of drug cartel-associated violence is significantly increasing,* ***one can logically expect it to spill outside the areas where it is presently reported.***
- *Because the informant has reported with 100% reliability for three years,* ***he will likely report reliably in the near future.***
- *If the enemy has advanced radar technology capability and does not have a supporting R&D program,* ***they likely got the technology from other sources.***

The conclusions arrived at by inference may then be used in further inference. The inference is often denoted by phrases such as "implies that" or "therefore."

Stage Three: Conclusion

Finally, after the argument, we arrive at another proposition. The conclusion is often stated as the final stage of inference. It is affirmed based on the original premises and their inference. Conclusions are frequently indicated by phrases such as "therefore," "it follows that," "we conclude," and so on.

The conclusion of the argument is bolded in the following examples:

- *Since the volume of drug cartel-associated violence is significantly increasing, one can logically expect it to spill outside the areas where it is presently reported.* ***Therefore, we expect a marked rise in the volume of drug cartel-associated violence outside the areas where it is currently being reported.***
- *Because the informant has reported with 100% reliability for three years, he will likely report reliably in the near future. Provided he continues to have required access,* ***we conclude that he will continue to report reliably.***
- *If the enemy has advanced radar technology capability and does not have a supporting R&D program, they likely got the technology from other sources. Without a working R&D effort,* ***the enemy will continue to seek outside assistance or covert procurement means to maintain or improve their radar technology capability.***

7. Exhibiting Consistency of Analysis over Time or Highlighting Changes and Explaining Rationale

Consistency enhances credibility. Analytic products should state how their judgments on a topic are consistent with or represent a change from those in previously published analyses or represent initial coverage of a topic. Products need not be lengthy or detailed in explaining change or consistency. However, they should avoid using boilerplate language and make clear how new information or different reasoning led to the judgments expressed in them. Recurrent products, such as daily crisis reports, should take note of any changes in judgments or absent changes, and recurrent products need to confirm consistency with previous editions. Significant differences in analytic judgment, such as between two IC analytic elements, should be fully considered and brought to customers' attention.[2] Analysts should:

- Confirm agreement with previous reporting or explain changes.
- Detail how new information or insights led to revised judgments.

Guidance on Consistency of or Explaining Changes to Analytical Judgments

There are only three approaches open to the analyst:

- You agree with previous reporting and explain and support why you agree
- You disagree with previous reporting and explain why and support why you disagree; and last
- This is new coverage on a topic not previously reported on

You Agree with Previous Reporting

Consistency of analysis over time directly relates to appropriately expressing uncertainties and significance. Consistency ultimately builds confidence and credibility with the intelligence consumer. This begins with the analyst self-policing their work and asking: Are my (or the previous analyst's) judgments still valid? Does your analysis provide any new insights if it is consistent with previous products? Do not waste the intelligence consumer's time by making them read another product that does not add to their understanding.

You Disagree with Previous Reporting

Again, the analyst asks whether my (or the previous) judgments are valid. However, this time the answer is "no." This leads to the next question: Why? Now the analyst has an obligation to find why the previous reporting was erroneous (e.g., they/you missed something or collections' sensors were fooled, etc.) or perhaps the right answer just changed (e.g., the enemy moved to another location, the previous leader of a crime organization was usurped, etc.). In either case, the analyst highlights the change and explains and supports the rationale for change and possible implications associated with the change.

New Coverage on a Topic Not Previously Reported On

When reporting on a topic not previously covered, the process is much the same as with topics that have previous reporting associated with them. It still requires the analyst to self-police their own work and ensure their judgments are valid. However, in this case, there is a higher level of due diligence in the sense that everything is done from scratch. There are no previous assessments to review and gain potential insights. The analyst must look at every piece of data and build the assessment from the ground up.

Applications

- **Military Intelligence:** Track shifts in enemy tactics over time and update predictions accordingly.
- **Law Enforcement:** Highlight changes in crime patterns and the implications for resource allocation.
- **Business:** Document and explain changes in customer preferences about product cycles.

8. **Making Accurate Judgments and Assessments**

Analytic products should apply expertise and logic to make the most accurate judgments and assessments possible based on the information available and known information gaps. In doing so, analytic products should present all judgments that would be useful to customers and should not avoid complex judgments to minimize the risk of being wrong. Inherent in the concept of accuracy is that the analytic message a customer receives should be the one the analyst intended to send. Therefore, analytic products should express judgments as clearly and precisely as possible, reducing ambiguity by addressing the likelihood, timing, and nature of the outcome or development. Clarity of meaning permits assessment for accuracy when all necessary information is available.[3]

Guidance on Making Accurate Judgments and Assessments

Analysts, like most professionals, pride themselves on doing the job right. In contrast to most other professionals, an analyst's mistake may result in significant loss of life, property, or even the defeat of a nation. The possible magnitude and significance of a wrong judgment or assessment impel the analyst to be clear, expeditious, and precise, and get it right the first time and every time. It is impossible to be correct every time, but it is the goal.

So, how is it done? Individual intellectual honesty and the recognition that no one is right all the time, along with critical and independent reviews, will significantly enhance the quality of analysis and the accuracy of the products that result from the process. If analysts and agencies across the IC wholeheartedly adopt and train to the standards laid out in ICD 203, analytic processes and analytic product accuracy should improve significantly. Analysts must strive for accuracy by:

- Applying rigorous logic and expertise.
- Communicating judgments with precision and clarity.

Applications

- **Military Intelligence:** Produce precise threat assessments to guide mission planning.
- **Law Enforcement:** Generate accurate profiles to identify and apprehend suspects effectively, as shown in Figure 15.8.
- **Business:** Deliver precise forecasts to inform product development or financial strategies.

9. **Incorporating Effective Visual Information Where Appropriate**

Analytic products should incorporate visual information to clarify an analytic message and complement or enhance data and analysis presentation. In particular, visual presentations should be used when

FIGURE 15.8 Law enforcement generating suspect profile (www.shutterstock.com).

information or concepts (e.g., spatial or temporal relationships) can be conveyed better in graphic form (e.g., tables, charts, images) than in written text. Visual information may range from plain presentation of intelligence information to interactive displays of complex information and analytic concepts. All of the content in an analytic product may be presented visually. Visual information should always be clear and pertinent to the product's subject. Analytic content in visual information should also adhere to other analytic tradecraft standards.[4]

Guidance on Incorporating Effective Visual Information Where Appropriate

If the visuals you plan on incorporating do not improve, confuse, or distract from the analytic story you are trying to present, lose them. If you are confident that they help the message, keep them simple and clear. Avoid using too many distracting colors, images, or confusing text. The visual should be consistent with the written portion of the product and complement, simplify, and strengthen product findings. Visuals are best used when tied to the assessment's main judgment.

TIPS FOR INCORPORATING VISUALS INTO INTELLIGENCE PRODUCTS

- *If visuals confuse or distract from the message, do not use them.*
- *Use visuals where they can best support the primary findings/judgments of an analytical product.*
- *Keep visuals simple, uncluttered, clear, and concise.*
- *Visuals should agree with the written text and reinforce the message.*

As discussed in Chapter 6, visuals communicate not only on a cognitive level but also on an emotional level. Visual clues help us decode text and attract attention to information or direct attention, increasing the likelihood that the audience will remember.[5] Graphics engage our imagination and heighten our creative thinking, leading to a more profound and accurate understanding of the presented material.[6,7] See Chapter 6 for more detailed information. Visual aids can enhance understanding by:

- Clarifying complex data relationships.
- Avoiding unnecessary or distracting elements.

Applications

- **Military Intelligence:** Use maps to illustrate enemy positions or anticipated movements.
- **Law Enforcement:** Create crime heatmaps to allocate patrol resources efficiently.
- **Business:** Develop dashboards visualizing sales trends, revenue growth, or market penetration.

Practical Application

By adhering to the standards in ICD 203, intelligence analysts can produce credible, relevant, and actionable products. Practical exercises, such as evaluating source reliability or distinguishing assumptions from conclusions, reinforce these best practices. For instance, analysts might compare multiple hypotheses using structured matrices or critique visual aids for clarity and relevance.

Reflection and Implementation

As intelligence work continues to evolve, so must the application of best practices. The IC ensures its assessments meet the highest analytical quality through rigorous adherence to standards, providing decision-makers with the reliable insights they require.

CHAPTER SUMMARY

This lesson explored the critical role of probability and analytic standards in intelligence assessments, focusing on the guidance provided by the Intelligence Community Directive (ICD) 203. The directive establishes nine analytical standards designed to enhance intelligence products' quality, reliability, and relevance. By adhering to these standards, analysts ensure their work is credible, actionable, and transparent.

Key Takeaways

1. **ICD 203 Analytical Standards:** These standards include describing source reliability, expressing uncertainties, distinguishing assumptions from intelligence, incorporating alternative analyses, and ensuring logical argumentation, among others. Each standard addresses common pitfalls in intelligence analysis and promotes rigor and clarity.
2. **Probability in Assessments:** Quantifying uncertainty using probability terminology improves clarity and enables decision-makers to understand the confidence levels associated with

analytic judgments. This practice helps bridge the gap between ambiguous statements and actionable insights.

3. **Source Reliability:** Accurate assessments depend on the reliability of the underlying sources. Analysts must evaluate source credibility, assess vulnerabilities to deception, and consistently document the basis for their judgments.
4. **Addressing Cognitive Biases:** Structured analytic techniques, such as **Analysis of Competing Hypotheses (ACH)**, are vital for mitigating biases and "groupthink." These methods help analysts consider alternative perspectives and reach balanced, well-supported conclusions.
5. **Logical Argumentation:** Presenting coherent arguments that link premises, inferences, and conclusions ensures the credibility and utility of analytic products. Logical reasoning builds trust with consumers and facilitates more informed decision-making.
6. **Effective Visual Information:** Visual aids such as charts, maps, and matrices enhance comprehension by clarifying complex relationships and supporting key judgments. Analysts should use visuals to complement rather than overshadow written analysis.
7. **Consistency over Time:** Demonstrating consistency or explaining changes in analysis strengthens consumer confidence. Any changes in judgment should be justified with new information or reasoning.
8. **Practical Applications:** The principles outlined in this lesson apply across disciplines, including military intelligence, law enforcement, and business. By tailoring their analysis to meet specific needs, analysts provide actionable insights that directly support operational goals.

Implementation in Practice

Intelligence assessments are high-stakes endeavors that demand precision, rigor, and adaptability. By applying ICD 203 standards, analysts can enhance the quality of their work, ensuring it meets the diverse needs of consumers in various fields. The integration of probability, transparency, and critical thinking fosters accurate but also credible and actionable products.

As intelligence work continues to evolve, so must the methods and best practices used to produce assessments. This adherence to standards ensures analysts can provide decision-makers with the reliable insights necessary for navigating complex challenges.

Key Concepts Covered

1. **Analytical Integrity:** Analysts must maintain objectivity and intellectual honesty in all intelligence assessments.
2. **Transparency:** Intelligence products should clearly explain evidence, assumptions, and reasoning.
3. **Structured Methodology:** Applying structured analytic techniques strengthens analytic rigor.
4. **Continuous Learning:** Analysts must continually refine their skills and update their knowledge.
5. **Collaboration and Peer Review:** Constructive feedback improves the quality of intelligence products.
6. **Adherence to Analytic Standards:** Best practices align with the analytic standards established by Office of the Director of National Intelligence.

Learning Objectives Accomplished

1. **Define** the concept of "best practices" in intelligence analysis and explain their significance.
2. **Identify** and **apply** the nine standards of ICD 203 to real-world scenarios.
3. **Evaluate** the quality and reliability of intelligence sources.
4. **Communicate** levels of uncertainty and confidence effectively.
5. **Construct** logical arguments and integrate alternative analysis techniques.
6. **Develop** visual aids that enhance analytic communication.

Practical Application

You examined examples illustrating:

- Applying analytic tradecraft standards in intelligence reporting.
- Conducting peer reviews to strengthen analytic conclusions.
- Maintaining objectivity when analyzing politically sensitive issues.

Reflection Questions

1. Why is transparency important in intelligence analysis?
2. How can peer review improve the quality of intelligence products?
3. What responsibilities do analysts have to maintain analytic integrity?

Adhering to best practices ensures that intelligence analysis remains credible, objective, and valuable to decision-makers.

GLOSSARY OF TERMS

Here is a glossary of key terms introduced and discussed in Chapter 15 to enhance your understanding of the material.

Analysis of Competing Hypotheses (ACH): A structured analytic method that compares hypotheses against evidence to avoid bias.
Assumptions: Unverified beliefs that analysts treat as true in forming judgments.
Cognitive Bias: Mental shortcuts or tendencies that skew perception and decision-making.
Confidence Level: An expression of how certain an analyst is in their assessment, often linked to probability (e.g., 70% likely).
HUMINT: Intelligence derived from human sources, often vulnerable to deception or misinterpretation.
ICD 203: Directive issued by the Director of National Intelligence outlining standards for analytic integrity and rigor.
Inference: A logical deduction based on premises.
Judgment Pedigree: The analytic traceability of conclusions to their source material and reasoning.
SIGINT: Signals Intelligence; derived from intercepted communications or electronic emissions.
Visual Aids: Charts, maps, or graphics used to clarify complex relationships and patterns.

This glossary serves as a quick reference for understanding key terms and concepts from the chapter. Feel free to revisit it as you progress through the material!

NOTES

1. Office of the Director of National Intelligence, *Analytic Standards*, Intelligence Community Directive 203 (ICD 203), 2007.
2. Office of the Director of National Intelligence, *Analytic Standards*, Intelligence Community Directive 203 (ICD 203), 2007.
3. Office of the Director of National Intelligence, *Analytic Standards*, Intelligence Community Directive 203 (ICD 203), 2007.
4. Office of the Director of National Intelligence, *Analytic Standards*, Intelligence Community Directive 203 (ICD 203), 2007.

5. W. H. Levie and R. Lentz, "Effects of Text Illustrations: A Review of Research," *Educational Communications and Technology Journal*, 30, 195–232, 1982.
6. D. Bobrow and D. Norman, *Some Principles of Memory Schemata, Representation and Understanding: Studies in Cognitive Science*, New York: Academic Press, 1975.
7. D. Rumelhart, *Schemata: The Building Blocks of Cognition, Theoretical Issues in Reading Comprehension*, Hillsdale, NJ: Lawrence Erlbaum Associates, 1980.

CHAPTER 16

OPSEC

Protect What Matters Most

INTRODUCTION

From Battlefield Blunders to Boardroom Breaches: Why OPSEC Still Matters

In 2011, U.S. Navy SEALs raided a compound in Abbottabad, Pakistan, killing Osama bin Laden. That operation was possible not just because of brave operators or cutting-edge technology, but because the mission's operational security (OPSEC) worked. Critical planning details were locked down. No media leaks. No traceable patterns. No social media chatter.

Compare that to a Russian soldier's selfie in 2022, which revealed his unit's position to Ukrainian artillery. Or a LinkedIn post from a defense contractor casually referencing a sensitive AI program. These seemingly small lapses illustrate a simple truth: Operational Security is not optional, as Figure 16.1 shows.

FIGURE 16.1 Examples of poor OPSEC.

 DOI: 10.4324/9781003561712-16

Whether on a battlefield, in a government agency, or managing a tech startup, understanding OPSEC is the line between mission success and catastrophic failure. This chapter explores how a disciplined approach to protecting information ensures security in a world where data moves faster than bullets.

In today's interconnected world, information is power. Operations Security (OPSEC) is vital to intelligence and counterintelligence efforts to protect critical information from adversaries. Whether you are a soldier on a mission, a CEO launching a new product, a law enforcement officer investigating a crime, a government agency working on sensitive programs, or even an individual protecting their privacy, understanding and practicing OPSEC is paramount. OPSEC originated as a military strategy but has since been widely adopted by law enforcement, businesses, and other entities. Through its structured framework, OPSEC ensures that sensitive data is safeguarded, thereby maintaining strategic advantages and minimizing risks, as illustrated by the two covert operatives in Figure 16.2. This lesson will provide a foundation for understanding and implementing OPSEC across various domains.

FIGURE 16.2 Two figures using sign and countersign to ensure OPSEC.

LEARNING OBJECTIVES

1. **Define** Operational Security (OPSEC), its core principles, and its importance in intelligence and counterintelligence.
2. **Analyze** the five-step OPSEC process for identifying and mitigating risks to critical information.
3. **Recognize** how adversaries exploit indicators and how OPSEC practices prevent this.
4. **Examine** historical and contemporary examples of OPSEC successes and failures.
5. **Recognize** common vulnerabilities across different sectors.
6. **Apply** OPSEC principles to hypothetical and real-world scenarios to enhance information security awareness.
7. **Develop** mitigation strategies for identified vulnerabilities.
8. **Appreciate** the continuous nature of OPSEC and its role in proactive risk management.

THE CORE PRINCIPLES OF OPSEC

Our adversaries follow friendly operations, the internet, and the open press to know when a piece of information relating to them or their operations has been released. Often, they know how many people and even who the individual people involved were, who had access to that information. In many cases, all they need is a single bit of data, released inadvertently by someone who did not practice appropriate OPSEC, and an adversary can identify that individual, their organization, location, and much more. No one can protect all information from compromise, so there must be a determination of what portion of information is critical, and that explicit part must be protected.

So, at its core, OPSEC focuses on identifying, analyzing, and protecting critical information, then determining if an adversary has the wherewithal to compromise critical information. This is not limited to the military; businesses, law enforcement, governments, and some individuals rely on OPSEC to protect their operations and assets. OPSEC core principles are:

- **Critical Information:** This includes operational plans, personnel identities, technological capabilities, and any information that could compromise missions or give adversaries an advantage.

- **Adversary Tactics:** Sophisticated adversaries can extract intelligence from seemingly innocuous data. For example, small pieces of leaked information can be pieced together to uncover larger secrets.

THE OPSEC PROCESS

The OPSEC process consists of five essential steps:

1. **Identification of Critical Information:** What information or activities must be protected?
2. **Analysis of Threats:** Who are the potential adversaries, and what are their capabilities and intentions? Adversaries can range from competitors and hackers to foreign governments and criminals. Understanding their motives is crucial to assessing the risk. This step includes assessing who would benefit from obtaining the information or disrupting your operation.
3. **Analysis of Vulnerabilities:** Where are we susceptible to exploitation by these adversaries? Vulnerabilities are weaknesses or gaps in our systems, processes, or behaviors that can be exploited. They may include physical security flaws, digital security gaps, or even social media postings by employees or team members.
4. **Risk Assessment:** What is the likelihood that a vulnerability will be exploited, and what would be the potential impact? This step combines threat analysis and vulnerability analysis to understand the level of risk. A risk matrix can be a useful tool to document and rate the threat and the risk.
5. **Application of Appropriate Countermeasures:** What actions can we take to eliminate or mitigate identified vulnerabilities? This is the most important step! These countermeasures include physical security enhancements, cybersecurity measures, policy changes, personnel training, and awareness programs.[1]

AUTHOR'S NOTE

Throughout this chapter, remember that adversaries—whether military, criminal, or business—especially the more sophisticated ones, mirror everything we do to gain intelligence advantages and to prevent us from achieving the same advantages over them. In essence, everyone aims to implement and ***practice good OPSEC.***

FIGURE 16.3 The most critical step.

Identify Critical Information

This is the most critical step. It involves determining what specific information needs to be protected to ensure operational success or safeguard assets. Critical information varies by sector and is defined by its potential value to adversaries and the harm its compromise could cause.

Examples: Refer to Figure 16.3 as examples of critical information are discussed.

- *Military: Locations and times of troop deployments, operational plans, technological capabilities, and supply chain routes. Soldiers must be mindful of their social media posts, public conversations, and even discarded equipment, as these can be exploited to gather intelligence.*[2] *For example, posting a picture of a unique landmark near a deployment location would be a critical OPSEC violation.*
- *Government: Policy development, conflict or trade negotiation positions, or foreign relations.*
- *Business: Trade secrets, R&D plans, proprietary algorithms, client data, and financial reports.*
- *Law Enforcement: Details of ongoing investigations, case files, planned criminal raid locations and timing, investigative techniques, and informant identities.*
- *Individual: Personal identifiable information (PII) such as Social Security numbers, bank account details, passwords, personal schedules, location data, and financial details.*

Analyze Threats

This step identifies potential adversaries, their intentions, and the methods they might use to obtain the critical information. This requires understanding both direct and indirect threats.

Examples:

- *Military: Foreign intelligence agencies using surveillance drones or hacking military networks.*
- *Government: Foreign government agencies and unethical domestic defense contractors are interested in sensitive policy discussions and classified information for national security reasons and economic rewards.*
- *Business: Competitors engaging in industrial espionage or cyberattacks to steal proprietary data.*
- *Law Enforcement: Organized crime groups bribing insiders, intercepting communications, surveillance or contamination of active crime scenes.*
- *Individual: Phishing attacks, social engineering, or identity theft attempts.*

Analyze Vulnerabilities

This involves assessing the weak points in systems, operations, or behaviors that could allow adversaries to access critical information. Vulnerabilities can be technological, procedural, or human.

Examples: Refer to Figure 16.4 as examples of vulnerability analysis are discussed.

- *Military: Insecure communication channels, outdated encryption protocols, or over-sharing during personal conversations.*
- *Government: Civilian government agency personnel using unsecure communication methods, having sensitive policy discussions in unsecure locations, and carrying classified information outside secure areas.*
- *Business: Employees using weak passwords or leaving sensitive documents in open spaces, thus precipitating a loss if the upcoming product specifications are leaked to competitors before the release.*
- *Law Enforcement: Lack of physical security at evidence storage facilities or compromised devices used in the field, accessible active crime scenes, unsecure communications.*
- *Individual: Sharing too much personal information on social media or using public Wi-Fi without a VPN.*

Assess Risks

This step evaluates the likelihood of vulnerabilities being exploited and the potential impact of such exploitation (see Figure 16.5). The goal is to prioritize threats based on their severity and probability.

FIGURE 16.4 Analyzing weak points in the organization.

Examples:

- *Military: The risk of an adversary intercepting communication about an upcoming mission could result in high casualties or mission failure.*
- *Government: An adversary monitors an unsecure communication channel where sensitive policy discussions take place, which may compromise national security. Leaked information could be used to exploit foreign relations or even impact future military operations.*
- *Business: A data breach exposing client information could lead to lawsuits, reputational damage, and financial losses. A cyberattack targeting financial data could have disastrous consequences.*
- *Law Enforcement: A leak about an undercover operation could endanger officers and compromise the mission.*
- *Individual: A compromised bank account could lead to financial loss and identity theft.*

Apply Countermeasures

Implement strategies and tools to mitigate the identified risks. These measures should be tailored to address specific vulnerabilities and effectively protect critical information, as shown in Figure 16.6.

FIGURE 16.5 Assessing risks.

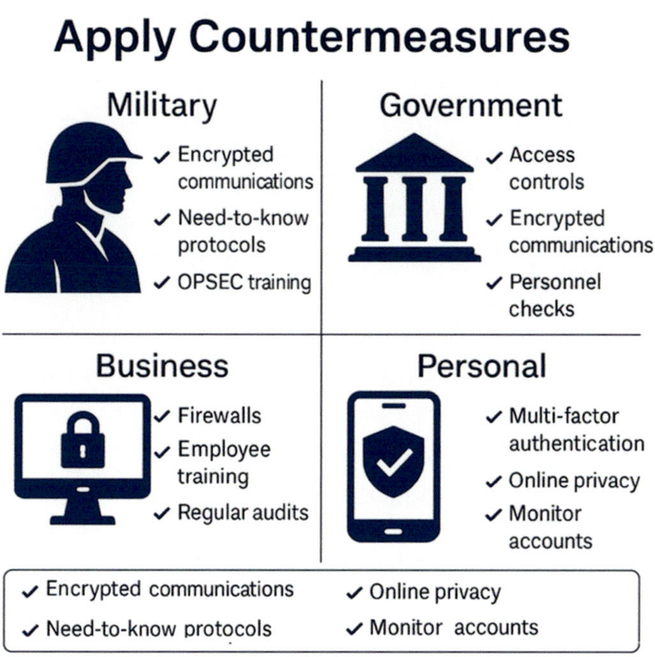

FIGURE 16.6 Applying countermeasures.

Examples:

- *Military: Use encrypted communications, implement need-to-know protocols, and conduct regular OPSEC training.*
- *Government: OPSEC may involve rigorous access controls, encrypted communications, and thorough personnel background checks.*[3]
- *Business: Introduce cybersecurity measures such as firewalls, employee training, and regular audits of IT systems. Proper document management, cybersecurity, and employee awareness about information sensitivity are vital.*[4]
- *Law Enforcement: Secure communications using encrypted radios, maintain strict chain-of-custody protocols for evidence, and vet informants carefully.*
- *Individual: Use multifactor authentication, avoid sharing sensitive information online, and regularly monitor financial accounts for unauthorized activity. Even seemingly benign location information and family pictures can be used to create a pattern of life (POL), which a criminal or an adversary can use.*

INTELLIGENCE AND COUNTERINTELLIGENCE

Intelligence involves gathering information about adversaries, while counterintelligence aims to protect one's information from exploitation. OPSEC plays a crucial role in both domains by:

- Denying adversaries access to critical data.
- Enhancing the overall security framework for operations.

Historical Perspective: "Loose Lips Sink Ships"

During World War II, civilians were educated about OPSEC through campaigns like "Loose Lips Sink Ships," underscoring the need for vigilance in daily conversations (see Figure 16.7). Such awareness campaigns remain relevant in today's digital age.

Everyday Examples

The direct connection between OPSEC and "awareness" is obvious. One must always be aware of whom they are interacting with and the level of that interaction when anything remotely connected to our nation's security is discussed or contemplated. Though OPSEC training and emphasis are most prevalent among our armed forces and government agencies,

FIGURE 16.7 WWII OPSEC poster (U.S. Archives).

such as the State Department and Department of Defense, it is an issue we all must be mindful of and conscious of (see Figure 16.8).

Family members, close friends, and associates of individuals involved in national security constantly come into possession of subtle pieces of

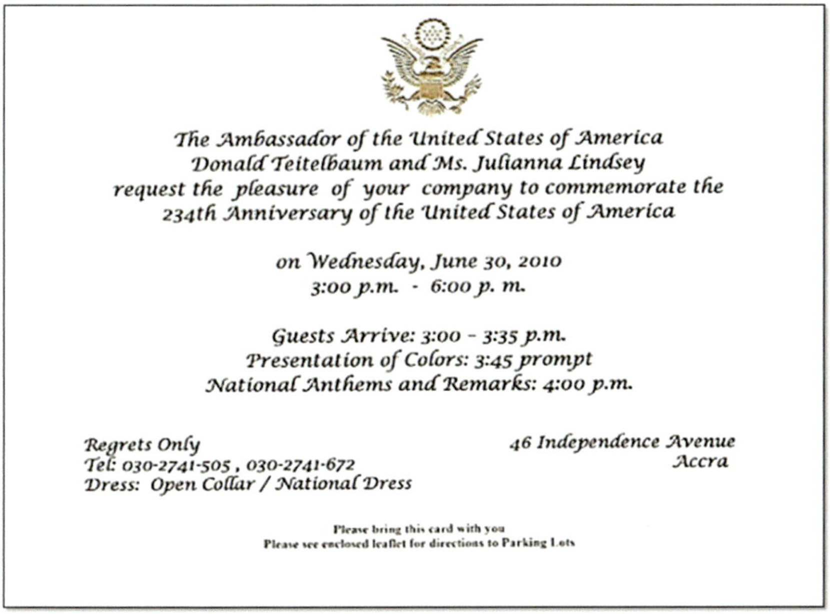

The Ambassador of the United States of America
Donald Teitelbaum and Ms. Julianna Lindsey
request the pleasure of your company to commemorate the
234th Anniversary of the United States of America

on Wednesday, June 30, 2010
3:00 p.m. - 6:00 p. m.

Guests Arrive: 3:00 - 3:35 p.m.
Presentation of Colors: 3:45 prompt
National Anthems and Remarks: 4:00 p.m.

Regrets Only
Tel: 030-2741-505 , 030-2741-672
Dress: Open Collar / National Dress

46 Independence Avenue
Accra

Please bring this card with you
Please see enclosed leaflet for directions to Parking Lots

FIGURE 16.8 Invitation to Department of State dinner party (U.S. Department of State).

FIGURE 16.9 OPSEC in personal communications (U.S. Department of Defense).

information, from which an adept adversarial counterintelligence operator can derive more complex and detailed data. For example, a service member or member of one of the aforementioned agencies, who may be separated from family or friends, and communicating by letter or digitally, almost always adheres to a simple principle of human interaction; we always want our friends and loved ones to know, "where we are" (see Figure 16.9).

Other Real-World Examples

Each following example demonstrates the practical application of the OPSEC process in different contexts, highlighting its versatility and necessity across domains.

Military

- *Situation*: During a military operation in a conflict zone, troop movement schedules are critical.
- *Threat*: An adversary monitors open communication channels.
- *Countermeasure*: Encrypt all communications and limit access to deployment details to essential personnel only.

Business

- *Situation*: A tech company is about to launch a new product.
- *Threat*: Competitors deploy spyware to gain access to internal meetings.

- *Countermeasure*: Conduct regular cybersecurity audits and enforce strict policies on external device connections.

Law Enforcement

- *Situation*: A police department is planning a large-scale raid on a drug cartel.
- *Threat*: A mole within the department leaks the plan to the cartel.
- *Countermeasure*: Conduct background checks on team members and limit access to raid details to need-to-know personnel.

Individual

- *Situation*: A person posts vacation photos online in real-time, revealing they are away from home.
- *Threat*: Burglars monitor social media to target vacant homes.
- *Countermeasure*: Post photos only after returning home and use privacy settings to limit access to personal posts.

Enforcing Operational Security in a Complex World

The Ubiquitous Nature of OPSEC

The mantra "OPSEC is everyone's responsibility" is not merely a slogan; it is a fundamental principle for safeguarding sensitive

AUTHOR'S NOTE/TRIVIA

There exists a large community of Civil War "relic hunters"' in southern states, particularly. When preparing to search for places to "dig," these hunters first read and review the hundreds, sometimes thousands, of letters available that were written by soldiers fighting in particular battles. Even these soldiers, so many years ago, followed that simple human need to let their loved ones know exactly where they were at the time of writing the letter.

Soldiers would always start a letter home with sentences such as, "We are camped 200 yards south of a creek that runs east and west through a corn field just north of the town of Clarksdale," or something to that effect.

Similarly, nowadays, internet researchers (particularly family and friends of Russian soldiers) use social network postings to determine their loved one's location, needs, and present status.

Information that informs and comforts loved ones—and future amateur treasure hunters—can simultaneously provide an adversary with information to seal one's fate.

FIGURE 16.10 Individual's role in OPSEC.

information and ensuring operational success, especially within the military. Every individual associated with military operations, whether directly or indirectly, possesses information that could be of value to an adversary. Even if seemingly innocuous, this information can be pieced together to create a detailed picture of our capabilities, vulnerabilities, and intentions.[5] OPSEC is a continuous process, not just one event or procedure, but rather a culture.

The Individual's Role in OPSEC

Individuals at all levels, including those with the least sensitive security classifications, often have access to vital operational details, as shown in Figure 16.10. These details range from troop movements and strength to morale, leadership changes, and seemingly minor operational data. Even an overheard conversation in a public setting or a seemingly harmless social media post can reveal critical information to an adversary with the capability to exploit it.[6] OPSEC is not a function limited to intelligence analysts in secure facilities; it is equally incumbent on all personnel to remain vigilant and protect sensitive information.

Counterintelligence: The Guardian of OPSEC

In the military, Counterintelligence (CI) is primarily responsible for ensuring that everyone maintains OPSEC. While intelligence operations focus on gathering and analyzing information about adversaries, counterintelligence is dedicated to preventing adversaries from obtaining similar information about our own operations and personnel.[7] This makes CI inherently responsible for ensuring OPSEC compliance (see Figure 16.11).

FIGURE 16.11 Military OPSEC.

CI's Multifaceted Approach to OPSEC Enforcement

CI operations employ a variety of methods to protect sensitive information. The term euphemistically titled "dumpster dive," well-known in the intel community, is also responsible for counterintelligence operations. Dumpster diving involves going through the trash and discarded items of a functioning sensitive compartmented information facility (SCIF) or other department charged with dealing with classified items to see what is being discarded and determine whether these items could be used to gain information (see Figure 16.12). CI's responsibilities encompass detecting, identifying, assessing, and neutralizing a wide array of threats. This includes adversarial efforts to exploit vulnerabilities and unintentional or deliberate actions by personnel that compromise OPSEC.[8]

While CI cannot directly control open-source intelligence (OSINT), all other avenues for information release can be monitored and controlled to a certain extent. Furthermore, if classified information is illegally released through open sources, CI can intervene, potentially leading to criminal charges. It is important to note that OSINT is information obtained from sources that are available to the public. However, it is not necessarily "public" information. Non-disclosure agreements (NDAs) are formal processes used to ensure all parties involved understand their OPSEC responsibilities. Government, business, and private entities use NDAs. An NDA specifically focuses on an individual's or organization's information privacy, which differs from other business

FIGURE 16.12 CI officer searching through trash (U.S. Department of Defense).

contracts like service or sales agreements that focus on the terms and conditions of service or transactions.

The case of Aldrich Hazen Ames (see Figure 16.13), a former CIA analyst who was convicted of spying for the Russian KGB, highlights the importance of robust counterintelligence practices. CI is also responsible for developing and modifying training materials used throughout the military and civilian government agencies to help individuals avoid unintentional information disclosures.[9]

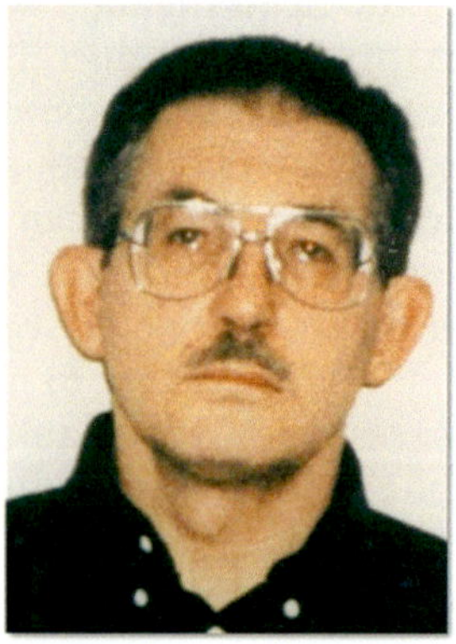

FIGURE 16.13 Aldrich Hazen Ames (Federal Bureau of Investigation).

Practical Applications of Counterintelligence

- **Dumpster Diving:** This practice involves inspecting discarded items for potentially sensitive information from secure facilities. While it might seem mundane, this activity is critical to CI's efforts to identify and mitigate vulnerabilities.
- **Red Teaming:** These exercises involve undercover teams testing and exploiting an organization's operational security procedures to highlight weaknesses and improve training. Though these teams often comprise special operations personnel, CI usually oversees these exercises.
- **Cybersecurity:** Given the prevalence of cyberattacks, CI must also monitor and protect government and military networks. Data breaches and insider threats are equally important to CI.
- **NDAs:** NDAs, or non-disclosure agreements, are legally enforceable contracts that create a confidential relationship between a person with sensitive information and a person who will gain access to that information (see Figure 16.14). A confidential relationship means one or both parties have a duty not to share that information.

The Impact of Open-Source Intelligence (OSINT) on OPSEC

OSINT, while generally unclassified, plays a significant role in both intelligence and counterintelligence. OSINT often supplements or substantiates classified information. However, OSINT can also serve as a valuable source of information for adversaries if not properly managed and secured.[10] Freedom of information policies in many countries prevent CI from controlling the release of information obtained by news outlets. Adversaries also face similar challenges in controlling OSINT, making it a valuable source for our own intelligence. The challenge arises when seemingly innocuous details obtained from OSINT can be combined and aggregated with other information to provide our adversary a more complete picture.

Controlling OPSEC Violations

All other areas of potential OPSEC violations (beyond OSINT) are more easily monitored and controlled, particularly when military personnel or Department of Defense (DoD) employees are involved. The most effective control method is comprehensive training. All service members receive regular OPSEC briefings and are often required to sign non-disclosure agreements (NDAs) acknowledging their understanding of OPSEC and the penalties for divulging sensitive information (see Figure 16.15). Additional NDAs may be necessary for specific missions.

United States General Accounting Office

GAO

Fact Sheet for the Chairman, Legislation and National Security Subcommittee, Committee on Government Operations

January 1991

INFORMATION SECURITY

Federal Agency Use of Nondisclosure Agreements

143616

RELEASED

RESTRICTED— Not to be released outside the General Accounting Office unless specifically approved by the Office of Congressional Relations.

GAO/NSIAD-91-106FS

FIGURE 16.14 Federal NDA regulations.

FIGURE 16.15 Controlling OPSEC violations.

FIGURE 16.16 Navigating social media and the modern information age (www.shutterstock.com).

OPSEC Challenges in the Modern Information Age

The current information environment poses considerable challenges to OPSEC, primarily due to the ubiquitous sharing of information on social media (see Figure 16.16). Individuals openly share intimate details of their lives online, making it easier for adversaries to gather information and potentially exploit vulnerabilities.[11] This necessitates that everyone is trained to understand and implement best practices for OPSEC.

SUMMARY (OPSEC: PROTECT WHAT MATTERS MOST!)

What Is OPSEC?

Operational Security (OPSEC) is a proactive process focused on protecting critical information, actions, and capabilities from potential adversaries. It's about identifying vulnerabilities and taking steps to mitigate risks before they can be exploited. OPSEC is not just about keeping secrets; it is about ensuring the success of your operations, projects, and even daily life. It is a continuous process that demands vigilance and adaptation (see Figure 16.17).

FIGURE 16.17 Five steps of OPSEC.

The Five Key Steps of OPSEC

1. **Identify Critical Information:** What information or activities need protection? This step is the foundation of effective OPSEC. Consider what information would be harmful if exposed to the wrong people.
   - *Examples:* Sensitive project details, financial data, personnel information, personal location, travel plans, etc.
2. **Analyze Threats:** Who might seek to exploit your information, and what are their capabilities and intentions? Understand the various threat actors relevant to your situation.
   - *Examples:* Competitors, hackers, criminals, foreign governments, unauthorized individuals, casual observers, etc.

3. **Analyze Vulnerabilities:** Where are you susceptible to exploitation? Identify weaknesses in your systems, processes, and behaviors that could be targeted.
   - *Examples:* Weak passwords, unencrypted data, oversharing on social media, insecure networks, inadequate physical security, etc.
4. **Assess Risk:** What is the likelihood and potential impact of a vulnerability being exploited? Determine the overall risk to your critical information and operations.
   - *Consider:* Likelihood of an exploit, severity of consequences, potential financial loss, damage to reputation, physical harm, etc.
5. **Apply Countermeasures:** What actions can you take to eliminate or mitigate identified vulnerabilities? Implement practical measures to reduce risks to an acceptable level.
   - *Examples:* Strong passwords, encryption, privacy settings, security awareness training, multifactor authentication, physical security enhancements, etc.

OPSEC in action across Sectors (and in Your Daily Life!)

- **Military:** Secure troop movements, equipment, and communications. Avoid location-based social media posts and open discussions in public.
- **Business:** Protect intellectual property, financial data, and customer information. Implement robust cybersecurity measures and provide employees with training.
- **Government:** Safeguard classified information, policy discussions, and sensitive operations. Rigorous access controls and secure communication channels are essential.
- **Law Enforcement:** Protect investigative techniques, informant identities, and case files. Limit access to sensitive information and maintain confidentiality.
- **Individual:** Secure online accounts, personal data, and physical spaces. Use strong passwords, avoid phishing scams, and be mindful of social media usage. Be aware of your surroundings.

Practical OPSEC Tips You Can Use Now

- **Think Like an Adversary:** Consider how your information could be used against you.
- **Minimize Your Digital Footprint:** Be mindful of what you post online and the data you share.

- **Practice Good Password Hygiene:** Use strong, unique passwords and a secure password manager if needed. Use multifactor authentication whenever possible.
- **Secure Your Devices:** Keep software updated and use antivirus protection.
- **Be Observant and Aware:** Pay attention to your surroundings and your discussions in public places.
- **Use Secure Connections:** Use HTTPS for websites with sensitive information.
- **Regular Review:** Periodically review and update your OPSEC habits and procedures.

FINAL AUTHOR'S NOTE

Operational Security is a crucial responsibility shared by all. It is the collective effort of all personnel to protect information, operations, and personnel. Counterintelligence plays a vital role in enforcing OPSEC, but its success depends on the vigilance of all individuals. Effective OPSEC requires continuous training, awareness, and the understanding that even seemingly insignificant information can be harmful in the wrong hands. By understanding the threats, vulnerabilities, and the importance of individual actions, we can proactively safeguard our information and protect our interests.

OPSEC is a Continuous Journey – Stay Vigilant, Stay Secure!
Remember: You are your best security asset!

Key Concepts Covered

1. **Operational Security (OPSEC):** OPSEC protects sensitive information that could be exploited by adversaries.
2. **Critical Information Identification:** Analysts must identify information that could reveal vulnerabilities or operational intentions.
3. **Threat Awareness:** Understanding adversary capabilities helps determine what information must be protected.
4. **Risk Assessment:** Analysts evaluate vulnerabilities and implement measures to reduce exposure.
5. **Information Protection:** Proper handling of classified and sensitive information prevents intelligence compromise.

6. **Operational Discipline:** Maintaining OPSEC requires continuous awareness and adherence to security procedures.

Learning Objectives Accomplished

1. **Define** Operational Security (OPSEC), its core principles, and its importance in intelligence and counterintelligence.
2. **Analyze** the five-step OPSEC process for identifying and mitigating risks to critical information.
3. **Recognize** how adversaries exploit indicators and how OPSEC practices prevent this.
4. **Examine** historical and contemporary examples of OPSEC successes and failures.
5. **Recognize** common vulnerabilities across different sectors.
6. **Apply** OPSEC principles to hypothetical and real-world scenarios to enhance information security awareness.
7. **Develop** mitigation strategies for identified vulnerabilities.
8. **Appreciate** the continuous nature of OPSEC and its role in proactive risk management.

Practical Application

You explored real-world OPSEC scenarios such as:

- Identifying vulnerabilities in military operational planning.
- Protecting sensitive intelligence sources and methods.
- Assessing risks associated with public information exposure.

Reflection Questions

1. Why is operational security essential in intelligence operations?
2. How can seemingly minor information disclosures create security risks?
3. What steps can analysts take to protect sensitive information?

Protecting sensitive information is a responsibility shared by every intelligence professional. Continue refining your analytical and security awareness skills as you progress through your studies.

GLOSSARY OF TERMS

Here is a glossary of key terms introduced and discussed in Chapter 16 to enhance your understanding of the material.

Adversary: Any entity that seeks to obtain, disrupt, or compromise your information or operations.
Counterintelligence (CI): Efforts to protect an organization from espionage, insider threats, or unauthorized disclosures.
Countermeasures: Actions taken to eliminate or reduce security vulnerabilities.
Critical Information: Specific facts about intentions, capabilities, or activities that, if revealed, could harm an organization.
Dumpster Diving: The practice of sifting through trash to find unprotected sensitive data.
NDAs (Non-Disclosure Agreements): Legal contracts preventing individuals from sharing specified sensitive information.
OPSEC (Operational Security): A systematic process for denying adversaries access to critical information.
OSINT (Open-Source Intelligence): Intelligence derived from publicly available sources.
Red Team: A group assigned to mimic adversaries and test defenses.
Vulnerability: A weakness that could be exploited to compromise critical information.

This glossary serves as a quick reference for understanding key terms and concepts from the chapter. Feel free to revisit it.

NOTES

1. U.S. Department of Defense (DoD), *Joint Chiefs of Staff, Operations Security*, Joint Publication 3-13.3, 2017.
2. U.S. Army, *Operations Security*, AR 530-1, 2020.
3. U.S. Central Intelligence Agency (CIA), *CIA Handbook of Security*, 2017.
4. National Institute of Standards and Technology (NIST), *Protecting Controlled Unclassified Information in Nonfederal Systems and Organizations*, NIST Special Publication 800-171, 2018.
5. U.S. Department of Defense (DoD), *Joint Chiefs of Staff, Operations Security*, Joint Publication 3-13.3, 2017.
6. U.S. Army, *Operations Security*, AR 530-1, 2020.
7. U.S. Department of Defense (DoD), *Counterintelligence*, Department of Defense Directive 5240.06, 2016.
8. U.S. Central Intelligence Agency (CIA), *CIA Handbook of Security*, 2017.
9. M. M. Lowenthal, *Intelligence: From Secrets to Policy*, CQ Press, 2018.
10. J. M. O'Leary, *Open-source Intelligence (OSINT): Tools and Techniques*, Rowman & Littlefield, 2018.
11. Palgrave Macmillan, Lusthaus, C., and Zuber, A., *The Social Media Threat Landscape*, 2021.

Index

For Product Safety Concerns and Information please contact our EU representative GPSR@taylorandfrancis.com Taylor & Francis Verlag GmbH, Kaufingerstraße 24, 80331 München, Germany

Batch number: 10731111

Printed by Printforce, the Netherlands